Ernst Ulrich Grosse
Heinz-Helmut Lüger

Understanding France in Comparison with Germany

An Introduction

This book has been translated by
Deborah Anne Vester, Matthew Wyneken and Peter Spaeth

PETER LANG
Berne · Berlin · Frankfurt/M. · New York · Paris · Vienna

Die Deutsche Bibliothek – CIP-Einheitsaufnahme

Grosse, Ernst-Ulrich:
Understanding France in comparison with Germany : an introduction / Ernst Ulrich Grosse ; Heinz-Helmut Lüger. This book has been transl. by Deborah Anne Vester ... - Berne ; Berlin ; Frankfurt/M. ; New York ; Paris ; Vienna : Lang, 1994
Einheitssacht.: Frankreich verstehen <engl.>
ISBN 3-906753-03-4
NE: Lüger, Heinz-Helmut:

Cover design: Süddeutsche Zeitung, 9 March 1962

Figures 62, 63, 83, 84, 85, 86, 87:
Adolf Benjes, Ingenieurbüro für Landkartentechnik, Alemannenstrasse 20, D-79227 Schallstadt

The Original German edition appeared 1987 (1st edition) and 1989 (2nd edition) as "Frankreich verstehen. Eine Einführung mit Vergleichen zur Bundesrepublik" Wissenschaftliche Buchgesellschaft Darmstadt.

Translated from the 3rd revised and extended edition, 1993:
"Frankreich verstehen. Eine Einführung mit Vergleichen zu Deutschland".
Translated by Deborah Anne Vester, Matthew Wyneken and Peter Spaeth.

Printed in Germany

Understanding France
in Comparison with Germany

Contents

Abbreviations

A2	Antenne 2 (now called FR2)
CAPES	Certificat d'Aptitude au Professorat de l'Enseignement du Second Degré
CAPET	Certificat d'Aptitude au Professorat de l'Enseignement Technique
CDS	Centre des Démocrates Sociaux
CERES	Centre d'Etudes, de Recherches et d'Education Socialistes
CFDT	Confédération Française Démocratique du Travail
CFTC	Confédération Française des Travailleurs Chrétiens
CGC	Confédération Générale des Cadres (official abbreviation: CFE-CGC)
CGPME	Confédération Générale des Petites et Moyennes Entreprises
CGT	Confédération Générale du Travail
CID-UNATI	Comité d'Information et de Défense – Union Nationale des Travailleurs Indépendants
CNCL	Commission Nationale de la Communication et des Libertés
CNI	Centre National des Indépendants
CNPF	Conseil National du Patronat Français
CNRS	Centre National de la Recherche Scientifique
CODER	Commissions de Développement Economique Régional
CSA	Conseil Supérieur de l'Audiovisuel
DATAR	Délégation à l'Aménagement du Territoire et à l'Action Régionale
DEA	Diplôme d'Etudes Approfondies
DEUG	Diplôme d'Etudes Universitaires Générales
DOM	Départements d'Outre-Mer
ENA	Ecole Nationale d'Administration
ENS	Ecole Normale Supérieure
FEN	Fédération de l'Education Nationale
FLNKS	Front de Libération Nationale Kanak Socialiste
FN	Front National
FNSEA	Fédération Nationale des Syndicats d'Exploitants Agricoles
FO	Force Ouvrière (official abbreviation: CGT-FO)
FR2	France 2
FR3	France 3
GE	Génération Ecologie
HEC	Ecole des Hautes Etudes Commerciales
IFOP	Institut Français d'Opinion Publique
INSEE	Institut National de la Statistique et des Etudes Economiques
IUFM	Institut Universitaire de Formation des Maîtres
IUP	Institut Universitaire Professionnel

IUT	Institut Universitaire de Technologie
MRG	Mouvement des Radicaux de Gauche
MRP	Mouvement Républicain Populaire
M6	Métropole télévision 6
ORTF	Office de Radiodiffusion-Télévision Française
PCF	Parti Communiste Français
PDG	Président-Directeur Général
PFN	Parti des Forces Nouvelles
PR	Parti Républicain
PRS	Parti Radical-Socialiste
PS	Parti Socialiste
PSD	Parti Social-Démocrate
PSU	Parti Socialiste Unifié
RMC	Radio Monte-Carlo
RPCR	Rassemblement pour la Calédonie dans la République
RPF	Rassemblement du Peuple Français
RPR	Rassemblement pour la Republique
RTL	Radio-Télévision Luxembourg
SFIO	Section Française de l'Internationale Ouvrière
SMIC	Salaire Minimum Interprofessionnel de Croissance
STS	Section de Techniciens Supérieures
TF1	Télévision Française 1
TGV	Train(s) à Grande Vitesse
TMC	Télé Monte-Carlo
TOM	Territoires d'Outre-Mer
UDC	Union du Centre
UDF	Union pour la Démocratie Française
UDR	Union des Démocrates pour la République
UNR	Union pour la Nouvelle République
UPF	Union pour la France
ZEP	Zone d'Education Prioritaire

Preface

> The majority of the French have Celtic, Roman and Frank forefathers and have retained both the positive and negative traits of the old Gauls. The French possess a great intellectual propensity. They are brave, chivalrous, warm, extremely flexible and eloquent in speech. The French are passionate politicians. They never fail to demonstrate an unequivocal national enthusiasm and a willingness to make sacrifices for the might and reputation of their country. However, they often lack toughness and a contemplated calmness. (v. Seydlitz 1912, p. 123)

> ...our country, which has fully devoted itself to social and political democracy, has a weakness for brilliant individuals. Its inhabitants, although diligent and hardworking, appear frivolous. Its tradition of revolutions has made the French a conservative people - in contrast to what they believe and what others might believe. It is possible that our individualism, which some call excessive, has been inherited from the Celts. (Roche 1961, p. 21)

The ways of looking at the history of civilization, which are more or less confined to the emphasis of national traits, are no doubt a thing of the past. Views, which presuppose a continuity of the Gallic character or try to revive the old chauvinistic arch enemy cliché, are most likely to be ridiculed today. However, even when such crass simplifications of how we see others and ourselves seem to be largely overcome, this naturally does not rule out the continued existence of certain national stereotypes. This is well evidenced by journalistic reportage, for example, or the presentation of another country in different language textbooks. In such instances, not only do various expectations and standards become effective but also – and one may assume – a certain social-psychological need to confirm the identity of one's own group with corresponding generalizations and differentiations.

Relapses into antithetical stereotypes are therefore very possible in situations which are perceived as conflicts or confrontations. Just thinking back to the widely discussed games between France and Germany during the last World Cups in soccer: How easy was it to use phrases such as “athletics, team discipline versus the art of playing, imaginativeness” or “the German fighting spirit and muscle men versus the light- footedness, liveliness and latinity of the French (cf. Keller 1983). Similarly, German journalists are likely to employ simplifying stereotypes whenever they comment on issues concerning French economic policy. And conversely, did not the airing of various old resentments and fears follow hard on the heels of German reunification? Be that as it may, these examples are indicative of the general tendency to interpret particular occurrences and developments by applying national or group-specific categories. Thus, a mechanism is involved which from the outset selectively steers the perception of events and assimilation of information. It is also not possible to simply abstract from such substantiated ethnocentric patterns of judgement. People must be made aware of these patterns and see them in relative terms so that the result might be an improved transnational understanding. For this reason, systematic insight into the circumstances of another country (without disregarding its historic background) and explicit comparisons with one’s own cultural situation are dispositive. This volume is dedicated to such principles.

Factual information, explanatory comments as well as statistics and illustrative material on a group of selected topics have been compiled in order to provide the reader with a basic framework. The explanation for this is that a certain elementary knowledge of historical and sociopolitical conditions is indispensable for anyone’s grasp of current developments and problems in France. Naturally, the contours of such a frame of reference are doomed to remain vague and subjective. There is not even a clearly defined canon of data concerning France. Nevertheless, topics have been selected in such a way that their discussion should offer broader access to an understanding of France.

The individual chapters do not have the sole purpose of disseminating isolated facts on “nation and people” as the case is in traditional social studies curricula. Instead, they attempt to elucidate specific and common developmental trends of France and Germany. The described phenomena should be easy to understand from the specific context of each country. This will ultimately allow the German reader to discuss the problems connected with these issues in addition to looking at them with a critical eye (cf. Bock 1974, Schüle 1983).

In this sense, the *references to contrasts* play an important part in the depiction of such phenomena since unusual features and characteristics of a country often do not become clear until comparisons are made. Nevertheless, the chapters in this book primarily focus on the portrayal of the France of today, even when parallels to Germany are occasionally described in greater detail. Our methodological approach aims at avoiding direct comparisons which disregard the function or particular importance of a phenomenon within the specific context of the country in question. All comparisons must take into account that the features of society A can never fully correspond to the features of society B and, as a rule, isomorphic assignments lead to inappropriate simplifications (as shown in detail by Müller 1980, Spillner 1978). A typical example of such a misleading way of drawing comparisons is the statistics on strike frequency: Such statistics state, for instance, that there are essentially more strikes in France than in the Federal Republic of Germany. This assertion would only be reasonable if it considered the distinct circumstances of each country, especially the vastly different working conditions and the existence of disparate arbitration procedures.

The following chapters attempt to familiarize the reader with the subject matter in such a way as to avoid those difficulties which typically arise in the assimilation and conveyance of cultural information. The contents of this study are limited to a group of so-called standard topics: political institutions, party systems, economy, social structures, education systems, mass media and German-French relations. Thus, this book does not contain "everything but the kitchen sink", as Herbert Christ recently complained. In our opinion, the *civilisation quotidienne* would have to be treated in a separate discussion (cf. e.g. Kalmbach 1990 or Passet 1990).

One problem particular to publications dealing with culture-related topics is that available information becomes obsolete relatively quickly: Just think of the change of political priorities in France since 1981, 1986 or 1988. For this reason, descriptions in this book are not based on a rigid notion of topicality but are more directed towards structural trends in the longer term.

Owing to the limited array of topics, it is not possible to address theoretical views generally related to the prerequisites (and problems without solution) of French social studies. The same applies to didactic issues. Therefore, we have made reference to a variety of specialized literature. The following aspects in particular have been left aside:

- an outline of the *history of French social studies and research on France* (see Hinrichs/Kolboom 1977a-c),

- a discussion on currently published literature on *France* (see Weller/Wenger 1983, Christ 1985, Fricke/Weller 1989),
- an overview of the approaches and models designed for teaching *French social studies* (see Baumgratz et al. 1978, Christ 1979, Schüle 1983, Melde 1987, Lüger 1991) and finally
- references to *material and dossiers on topics related to French social studies* (see Melde 1980, Bauer/Walter 1984).

The designations of the individual chapters purport to reflect different positions within the particular subject matter.

We would like to express our gratitude to Mr. Ernst Seibold for the numerous graphics he has prepared. We are also indebted to the Wissenschaftliche Gesellschaft Freiburg for its financial support.

We request that any forms of critique and suggestions of improvement be submitted to the publishing house.

Freiburg i. Br./Gosheim, March 1992

Ernst Ulrich Grosse — Heinz-Helmut Lüger

1. Political institutions in France and Germany

Heinz-Helmut Lüger

Two features are often used in characterizing the French form of government, features that appear to be very typical of it. The first of these two features is the strongly centralized organization of the governmental system. One consequence of this centralistic structure is that planning and decision-making processes affecting even the remotest areas of the country take place in the capital city, Paris. The second feature is a form of government that strikes one as being quite autocratic when compared to the system in the Federal Republic of Germany. In this system the president is assigned a dominating position while the parliament plays only a subordinate role. This situation is fittingly described by the term *monarchie républicaine* (cf. Duverger 1974, Zürn 1965). Despite the fact that these two aspects, centralism and presidential government, have their origin in two different periods in the history of the country, both of them have a decisive influence in making France what it is today. Their significance reaches far beyond the scope of constitutional law and administration.

Despite the numerous effects that the mentioned structures have in general on governmental dealings and political decision-making processes, it would be neither appropriate nor adequate to presume that a comparison between France and Germany will entail nothing but contrasts. Dualistic oppositions such as centralism vs. federalism or the presidential vs. the parliamentary system may come to mind quite readily, but they nevertheless neglect the relevance of developments in the opposite direction, e.g. movements towards decentralization in France or tendencies towards centralization in Germany. In the following description of the political systems in these two countries it will be important not only to take into consideration these changes in the institutional systems and the continuous adaptation to the changing problems of society but also to seek explanations based on the historical conditions peculiar to each country.

1.1 *Centralism and historical heritage in France*

1.1.1 Traditional administrative structures

The primary manifestation of centralism in France is that all decision-making paths converge in the centralized government agencies in Paris. At the same time, the decision-making responsibilities of local authorities are kept at a minimum. This system, which has begun to change somewhat only in the last few years, is based on the deeply rooted notion of a homogeneous and indivisible nation whose central administration embodies, as it were, the public welfare and guarantees the preservation of national unity.

For a long time – up to 1982 – the crucial link between the centre and the periphery was the prefect. Prefects were appointed by the head of state, acted as representatives of the government at the *département* level and saw to it that decrees from the government were carried out. In their capacity as supervisory officials (tutelle administrative), *préfets* had wide-ranging authority; in particular, they supervised the activities of the administrative authorities, up to and including the dealings of the mayors. Any administrative action from passing a communal budget to building a road was in principle subject to the

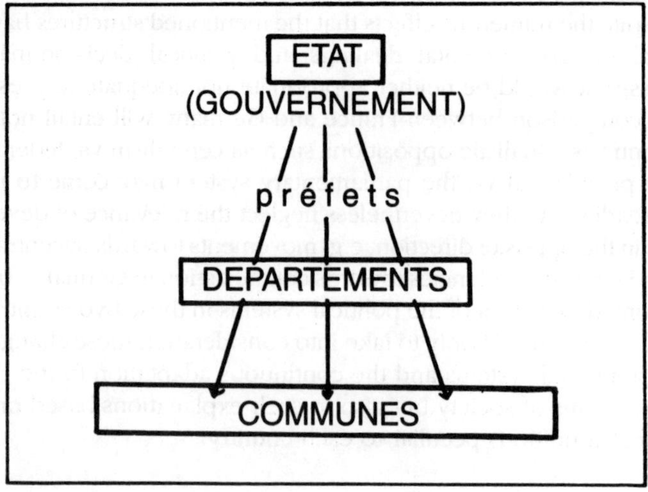

Fig. 1: Administrative centralism in France

supervision and authority of the responsible prefect. He was furthermore also in charge of the police. A greatly simplified rendering of the traditional administrative structure can be seen in *Fig. 1* (cf. I.3 for further duties of prefects and for changes after 1982).

Obviously, rigid administrative centralism of this kind left little room for autonomy or regional initiative. And this is probably not an effective means of promoting willingness on the part of the majority of the population to partake actively in politics. Furthermore, the ubiquitous French government is frequently associated with the Frenchman's reputed disposition to resist any form of governmental authority.

Admittedly, neither the unity of the French nation nor the equation of government and nation have ever been seriously called into question; nevertheless, the shortcomings of the centralistic administrative apparatus have not gone unnoticed and have been publicly criticized time and again. Napoleon III, for example, was one of the first to lament the bureaucratic excesses given rise to by the system: even the simplest of communal projects required a processing time of at least two years – even if the project met with no objections – for the simple reason that a dozen governmental agencies were involved in the process. In 1870 he even set up a *commission de décentralisation.* This commission, however, was as void of practical consequences as were the various attempts at reform undertaken during the following Third Republic. «Les hommes politiques proposent, l'inertie des mentalités dispose», as A. Peyrefitte (1976, p. 439) fittingly summed up.

Critique of centralism continued to be heard after 1945 and, as can be seen from the two excerpts, T. 1 and 2, was not restricted to any single party.

T. 1:
Notre administration est centralisée à l'extrême. On observe depuis une trentaine d'années une constante augmentation des bureaux parisiens et de leur tâche aux dépens des communes, des départements et des services extérieurs de l'Etat. Cette centralisation, contraire à l'esprit de liberté, a diverses causes. Elle est due à l'action parlementaire dont la tendance profonde est l'uniformité, donc à la cen-

T 2:
Cette façon d'uniformiser par la règle, jusque dans les moindres détails, tous les comportements sociaux et toutes les interventions des collectivités locales sur l'ensemble du territoire national est une des manifestations les plus insupportables de notre centralisme étatique. C'est la négation de toute initiative locale, de tout droit à la différence et à l'expérimentation.

tralisation. Elle est due aussi à des causes techniques: le caractère de maints travaux et services rend aujourd'hui plus difficile la tâche des autorités locales qui n'ont pas les collaborateurs compétents. Elle est due enfin à des causes financières qui sont peut-être les plus importantes. La première marque d'un Etat, ou en tout cas d'un Etat dont les finances sont délabrées, est qu'il prend la part du lion dans les recettes publiques. De ce fait, tout l'argent est à Paris, et c'est à Paris qui répartit l'impôt et le crédit.

Cette centralisation est nocive. Du point de vue politique, les libertés locales sont la meilleure éducation civique des électeurs et des élus. Du point de vue de l'administration, une centralisation peut ne pas nuire à l'efficacité des services publics quand ils sont commandés par un pouvoir stable et autoritaire: ce n'est pas toujours le cas en démocratie. Alors la centralisation aboutit à l'absence de décisions et d'activité, en un mot, au sommeil.

(Debré 1950)

Les élus locaux étouffent sous le poids des règles, décrets, arrêtés, circulaires ... auxquels ils sont soumis. Pour eux, ce n'est même plus Courteline (*), c'est Kafka!

(Mitterrand 1980, quoted from: CF 204/1982, 45)

(*) Georges Courteline, 1860-1929, French writer and dramatist, chiefly satirized petit-bourgeois behavior and the bunglings of the narrow-minded mentality common to bureaucrats (cf. e.g. *Un Client sérieux, Le Gendarme est sans pitié, Messieurs les Ronds-de-Cuir*).

Whereas the Gaullist Debré considers centralism to be justified by its efficiency as long as authority is intact, the Socialist Mitterrand maintains that any «centralisme étatique» has, by its very nature, a stifling influence and is predisposed to absurdity. Both of them, however, are in agreement as to its tendency to curb innovation and as to the poor manner in which it promotes decentralized initiative.

1.1.2 National unity and the expansion of central power (from the Capetians to the Third Republic)

As has already been alluded to, the system of government peculiar to France has developed and consolidated in the course of several centuries. It is closely tied to the emergence of a unified French nation and can only be explained in light of this.

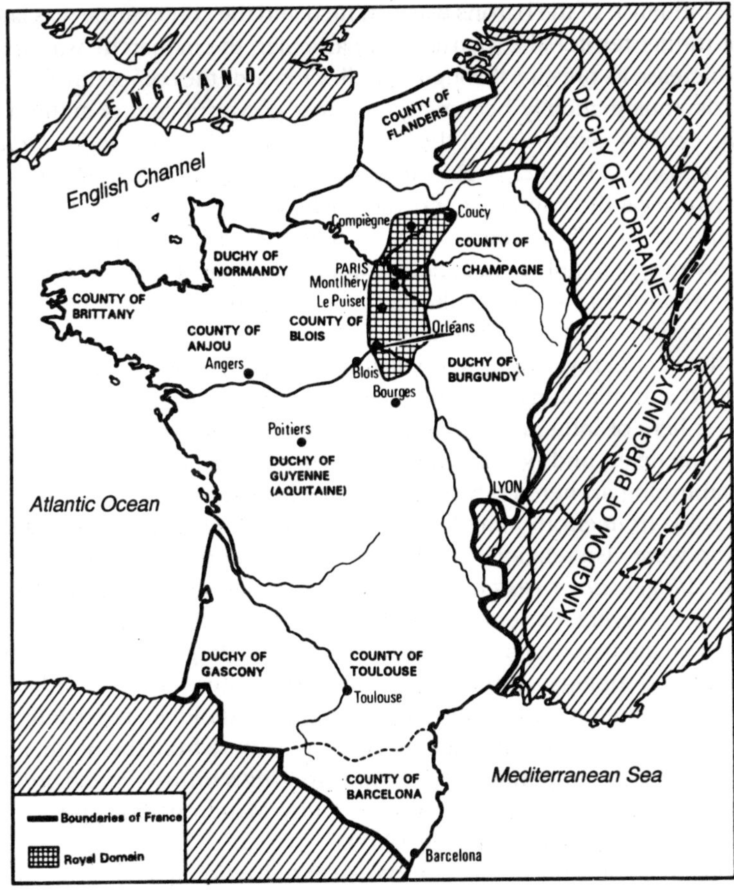

Fig. 2: France at the beginning of the 11th century
(Source: Bertier de Sauvigny 1980, 64)

The beginnings can be traced back to the *Capetian monarchy.* In 987, after the demise of the Carolingian dynasty, *Hugh Capet* was elected king of France. This event is significant inasmuch as his royal dominions (lands located in the Ile-de-France, including Paris and Orléans) formed the core for what was later to become France (cf. *Fig. 2*). His successors were able to consolidate their holdings and secure the royal crown for several generations of Capetians. Their sphere of influence was further enlarged at the beginning of the 12th century;

the influence of the barons was curtailed and the cornerstone was laid for further territorial expansion. In particular, the monarchy was able to increase its prestige through its policy towards the competing feudal lords, thus gradually becoming the most powerful central authority. The decisive expansion of the royal domains took place under *Philip II Augustus* (1180-1223). He successfully pushed back English predominance on the continent and vanquished the troops of the German emperor, the ally of the English, at *Bouvines* in 1214. The victory of Bouvines, generally held to be an important step in the rise of a *feeling of national unity*, also resulted in a fourfold increase in the territorial possessions of the crown and strengthened the predominant position of the central royal authority. The further endeavours of Philip II were aimed at diminishing the influence of his vassals, securing control in his sphere of influence by increasing the efficiency of his administrative agencies, and permanently stabilizing the political status quo by establishing an hereditary monarchy for his successors.

Aside from efforts aimed at territorial and administrative unification there were also religious conflicts of great consequence, in particular the *Albigensian Crusade* (1209-29) (for more details see Madaule 1973). In several extremely brutal campaigns it was not only possible to crush the heretical movement started by the Albigensians (*Cathari*), but also to subjugate most of the Languedoc. In this way the (northern) French kingdom had established a firm foothold in the south of France, a region differing in language and culture from the north, and it had taken an important step towards *forging a united French nation* (Köller/Töpfer 1978, p. 96f.; also cf. Duby/Mandrou 1968 and – in a european context – Duroselle 1965).

One can thus note that attempts at centralization in France resulted as early as the 13th century in feudal territorialism being overcome to a certain degree in favour of a strengthened monarchy. Of course, this trend did not progress without resistance and setbacks. Above all, the conflict with England (the Hundred Year's War, 1339-1453) repeatedly challenged the king's sovereignty; after this long period of political uncertainty, however, the French monarchy finally reemerged strengthened under *Charles VII*, and even more under his successor *Louis XI* (1461-83). The latter forced royal authority back on the rebellious territorial lords and also succeeded in adding several new large regions (Provence and the Duchy of Burgundy, among others) to his domain. The formation of a unified nation was thus practically complete by the time *Francis I* (1515-47) set out to establish a centralized civil service for administrational purposes and the collection of taxes, and when he decreed in the *Edict of Villers-Cotterêts* of 1539 that henceforth the official written language was to be French (more precisely, the dialect spoken in Ile-de-France, the ancestral holdings of the Capetians) and no longer Latin. This did not mean a levelling of contrasts, which were quite considerable in part: legal and fiscal differences continued to exist among the individual provinces as well as between the regional privileges of nobility, and even the edict on the unification of the official language did not automatically lead to a decline in regional languages.

In the second half of the 16th century and at the beginning of the 17th, several religious wars (above all with the Huguenots) and revolts of the nobility again placed the authority of the monarchy under a great amount of pressure. The power of the monarchic system, however, was re-established thanks to *Henry IV's* (1589-1610) policy of intercession and the energetic tactics of *Richelieu*, who had been appointed by Louis XIII in 1624 and who succeeded in breaking the resistance of the Protestants and quashing the reaction of the aristocracy. In the process, the use of extremely brutal methods (the establishment of special tribunals, liquidation of leaders in the aristocratic opposition, razing of citadels in the provinces, quelling of uprisings) sometimes proved unavoidable in realizing the centralistic goals. The use of *intendants* turned out to be especially efficacious in strengthening (and unifying) the central authority. Intendants were extraordinary officials directly appointed by the king and bestowed with particular powers for certain undertakings; their office, however, could be revoked at any time. Their basic purpose was to replace the deposed territorial lords in managing supervisory and administrative affairs in accordance with the king's wishes. (Later observers often compared the role of the intendants to that of the prefects.)

The principles of *national unity* and the *indivisibility of royal authority* reached its zenith during the absolute monarchy of *Louis XIV* (1643-1715). Aided by *Colbert*, he pushed through the completion of an all but omnipotent central administration, forced the nobility out of power and replaced them with intendants, who from now on had permanent positions in the provinces (primarily members of the bourgeoisie were now appointed to these offices). Any type of particularism, including religious dissidence, was suppressed with pitiless severity. The reign of Louis XIV was based on the notion of establishing a complete monopoly of power for the king as the incarnation of the state. It is interesting to note that this tendency to absolute authority of the state and the accompanying basic distrust of

Fig. 3: The traditional provinces of France
(Source: CF 204/1982, 13)

all movements towards decentralization have by far outlasted the 17th century: "Sovereignty is thus concentrated in the government: aside from it, there is no legitimate power." This statement by René Rémond (1978a, p. 23) would seem to reflect a French view of government widely held up to this very day.

The territorial extent of the French nation can be seen in *Fig. 3.* (The dates refer to the years in which the provinces were acquired by the crown.) Only few territorial changes have come about since the *Ancien Régime* (Savoy and Nice 1860).

The *French Revolution* brought a new turning point in 1789. It, however, did not, as one might presume, bring about the dissolution of the concentration of power typical of the *Ancien Régime*; administrative centralism in particular, if anything, even increased. The *Constituante* initially pursued a program of decentralism by replacing the traditional provinces, reminders of the monarchy, in 1790 with 83 new administrative entities called *départements*, all of roughly the same size (an organization still in existence today, except that the number of *départements* has been increased to 96; cf. *Fig. 4*). At the same time, the *Constituante* provided for elected representatives at the *département*, district and communal levels. In 1793, however, the Jacobins forced the *Convention* to suspend these elections and to revoke the newly granted autonomy. The reason for this was that in various *départements*, royalists and Girondins had entered into league with each other against the Revolutionary Government in Paris, and also that the Sansculottes with their radical democratic activities had become a further dangerous opposition group. In order to save the revolution, the Jacobins and the National Convention became proponents of central government:

> La Convention est placée devant un simple choix qui ne doit pas être déformé: ce n'est pas fédéralisme ou jacobinisme, mais arrêt de la Révolution ou poursuite de la Révolution; ce n'est pas centralisation ou décentralisation, mais contre-révolution ou révolution ... Par nécessité révolutionnaire, le jacobinisme devient centralisateur. (Flonneau 1982, 103)

This meaning of the term *jacobinisme* has been preserved in political parlance. Thus regardless of the role played by the Jacobins in the French Revolution as a whole, the usage of the phrase "Jacobinic tradition" in France refers primarily to an attitude which favours a centrally organized, tightly run unitary state. This state embodies at the same time the principle of popular sovereignty as a form of Rousseau's *volonté générale*; decentralizing or federalist tendencies are therefore looked down on as assaults on this principle.

Some of the structures which were set up during the revolution lasted until after the coup by *Napoléon Bonaparte* on 9 November (= 18 Brumaire) 1799, in particular the overall division of the country into *départements*. In the very first year of his consulate (1799-1804), however, Napoleon replaced the elected representatives of the regional administrative units with functionaries appointed by the government. For this purpose, the institution of the *prefect* was brought into being to function as an executive and supervisory agency of the central authorities at the level of the *départements*. (The term chosen reflects the revival of names and symbols from the time of the Roman Empire.) In the *arrondissements* and *communes*, the *sous-préfets* and *maires* were also appointed to represent the government. Similar to the kings in the times of the absolute monarchy, Napoleon had all the forces he needed to rule the country under his sole control. After further consolidation of the centralistic administrative system under Napoleon, the system remained practically unchanged until the end of the

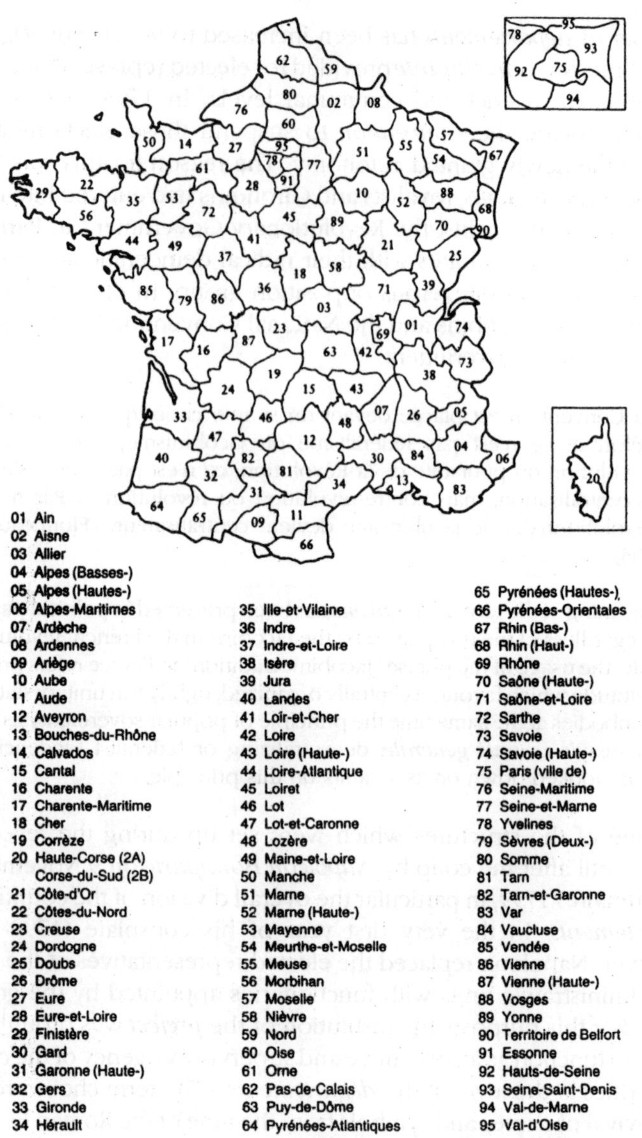

(The *départements* Haute-Corse and Corse-du-Sud both have the number 20. The so-called *Départements d'Outre-Mer* [DOM] and *Territoires d'Outre-Mer* [TOM], i.e. overseas *départements* and territories, of which there are six respectively five, are not included in this list. The numbers of the *départements* are in addition incorporated into the zip codes and license plate numbers.)

Fig.: 4: The French Departments

Third Republic and after the Second World War formed the institutional basis for the tentative attempts at decentralization of the time.

Looking back at French history, one can see that efforts toward national unity and toward building up a strong, centralistically oriented system of government played a prominent role in all time periods. Furthermore, the unbroken *tradition of a unitary state* can with good reason be viewed in this respect as one of the given historical conditions which are characteristic of France and which continue to have an effect even on modern politics:

> C'est sans doute le point sur lequel la comparaison entre la France et l'Allemagne fait ressortir le plus nettement la singularité du cas français. L'Etat a-t-il forgé l'unité nationale ou le sentiment national a-t-il précédé l'apparition de l'entité politique? La question est vaine et la controverse sans intérêt pour l'intelligence du présent: ils se sont identifiés l'un à l'autre depuis des siècles. L'unité nationale s'est exprimée dans une construction politique qui a en retour consolidé l'unité. Tour à tour la monarchie d'Ancien Régime, les jacobins de la Révolution, la centralisation consulaire, la République parlementaire ont travaillé à unifier la communauté nationale. La France est, au terme de ce travail des siècles, une des nations les plus unifiées qui soient. (Rémond 1978b, 18)

1.1.3 On the situation of regional languages

As has already been mentioned, the development of the French nation went hand in hand with the suppression of regional independence and with the propagation of French as the common language. An important step in this *Frenchbification* was the *Edict of Villers-Cotterêts*, in which the dialect of the Ile-de-France was introduced as the official language (cf. pg. 7).

This standardization of the language was effectively promoted by efforts towards centralization in the 17th century and especially by the revolution of 1789. The regional languages were viewed as relics of the *Ancien Régime* and as contradicting the idea of a "single and indivisible" republic. («La République française est une et indivisible» was the motto in 1729.) From then on French became the sole written language and increasingly superseded the other regional languages.

The trend toward levelling language differences was given further impetus when compulsory school attendance was introduced (1881/82), for the only language tolerated in the classroom was French.

The use of the local language, so-called *patois*, in everyday situations at school was strictly forbidden and punished accordingly with pedagogic methods. For example, one common punishment in Brittany until the 1950's was *la vache*, a figure that a student who had been caught speaking Breton had to wear around his neck until a new "victim" was found.

The decline of regional languages is a process that has continued to this day, and it seems highly unlikely that this trend will be reversed. Neither attempts at artificially reviving such languages (such as those undertaken in the 19th century by Mistral and by the Occitan group of poets called *Félibrige*, or such as are being made by current regional movements) nor certain liberalizing measures (e.g. the *Loi Deixonne* from 1951, which made possible the introduction of certain regional languages as an elective subject in schools; the prestige of such languages at schools and universities has been further improved since 1981) are likely to affect this negative prognosis. One crucial reason for this is the mere fact that French has secured such a strong position and has become customary for both written and spoken communication in most areas of life; in view of this, the chances that bilingualism (common language French and local language) will continue to exist in certain regions of France are becoming smaller and smaller.

"According to the *economic principles* of linguistics, the aim of spoken language is to obtain a high degree of communication between speaker and listener while using a small amount of linguistic means. Bilingualism by its very nature requires that two systems of communication be available at all times. If, however, experience shows that the French language shared by the whole nation fills all communication needs perfectly, maintaining an additional, regional language is a luxury (*linguistic redundancy*) when viewed pragmatically. A *langue régionale* – either French or non-French – has a realistic chance of survival only as long as it offers its speakers some kind of advantage over the *langue commune*." (Müller 1975, p. 8f.)

A simplified view of the distribution of regional languages in France is depicted in the following map (*Fig. 5*).

To begin with, France can be divided into two large linguistic areas, the *langue d'oïl* and the *langue d'oc* regions (named after the ancient words for "yes", *oïl* and *oc*, in the respective regions). As a result of the above-mentioned process of language levelling, the border between the two regions has gradually been shifting southwards. What this diagram does not show is that French, originally restricted to the north of France, is now the common language of the entire country. The regional variants and dialects of French are not reflected in this map either.

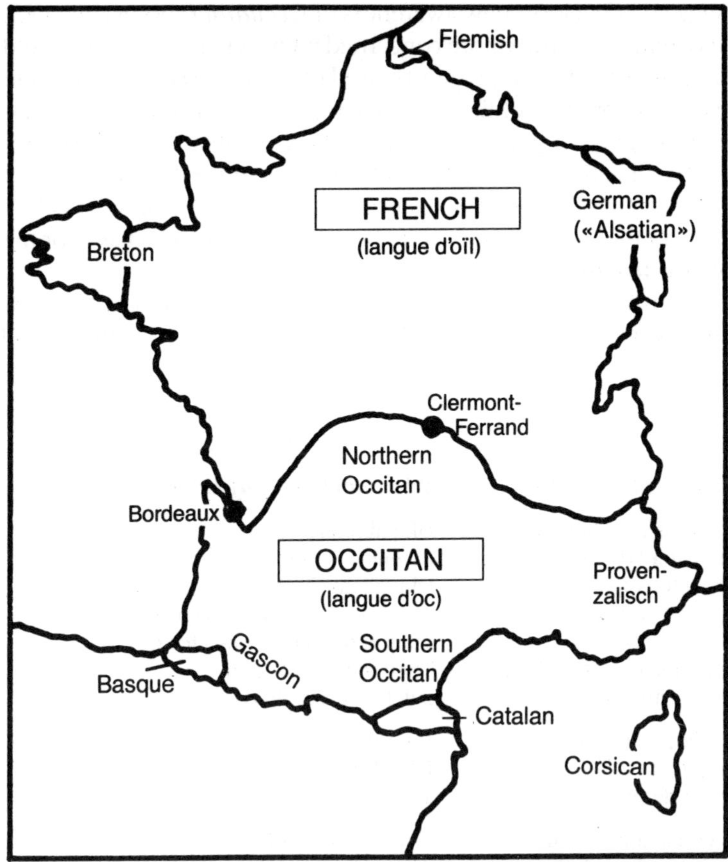

Fig. 5: Distribution of languages in France

Langue d'oc is equivalent to modern *Occitan* with its four main dialects, Gascon, Northern Occitan, Southern Occitan, Provençal. (A somewhat different classification can be found in Berschin et al. 1978, p. 267.) The culture at the Occitan courts and the lyric poetry of the troubadours were highly influential in medieval Europe. The Albigensian Crusade and the end of the Raimondine dynasty (Counts of Toulouse), however, ushered in the downfall of southern predominance. The present-day Occitan movement is, among other things, trying to rediscover the medieval origins of the region, carry on this heritage and develop a new awareness of *Occitanie* (abbreviated *OC*); the movement is furthermore concerned with increased economic and political self-determination (as opposed to *colonialisme intérieur*) and with the preservation of the Occitan language (establishing a standardized orthography, publishing the works of Occitan authors, sponsoring cultural activities). The *mouvement régionaliste* benefited greatly from the events of May 1968, the ecological movement and the Larzac protests in the 1970's. Since then, though, such activities have for the most part lost their élan.

The lyrics of the following song may serve as an example of the loss of identity felt by the populace and of its alienation from language and culture.

T. 3:

Perque m'an pas dit?	*Why didn't anybody tell me?*
Coma totis los mainatges	Like all children
Som anat a l'escòla	I went to school
Coma a totis los mainatges	Like all children
M'an aprés a legir	They taught me how to read
M'an cantat plan de cançons	They sang many songs for me
M'aprenguèron tant d'istòrias:	They told me so many stories
Lutèce...Paris...Paris...	Lutetia...Paris...Paris...
Mas pérqué, pérqué	But why, why
M'an pas dit a l'escòla	Didn't they tell me in school
Lo nom de mon païs?	The name of my country?
Nos contava lo regent	The teacher told us
Aquel grand rei de França	About this great king of France
Acatat davant los paures	Bowing down to the poor
Un sant òme aquel Sant Loïs	A holy man, this Saint Louis
Aimava tota la gent	He loved all of his people
E voliá pas la misèria	And he wished no misery
Un sant òme aquel Sant Loïs	A holy man, this Saint Louis.
Mas pérqué, pérqué	But why, why
M'an pas dit a l'escòla	Didn't they tell me in school
Qu'aviá tuat mon païs?	That he killed my country?
E quand forguèrem mai grands	And when we were older
Nos calguèt parlar tres lengas	We had to learn three languages
Per far un bon tecnician	In order to become good technicians
Nos caliá cargar tres lengas	We had to load ourselves down with three languages
E l'anglés e l'alemand	English and German

e çò que s'escriu a Roma	And what they write in Rome
Per far un bon tecnician	In order to become good technicians.
Mas pérqué, pérqué	But why, why
M'an pas dit a l'escòla	Didn't they tell me in school
La lenga de mon païs	My country's language?
...	...

(Claude Marti 1975)

Aside from French and Occitan, there are two other Romance languages spoken in certain regions of France:
- Catalan (basically the area of the *département* Pyrénées-Orientales),
- Corsican (a Tuscan dialect spoken on Corsica; approximately 50% of the population speak this language).

The non-Romance languages shown in *Fig. 5* are:
- Flemish (found in the *département* Nord; losing ground rapidly),
- Breton (a Celtic language spoken in the western section of Brittany; numerous organizations are promoting regional awareness),
- Basque (a non-Indo-European language found primarily in the *département* Pyrénées-Atlantiques; Basque is similar to Catalan in the southeast of France in that most speakers of these languages live in Spanish territory; there is relatively strong resistance on the part of the Basque population to being Frenchified.
- German or so-called Alsatian (including the Moselle Franconian dialects in eastern Lorraine and the High and Low Alemanic dialects in Alsace, all of which are usually subsumed by the French under the term *l'alsacien*; it is estimated that there are about 1.2 million speakers of German in France; due to the historical background of the region and its difficult "sandwich position" (Keller 1986a), there is hardly any politically oriented regional awareness here).

Cf. e.g. Kremnitz 1975, Garrisson 1987 for further details concerning ethnic minorities and regional languages in France.

1.1.4 The DOM-TOMs

The outline of the structure and extent of the French national territory given in chapter 1.1.2 is incomplete without also mentioning the *Départements d'Outre-Mer (DOM)* and the *Territoires d'Outre-Mer (TOM)*.

A relic of the past colonial empire, France still maintains control over a number of overseas territories (cf. *Fig. 6*), including:
- Guadeloupe
- Martinique
- Guyane
- la Réunion

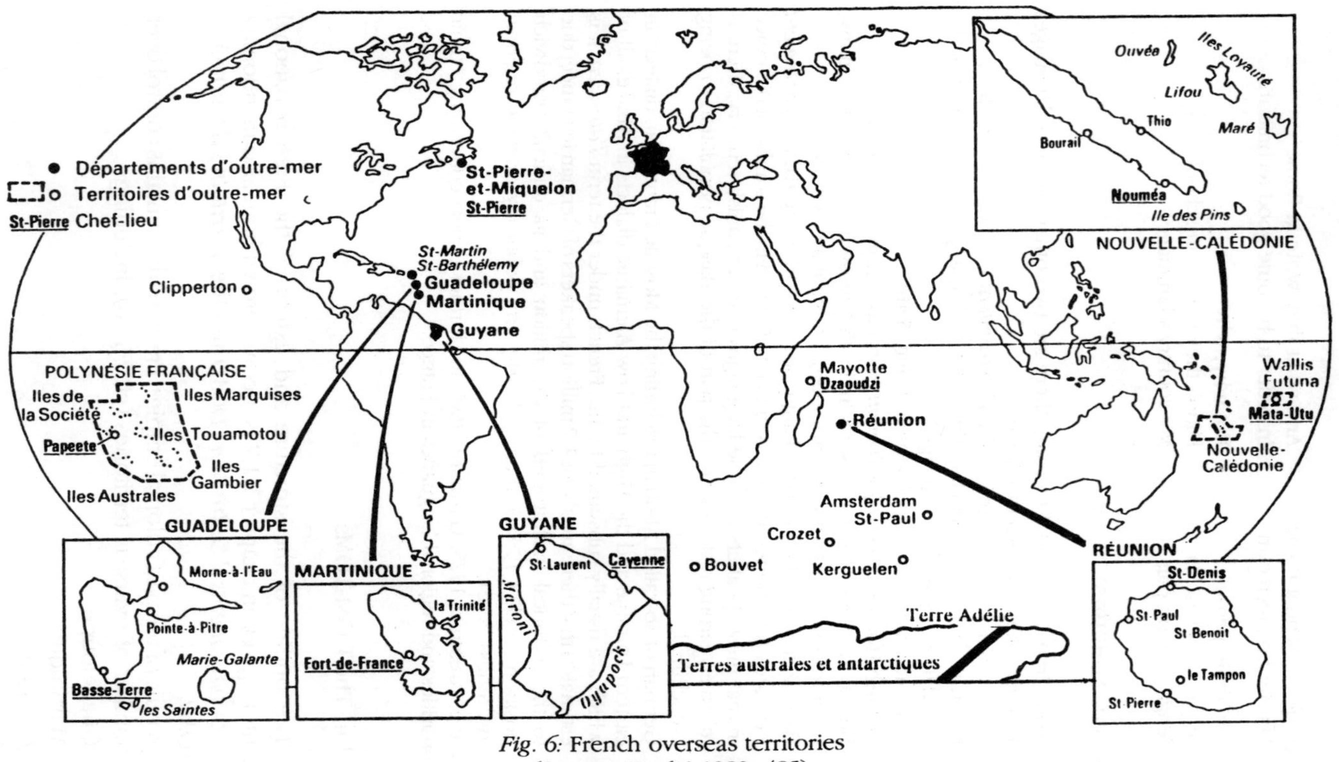

Fig. 6: French overseas territories
(Source: Verdié 1989, 485)

All four territories, which are also part of France's oldest colonies dating back to the 17th century, were given the status of *départements* in 1946. In addition, the islands

– Saint-Pierre-et-Miquelon
– Mayotte

are also controlled like *départements* (since 1976), although with some special internal regulations. Finally, among the *Territoires d'Outre-Mer* are

– Nouvelle Calédonie [New Caledonia]
– Polynésie française [French Polynesia]
– Wallis-et-Futuna
– Terres australes at antarctiques françaises (above all Terre Adélie) [Australian and Antarctic Territories]

The *territoires* differ quite significantly in their status, but, in contrast to the DOM, they generally enjoy a greater degree of autonomy. All the territories are under the administration of the *Ministère des départements et territoires d'outre-mer* in Paris. The DOM-TOMs in their entirety cover an area of about 420,000 square kilometres, with a total population of less than 2 million.

The standard language and the language of the educated in the DOM-TOMs is French, mainly to convey the idea that all their inhabitants are *citoyens* of the *République française*. In spite of many upheavals, very little has changed in this time-honoured aim. The vernacular spoken in the four Caribbean islands is Creole (based on French vocabulary), while Polynesian languages dominate in the South Sea territories.

The idea is put forward at times that it could not possibly, or no longer, be economic considerations that would explain France holding on to her overseas territories. In fact, a number of these territories are faced with formidable economic and social problems. Unemployment figures are soaring (Guadeloupe and Martinique: 30%, la Réunion 40%), with illiteracy almost as dramatic. Economic dependence on the mother country is steadily increasing, particularly since some of the initially profitable production sectors (e.g. agriculture) have declined. In some cases exports hardly cover 15% of imports; investments require vast subsidies, and allowances and tax benefits must be granted to the workforce in the tertiary sector (e.g. administration officials) (cf. Ripert 1990).

Although the general economic situation may not generally be so bleak, it is certainly not economic factors alone that explain the continuing interest in the overseas territories. *Military and geopolitical aspects* are more likely to play a significant role. Thanks to its DOM-TOMs, France is capable of maintaining a relatively strong *military presence* in the Indian Ocean (Mayotte, la Réunion, Terres australes) and in the Pacific Ocean (Polynesia, New Caledonia, Wallis-et-Futuna), as well as its *political influence* in potential trouble spots. It seems one way of keeping vestiges of the old position of world power (cf. Moutoussamy 1988).

Keeping a nuclear arsenal is one of the cornerstones of French military doctrine. Sparsely populated areas far from Europe offer virtually ideal conditions for testing new weapons. Not surprisingly, one of the most important test centres was established in the sporadic islands of French Polynesia, the *Centre d'expérimentation du Pacifique (CEP)*, the site of regular atom bomb tests on the Mururoa Atoll that the French government still considers necessary in spite of vociferous international protest. In economic terms, the CEP has brought about a certain economic recovery in the region. But the development begins to show its ugly side: disproportionate expansion of the tertiary sector, severe price increases, the destruction of indigenous economic structures, high unemployment figures, in turn leading to permanent social tensions. Moreover, criticism of France's nuclear policy is growing.

Strong independence movements in some areas are another issue difficult to appraise by the French DOM-TOM policy. This is particularly evident when ossified colonial structures lie in the way to a peaceful solution, as demonstrated by the example of New Caledonia.

The territory *Nouvelle Calédonie*, a group of islands in the South Pacific east of Australia, was colonized about 150 years ago. The first "settlers" were convicts deported from France. Their descendants, the *Caldoches*, together with the *Métropolitains* (later arrivals from France) account for the second largest population group (approx. 36%). About 21% are made up from immigrant populations from other islands (mainly Polynesians from Wallis [Wales]). The largest population group with 43% are, however, the *Canaques*.

The economic wealth of New Caledonia rests primarily on its mineral resources: chromium, cobalt and about 25% of the world's nickel reserves. Like the large plantations, they are exclusively owned by the white *Caldoches*. This distribution of wealth and the deterioration in the living standards of the indigenous population have in the past repeatedly led to tensions and bloody conflicts. The Canaques, increasingly made to feel like strangers in their own homeland, responded by forming the *FLNKS* (*Front de Libération Nationale Kanak Socialiste*) and now demand the establishment of *Kanaky*, an autonomous country independent from France. They are opposed by the *anti-indépendantistes*, in their majority whites who advocate staying with France, organized in the ultraconservative *RPCR* (*Rassemblement pour la Calédonie dans la République*) or the extreme right-wing *Front National*.

The demand for independence voiced by the FLNKS that was also endorsed by the UN General Assembly in 1986 has changed the situation drastically. The French government saw itself compelled to grant the Canaques some degree of codetermination by redistributing the territory and to promise changes in their autonomy status. The political efforts aimed at striking a reasonable balance suffered a severe setback in 1986-88, when the Chirac government inaugurated a new stage of *colonial restoration*.

At first, most of the measures designed to strengthen the position of the FLNKS and the population represented by it were revoked. In particular, the regions dominated by the FLNKS (3 out 4) were incapacitated by simply refusing financial assistance and reinforcing control in the Canaque settlements with the establishment of new military bases. The FLNKS, boycotting a referendum planned for 1987, was simply declared non-existent and massively obstructed in its political activities.

> «La revendication indépendantiste en Nouvelle-Calédonie est ultra-minoritaire et sans fondement. Les indépendantistes n'auraient jamais trouvé d'écho sns le laxisme soxialiste. Le FLNKS n'existe pas. Donc il ne peut pas manifester», said DOM-TOM minister Bernard Pons in 1987.

By taking this approach the government succeeded in re-establishing the colonial dominance of the white population, but also creating a quasi-civil war situation and ultimately driving the Canaques into radicalism.

The situation finally culminated in the Ouvéa massacre: in an attempt to free some hostages three days before the second ballot for the presidential elections on 8 May 1988, Chirac decided to opt for a violent solution, a decision ending in the loss of twenty lives and exacerbating the situation even further.

The hostile parties did not meet again until after Mitterrand's reelection for president of state. Prime Minister Michel Rocard and the representatives of the RPCR (Jacques Lafleur) and the FLNKS (Jean-Marie Tjibaou) arrived at an agreement that, in simple terms, aimed at the "decolonization of New Caledonia within the institutions of the French Republic". The result of the negotiations was endorsed by 80% of the votes in favour in a referendum held in November 1988 (with an election turnout of only 37%). The central agreement, however, is

Fig. 7
(From: Libération 27 June 1988)

not to be redeemed until 1998: that is the year when a general referendum will be held to decide a) on the restructuring of the territories into three provinces and b) on the self-determination (*autodétermination*) of New Caledonia (on the issue of self-determination from the point of view of the indigenous population, see *Fig. 7*).

The 1988 agreement certainly went some way toward defusing the situation. But the question remains whether a sustainable solution pleasing all population groups will be reached. Some serious setbacks (e.g. two of the leading FLNKS representatives being assassinated in 1988) give rise to a certain pessimistic outlook.

The quest for democratically legitimized participation models is obviously an important subject in the other overseas territories, too. This is shown by the large number of organizations striving for independence. Sooner or later, France will have to come to a settlement with these groupings and find new forms of co-operation somewhere between *indépendance* and *autonomie*.

1.2. *Particularism and the federal tradition in Germany*

Whereas the development in France has been determined to a crucial degree by the concentration of all governmental powers and by resistance to decentral tendencies, *German history* since the end of the Middle Ages has been characterized by more or less the opposite tradition. The observation that territorial powers have overshadowed central authority in Germany, and that "as opposed to conditions in France, a unified, a concrete continuity with regard to national development [has been lacking] in Germany" (Mommsen 1978, p. 31) has all but become commonplace in comparisons between Germany and France.

Although in France it was possible for, e.g., Philip II Augustus to consolidate royal predominance as early as the beginning of the 13th century, and for Philip IV (the Fair) to control even the Papacy after 1300, it was the territorial lords, both secular and ecclesiastical, who plainly held the power in Germany. The king lacked military might; according to the German feudal system, one pledged fealty to the individual lords and not to a central monarchy. The German electors had achieved the right to elect the king, the Papacy retained its influence – due at least in part to the outcome of the Investiture Controversy –, and it was not possible to develop a unified system of government because of the sovereignty of the lords. The decision to elect Rudolph of Habsburg king was symptomatic of the distribution of power at the time and of the desire to prevent the rise of a strong central authority no matter at what cost. The position of the lords, initially set down in the *Confoederatio cum principibus ecclesiasticis* (1220) and *Statutum in favorem principum* (1232), was confirmed repeatedly (1356 the Golden Bull, 1648 Peace of Westphalia), thus further reinforcing the king's or emperor's impotence and the condition of political territorialism. In the 17th century, the Holy Roman Empire was not much more than an alliance of sovereign states held together by the imperial crown. (At the very same time France, united as a single nation, was attaining European supremacy under the absolute monarchy of Louis XIV.) The German *Reich* had no foundation on which to base an extensive central administrative system patterned after the French; only in certain individual states comprising the *Reich* did comparable developments take place (cf. the centralized civil service in Prussia since Frederick William, the "Great Elector").

Fig. 8: German Confederation (1815), German *Zollverein* (1834)

German particularism was at first able to survive both movements towards national unification and various reorganizations of the *Reich*: the German Confederation of 1815 was only a loose federation (*Fig. 8*), the German *Zollverein* (1834) had a solely economical purpose and, like the North German Federation of 1866, did not even take in the whole *Reich*. This particularism did not diminish until after the Franco-Prussian War of 1870/71, at which time Germany was united under Prussian leadership in the form advocated by the "Little German" party. The *Reich* under Bismarck was, admittedly, nothing but a "superimposed confederation" (Wehler 1980, p. 60; cf. *Fig. 9*) that came into being through treaties with the southern German states and that lacked

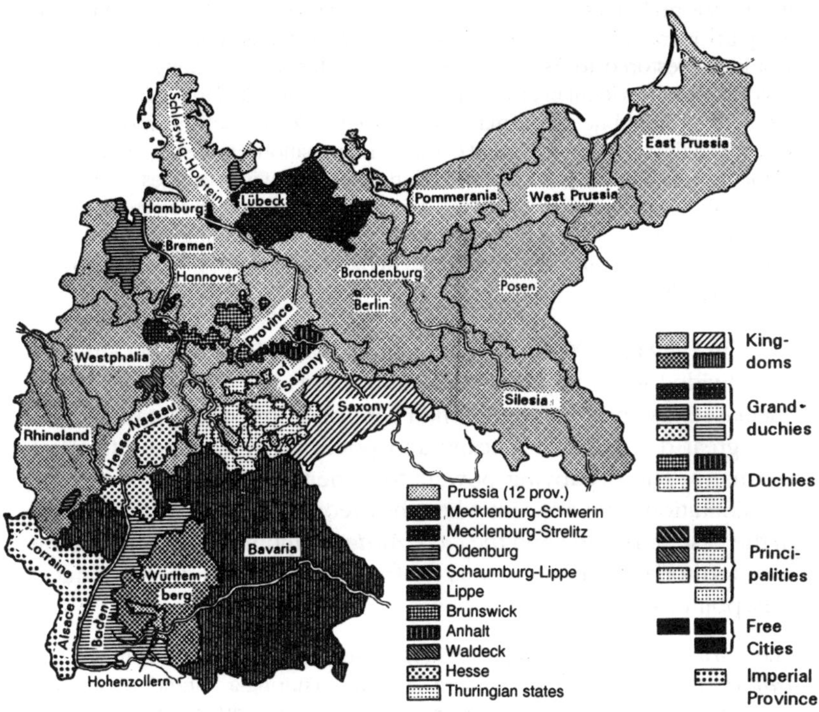

Fig. 9: The German *Reich* 1871

any real sovereignty. Nevertheless, an increasing degree of national awareness and the idea of a *Reich* headed by the German *Kaiser* gradually overcame the individual interests of the member states. The German *Reich* thus developed into a relatively unified nation, albeit much later than France, England and Spain. The basis of this new nation, however, continued to be the *federal principle*; this continued to be the case after World War I in the Weimar Republic.

This system of organization based on political entities of historical origin was brought to an end by the unitary policy of the Nazis. After the collapse of Nazi Germany in 1945 and the territorial reorganization agreed upon by the Allies in the Yalta and Potsdam Conferences, federalism resumed its course in 1949 with the newly founded Federal Republic of Germany (West Germany) (cf. e.g. Rupp 1982, Grosser 1981).

It was thus no longer possible to refer to a unified nation despite the fact that the participants in the Potsdam Conference had still assumed that Germany would be restored to its 1937 boundaries – this kind of unity was and is historically self-evident in France, for example. As a result of this legal situation, the Federal Republic of Germany initially considered itself no more than a (provisional) partial embodiment of the German nation. However, as the paths of the two constituent parts diverged during the following decades, and as the economic boom in West Germany and the West German rejection of the political system in East Germany started to form the basis of a new feeling of national awareness, the reestablishment of past national unity became less and less compelling.

From 1949 to 1990 the territory of the Federal Republic of Germany was divided into ten federal *Länder* (cf. *Fig. 10*). West Berlin had a special status and was under Allied control despite the fact that it was to a great degree economically and politically integrated into West Germany. The occupying powers took neither historical nor ethnic considerations into account when they reorganized the states (except in the case of Bavaria and the city-*Länder* Hamburg and Bremen); the new territorial distribution was far from perfect from an economical viewpoint as well.

The *German Democratic Republic* (*East Germany*) consisted initially of five *Länder*: Mecklenburg-Vorpommern, Saxony, Thuringia, Brandenburg and Saxony-Anhalt. They were represented in the *Länderkammer*, which was composed of members of the individual state legislatures. Although the *Länderkammer* did not have the same status as the *Volkskammer* (People's Legislature), the system was clearly federative. When the country was reorganized into *Bezirke* (districts) in 1952, however, the *Landtage* (state legislatures) and the *Länder* themselves were abolished; the *Bezirkstage* (district councils) which were then established were governmental administrative agencies more or less equivalent to the West German *Regierungspräsidien*. In this way, federalism was abolished and replaced by the structures of a centralized, unitary state.

German reunification in 1990 brought about new changes: the fundamental upheavals taking place in eastern Europe and the consent of the four Allied powers allowed the German Democratic Republic to join the "territorial scope of the [German] Constitution" (pursuant to Article 23 Basic Law) (cf. v. Beyme 1991 for greater detail). The unification agreement expressly stated that the *Länder* dissolved by the GDR in 1952 will be reconstituted. From the date this provision came into effect (3 October 1990) the Federal Republic of Germany is made up of 16 federal *Länder*.

Although it is not always easy to draw a line between the authorities of the federal government and those of the *Länder* in West Germany, the legislative powers of the states consist chiefly of the following

Fig. 10: Federal system v. unified state (until 1990)

areas: cultural affairs (advancement of the arts and sciences, legislation concerning media, jurisdiction over the school and university system, this latter jurisdiction being restricted by the federal government inasmuch as it establishes guidelines and is involved in financing), the police force (unless supplemented by the authority and organizations of the federal government), questions dealing with regional planning and ecology (again, partially subject to regulations set by the federal government). Another, no less important duty is that federal laws are to be executed and enforced by the states' administrative bodies; this results in a large degree of latitude for the state bureaucracies, a freedom of action which is to a large extent exempt from political control (cf. Ellwein 1977, Schnabel 1980). Finally, the states are represented in the *Bundesrat* (Federal Council), where they can take part in legislation at the federal level. Despite all this, the overall emphasis has clearly been shifted to the federal government. More and more problems require regulative measures that extend beyond the borders of the individual states. These problems necessitate not only a concentration of financial means but also the centralization of decision-making processes.

It is because of this, but also "primarily because of tendencies toward centralization given rise to of necessity by industrial society, that the importance of the federal government in the relationship between the federal level and the *Länder* has become much stronger than was intended by the authors of the constitution. Due to the levelling effect of industrial society, the Länder today hardly have a chance any more to develop their own kind of political identity and their own differentiated qualities of government." (Sontheimer 1985, p. 250)

1.3 *Reforms in French centralism and the movement to decentralization*

In the same way that the federative principle is increasingly being overshadowed in West Germany by centralizing forces, tendencies steering away from the centralistic system are also emerging in France. As a rule, the local civil servants, in their capacity as representatives of the central government, and the elected representatives of the local administrative units (*départements, communes*) were able to establish a good atmosphere of co-operation, a kind of working agreement between the central and peripheral authorities. Since both parties were constantly dependent upon each other – the administrative offices needed contact persons in order to carry out governmental decrees in a flexible manner and with as little conflict as possible; the local representatives were concerned with looking after the interests of their constituency, again with as little conflict as possible – the hierarchical nature of the formal structures became partially obscured. This intertwining of administration and personnel resulted ultimately in undermining to a certain extent the centralistic principle at the periphery (Grémion 1980, p. 104).

These tendencies in the opposite direction, however, could not cover up the continuing imbalance in the distribution of authority. The tutelary role of the central government with the well-known *remontée des dossiers sur Paris* was present at all times and was a hindrance to making local planning and decision-making possible. The outcry for decentralization is thus by no means a phenomenon typical of the 1980's alone, but rather can be traced, as indicated above, to as far back as the last century.

The necessity of counteracting the centralistic orientation in France with far-reaching structural reforms became increasingly apparent subsequent to World War II. Steps for a regional reorganization were devised, in particular with the goal of decreasing the economic and social differences between the region around Paris and the French province (cf. the program presented in *Paris et le désert français* by Jean F. Gravier [1947]); the catchword of the times was: *aménagement du territoire.* The wide-ranging program subsumed various projects under this phrase: stimulating the development of economically neglected regions by expanding their infrastructures and by a concerted action aimed at attracting new industry; stopping migration out of these regions; the long-range goal of disentangling or at least stabilizing the densely populated area in and around Paris (Delmas 1962, Monod/Castelbajac 1973). The new regional policy was closely tied to the government's four-year plans (*planification*, cf. 3.5), in which were specified the key economic goals for the period of reconstruction and later also for the structural changes in industry. Planning and coordination of projects were aimed at *regional needs*, for which express reason 22 economic program regions (*régions de programme*) were created in *1956*.

The economic regions usually comprised several *départements.* Their status was at first vague and they had no agencies or authority of their own. This division into economic regions – although it was set up by the central bureaucracy in Paris without any conferral with the population whatsoever and with no regard to historical and cultural ties – has been maintained up to the present and was not substantially modified by any of the subsequent reforms (exceptions: Corsica is now a region on its own, Rhône and Alpes have been combined; cf. *Fig. 11*).

There had also been a somewhat comparable regional organization during the Vichy regime, although this had been intended more to revive the old provinces. This fact was later used for a long time to further discredit regionalist demands – in addition to the familiar Jacobin argument that any form of decentralization would endanger the *République une et indivisible.*

Fig. 11: The regional organization of France

The institution of the economic regions was reinforced in *1964*, on the one hand by the appointment of regional prefects (*préfets de région*), on the other by the creation of the *Commissions de Développement Economique Régional* (CODER). The primary duty of the so-called *super-préfet*, who was at the same time the *prefect* of a *département*, consisted of seeing to it that governmental decisions concerning regional planning were carried out in his economic region and of coordinating the realization of such decisions with the other *département* prefects. It should be noted, however, that all important steps in the planning stages, including the allocation of finances, were taken care of by the central administration, as of 1963 by a central regional planning authority (*Délégation à l'Aménagement du Territoire et à l'Action Régionale*, DATAR); thus the regional prefects were responsible for nothing but the execution of the plans. The CODER as well had a merely advisory status; a quarter of the members in these commissions were indirectly elected (mayors, members of the general councils), 50% represented professional organizations (business and industry, unions), and the remaining quarter was appointed by the government.

The success of this regional planning policy was very limited. It proved to be impossible to reduce the large economic disparity between individual economic regions and the resulting differences in living conditions. Above all, however, these measures achieved nothing in the way of decentralization (cf. the assessment in T. 4 made in 1964 by Mitterrand, at that time in the opposition).

T. 4:
... la Ve République procède, en réalité, à un extraordinaire durcissement du système napoléonien. Non seulement aucune mesure décentralisatrice n'a été prise, mais les pouvoirs des assemblées municipales et départementales sont inexorablement réduits au bénéfice des fonctionnaires placés par le gouvernement à la tête des régions-programmes. Tel est le circuit: les experts du Plan conçoivent, élaborent. Les experts de l'Aménagement mettent en oeuvre et répartissent les «tranches opératoires». A l'échelon de la région un fonctionnaire, le préfet coordinateur, exécute. Des fonctionnaires, les préfets, réunis sous la présidence du super-préfet en conférence interdépartementale, affectent les investissements. Ni le Parlement ni les Conseils généraux n'interviennent ... Au gré des préférences politiques, le ministère de l'Intérieur guide le choix de ses agents qui déversent la manne sur les communes qui votent bien et stérilisent les communes qui votent mal. (Mitterrand 1984, 168)

Criticism, however, was not the sole domain of the parliamentary opposition, and the time seemed almost more than ripe for relaxing the strictness of the anachronistic central decision-making and administrative system. It was under these circumstances that *de Gaulle* finally devised plans for an extensive regional reform at the end of the 1960's. The heart of these plans consisted of turning the economic regions into independent administrative units (*collectivités territoriales*) with budgets of their own, with assemblies, part of whose members were to be elected directly, and with extensive powers.

The project was not only inspired by de Gaulle's notion of a participative society, it also bore in mind certain political tendencies of the time: the demand for more direct democracy (above all following the events that took place in May 1968) and the growing movements in favour of regionalism.

(The term *régionalisme* – as opposed to *régionalisation* – refers primarily to the efforts and activities of ethnic and language minorities who are opposed to total Frenchification and the political predominance of the centralist state and who advocate a greater amount of regional independence [cf. 1.1.3 as well as Lafont 1967 and the survey in Schmidt et al. 1983, pp. 267-275]. Regionalization, on the other hand, designates a form of decentralization which uses the economic regions as a starting point.)

Fig. 12
(Source: CF 204/1982)

De Gaulle's plans, worked out in detail in the *Projet Jeanneny,* were a reform that truly went far beyond the measures that had been taken up to then and were without a doubt intended to curtail central power and enhance the power of the periphery. Furthermore, the reforms were aimed at abolishing the Senate, the second chamber of Parliament; it was to be replaced by an assembly made up of representatives of social and professional interest groups, again modelled after the participative concept mentioned earlier (for more details see: Grémion 1980, p. 112ff.; CF 204/1982, p. 20ff.). The project had been conceived practically behind closed doors and when de Gaulle submitted it to a referendum on 27 April 1969, the general populace was not really able to assess its complexity or its significance (especially with respect to the Senate reform). The referendum resulted in 53.2% voting against the project and 46.7% voting for it.

When analyzing these results, one should naturally not overlook the fact that de Gaulle also had other motives in calling this referendum, motives of a tactical nature stimulated more by day to day politics. By winning the referendum de Gaulle was hoping to increase his popularity after the riots of 1968 and to reaffirm the legitimacy of his presidency. On the other hand, rejecting this bill was practically the only way that the opposition could make de Gaulle resign. Thus, the election results cannot be construed solely as a negative vote for the reform project.

After the failure of de Gaulle's reforms, the *regional legislation* of 1972 introduced by his successor, *Pompidou*, brought about no significant structural changes: the economic regions were not turned into independent administrative units but were instead only given the status of *établissements publics* ("public agencies"); in this way they had now merely become a sort of joint authority for several *départements*, had no administration of their own and could not intervene in the legal domains of other political subdivisions (*départements, communes*). A *conseil régional* was established, a representative body whose members were elected indirectly. The composition of this new body further reinforced the position of the local notables, whose influence had been under discussion in the previously planned senate reform. The economic and social committee (*Comité économique et social*) had an advisory function and was made up of, among others, representatives of business and industry, unions, chambers of commerce, self-employed professionals, health and welfare institutions. The influence of these boards had been deliberately kept in check; in particular, governmental supervision had been left unchanged so that it was not possible for any decentralizing effects whatsoever to come of Pompidou's "mini-reform".

The way for a fundamental change in this respect was not paved until 1981, when the political Left won the elections. A policy of decentralization – a *révolution tranquille* – was declared one of the priorities of the following legislative period.

The political motivation behind decentralizing measures was not only to increase effectiveness in administration and economy, instead the main thrust – at least according to the political platform from 1972 on – was aimed at granting more autonomy to local authorities and at improving the opportunities for active and direct participation in politics:

> La France vit encore sous Napoléon. Une centralisation extrême de toutes ses structures étouffe les initiatives et l'esprit de responsabilité. L'Administration jusque dans les services les plus reculés et jusque dans les marchés les plus lointains pullule de petits Napoléon...
>
> La décentralisation est une nécessité car les citoyens doivent se sentir concernés par la chose publique.
>
> La question principale est d'accroître la démocratie, de briser la domination de l'Etat centralisé et de la haute Administration. Une décentralisation poussée à tous les niveaux répondra à cette exigence.» (Parti socialiste 1972, 103 f.; similar: Programme commun 1973, 73 ff.)

Probably the most significant changes brought about since 1982 by G. Deffere's decentralization laws were:

- the *economic regions were turned into autonomous administrative units* (with a directly elected *Conseil régional*) and
- the *tutelle administrative*, i.e. administrative control by the central authorities, was abolished.

The prefects lost a great deal of their previous functions, in particular their power of directive over the regional authorities. In their capacity as *commissaires de la République*, their chief duty now is to supervise the legality of administrative activity (*contrôle de légalité*), i.e. they may cause decisions made in their districts to be reviewed *afterwards* by the administrative courts and, if necessary, to be revised. The executive power, however, is unequivocally in the hands of the chairpersons or presidents of the elected assemblies, namely the *Conseil régional* or *Conseil général*; resolutions passed by the city council (*Conseil municipal*) no longer require the consent of a governmental supervisory authority either. The system for the allocation of funds was also reorganized at the same time that regional authority was extended. The success of these decentralization efforts probably depends not least of all on the manner in which government subsidies are appropriated – regardless of shifting majorities in the government – and on the extent to which the regional authorities have access to their own sources of tax income.

The following is a brief résumé of how jurisdiction is distributed among the individual regional authorities. Additional explanations and historical background information can be found in CF 204/1982, 220/1985, Verdié 1987, 94ff.; Gontcharoff et al. 1983ff. offer an exhaustive commentary on the laws concerned; see Uhrich 1987, Albertin 1988, Verdié 1989, 138ff., Min. de l'Ind. et du Comm. ext. 1991 for the effect on economic development.

	Bodies	Functions
Région	*Conseil régional* (elected directly) *Président du conseil régional* (= executive power)	Draws up the economic plan for the economic regions, in drafting the national plan
	Comité économique et social (= advisory board, made up with representatives from various societal groups)	Activities in the areas of economy, social welfare, culture (e.g. promoting certain branches of industry, coordinating

	Commissaire de la République de région (= representative of the government, supervision of legality)	specific projects for supporting individual firms and vocational training. Ecology.
Département	*Conseil général* (elected directly)	Jurisdiction in the areas of economy and social welfare
	Président du conseil général (= executive power) *Commissaire de la République/ Préfet* (= representative of the government, supervision of legality)	Supplements governmental social policy (in particular social benefits)
Commune	*Conseil municipal* (elected directly) *Maire* (= executive power)	Zoning, building-permits Jurisdiction in the areas of economy, social welfare and the arts Resolutions passed by the city council can be carried out immediately without previous consent of a governmental supervisory authority

It is still unclear whether France will actually succeed in overcoming its old Jacobinic background and be able to initiate the formation of a «nouvelle citoyenneté», as Pierre Mauroy announced in 1981. At any rate, the measures which have been taken since 1982 leave earlier attempts at reform far behind; and the fact that the *tutelle administrative* has been abolished and that the regional authorities have been granted greater powers at all levels cannot be rated high enough in view of the firmness with which centralistic institutions are rooted in French history. For this reason it would be dreadfully inappropriate to term these measures mere "cosmetic surgery" or "marginal reforms" whose goal is merely "to update the central government without calling the distribution of power into question" (cf. Brauner 1986). Granted, we shall have to see if and how the policy of decentralization will be continued in the coming years.

1.4 *Problems and reforms in the federalistic system of Germany*

The problem of decentralization is, for obvious reasons, irrelevant in the Federal Republic of Germany. Questions of territorial reorganization, too, arise from completely different considerations. For instance, there were prolonged discussions in West Germany about reorganizing the *Länder* – an act, by the way, which was originally declared obligatory in Article 29 of the West German constitution. The motivation behind this discussion, however, was to do away with existing inequities, for the in part substantial degree to which the individual *Länder* differed in size, population and economic strength could not help but result in them developing in divergent directions. All of the suggestions for reorganizing the system, however, failed because of the interests of the states themselves, the sole exception being the merger of Baden, Württemberg-Baden and Württemberg-Hohenzollern in 1951 to form Baden-Württemberg. As a result of this situation, the passage in Article 29 of the constitution was altered in 1976 from a stipulation to a permissive provision. ("The territory of the Federal Republic may be reorganized to ensure that the *Länder* are capable of fulfilling their duties commensurate with their size and economic efficiency.") A new opportunity to reorganize arose in 1990 during the preparations for the unification agreement, but it was again allowed to lapse without action. The only step taken was the reconstitution of the old *Länder* Mecklenburg-Vorpommern, Saxony, Thuringia, Brandenburg and Saxony-Anhalt in the "joining territories", previously dissolved by the GDR in 1952. A territorial option involving two or three *Länder*, which would take account of the differences in economic power of the appropriate regions, was not feasible under the prevailing circumstances. Other proposals such as the formation of "cross-border" *Länder* (for instance, Schleswig-Holstein/Mecklenburg or Hesse/ Thuringia) were also dropped eventually.

The task of the Federation involving *regional planning policies* for all the states is a completely different matter. This policy is intended to ensure as much as possible similar living and working conditions throughout the country. This includes, for example, measures for rectifying weak spots in the economic structures of an area, providing aid for economically underdeveloped regions, and ecologically oriented improvements in highly industrialized and densely populated areas. It is quite appropriate to draw a parallel between what has just been mentioned and the French *aménagement du territoire.*

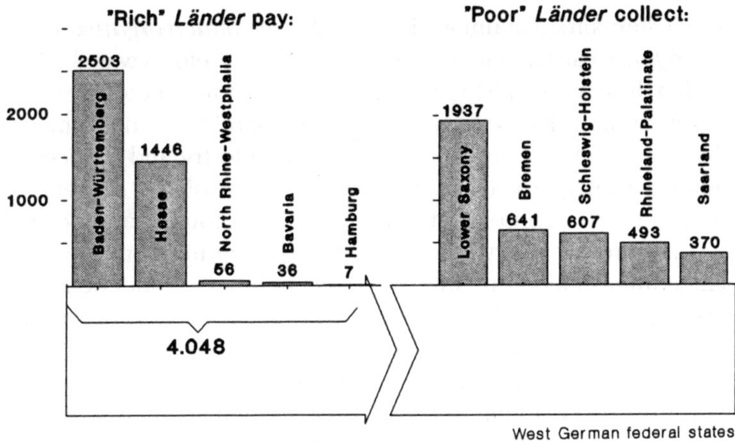

Fig 13: Financial compensation among the states
(Revenue sharing 1990 in millions of DM)

A further means of integration is the system of (horizontal) *revenue sharing between the Länder*. Because of the disparate geographical distribution of the *Länder* and because of their differing degrees of economic development, the economic differences between the individual *Länder* turn out in part to be quite substantial. Attempts are then made to rectify these differences by annual compensation payments ("Uniformity of living conditions"). The basis for this system is Article 107 of the constitution, according to which *Länder* that are financially better off are obliged to make compensation payments to *Länder* with a poorer financial situation; this is then supplemented by additional allotments from the federal government.

Thus in 1990, Baden-Württemberg, Hesse, North Rhine- Westphalia and Bavaria were classified as economically stronger and were therefore the payers for the financial compensation. The rest of the states were "entitled to compensation" (cf. *Fig. 13*). In 1970, by contrast, North Rhine-Westphalia was "number one" of the "rich" states. There is very little agreement as to the proper way of determining the financial strength of the individual *Länder*, threats of constitutional complaints are therefore not infrequent.

The East German federal states will not be included in the revenue sharing between *Länder* until 1995. The immediate integration, originally stipulated, would certainly have meant the financial collapse of the old states. Instead, the first stop to overcome the west-east gradient was to introduce a provisional fund called "German Unity". It is also envisaged to participate the new states in the distribution of the turnover tax (Value Added Tax) according to their population sizes.

Another step aimed at unification was the *regional reorganization* (*Gebietssreform*) carried out from 1965 to 1979. This reform was chiefly intended to dissolve the historical communal structures (note that 95% of the communities had a population of less than 5000) and to meet "the demands of a modern society based on industry and services". The guiding principle was to create at the levels of the *Gemeinde* (community), *Kreis* (approximately equivalent to a county) and *Bezirk* (district) new regional structures tailored to a size most suitable for efficient administration. In this way, the number of independent communities was reduced from about 24,000 to 8500. (In comparison, France has nearly 37,000 independent *communes*, about 60% of which have a population of less than 500; communal reforms have not as yet gone beyond the planning stages.) Even though there was much dispute as to how to carry out this regional reorganization, dispute which resulted in procedures varying sometimes from state to state, the overall effect was certainly that of contributing to the unification of the administrative structure – and thus to reinforcement of certain centralizing tendencies as well. However, opinions differ as to whether the other goals, such as improving communal autonomy or increasing efficiency and lowering costs, have been achieved.

1.5 *Political institutions of the Fifth Republic*

The constitution of the Federal Republic of Germany reflects the experiences of the Weimar Republic and of the period of German fascism by trying to prevent the same mistakes from being repeated. In a similar fashion, it can be seen that the current political system in France, the Fifth Republic, is closely related to the events that preceded it. It is thus necessary to account for these events, particularly the postwar period in a France fraught with changes and crises, when portraying the current political institutions.

1.5.1 Crisis and failure of the Fourth Republic

Following the *Libération* and in the 1950's there were two dominant topics in French politics: first of all, economic reconstruction and changing the industrial orientation of the country, and secondly, the colonial question (wars in Indochina and Algeria). The *Fourth Repu-*

blic succeeded the provisional governments after the new constitution went into effect in 1946. Whereas the governments of the new republic were highly successful in economic affairs and in the area of European politics, they failed when it came to solving the colonial problem. A very important reason for this was that the governments were in an uninterrupted state of crisis. This, in turn, was due to the institutional system of the Fourth Republic.

As had been the case in the Third Republic (cf. the succession of republics in the following chronology), the constitution of 1946 had granted the *Assemblée nationale* far-reaching powers but it had only accorded a relatively weak position to the Government. This had practically reinstated parliamentary rule, the *régime d'assemblée* of the prewar period (detailed discussion in Fauvet 1959). The authors of the constitution intended this to forestall the possibility of anti-republican tendencies in the event of a strong figure at the head of the executive branch. The situation was aggravated by the fact that the profusion of parties – again, similar to the Third Republic – made it difficult from the very start to form a majority capable of governing. Unstable coalitions and frequent changes of Government were commonplace: more than twenty Governments followed each other in rapid succession in a time span of not quite twelve years. The lack of continuity in government and of an executive branch capable of action finally brought about the fall of the Fourth Republic during the Algerian War and resulted in *de Gaulle coming to power in 1958.*

Chronology 1: First to Fifth Republics

1792-1804 FIRST REPUBLIC

1792 Monarchy abolished and the republic proclaimed by the national convention

1793 "Jacobin constitution" ratified (e.g. universal suffrage, popular sovereignty, plebiscite) but not put into effect due to state of war

1795-99 The *Directoire* follows the Reign of Terror

1799 Coup by Napoleon Bonaparte, consular constitution, dictatorial powers for Napoleon as the first consul

1804 Consular dictatorship changed to a monarchy (*Premier Empire*)

1848-1852 SECOND REPUBLIC

1848 February Revolution (chief reasons: economic crisis and income restrictions on the right to vote), bourgeois monarchy under Louis-Philippe overthrown; universal suffrage and social concessions established, only to be partially repealed soon afterwards; revolt of the Parisian workers (June 1848) brutally suppressed. Louis Napoleon Bonaparte elected President of the Republic

1851 Coup, new regime confirmed by plebiscite

1852 Monarchy reinstated by Louis Napoleon (*Second Empire*)

1870/75-1940 THIRD REPUBLIC

1870 Republic proclaimed after the collapse of the empire in the Franco-Prussian War

1871 The Paris Commune suppressed

1873 The royalist Mac-Mahon's term of office as head of state extended by 7 years (*septennat*) after an attempt to reinstate the monarchy failed

1875 Ratification of constitutional laws that only indirectly safeguarded the republican principle

1877 Parliament dissolved by Mac-Mahon; when the republicans came to power it became an unwritten law that presidents should never make use of their right to dissolve Parliament; the *régime d'assemblée*(s) begins

1884 Constitution revised, e.g. the return to monarchy is prohibited by constitutional law; consolidation of the republic continues despite numerous crises (e.g. 1887/89 possibility of coup by Boulanger, 1894-99 Dreyfus affair, 1914-18 World War I)

1936/37 Government by Popular Front under Léon Blum

1940 Military collapse of France, Vichy Regime begins

1946-1958 FOURTH REPUBLIC

1946 (5 May) First draft of constitution rejected by plebiscite (13 Oct.) Second draft of constitution ratified by only 53% of the actual voters (= 36% of the population entitled to vote); the constitution has features of the Third Republic (predominance of National Assembly, weak executive branch)

1947 Communists excluded from the government

1954 Algerian War begins, thus initiating the downfall of the Fourth Republic

1958 (13 May) Assault on the *gouvernement général* in Algiers, "welfare committee", possibility of civil war, (27 May) de Gaulle's take-over proclaimed, (1 June) de Gaulle elected head of government, (3 June) Parliament "recessed", particular powers for de Gaulle

1958 to present FIFTH REPUBLIC

1958 (28 Sept.) New constitution ratified by a large majority (chief characteristics: power of Parliament is lessened, strong position of the President of the Republic), (4 Oct.) Constitution goes into effect, start of the Fifth Republic, (21 Dec.) De Gaulle elected president

1962 Constitution amended to stipulate direct elections for president

1969 De Gaulle resigns after regional and Senate reform defeated in referendum

1969-74 Georges Pompidou in office
1974-81 Valéry Giscard d'Estaing in office
since 1981 François Mitterrand president
1986-88 *cohabitation* (president belonged to different party than majority in Parliament)

«Elle n'est pas tellement mauvaise, mais elle souffre d'une faiblesse de constitution, de son goût totalement hors de saison pour les guerres coloniales ruineuses, immorales (Indochine, Algérie), qui la perdront, et des convoitises de l'ogre de Colombey, qui l'épouvantera, la fascinera et la mangera.»
(Marianne's disproportioned figure in this cartoon might be an allusion to the disparaging name «Mademoiselle Q» coined by *Le Canard enchaîné* for the Forth Republic = *Quatrième* République.)

Fig.: 14
(Source: Le Canard enchaîné 5 March 1986. supplém. [= reprint])

The crisis of the Fourth Republic came to a head when on *13 May 1958* the *gouvernement général* in Algiers was occupied and a "welfare committee" (the name was supposed to evoke the *comité de salut public* of the French Revolution) was formed to protest against French policy in Algeria. Gaullists had participated in preparing the riots and shortly thereafter demands were heard in Algeria and Paris to have de Gaulle take over control. In a press conference the general said he was willing to do so and started negotiations with Prime Minister *Pflimlin* after paratroopers from Algeria had landed on Corsica on 24 May giving rise to fears that other actions by insurgent military units were in the offing. One day later, de Gaulle – although Pflimlin was still in office and their conference had been without success – published a communiqué with a sentence that would later be frequently quoted: «J'ai entamé hier le processus régulier nécessaire à l'établissement d'un gouvernement républicain capable d'assurer l'unité et l'indépendance du pays ...»

De Gaulle was successful with this unorthodox approach: after Pflimlin had been forced to resign, the National Assembly elected de Gaulle head of government on *1 June 1958*. Two days later it granted him particular powers in the face of an imminent civil war and entrusted him with the task of drawing up a new constitution. This sealed the fate of the Fourth Republic. (A clear résumé of the historical context of the time can be found e.g. in Weisenfeld 1982, Rioux 1983, Loth 1992; cf. also the pamphlet *Le Coup d'Etat permanent* by François Mitterrand.)

One final point must be added to qualify somewhat the events that have just been related. The events of 1958 should not be viewed as being causally involved in bringing about the fall of the Fourth Republic; on the contrary, the fall was inevitable right from the start. The constitution of the Fourth Republic repeated substantial mistakes of the Third Republic and had only met with the agreement of 36% of the population entitled to vote (with 30% refraining from voting). Instability, frequent changes of Government and inability to do anything about the problems waiting to be solved finally deprived the system of any backing it might have had left in the population.

1.5.2 Political stability and presidential power: «L'Etat, c'est lui«

The new constitution of 1958, which was ratified by an overwhelming majority of 79% of the plebiscite votes, is in certain regards in direct contrast to the principles of the Fourth Republic. It calls for substantial reinforcement of the executive branch and places the President of the Republic in a central position. At the same time, the powers of Parliament are curtailed by a series of restrictions. The prominent position of the president is further underscored by his ability to call on the population directly by means of referenda. The authors of the constitution (basically M. Debré, then Attorney General, and de Gaulle himself) intended for this shift in emphasis towards the executive branch to ensure stability in government and to preclude a relapse to the period of crisis that was the Fourth Republic. The nature of the constitution was at first by no means uncontroversial, meeting with vehement criticism especially from the Socialists and the Communists. It can safely be said, however, that no sizable political grouping in France today has fundamental reservations concerning the institutional system of the Fifth Republic; the only party demanding that presidential authority be cut back is the Communist Party.

Since it is not possible to give a detailed description of the individual institutions in the present context, we would like to refer the reader to several, more exhaustive works: Aron 1959, Goguel/ Grosser 1976, Duverger 1974, 1990, Richard 1979, Zürn 1965, Haensch/Tümmers 1991, Kempf 1980, 1989; a short comparison of the institutions in the Fourth and Fifth Republics can also be found in Menyesch/Uterwedde 1982, p. 136ff.

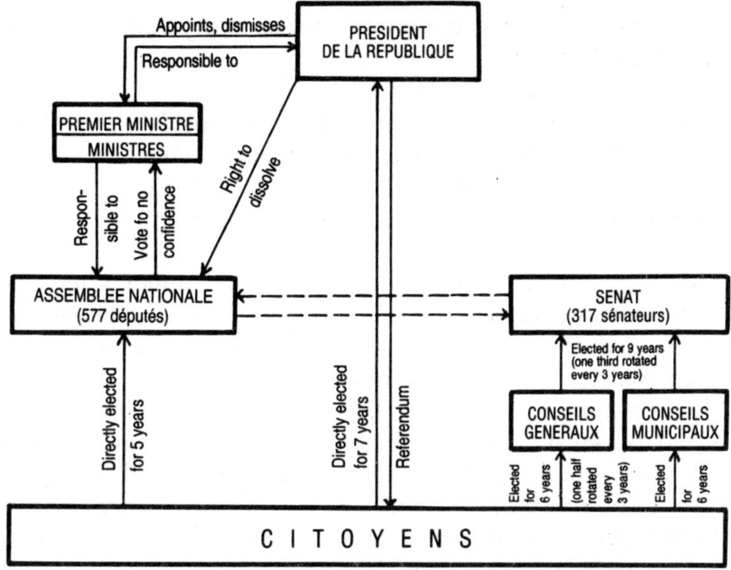

Fig. 15: France's system of government

According to Art. 5 of the constitution, the *French President of the Republic* (*Président de la République*) is supposed to serve as a sort of arbitrator, set off from the parties and day-to-day-politics; he makes sure that the constitution is complied with and guarantees national independence:

> Article 5
>
> Le Président de la République veille au respect de la Constitution. Il assure, par son arbitrage, le fonctionnement régulier des pouvoirs publics ainsi que la continuité de l'Etat.
> Il est le garant de l'indépendance nationale, de l'intégrité du territoire, du respect des accords de Communauté et des traités.

This office is endowed with far-reaching authority, especially when compared to other democratic systems of government. The president

- appoints the Prime Minister and dismisses him if he tenders his resignation; appoints the other members of the cabinet after they are nominated by the Prime Minister (Art. 8),
- presides over the Council of Ministers (Art. 9),

- promulgates laws, has the power of suspensory veto against the parliament (Art. 10),
- may call referenda (Art. 11),
- may dissolve the National Assembly after consultation with the Prime Minister and the president of Parliament (Art. 12),
- is commander-in-chief of the armed forces (Art. 15),
- has special powers in exceptional circumstances (Art. 16).

The president is not responsib1e to Parliament and cannot be removed from office during his seven-year term (*septennat*). In addition, ever since the *constitutional revision of 1962* he has been directly elected by the people (no longer by an electoral college).

The constitution was largely tailored to de Gaulle himself and reflected to a great extent ideas that he had propagated in 1946 in his well-known speech in Bayeux (this speech is reprinted in Goguel/Grosser 1976; cf. also the excerpt in T. 5). The concentration of power in the presidency and de Gaulle's claim to absolute leadership brought to politics an increasing degree of personal orientation. Other factors which were not inconsequential in contributing to this new *"personalization"* were the performance of certain rituals and the image of the presidency encouraged by the president himself, an image sometimes reminiscent of monarchic times. Thus, the accusation that this course was leading to a «présidentialisation du pouvoir» or a «monarchie élective», and voices that compared the Elysée to Versailles were not unfounded. However, this criticism can be applied just as well to de Gaulle's successors up to and including Mitterrand.

T. 5:
Suivant moi, *il est nécessaire que l'Etat ait une tête, c'est-à-dire un chef, en qui la nation puisse voir, au-dessus des fluctuations, l'homme en charge de l'essentiel et le garant de ses destinées.* Il faut aussi que l'exécutif, destiné à ne servir que la seule communauté, ne procède pas du Parlement qui réunit les délégations des intérêts particuliers. Ces conditions impliquent que le chef de l'Etat ne provienne pas d'un parti, qu'il soit désigné par le peuple, qu'il ait à nommer les ministres, qu'il possède le droit de consulter le pays, soit par référendum, soit par élection d'assemblées, qu'il reçoive, enfin, le mandat d'assurer, en cas de péril, l'intégrité et l'indépendance de la France. En dehors des circonstances où il appartiendrait au Président d'intervenir publiquement, Gouvernement et Parlement auraient à collaborer, celui-ci contrôlant celui-là et pouvant le renverser, mais *le magistrat national exerçant son arbitrage et ayant la faculté de recourir à celui du peuple.* (de Gaulle 1959, p. 240; italics by H.H.L.)

Déclaration de politique générale
du gouvernement Chirac
à l'Assemblée nationale.
(5 juin 1974.)

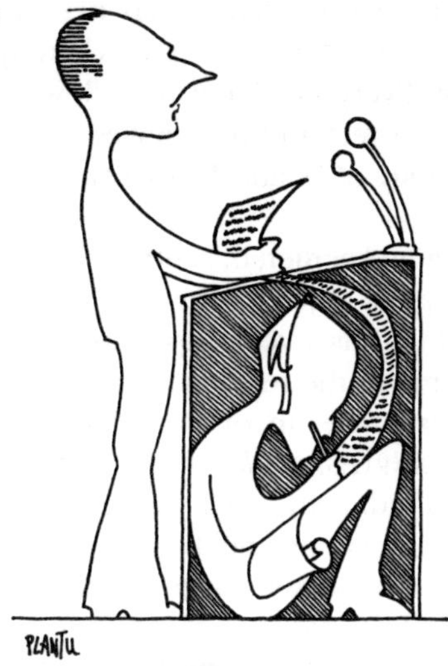

Fig. 16
(Source: Le Monde 1975, 20)

The second face of the Januslike executive branch is the *Government* headed by the Prime Minister. According to the constitution (Art. 20), its duty is to determine and conduct the politics of the nation. In actuality, though, up to 1986 it was the president who dictated the scope of action and the points of emphasis while the Government took charge of concrete execution and implementation. The Government, i.e. the Prime Minister, was thus quite often confined to the role of a performative agency (as alluded to in *Fig. 16*, which depicts President Giscard d'Estaing and Prime Minister J. Chirac).

The Government is responsible to Parliament but appointed by the President following the Prime Minister's proposal, with the President having to take into consideration that the Government must be supported by a majority in the National Assembly. If there is no such majority, the Government can be forced to resign by a vote of no confidence (*motion de censure*, Art. 49/50), something which has occurred only once to date in the Fifth Republic. On the other hand, if the President wishes to dissolve the Government, e.g. because he feels it has been 'worn out' by the disputes of day-to-day politics or because it is losing popularity, the constitution stipulates that he must first wait for the Prime Minister to tender his resignation. In actuality, however, the normal procedure has been that the president would urge the Prime Minister to resign, whereupon the Prime Minister would comply. Every president has allowed himself a great deal of latitude in this respect and has viewed changes of Government as a tool in the strategy of political survival.

As was explained earlier, the authors of the constitution for the Fifth Republic took great pains to prevent the reinstatement of the *régime d'assemblée(s)*. This is a very important consideration when trying to understand some of the restrictions on *Parliament*.

Parliament is made up of two chambers: the (more important) *National Assembly* (*Assemblée nationale*) and the *Senate* (*Sénat*). The latter is elected indirectly, i.e. by an electoral college; elections for a third of the members are held every three years (cf. *Fig. 15*). The electors consist of representatives and delegates from the general and city councils and are chosen according to a certain system. Since the number of representatives from the thinly populated rural districts is proportionally high, the Senate traditionally tends to be a rather conservative chamber. The members of the National Assembly are elected directly and hold office for five years. The system of elections established in 1958 was another measure intended to facilitate a stable majority in Parliament and is based on the principle of majority vote (*scrutin majoritaire uninominal*) with two ballots. When Mitterrand introduced an election reform calling for proportional representation (*scrutin proportionnel*) for the 1986 elections, many politicians and commentators had a foreboding of the imminent collapse of the Fifth Republic: «Mitterrand choisit la pagaille» (France-Soir), «Incompatibilité avec la Constitution» (Alain Poher), «L'ingouvernabilité de la France» (Giscard d'Estaing); Rocard, a member of the Socialist Party, resigned his post as minister. After the change in Government in 1986, however, the majority vote system was restored.

The National Assembly and the Senate are jointly involved in the process of passing laws. Both of them must ratify a bill in precisely the same wording. If this is not possible, the versions are sent back and forth up to three times (*navettes*) and if necessary, submitted to a committee for mediation (*commission paritaire mixte*). If an agreement is still not reached, the National Assembly may decide the issue if the Government so requests. In addition to the above procedure, both chambers are entitled to appeal to the highest instance of judicial review, the *Conseil constitutionnel*, which is comparable to the German Federal Constitutional Court or the American Supreme Court.

Until 1974, the *Conseil constitutionnel* could only be called on by the president or by the presidents of the National Assembly or Senate. To all practical extent, therefore, the opposition had no means of initiating steps to determine the constitutionality of laws. It was not until the ratification of a constitutional amendment that Representatives and Senators (when supported by at least 60 other persons) were also granted this right. A third of the nine members of the *Conseil* are appointed every three years by the president, the president of Parliament and the president of the Senate – a procedure which does not preclude "political" appointments based on the current majority.

Bills may be initiated by the Prime Minister and by both chambers. However, the legislative activities of the two chambers are regulated at significant points and limited by those of the executive branch:

- The types of laws for which Parliament is responsible (*lois ordinaires*) are minutely detailed in Art. 34 of the constitution (e.g. constitutional rights, questions of citizenship and nationality, matrimonial law, education, labour law, etc.). All other matters are subject to *governmental power of decree*, i.e. the Cabinet makes direct decisions (so-called *ordonnances*) without them being put to vote in Parliament. Furthermore, Parliament may empower the Government to issue decrees in matters normally under parliamentary control. This is done frequently to hasten the progress of certain measures.
- If the Government wants to shorten the debate over one of its bills (*projets de loi*) or to circumvent amendments (*amendements*), it may force a vote on the complete bill or parts of it (*procédure du vote bloqué*), or it may declare that the passage of the bill is to be treated as a vote of confidence (*question de confiance*). This last case is covered in Art. 49-3 of the constitution. There it is stipulated that a bill is considered adopted if a motion of no confidence (*motion de censure*) does not obtain an absolute majority within the next 24 hours. This not only speeds up the process but has the additional advantage for the Government that any dissent in its own ranks is silenced. For with *recours à l'article 49-3*, a bill can be ratified without any discussion and without a vote being taken. Above all, this means that the opposition is not given an opportunity in Parliament to express its own views on the matter. Thus if the Government has a precarious majority in Parliament, Art. 49-3 is one way of bypassing the representatives for the most part and quickly forcing through a project of the Government – a practice made use of with particular frequency by the Government of Prime Minister Chirac (1986-88).

Fig. 17
(Source: Le Canard enchaîné 19 March 1986)

- The *time limit set for the two legislative sessions* is another limitation imposed on Parliament. Under certain circumstances it is possible to invoke a special session, but it is the president who decrees when it shall start and end.
- The above-mentioned ability of the National Assembly to propose a *vote of censure* is, on the one hand, restricted by several conditions and, on the other hand, countered by the president's right to dissolve Parliament. (Up to now there has been only one successful vote of no confidence in the Fifth Republic. Without consulting Parliament, de Gaulle called a referendum in 1962 to vote on a constitutional amendment calling for direct elections of the president. Parliament responded by ousting the Government led by Pompidou, upon which de Gaulle dissolved the National Assembly.)

Each of these items illustrates the degree to which the function of Parliament has been restricted. The reinforcement of the executive branch has undeniably opened up new potential ways of abusing power, as can be seen, for example, in the Government's power of decree or in the practice of *vote bloqué*. Furthermore, the constitution seems to be based on the implicit assumption that the president and the majority in Parliament automatically come from the same party. For this reason, the situation that arose in 1986 for the first time – a Socialist president and a majority in the National Assembly made up of the parties of the Right – appeared to many observers to be the outset of a constitutional or governmental crisis (*Fig. 17*). Other commentators were more calm in their appraisal of the approaching "diarchy" in the executive branch, seeing in it more or less a test of the constitution of the Fifth Republic. In any event, the two-year period of *cohabitation* came to an end without the expected crisis taking place. What did happen was that the roles of Parliament and Government on one hand and that of the president on the other were redefined. After a period from 1958 to 1986 bearing a distinctly presidential stamp, the Government was now in the hands of the opposite political faction and provided a forceful counterweight: the president was restricted to his determinative role in foreign policy and national security while the Prime Minister and his Cabinet were responsible for all other areas (hence the characterization of the French governmental system as "semi-presidential"). For example, the Government was able to repeal various reforms which had been passed in the previous legislative period (such as changing the electoral system or denationalizing enterprises that had recently been nationalized). This experiment, *cohabitation*, was backed by a relatively large segment of the population, and at no time was there any danger of the parties regaining their erstwhile predominance. There was no truth to the updated saying «Quand le chat dort, les souris dansent, quand la cohabitation affaiblit le Président, les partis se réveillent». On the contrary, it had been clear from the start that *cohabitation* would merely be a temporary situation, and in the end, as Duverger (1987, p. 209f.) points out, it brought about a new way of passing political power from one party to the other:

> Après avoir pratiqué la grande alternance en 1981, qui porte à la fois sur la Présidence de la Républigue et sur l'Assemblée nationale, les électeurs ont expérimenté la petite en 1986, qui joue sur l'Assemblée nationale seule. L'une et l'autre s'étant avérées raisonnables, ils se souviendront de la gamme des procédés leur permettant de nuancer le changement. Pourquoi se priveraient-ils de l'un d'eux, qui a montré sa valeur?

1.5.3 Main political differences between France and Germany

There are but few similarities between the systems of government in France and Germany. It seems to be especially difficult to find analogies to the concentration of power that distinguishes the French presidency.

The only thing that might be comparable – as has been suggested, for example, by Grosser – would be the *constitution of the Weimar Republic*. "The basic structure is the same: a president directly elected by the people, a national assembly (the German *Reichstag*) which represents the people to at least the same degree as the president does – and in between, a government with a

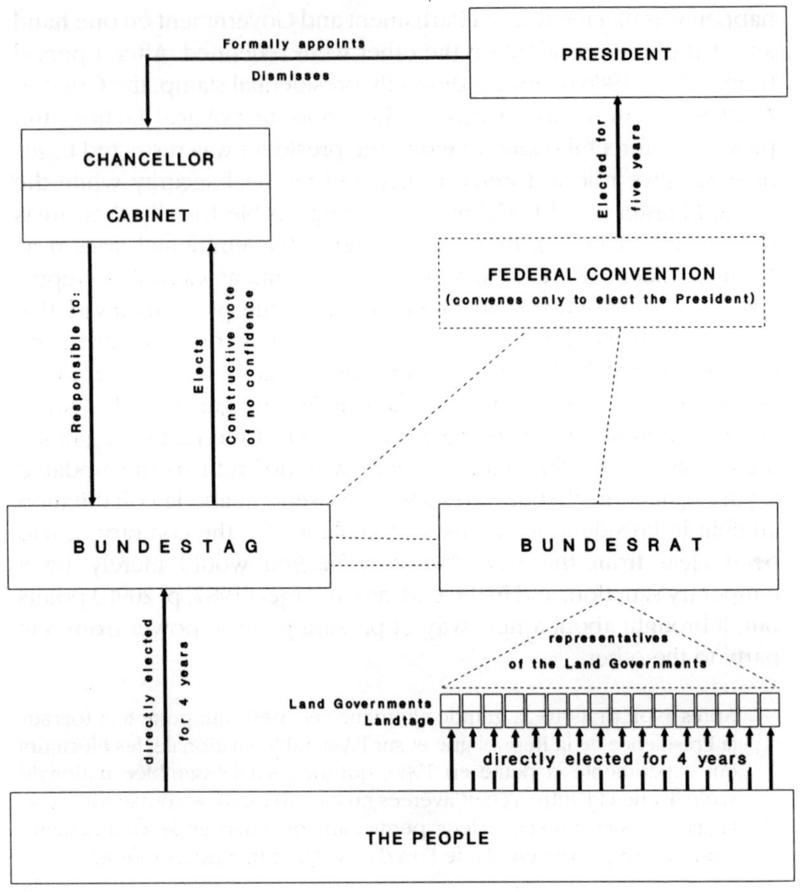

Fig 18: System of government in Germany

prime minister (the German *Reichskanzler*), whose exact status is unclear" (1986, p. 12; cf. also 1981, p. 24ff.). This parallel is not only helpful in pointing out an historical precedent for the French *cohabitation* of 1986; in this light, the latter occurrence would be tantamount to the parliamentary reading of a constitution that had hitherto been applied presidentially. It would also be instructive to take notice of the *direction* of development: France would thus have developed towards strong presidential power, Germany away from it. This comparison, however, should not be taken too far.

In the institutional structure of Germany, the functions of the executive branch are the province of the chancellor alone (*Fig. 18*). The

Government is answerable solely to the directly elected *Bundestag* (Federal Parliament) and sets policy on its own (this right to set guidelines is called the chancellor's *Richtlinienkompetenz*). The chancellor is nominated by the President – in accordance with the majority in Parliament – but elected by the *Bundestag*. It is possible to oust the government, e.g. if the constellation in Parliament changes, by means of a constructive vote of no confidence ("constructive" means that a successor must be designated before the motion of censure is put to a vote) and at the same time elect a new chancellor (this has only occurred once, namely in 1982 when Chancellor Schmidt lost power).

As a whole, therefore, it is more the principle of parliamentary representation and not the strength of executive power that is emphasized; this power is subject in its entirety to parliamentary control. In contrast, a vote of no confidence in France can only oust the Prime Minister or the Government, not the president.

The introduction of the "constructive" vote of no confidence was a result of experiences in the Weimar Republic, as is also the fact that the constitution does not allow referenda to be held. Legislation is passed by the *Bundestag*. If a bill deals with matters in the jurisdiction of both the federal *and* state governments, it must additionally be ratified by the *Bundesrat* (Federal Council). The *Bundestag* is not subject to restrictions in legislative power comparable to those in effect for the French parliament, e.g. limited jurisdiction and means of circumventing parliamentary influence.

2. Blocs and divergences: the political parties

(Ernst Ulrich Grosse)

One difference between the spectrum of political parties in France and in Germany is that the French system has been characterized by numerous changes ever since the beginning of the Fourth Republic. Important forces of the Left, the liberal[1] Centre and the Right have either disappeared or no longer play the prominent role they once used to; a good many alliances between parties have fallen apart while others have been cemented. It was the Fourth Republic in particular that was known as the era of "party rule": shifting coalitions resulted in 19 governments over a period of 12 years. It was because of this that de Gaulle laid the foundations of the Fifth Republic in 1958 with the express goal of counteracting the unstable *«système» (des partis)* which he had been struggling against since 1946. A new constitution was drawn up for this purpose and ratified by a referendum. Article 4 of this constitution names (for the first time in French history) political parties, but reduces their role in politics to mere participation in elections:

> Les partis et groupements politiques concourent à l'expression du suffrage. Ils se forment et exercent leurs activités librement. Ils doivent respecter la souveraineté nationale et la démocratie.

The last sentence is aimed at, for example, "anti-French" separatist movements in the overseas départements and territories (*départements d'outre-mer and territoires d'outre-mer*) and in the French homeland. It is also to be understood as a warning to the parties of the Far Left and Right. However, only two parties have been banned up to now on the basis of Art. 4 – the Trotskyist *Ligue communiste* and the radical right-wing party *Ordre nouveau*, both in 1973; for other "organisations dissoutes", see Quid 1992, p. 700. In contrast, any "extreme" party or group in Germany has to reckon with being banned as an unconstitutional organization, a fact which has already affected several parties and groups. The disparity between the constitutional norm and constitutional reality is not as great in Germany as it is in France, due presumably for the most part to the German experiences in the 1920's and 30's. In this connection one

---

1 The term "liberal" is used throughout this book not as an antonym of "conservative" but rather to denote a political attitude which advocates economic, political and personal freedom.

can see how characteristic it was of the French to react with a wave of protest to the German *Extremistenerlaß* (a decree against political extremism which prohibited a person from being employed by the state because of his political affiliations) and other associated events of 1977/78. Prominent politicians of the parties of the Left, among them Mitterrand, demanded at the time that this decree be repealed immediately (cf. 2.6 and 7.2.1).

The French parties in the Fifth Republic - so it would *seem - have less influence at a national level* than their German counterparts. On the one hand, French policy is determined by the directly elected president and his appointed Prime Minister, and on the other, the powers granted to the National Assembly are more restricted than those of the German *Bundestag* (cf. 1.5.2). Germany is a "party-ruled state", both "by law and in reality"; this situation has resulted in so-called *Staatsverdrossenheit* in the population - this may be approximately translated as "vexation with and disappointment in the system of government" (see Lammert 1979, p. 4 on this widely discussed topic). A consequence of this dissatisfaction has been an increase in the number of citizens' action groups, a phenomenon which in particular led to the rise of the (German) Green Party (von Krockow 1983). As a result of all this, Germany seems to be in stark contrast to France and its *monarchie républicaine* moulded by presidential authority. Some foreign observers and certain persons involved in French politics were afraid that the French parties would degenerate to mere election machines voting for or against bills, most of which would be submitted by the Government. In their opinion, it was precisely the stable majorities in parliament, a result of *scrutin majoritaire*, that were bringing about this state of affairs (Schmidt et. al. 1981, p. 68; Morawe 1983; Marchais 1985, pp. 16-26, p. 78f.).

One must, however, emphasize the following points that contradict this view:

1. The parties provide effective support for the presidential candidates during the campaign, and the composition of the Government depends on the results of the elections for the National Assembly. This has been especially apparent ever since 1981 when Mitterrand and the *gouvernement de la gauche* came into power (cf. T. 7).

2. The phenomenon of the *Union pour la Démocratie française* (UDF) illustrated quite clearly the president's dependency on a solid "party base" (cf. 2.5).

3. The opposite conclusion is just as valid. Persons aspiring to the presidency and well-known candidates in the *élections législatives* have little prospect of success unless they possess a sufficient degree

of "party backing" and enough ability to mobilize people within their own party or alliance of parties (consider, for example, the somewhat pitiful showing of the former Prime Minister Raymond Barre - the favoured candidate of many French tycoon - in the *législatives* of March 1986 and the *présidentielles* in April/ May 1988, cf. Kempf 1988, p. 89f. and Kempf 1989a, p. 166).

4. The importance of the parties, especially at the decision-making levels of the *départements* (*conseils généraux*) and *régions* (*conseils régionaux*), has been augmented by decentralization.

Both decentralization and the system of proportional representation, introduced for the first time in the elections for the *Assemblée nationale* and the *conseils régionaux* in 1986 and entailing hierarchically ranked party lists in each *département,* have their origins in a Socialist strategy agreed upon by President Mitterrand and his party. The proportional elections have led to an increase in the importance of the party machines, an effect which is veritably changing the system of the Fifth Republic (cf. Colard 1986, pp. 18-23). To be sure, the majority rule principle was restored by the RPR/UDF Government in 1986, but the party machines as well as the parliamentary groups of the Gaullists and the "liberal" UDF have maintained as much as possible of the power they had been able to acquire.

The question remains whether the Fifth Republic will eventually develop back into a "party-ruled state". Tendencies towards this development were discernible quite early on. It can be traced as far back as to the presidencies of de Gaulle, Pompidou and Giscard d'Estaing. The most conspicuous signs of this development are various scandals caused by rivalry and indiscretions, the whole situation thus being reminiscent of that in the Fourth Republic. It became apparent that political membership in or political affinity for the proper party was an important consideration when it came to the time to grant subsidies, confer posts in the executive branch, appoint loyal judges to the highest supervisory bodies (*Conseil constitutionnel* and *Conseil d'Etat*), and fill managerial positions in state-run enterprises and state-operated television. The term *Etat-UDR* was used to describe the situation (cf. 2.4). Later, after Giscard d'Estaing came to power, some people began asking whether an *Etat-UDF* had not come into being in analogy to the former Gaullist government (cf. 2.5). The gap between the constitutional norm and constitutional reality was thus not restricted to the astoundingly tolerant manner in which extremist parties were dealt with; a similarly incontrovertible gap had come into being in this area as well. It was indeed no longer possible to speak of a *«séparation des pouvoirs»*, i.e. separation of powers between the legislative, executive and judiciary branches, the system of checks and balances as described in Montesquieu's theory of government. The grand ideals were replaced by the political reality of presidential predominance and – especially from Pompidou's last years on – a system based on party membership or even favouritism. The Fourth Republic had in this respect an obvious and undeniable influence on the attitudes and behavior of the so-called *classe politique* in the Fifth Republic, despite the new stability and completely different balance of power in the new republic. This influence was due in part to the simple fact that many veteran politicians from both the "Right" and the "Left" were kept on "in the best interests of the nation" ... In contrast to this, the period of government by the Left (1981-1986) started off with many a laudable resolution. So many examples of relapses into "party-based" bestowal of subsidies, posts and offices soon came to light, however, that references to an *Etat-PS* would have been completely warranted. The "equilibrium" in this situation was based more on a carefully calculated balance of influence between the different *courants* or currants (cf. 2.6) within the party itself on the one hand, and between the PS as a dominating whole and the members of its smaller partners - PCF until 1984, MRG, PSU, *divers gauche* (cf. 2.8.4) – on the other. Regardless of what had become of the "new" political ethics, however, the Government formed by Chirac after the March elections of 1986 was constrained to concede to Parliament - and thus to the parties as well - a role much greater than had ever been the case since 1958 (Sandoz 1986, p. 210f.). The new situation of *cohabitation* in the years prior to the presidential elections in the spring of 1988 even resulted in the text of the constitution of 1958 being reinterpreted: a parliamentary interpretation instead of the previous "monarchically" presidential interpretation. By observing the changing situation, Weisenfeld (1986, p. 10) had been able to predict this development: "Any new reading of the constitution will give the Government, the Parliament and thus the parties as well more leeway."

Where, then, is the "root of this evil"? To be sure, this question is based on the assumption that it is possible to term "evil" as an overt or concealed, a latent or obviously expanding system of party rule in a situation where it is possible for power to change hands. Might it not be more appropriate to consider this the normal state of affairs in Western democracies, a situation which varies "outwardly" from country to country and period to period, often in ways peculiar to time and place? Be this as it may, if a person is searching for "roots" he must expect to meet complicated and divergent answers. The author considers one of these "roots" to be the Fourth Republic - as has already been detailed. An additional consideration is a dialectic or interdependence between the "party base" and a "leadership superstructure" which in this age of electoral and television democracy must be outfitted with "leader images" suitable for the media - this is, however, a matter which cannot be dealt with in detail here. (This is the reason why politics as a whole, especially in France, is apparently becoming more and more attached to individual personalities; the "anticipatory" influence of the media, both direct and indirect - the indirect influence starts with the very process of selecting the candidates - is responsible to a considerable degree for this phenomenon.) The increasing importance of the political parties in France can also be attributed to a combination of two other factors: to the fact that the president is elected directly and to the electoral system of *scrutin majoritaire.* These factors are stressed by the political scientist Olivier Duhamel. According to him, they were instrumental in strengthening the position of the parties long before 1981, even though this was neither intended nor perceived in advance by de Gaulle (T. 7).

T. 7:

> Le système politique français est devenu majoritaire ... La mutation majoritaire s'est opérée du temps du Général, mais à son corps défendant. Elle résulte inéluctablement de l'élection directe du président. A partir du moment où le peuple désigne le titulaire du pouvoir suprême, les partis politiques sont contraints de se structurer en fonction de cette échéance décisive. L'organisation gaulliste doit prendre corps, pour soutenir son guide; la gauche non communiste, se regrouper, sous peine d'être condamnée à l'opposition permanente; la droite non gaulliste, se fédérer en un mouvement libéral, sous peine d'être réduite à la marginalité permanente. Voilà pour la bataille du premier tour. Quant au second, il ne laisse que deux hommes pour le choix ultime: le jeu politique ne peut que se bipolariser entre deux grandes coalitions, et redonner vie à l'affrontement multiséculaire entre droite et gauche.
>
> Tel est le paradoxe: Don Quichotte à la poursuite du régime des partis, qui n'existait pas, est celui-là même qui a substitué aux factions parlementaires, s'épanouissant sur la débilité des partis, d'authentiques machines politiques, conduites par un chef appelé à régner grâce à elles. (O. Duhamel, in: L'Express 21 June 1985, p. 26)

De Gaulle did notice the changes, however. He even recognized similar tendencies in his own ranks and attempted to check them by censuring them in a masterful speech given in December of 1965 (T. 8):

T. 8:
Si, malgré l'enveloppe, malgré les termes, malgré l'esprit de ce qui a été voté en 1958, les partis se réemparent des institutions, de la République, de l'Etat, alors, évidemment, rien ne vaut plus! On a fait des confessionnaux, c'est pour tâcher de repousser le diable! Mais si le diable est dans le confessionnal, cela change tout! ... Car, comment peut marcher la Constitution de 1958, et comment marche-t-elle, et marche-t-elle bien, depuis sept ans? Elle marche grâce à un chef d'Etat qui n'appartient pas aux partis; qui n'est pas délégué par plusieurs d'entre eux, ni même, à plus forte raison, par tous. (Ch. de Gaulle, quoted from: L'Express 21 June 1985, p. 26)

Today, the function of the French political parties is remarkable in three respects:
1) Party support is imperative in the *elite recruitment* for high political offices, although it is not, as a rule, acquired through a long-winded career within one's own party (the «*Ochsentour*», or the "long slog", as the Germans call it). The decisive factor is rather the training at one of the *Grandes Ecoles* (cf. 5.3.1) and the joining of a party in time before or after completing school.
2) Although the government may be endowed with more rights than parliament (cf. 1.5.2), the actual *legislative act* is still the domain of parliament and hence of the political parties. The degree of the government's dependence on the party rank and file was shown after the 1988 parliamentary elections. With the slogan "creating an opening to the Centre" and by appointing Michel Rocard as Prime Minister and several non-socialist ministers, President Mitterrand tried to obtain the support of the Centrists (CDS) for participating in a socialist minority government. In fact, "legislative coalitions between PS and CDS were quite common" (Kimmel 1991, p. 8) in the National Assembly. This platform began to crumble, especially "from 1990 on, the Centrists continued their return to an alliance with the Giscardists and the Gaullists" (ibid., p. 9). In May 1991 Mitterrand tried to revive the "reorientation of the Left Union" by appointing Edith Cresson as Prime Minister (ibid., p. 9), but the expected parliamentary backing from the Communists failed to materialize more often than not. This is why another government reshuffle, this time with Pierre Bérégovoy, was necessary in 1992. All these details show that both the president and the government, in spite of their far-reaching constitutional powers, still remain dependent on political parties or certain party constellations.
3) The role of the political parties in "mobilizing the electorate" and the nomination of candidates for the parliamentary elections and candidate support during the *présidentielles* was mentioned above.

Two laws (11 March 1988 and 15 Jan. 1990) on the state funding of political parties and of election campaigns led to noticeable improvements in the financial situation of the political parties in France, notoriously suffering from lack of members and from shortage of funds. But the deficits in the cash-flow of the political parties continue to give rise to some semi-legal or plain illegal "fund-raising measures" (Le Monde, 22 Nov. 1991, p. 10). A number of hefty scandals and the "exceedingly generous amnesty" granted by the 1990 Funding Law have badly damaged the reputations of the political parties. 57% of the population object to the fact that they are now allowed "to enrich themselves through taxpayer's money" (Kimmel 1991, p. 15).

The constitutional norm and constitutional reality are not as far apart in Germany – this was demonstrated earlier by the example of how radical parties were treated in West Germany. According to Art. 21 of the German constitution, the political parties are involved in the "development of political objectives" (i.e. their function is not restricted to elections) and are granted certain privileges, e.g.:

- The government reimburses the parties for the costs accrued during election campaigns – this type of reimbursement is still highly inadequate in France (Kempf 1983, p. 227; Le Monde, 22 Nov. 1991, p. 10).
- The parties are entitled to sponsor regular programmes to support education and research, for example by means of "Stiftungen" or "foundations" (for example, the CDU has its Konrad-Adenauer-Stiftung and the SPD its Friedrich-Ebert-Stiftung); these organizations are funded primarily by the Ministry of the Interior; they may accept tax-deductable donations but are not allowed to misuse the funds, e.g. to launder donations for direct use by the party, as was done, for example, by the *Staatsbürgerliche Vereinigung*.
- The parties are represented in the Bundestag and thus indirectly have the power to elect the Chancellor or remove him from office by a *constructive vote of no confidence.* The French parties are in a similar position in the National Assembly by being able to submit a motion of censure (i.e. not a constructive vote of no confidence) against the Government – not against the president though (cf. 1.5.2).

2.1 *Degrees of organization*

The weak constitutional position of the French parties (as compared to the German parties) is reflected by their low degree of organization and by a status which up to now has been somewhat "extra-legal", thus preventing administrative agencies from gaining any insight into the actual number of members a party has. The reason for this is that parties and all other kinds of interest or pressure groups are governed solely by the lax association law of 1901. This law is very convenient for party financing and thus has never been changed (Le Nouvel Observateur 16 Aug. 1985, p. 26f.).

The number of actual members in the French parties is quite small, a feature shared by the French trade unions. Because of "[the parties'] own exaggeratedly fantastic statistics on membership" (Morawe 1983, p. 197) the real numbers can only be estimated: a realistic approximation might be at best somewhat more than a third of what is officially quoted by the parties (cf. Kempf 1983a, p. 35). This would mean that the large French parties (Gaullists, Communists, Socialists) can claim between 200,000 and 300,000 members each, compared to the much larger numbers – about 900,000 each – for the Christian Democrats (CDU and CSU together) and the Social Democrats in West Germany. (For more details see 2.9.1 and the sections devoted to the individual French parties). Ysmal (1989, p. 163) in her table covering the period 1958 to 1986 estimates that the actual membership figures of French political parties are even lower.

2.2 *Types of political parties and tendencies toward "catch-all parties"*

Another general feature of party development is that the individual political parties are undergoing certain changes. It used to be that the traditional dignitary party would nominate only respected public figures to be its candidates in election campaigns. The left-wing party, on the other hand, would be a class party or a "mass-based party" with a Marxist platform and wide support in the lower classes of society. Both of these groupings are changing into modern, well-organized "people's parties", "catch-all-parties" as Otto Kirchmeier so fittingly described them. They no longer consider themselves the representatives of certain social groupings but attempt to appeal to the population as a whole. This is a process typical of all Western countries. In France, however, it set in later than it did, say, in the United States or in West Germany, and the development is still far from complete. There still are some small dignitary parties (cf. 2.5.1 for CNI, 2.5.2 for CDS, 2.5.3 for PRS and MRG, 2.5.4 for PSD). Similarly, the French Communist Party adheres to its traditional view of its own role as a class party of the Left and the vanguard of the proletariat (Jäger 1978, p. 77f. and 125, Marchais 1985, pp. 6-9) while at the same time making deliberate attempts to reach other social classes, in particular salary earning classes. The Socialists and the Gaullists, though, have been in the process of turning into catch-all parties for quite some time now (Ehrmann 1976, pp. 159 and 167), and this trend has also manifested itself in smaller parties such as the Republicans (cf. 2.5.1). However, this tendency has been weakening over the last years. Financial scandals and internal power struggles of their leaders have cost the established parties a great deal of sympathy and popularity (Kimmel 1991, p. 15). An internal renewal seems the only way of re-establishing their previous lead as true people's parties.

2.3 *Tradition, change and invariable factors in the party system*

The changes in the French party system as described in this section can be summarized as follows: a multi-party system is changed to a system of bipolar blocs; these then diverge again, this time with strong competition between the groups in the centre, i.e. the typical catch-all parties. Despite certain traditions and constant factors, therefore, not only the types of political parties but also the whole political system has been altered.

At the beginning of the Fifth Republic the only two strong political forces among the numerous parties of the time were the Gaullists and the Communists. When de Gaulle introduced the system of majority vote – a system which by its very nature polarizes the votes in the second ballot – his plan was to give the French people the alternative of choosing between "Gaullism or Communism". De Gaulle's strategy, however, did not work. As the quotation taken from Duhamel at the beginning of this chapter shows, the Socialists, and later liberal-conservative forces as well, succeeded in establishing themselves as counterweights in the left-wing (cf. 2.6) and in the right-wing spectrum (cf. the party coalition UDF, cf. 2.5). They had sensed that the French citizens and voters, who had been mistrustful of any and all governmental authority ever since the era of absolutism (Hänsch 1973, p. 11f.; Ehrmann 1976, pp. 74, 79f., 83f., 145), might have an interest or even take great pleasure in sidestepping an alternative which had been "dictated" from above. The final stage of this process at the end of the 1970's was a situation with four groupings, each of which was approximately as strong as the other: Communists and Socialists, Gaullists and the UDF (cf. *Table 1*). Each of the parties in the same

Table 1: Results of parliamentary and European elections in France since the beginning of the Fifth Republic. (Only the European parts of France, i.e. excluding the overseas territories and départements; the percentages for the individual parties are the percentages of valid votes in the first ballot, the seats indicated refer to the final results)

Year	1958	1962	1967	1968	1973		1978		1979		1981		1984		1986		1988		1989	
Elect. participation*	75,1	66,6	79,1	78,6	79,5	AN	81,7	AN	58,0	EP	69,9	AN	56,7	EP	75,1	AN	66,2	AN	48,8	EP
Far Left[a]	–	2,4	2,2	3,6	3,3	–	3,3	–	3,1	–	1,3	–	3,6	–	1,5	–	0,3	–	–	–
PCF	19,2	21,7	22,4	20,0	21,4	73	20,6	86	20,6	19	16,1	44	11,2	10	9,7	32	11,1	24	7,7	7
PS and MRG	15,7	12,6	18,7	16,5	20,7	102	24,9	113	23,7	22	37,8	285	20,8	20	31,9	203				
Var. left-wing parties	1,2	–	–	0,6	1,0	–	2,9	–	–	–	0,6	–	–	–	0,9	8	}37,7	269	}23,6	22
Environmentalist movements	–	–	–	–	–	–	2,2	–	4,4	–	1,1	–	6,7	–	1,2	–	1,2	–	10,6	10
UDF (so called since 1978)	18,4	20,8[e]	13,4[c]	10,3[c]	23,4[b]	119	20,4	124	27,4	25	19,2	62				125		127		13
RPR (previously UNR, UDR)	20,4	31,9[f]	38,1[d]	46,0[d]	23,9	183	22,5	154	16,1	20	20,9	88	}43,0	}41	}42,0	142	}40,3[i]	123	}37,3[j]	13
Various right-wing politicians	22,1	9,6[h]	3,9	1,8	3,3	13	} 3,2	14	3,3[g]	–	2,7	12	3,1	–	2,7	12		11		6
Far Right	2,6	0,9	0,8	0,6	2,8	–			1,3	–	0,4	–	11,0	10	9,8	34	9,2	1	11,7	10

* Percentage of valid votes compared to number of registered voters
a Trotskyists and PSU
b 10.7% RI and centrists loyal to the government, 12.6% *réformateurs* from the opposition
c centrists from the opposition
d including RI
e 4.4% RI loyal to the government, 7.5% Radicals from the opposition, 8.9% Christian Democrats (opposition)
f only UNR/UDT (Gaullists in the strict meaning of the term)
g 1.9% Servan-Schreiber ballot (left-wing liberal right) and 1.4% Malaud (CNIP)
h »modérés« (conservatives)
i election coalition of UDF, RPR and various right-wing politicians
j 28.9% UDF/RPR (Giscard d'Estaing), 8.9% Centre (S. Veil)
AN = Assemblée nationale, EP = European Parliament

(Sources: Reif 1981, p. 3R; Kempf 1983a, p. 33; Chapsal 1984, pp. 905-910; Statistisches Bundesamt 1984, p. 154; Quid 1985, p. 13f.; Le Monde 18 March 1986, p. 3; Le Figaro 18 March 1986, pp. 1 and 24; Le Monde 14 June 1988, pp. 1 and 30; Quid 1989, p. 732; Quid 1992, p. 825; Membership list of the European Parliament 1991, pp. 3-75)

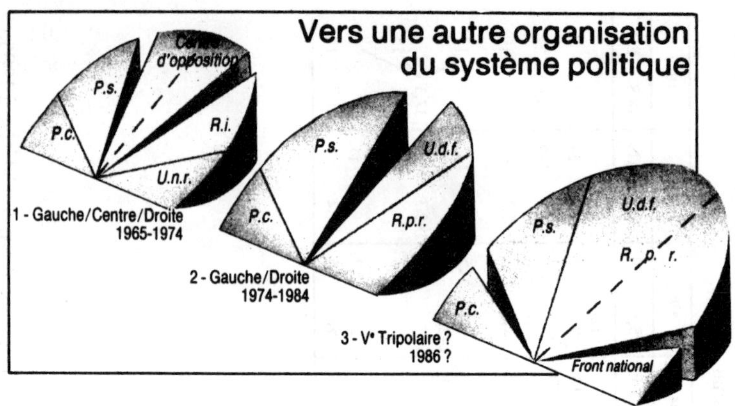

Fig 19: Changes in the French party system in the course of the Fifth Republic
(Based on: O. Duhamel, in: *L'Express* 18 Jan. 1985, p. 20)

wing, left or right, was continuously at odds with the other, due both to differences in programme and differences arising from competition – the Communists lost more and more voters to the Socialists, the Gaullists were envious of the rise of the UDF. Despite this, though, when it came to the second ballot, the two parties of the Left and the two of the Right would usually support the single candidate from the respective side with the best chance of winning, regardless of whether he came from their own party or from their "partner" party. It seemed that the existence of two blocs of about the same size, the *bipolarisation de la vie politique*, was to become a permanent fixture of the French political scene.

A book written by the political scientist René Rémond ([1]1954, [4]1982) aroused great interest in this situation. He put forward the proposition that the UDF and Gaullism were parts of two continuous lines which can be traced back to the bourgeois liberal Orleanists and Bonapartism respectively. For criticism of Rémond's theory see Bock 1978, Bluche/Rials 1983 and Rials 1985.

At present, though, the heyday of the bipolar arrangement of these four groupings has already come and gone. The *bipolarisation* will continue to exist because of the system of presidential elections, but it is on the wane. It is being superimposed by a three-part arrangement (or perhaps a modified four-part arrangement), the outlines of which are gradually becoming discernible (cf. *Fig. 19*):

- The Communists are to the far left, having become a marginal force due to loss of voters (cf. *Table 1*) and their fall-out with the Socialists in 1984.
- The Centre is occupied by the Socialists (PS) on the one hand and the Gaullists (now called RPR) and the UDF on the other; we must add to the Centre the *écologistes* since 1989 (cf. 2.8.2), a political force to be reckoned with, but which at present cannot be subsumed under the French "broad left".
- Finally, there is the *Front National* to the far right (cf. 2.8.3).

In other words, the PS, UDF and RPR are gradually approaching each other in the centre, even though the PS stresses the distance between itself and the two other parties (stage 3). Prior to this, the Socialists were the main group in the Left while the UDF parties and the Gaullists were the chief forces in the Right (stage 2). Up to 1974 the Centre was occupied by a small and unstable group of moderate parties between the Gaullists and Republicans on the one side and the two leftist parties on the other (stage 1). The social and structural causes for these changes will be discussed in the following sections.

Despite tendencies towards a *Ve République tripolaire*, it cannot be said that the distinction between Left and Right, a distinction so often declared extinct, is vanishing from the political scene in France. It seems to be ineradicable. What is the reason for this? This distinction has its roots in the political culture of the nation (Jäger 1980, p. 588). It is just as much a part of the heritage of the *Grande Révolution* as is Marianne, the motto *Liberté – Egalité – Fraternité*, the Tricolor or Bastille Day on 14 July. It has thus been engraved in the French soul by 200 years of tradition (shown clearly by Duverger [1985, p. 118] in his concise summary 1789-1980). Its institutional and terminological origins are to be found in the seating arrangement in the Assemblée nationale of 1789:

> «Les défenseurs d'un pouvoir fort du roi grâce à un véto absolu sur les lois se placèrent à droite par rapport au président de séance. Les partisans d'un exécutif amoindri, du rôle déterminant du Parlement, émanation de la souveraineté nationale, se situèrent à gauche.» (Defrasne 1975, p. 5)

The political meaning of the terms "right" and "left" have spread from France to all the languages of Europe (an example of the meaning of a word being borrowed from one language to another). The terms *droite, gauche* and later also *centre* were without a doubt well suited tags for the political tendencies in 19th century France. At a time when the Church still supported the monarchy and when there were still numerous, predominantly wealthy adherents of a strong executive power headed by an emperor, such tendencies could well be labelled 'right' while their anticlerical and republican opponents, coming from the workers and from part of the bourgeoisie, were rightly called 'left'. There were thus three issues which justified the distinction of Right from Left:

a) the question of whether the status quo with respect to income and property should be preserved or altered;
b) the question of whether the current system of government should be preserved or changed (monarchy vs. republic);
c) the attitude towards the power of the Church.

Once the republican system of government was firmly established with the Third Republic, and after the Church's influence had been diminished, particularly after the separation of Church and State had become law (1905), the differences between Right and Left became somewhat obscured. This distinction was justified only by the continued existence of serious social conflicts (criterion a) and was occasionally given new relevance by outbreaks of especially militant laicism (criterion c). The bipolarisation in the Fifth Republic put the differences between the two groups in a modern light and, one might say, even broadened the gap running between them along the line marked by the social struggle for redistribution. It is notable in this context that *gauche* and *droite* have become terms propagated chiefly by the "left-wing parties" (and often by the media since they are compelled to use concise formulations). The "right-wing parties", on the other hand, reject them as being obsolete on the grounds that the Right as well is interested in a "fair" distribution of income. Thus, as the classical social conflicts become less and less acute, the terms *gauche*, *centre* and *droite* degenerate more and more to empty phrases on a political chessboard dominated by the voter-oriented tendency of all of the large parties to turn into "catch-all parties" integrating all classes. These parties are in the process of losing their social and ideological home base (or expressed in a positive manner: they are gaining "mobility"). The more pragmatic and mobile a party is, the more successful the moves are on this chessboard.

Because of this tendency and because of the chances of starting a career that can culminate in a ministerial post or a leading party position, the number of flexible political managers coming from the elite universities (cf. 5.3.1), the breeding places of intellectual mobility (Jäger 1980, in particular p.593f.; Guédé/Rozenblum 1981, p. 992f.; L'Express 11 Jan. 1985, p. 86ff.; Schmitt 1991), is increasing in all of the French parties – except the PCF.

Another symptom is that: when older opinion polls are compared with more recent ones, one notices that an increasing number of the people polled decline to classify themselves as either left or right (1981: 20%, 1983: 22%, 1985: 27%). Furthermore, most of the persons asked considered the characteristic feature of the Left to be the belief in universal values such as *la justice, la générosité, la fraternité* (50%) instead of the struggle against capitalism in order to advance socialism or the fight to overcome social injustice (28%); 22% were uncertain (Libération 28 Jan. 1985, pp.2 and 6).

Therefore, different values are replacing the classical criteria for distinguishing Left from Right. These new values, however, also have a tradition of their own, for sympathy for humanitarian values has been widespread in the Left ever since the early stages of socialism and ever since Jean Jaurès. In the rhetorical condemnation of injustice it is the heart that speaks, no matter whether the topic is the long exclusion of the proletariat from the ballot, anti-Semitism (e.g. in the Dreyfus affair) or, for example, racial prejudice towards foreign workers in modern France. The emphasis placed on humanitarian values by the Left has made an impression on the French people and remains a traditional signal, especially in a period of political and social assimilation.

It is precisely this factor that helps to explain the rapid drop in popularity of the Socialists since 1990: scandals involving the party's dubious financial sources and personal rivalries at the Rennes Party Conference in March 1990 led to a drastic loss in trust (the economic policy of *austerité* is older; it alone does not account for this loss in trust). 31% of the people questioned in 1990 did no longer regard the PS as "left-wing" (Kimmel 1991, p. 10). After the profound changes taking place in Eastern Europe, it is now the PCF that tries hard to project an image of human values and moral integrity.

Let us now turn our attention to the individual political groupings.

2.4 *From Gaullism to neo-Gaullism*

For a long time the Gaullists were merely a "loosely structured dignitary party" (Kempf 1983, p. 130), a group centred around General de Gaulle and opposed to "party quarrelling". They benefited from the prestige of the former leader of the Resistance, the man who liberated France from the humiliation of the German occupation and who was a popular head of government until January 1946. With his "movement", the *Rassemblement du Peuple français*, de Gaulle wanted to regain power. He did not succeed. The RPF split and fell apart. It was not until the Algerian crisis and de Gaulle's return to power that a new Gaullist movement was formed: the UNR (*Union pour la Nouvelle République*), rechristened the UDR (*Union des Démocrates pour la*

République) in 1968. Their great success in elections - an absolute majority together with their smaller coalition partner, the "Independent Republicans", in the 1962 and 1967 National Assemblies - was attributable to the desire, embodied in de Gaulle, for stable government, for *"condamnation du régime désastreux des partis"* (Chapsal 1984, p. 259) and to a desire for worldwide recognition of the importance and self-determination of France. After the events of May 1968 the Gaullists were even able to win 46.4% of the votes in the first ballot of the new elections for the National Assembly and the absolute majority for themselves in the second ballot. This spectacular performance became the goal for following elections, but it was never again to be achieved.

The struggle for the *indépendance* and *grandeur* of France, an unchanging topic of Gaullist politics, must be considered in the light of several aspects. For one thing, it must be viewed as compensation for the loss of the colonies, including the Algerian *départements,* which until 1962 were legally part of the French homeland.

Secondly, this struggle is a reaction to the economic and technical superiority of the United States. This resentment also included Great Britain, which was held to be part of the American entourage by virtue of language, culture and politics. In addition, not only did de Gaulle and his successors never forget the occupation of France by German troops, but the condescending manner in which France had been treated during World War II by the Allies remained in their memories as well. In particular, they remembered how France, that is to say de Gaulle, had not been invited to the Yalta Conference in 1945, at which the boundaries of the power blocs in Europe had been mapped out in decisions of great historical consequence: «Le complexe de Yalta naît en France de cette offense, jamais digérée» (F. Rupfermann, in: L'Express 15 Febr. 1986, p. 10). The "Yalta" idea, however, is a completely unjustified illusion upon which all the French parties base their equally illusionary aspirations to *indépendance nationale*:

> T. 9:
> Le mythe de Yalta est enfin moribond en France: non, il n'y a pas eu partage de l'Europe entre deux Grands également dominateurs; non, le but suprême n'est pas de sortir d'un bloc dans lequel nous serions entrés par contrainte... Non, la France n'est pas une grande puissance. Elle n'est ni le nombril ni la lumière du monde. Mais elle est appelée à apporter une contribution réelle aux modifications du champ national ... Il se trouve que rien n'est plus favorable à la déresponsabilisation que l'invocation constante, par tous les partis, de la notion d'indépendance nationale.

Aucune nation n'est indépendante. (A. Grosser, in: L'Express 30 Aug. 1985, p. 17 f)

The collapse of the Eastern bloc in 1989/1990 was therefore seen by the French political parties and the media as *«la fin de Yalta»* and as an opportunity for French foreign policy to display greater independence.

The Gaullist aspirations to national *indépendance* and *grandeur* resulting from the above-mentioned reactions and need for compensation are reflected in their *economic policies*:

- government support for modernization, for the concentration of industry and for self-sufficiency in energy resources (especially nuclear power) in France itself, and
- in general: France was to be transformed from a country whose economy was predominantly based on agriculture and small business to a modern industrial nation under de Gaulle and Pompidou. This process was continued without change under both Giscard d'Estaing and Mitterrand. The development was and is intended to make France a competitive force in the Common Market and in the whole world.

However, these goals imply that *politics must have priority over economics*, at least in some areas.

The same tendency is reflected in *defense policy* by the build-up and expansion of the French nuclear *force de frappe* since 1959 and in the withdrawal of France's military forces from NATO command (cf. 7.2.2).

Gaullism projected the same aspirations into its *European policy* by striving for an independent – as far as this is possible – and thus powerful Europe positioned between the two superpowers, the U.S.A. and the U.S.S.R. At the same time, however, it was opposed to restrictions on French sovereignty imposed by a central European authority. De Gaulle is considered a pioneer in Franco-German reconciliation and European cooperation. It is, of course, hardly possible to deduce from de Gaulle's statements what he considered to be the proper role and significance of a European parliament since such a parliament did not come into existence until 1979. That is why this point is an item of great dispute among those parties which claim to base their positions on de Gaulle's standpoint in certain matters - not only as far as the European question is concerned (*Fig. 20*).

Fig. 20: "Mai 1979: élections européennes.
Les quatre grands partis revendiquent la filiation."
(*L'Express* 21 June 1985, p. 23)

(Simone Veil, at that time the leading candidate of the UDF and later president of the European Parliament, is at the upper right, next to her are Prime Minister Raymond Barre and President Giscard d'Estaing. Bottom right: Chirac. Upper left: Marchais. Bottom left: Mitterrand.)

The *domestic policy* of the Gaullists stresses not only independence but also the national unity of the French and the common destiny of the country, both in the past and in the present. These ideals constitute a part of their platform aimed at making the Gaullists "a factor of cohesion and integration at the political level, transcending class boundaries and social antagonism" (Lasserre 1976, p. 28). It is because of these values that it has also been possible for them to attract segments of the lower classes. Furthermore, the emphasis placed on national unity comes into play against all separatistic and "extreme" decentralistic tendencies. For example, when the questions of Corsica or the *départements et territoires d'outre-mer* are brought up, the Gaullists are the first to raise cries of *«intégrité du territoire national»* (cf. Kempf 1983, p. 255).

Lastly, the institutions of the Fifth Republic themselves, i.e. the strong position of the president and government and the weaker position of the parliament (a situation comparable to Bonapartism in the *Second Empire*) are considered Gaullist.

Equipped with these ideals and a solid majority in the National Assembly, the Gaullists appeared to be assured of continued rule over all branches of public life under Pompidou even after de Gaulle's resignation (1969). The term *Etat-UDR* was often used to describe this situation. After Pompidou's death in 1974, then, it was all the more surprising that a non-Gaullist, Giscard d'Estaing, was elected president – with the support of a group of renegade Gaullists centred around Jacques Chirac. The "movement" was able to survive the shock only due to the fact that the former dignitary party had already been transformed into a modern party machine under Pompidou. Giscard d'Estaing's attempts at depriving the Gaullists of important public functions (in the Government, economy, government-run audiovisual media etc.) and filling all positions of leadership with loyal personnel met with resistance from Chirac, who had advanced from Minister of the Interior to Prime Minister. Chirac resigned and subsequently formed a mass-based party in 1976, a party even more centralized and thoroughly organized down to each of the individual sections of the *circonscriptions législatives.* To be precise, he not only brought into being a structure which was democratic in form and hierarchic in function, he also led activities aimed at enlisting the great number of new members needed by a modern catch-all party, the foundations for which had been laid under Pompidou. The new name, ***Rassemblement pour la République***, was highly significant, especially since Chirac, the "renegade" of 1974, became the undisputed leader: it was supposed to evoke memories of the initial period under de Gaulle and at the same time – according to Kempf (1983, p. 138) – in order to emphasize that only a strong movement with support from all different directions would be able to prevent the "imminent socialist-communist takeover", a threat that had become acute since the left-wing coalition founded in 1972 started gathering more votes. (See *Fig. 21* for the changing names.)

This marked the beginning of neo-Gaullism. Its main characteristics were until 1988:

- a structured party machine with a relative increase in the number of members when compared to the first years of the Fifth Republic,
- complete subordination of this party machine to its president, Chirac, a subordination whose degree was highly uncommon in large parties of the Western world (Kempf 1983, p. 139; Rémond 1982 considers this to be a Bonapartist trait).

More recent studies by French political scientists (e.g. Passeron 1984, p. 27 and Guiol/Neveu 1984, p. 104) verify this subordination.

The ideal embodied by de Gaulle, Chirac's attainment of the office of Prime Minister (1974-76, 1986-88) and his being elected mayor of the capital city, Paris, in March 1977 have all contributed to this structure. Neo-Gaullism also evinces differences to Gaullism in its platform. Whereas both share the principles of ***indépendance***, ***grandeur*** and ***unité nationale***, the RPR leans towards "economic liberalism" based on the American economic model (Höhne 1984, p. 84): the *Plan de redressement économique et social* (RPR, 1983) and the course followed by Chirac's Government from 1986 on aimed at denationalizing numerous enterprises which had been nationalized prior to and after 1981; governmental interference in the economy was supposed to

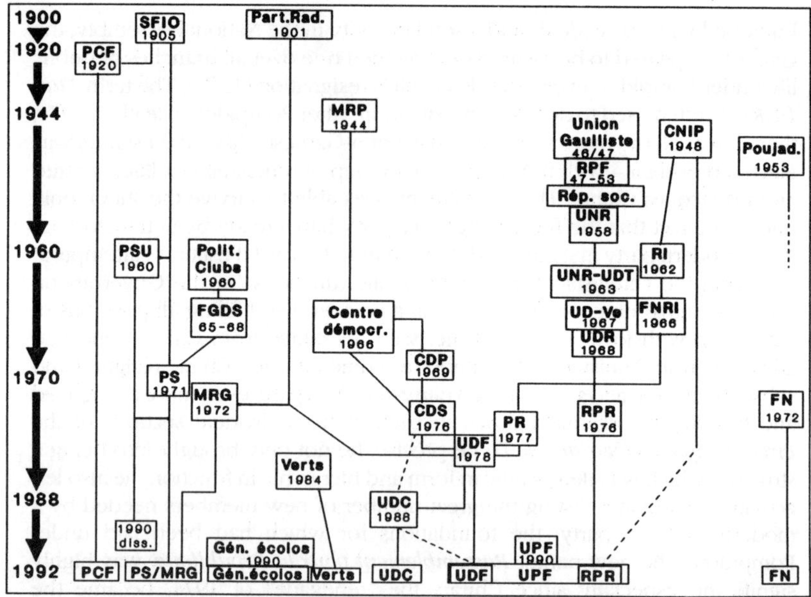

Fig. 21: Development of the French political parties
(Sources: Menyesch/Uterwedde 1983, p. 156; Duverger 1985, p. 118
and various press articles from 1988)

be reduced and unemployment was to be combated by granting tax benefits for investments from trade and industry and by extending part-time employment. These goals constituted an appeal directed at representatives of "modern" trade and industry, who make up a significant portion of the RPR voters (cf. *Table 2*). In contrast to this kind of "governmental retreat", de Gaulle had stressed the regulative and mediatory role of government. Furthermore, neo-Gaullism goes its own way in its policy towards Europe and armament: the RPR and Chirac advocate a joint European armament industry which is supposed to complement and by no means replace the American guarantee within NATO to defend Europe (Colard 1984, pp. 130-132). And the RPR supported the allied approach during the 1991 Gulf War. It is true that these positions of the RPR on economic and defense policy deviate greatly from those of de Gaulle, but it is essential to view them in the structural context of the French party system. As the catch-all parties tend to become increasingly similar to each other and as the Gaullist *héritage national* continues to place its stamp on the French parties under the presidential rule of the Fifth Republic, it becomes more and more necessary for the RPR to foster an image which sets it off from the other parties. It is this necessity that lies behind the current, more "pro-American" defense policy and in the "American" form of economic policy. However it would be just as possible for this necessity to effect a return to "authentic Gaullism" – as soon as "Gaullist" positions are relinquished by other groupings, in particular the Socialists and the UDF. Values and goals, in particular in the "Right" and "Centre" as depicted in Duhamels third model (cf. *Fig. 19*), appear to be nothing but pieces in a game of power, pieces to be manipulated at will over periods of time.

Chirac's failure in the 1988 presidential elections and his loss of office after the end of the *cohabitation* and after the parliamentary elections caused some ruptures in the party that had until now been organized along strictly hierarchical lines. A distinction must be made, however, between dissident ancient Gaullists and the "uprising of the young" against the "old Party Barons" (for details see Kempf 1989a, p. 172f. and Kimmel 1991).

There is an overabundance of management personnel (*cadres supérieurs*), members of trade and industry, self-employed, farmers and non-employed in the *constituency and membership roll* of the RPR, whereas workers are at a minority. A closer look at the membership shows that the old middle classes (*commerçants et artisans*) form the *point fort* of the RPR and that in contrast, the categories of the *salariés modestes* are the *point faible*, one might even say the «*talon d'Achille*» (Guiol/Neveu 1984, esp. p.97-99, cf. Menyesch/Uterwedde 1982, p. 167, and Kempf 1983, p. 186). The statistics on the structure of the membership, however, are just as unreliable as those on the number of members (Dec. '76: 285,256; Dec. '80: 667,453; 1986: 885,000) since they both come from the RPR itself and are used as a publicity measure. The actual number of members is estimated at around 150,000 to 200,000 (Kempf 1983a, p. 85) – which would be impressive enough for the former dignitary party. – The previously mentioned RPR economic plan and its updates are favourable to the wishes of the "independent" middle classes and big industrialists for liberalization, and their numbers are disproportionately high even in statistics from the RPR itself.

Opinion polls taken after national elections and based on representative samples of the population seem to be more trustworthy than the RPR's own statistics. The information given above on the dominating social and professional groups in the RPR voters was taken from such polls (cf. *Table 2*). What is particularly noticeable here when comparing the 1981 and 1988 presidential elections is the drop in figures of employees (*employés*) and workers, and the loss in votes in the age group 25 to 49 as opposed to gains in the age range above 50 – a clear age signal.

Another important factor is the religious affiliation of the voters: the RPR has its voter strongholds in the predominantly Catholic regions of western France (e.g. Brittany) and eastern France (e.g. Lorraine). It is also firmly rooted in Chirac's "bastions": in his home *département* Corrèze, in Cantal in the southern part of Auvergne and above all in Paris where he was able to attract many more voters for his party during his time in office as mayor.

The RPR and the UDF party alliance decided in June 1990 to form a joint parliamentary group, the *Union pour la France*, in the National Assembly. This was also the name they chose to enter the 1992 regional and cantonal elections. Future will tell whether both formations will join ranks even closer.

Table 2: Development of electorate structures in the French political parties (in % per category)

	Presidential elections 1988, 1st ballot							Regional elections 1992								Presidential elections 1981 (1st ballot in comparison)				
	div. li.	PCF	PS	Ver	UDF[1]	RPR	FN	ext. li.	PCF	PS[2]	GE	Ver	CPNT[3]	UPF[4]	FN	PCF	PS u. a.	Eco	UDF	RPR
Total	4	7	34	4	17	20	14	1,5	8	20,5	7	7,5	3	37,5	14	15,3	31,4	3,8	28,3	20,9
Sex																				
male	6	9	31	3	15	19	17	2	8	19	6	7	4	38	15					
female	4	5	37	5	18	21	10	2	8	23	8	8	2	36	12					
Age groups																				
18-24	4	5	35	5	19	17	15	2	6	18	13	8	4	36	12	20	37	6,5	19,5	17
25-34	6	9	39	6	16	13	11	2	10	20	8	10	4	32	13					
35-49	4	7	36	4	15	17	17	2	8	22	7	9	3	35	13	17,3	33,2	3,7	24	21,8
50-64	3	6	29	2	17	29	14	1	8	17	5	5	2	45	17	15,2	28	1,8	28,5	26,5
65 and older	1	9	29	1	17	31	12	1	7	24	3	3	2	42	17	5,5	24	1,7	48,8	20
Occupation																				
Farmers	5	2	20	3	16	36	18	1	3	12	3	7	13	47	12	7,5	11,5	1	35	45
Craft., bus.[5]	4	2	15	2	23	23	31	1	3	14	6	5	1	52	16					
Free professions																6	24,5	8	29,5	32
Cadre sup.	2	1	27	3	16	36	16	1	6	17	9	7	2	47	9					
Employees	5	5	39	4	18	14	16	2	9	24	9	9	2	29	19	13,5	41,5	5	21,5	17,5
Workers	7	17	43	3	7	7	16	1	11	21	9	10	7	22	19	28	37,5	2,5	18,5	13,5
Non-employed[6]	5	8	36	4	14	17	16	1	9	23	4	4	2	39	17	8,5	26	2,5	43	20

1 R. Barre was official presidential candidate for the UDF (cf. Kempf 1989a, p. 164; Quid 1992, p. 709), but the party did not give its unmitigated support.
2 PS, *Majorité présidentielle* and *Divers gauche*
3 CPNT = *Chasse-pêche-nature-tradition.* Mainly voters from the farming sector and agriculturally structured regions, predominantly coming from the left voter spectrum but now describing themselves as neither left nor right.
4 UPF = UDF, RPR and *Divers droite*
5 Craftsmen and businessmen
6 Retired people, non-working people and unemployed

(Source: Le Monde – Dossier et doc.: L'éléction présidentielle de 1988, May 1988, p. 41; Libération 24 March 1992, p. 5; Reif 1981, p. 40)

2.5 *The liberal-conservative party coalition UDF*

The *Union pour la Démocratie française* was founded on 1 Feb. 1978, in time for the parliamentary elections of that year. Although often termed a «*parti*» in the press, it is merely an election coalition made up of smaller parties, but it has succeeded in developing into a counterweight to the RPR. The name alludes to the pamphlet *Démocratie française* written by the President Giscard d'Estaing, and according to Kempf (1983, p. 154) was proposed by Servan-Schreiber. The alliance was supposed to provide Giscard d'Estaing with solid parliamentary backing in the face of his disputes with the Gaullists. The success of the UDF in the *législatives* of 1978 and the European elections of 1979 proved that the coalition was a good approach (1978: 124 representatives as opposed to 150 Gaullists, 1979: 25 vs. only 16 Gaullist representatives). After the Socialist victory in 1981 the UDF seemed to be without a leader. Nevertheless, the necessity of maintaining a significant grouping in the National Assembly and *Conseils généraux* to oppose the Gaullists and continued success in communal and cantonal elections kept the UDF together.

The UDF appeared more open to the political, economical and military build-up of Europe than did the RPR (Colard 1984, p. 127), and its economic policy also seemed to be more liberal (details will be given later). These two positions are closely linked, one might even say each of them is a consequence of the other: a group that wanted to expose France to economic competition with the products of other European countries also had to be an opponent of governmental intervention and protection, that is, an advocate of more economic freedom for business. This sort of freedom benefited above all the finance companies and big business during the presidential term of Giscard d'Estaing, a president who was on good terms with these groups even to the extent that he had relatives in these circles (cf. e.g. *Le Nouvel Observateur* 1 Dec. 1980, Enquête «Giscard et Cie»). This is why Kolboom (1978, p. 125; similarly Morawe 1983, p. 189) clearly classified the UDF as part of the "internationally-oriented financial and industrial bourgeoisie" as opposed to the RPR, which was the "political representative of the traditional small and medium-sized business bourgeoisie". A certain amount of scepticism towards simplified classifications of this kind is due, however. Admittedly, it would not be correct to deny completely the effects of socioeconomic factors and the tendency of political parties and groups to represent the interests of certain social classes – after all, the shift to catch-all parties in France is at the moment only a tendency which means that France is in a state of transition. Nevertheless, a "game model" would seem to describe this era of the rise of catch-all parties more fittingly, a "chess model" with competing parties and with values or positions on values being sought, taken possession of and propagated in a process of reciprocal give and take. This model will be even more appropriate in the future as the types of parties go through further changes (cf. 2.2 and 2.3).

This "chess model" explains why the RPR became more well-disposed toward Europe following its grave defeat in 1979 in the first European elections – this was the first time that the UDF received more votes and seats in an elected body than did the RPR (cf. *Table 1*). It also explains why the RPR is trying to outdo the UDF in liberalism and in its attitudes toward private property, namely in order to have a point in which its own economic stance can be distinguished from that of the UDF and – especially after 1983 – the Socialists, both of which had had liberal stances to begin with. This does not mean that the RPR has all of a sudden become a representative of the "financial and industrial bourgeoisie". Instead, it is merely attempting to leave the UDF and its successful position far behind by adopting a higher position on the scale ranging from governmental interventionism to liberalism, so as to reduce the UDF's "chances of ruling" and influence. This the RPR succeeded in doing from 1979 on, albeit to a lesser extent than had been hoped (cf. *Table 1*). For the time being, however, both the UDF and the RPR consider the Socialists their main, common foe. By introducing proportional representation, the Socialists made an attempt at attracting some of the UDF forces away from the bourgeois "Right" and into an alliance left of Centre with the PS, but this attempt failed prior to the parliamentary elections of March 1986.

Since the differences between the electorate of the RPR and that of the UDF were diminishing (cf. *Table 2*) – basically the only difference between the two "parties" is that the RPR is stronger in the agricultural popular section,in the self-employed petty bourgeoisie and in management –, it was only natural for them to begin to cooperate with each other in elections and for their official programmes to become increasingly similar. In 1984 the two groups ran for the second European elections on a joint ballot. In the *Convention libérale* of 8/9 June 1985 (cf. *L'Express* 26 July 1985, pp. 22-30) they objected to proportional representation in parliamentary elections as running counter to the "spirit" of the Fifth Republic. They joined forces to present a joint platform rejecting governmental intervention (including governmental regulation of prices and exchange rates) and calling for the denationalization of numerous enterprises which had been nationalized earlier. The RPR, UDF and independent groups of the Right again joined forces for the new parliamentary elections of 1988, calling themselves the «*Union du Rassemblement et du Centre*». For this reason, the present alliance (under the name *Union pour la France*, UPF, cf. 2.4.,) enjoys some tradition.

In the process, however, the UDF is also finding it necessary to preserve its own identity. If it continues to pursue a Gaullist course in defense and in domestic policy (cf. 2.4) and if changes of direction in the ranks of the Gaullists rob it of its individuality in European and economic policy, how is it going to keep its steady voters and attract new ones? It is at this point that it becomes manifest how difficult, perhaps even how impossible it is for an electoral alliance consisting of independent parties, each with its own organization, to cooperate to an even greater degree (cf. Kempf 1983, p. 155).
This was also shown by the reaction of one of the UDF member parties, the Centrists, who left the alliance after the 1988 parliamentary elections (cf. 2.5.2); the continued existence of the alliance is in grave danger.

Discussions on the future of the UDF continue. Three options seem probable (for details, see Kempf 1989a, p. 165 and *Le Monde* 12 Feb. 1992, p. 11):

- the continued existence of the UDF as multi-party alliance;
- strengthening the independence course, manifest in the Centrist parliamentary group, into a liberal and "European-minded" Centre party that would be capable (depending on the situation) of forming coalition governments both with the Socialists and the democratic Right;
- developing a major party of the moderate Right analogous to the existing joint parliamentary group consisting of RPR and the residual UDF.

The second option would be comparable with the (smaller) German FDP, while the third option would (with some reservation) correspond to the (larger) German CDU/CSU (cf. 2.9). All in all, the future of the UDF is still completely uncertain.

The individual UDF parties are presented in the following sections.

ne Republicans (PR)

'arti républicain emerged in May 1977 primarily from the ranks of the *…ration nationale des Républicains indépendants* (founded in 1966, later Giscard d'Estaing's centre of power), which in turn had been an offshoot of the anti-Gaullist bourgeois and farmer party *Centre national des Indépendants et Paysans* (CNIP); cf. *Fig. 21.* Ever since then the CNIP, now called CNI, has been of only marginal importance.

The name *Parti républicain* reflects the will of the party to detach itself from a union of relatively independent notables and dignitaries, this latter being a description still applicable to the CNI. The name was and still is intended to voice the wish for stronger party discipline and for a highly organized member party. At times the party even nourished dreams of "becoming a powerful catch-all party" (Kempf 1983, p. 153). The number of members reportedly grew from 60,000 in June 1977 through 165,000 at the beginning of 1980 (ibid., p. 153) to 190,000 in 1984 (Quid 1985, p. 612). This is also the level (185,000) given by Quid 1992, p. 707.

The platform of the PR, particularly with respect to European policy and the party's aversion to governmental protectionism, has left such a great mark on the programme of the UDF that the PR can no longer claim any distinguishing features whatsoever. The manner in which voters and new members are approached is correspondingly vague and based on individual personalities (for example, their 1986 election campaign was dominated by pictures of and quotations from the former head of the party, François Léotard). Nevertheless, they place their greatest hopes in the (growing) group of the wage-earning middle-class.

2.5.2 The *Centre des démocrates sociaux (CDS)*

The *Centre des démocrates sociaux* was founded in 1976 and can be viewed as a similar attempt to form a bourgeois-centre "third force" between the parties of the Left and the Gaullists. It is a Catholic party with notions of social reform that are similar to those of the *Sozialausschüsse* (committees responsible for social policy, workers' interests etc.) within the German CDU (Kempf 1983a, p. 37). The upper crust of the party – including the former chairman of the UDF, Lecanuet – originally came from the MRP, the important Catholic *Mouvement Républicain Populaire.* After the Second World War the MRP had joined with socialists and communists to form a coalition government under de Gaulle, and in June 1946 it even won 28.2% of the votes, so becoming the strongest French party for a while. After consistently losing votes to the Gaullists the MRP ceased to be a political factor even though it has not been officially dissolved to this very day. Only a few small remnants were able to survive – and currently live on in the CDS. The electoral base of the CDS is the same as that of the former MRP and can be found in the Catholic regions of eastern and western France in which a significant part of the population still participates in church activities. This means that the geographical areas in which they are politically strong coincide with the Gaullist strongholds. As is to be expected, however, the two groups of voters can be differentiated on the basis of church attendance. The results of polls which were taken after the 1978 elections (the last polls to take into account the individual parties constituting the UDF) indicated that 43% of the CDS adherents attended church regularly; this was the case for only 27% of the PR and 21% of the RPR voters (Kempf 1983, p. 180).

The CDS claimed to have 49,430 members in 1990 (Quid 1992, p. 701). After the parliamentary elections of 1988 the CDS, under the leadership of Pierre Méhaignerie, and its 41 representatives in the National Assembly (46 seats in 1986) withdrew from the parliamentary group formed by the UDF, leaving behind a mere "torso". The CDS group calls itself the *Union du centre* (UDC), the more common name also used in *Fig. 21.*

Even though the 41 *centristes* did not completely withdraw from the UDF, since the French system of majority vote forces all important parties, including the CDS, to be loyal to their blocs, they have – occasionally – supported Rocard's Government either by abstaining or by casting their votes in favour of the Prime Minister.The CDS has meanwhile showed stronger leanings back to the UDF and co-operated in the 1992 regional elections like the other UDF parties in the UPF alliance (cf. 2.4). Although the CDS presents itself independently in the National Assembly, it runs under the UPF umbrella otherwise – a "hermaphrodite" position it certainly cannot afford to keep up in the long run.

2.5.3 The Radicals

The oldest French party still in existence, on the other hand, is a *laicist* party: the *Parti radical-socialiste*, a party which was influential during the Third Republic from the turn of the century on. This name is easily misinterpreted outside of France but in actuality comes from the radical struggle against the influence of the Church, the struggle responsible, for example, for the separation of Church and State as set down in law in 1905 (Defrasne 1975, p. 72f.). The close contacts between radicalism and French Freemasonry date back to the time of the Dreyfus affair (1894-1906, cf. Miquel 1973 and Gallo 1984, p. 158ff.) and also to anticlerical movements before and after the party was officially founded in 1901.

Their policy in economic matters, however, was in line with their status as a party of the middle classes, the self-employed and some farmers as well. This was usually a liberal policy, but the party was at times also in favour of governmental intervention and nationalization. The only constant feature of the party was its laicism. This is the reason why the party oscillated throughout its history between alliances with the Right and Left, each shift occasioning the formation of internal factions (Rémond 1982, pp. 305-307). Not even noted "radical" politicians such as J. Ferry, Clemenceau, Daladier and Mendès-France were able to prevent this behavior. The Fifth Republic and its push towards bipolarization brought increased tension within the party. As a result, J. J. Servan-Schreiber's attempt at uniting the party with a "modern", anti-centralistic platform stressing private enterprise open to innovation was also doomed to failure. The crisis came to a head when the Radicals and Lecanuet's *Centre démocrate* united to form the *Mouvement réformateur*, an alliance hostile to nationalization. The left wing of the party was not in agreement with this step and the result was the breakup of the party.

The minority faction led by Maurice Faure and Robert Fabre assumed the name *Mouvement des Radicaux de Gauche* (MRG) and became the third force in the *Union de la Gauche* (PCF and PS) in 1972. Since then the MRG has been holding its own as the electoral and parliamentary partner of the Socialists, but not without difficulty. The majority of its voters are concentrated in the laicist and regionalist bourgeoisie of the southwest and Corsica.

The majority faction, on the other hand, retained the name associated with the long tradition of the party (the party is customarily referred to by the press as «*les Valoisiens*», so named after their headquarters at the Place des Valois in Paris) and later supported Giscard d'Estaing's presidential candidacy in 1974 and 1981. In the meantime, however, its political significance has dwindled to practically nothing. It claims 15,000 members while the MRG claims 25,000 (Quid 1992, pp. 703 and 707).

It can be seen that the Radicals failed to adjust their strategy to the new situation after the decline of the traditional middle class, their basis of power during the Third Republic.

2.5.4 Further constituents of the UDF

The *Programme commun de gouvernement* shared by the PS and the PCF induced a group of 4000 members of the PS to split off from the Socialists to form the *Mouvement démocrate socialiste* de France. Today this party is known as the *Parti social-démocrate* (PSD), claims to have 110,000 members and reckons itself among the social democratic parties of Europe. The PSD is one of the firm proponents of the economic and political unification of Europe and of decentralization in France (cf. Quid 1985, p. 612). This party joined the UDF shortly after its formation in 1978 and is an important factor, for example, in Alsace.

The *Clubs Perspectives et Réalités* (cf. 2.8.5) constitute a further member of the liberal-conservative alliance. They were called into being in 1965/66 by Giscard d'Estaing and are currently widespread throughout the country. Their members do not wish to commit themselves to one or the other of the three main constituents in the UDF. Both the PSD and these clubs are directly represented in the political council of the UDF by one of its four vice presidents.

2.6 *The Socialists (PS) and their relationship to the Communists*

The "fateful question" of who to enter into an alliance with in order to achieve one's own political goals has been even more central throughout the history of the Socialists than it was for the Radicals. Should they join forces

- with the Communists, i.e. in an *alliance à gauche*,
- or with the progressive-moderate parties in an *alliance au centre*?

This question is much more than a tactical consideration, it is a matter of principles and ethics. It has repeatedly been an item of vehement and bitter controversy. The SFIO (*Section Française de l'Internationale Ouvrière*), the precursor of the current party, had already been subject to shifting internal majorities and policy, and it is significant to note in this context that the SFIO was formed in 1905 by the union of the hard-line Marxist *Parti socialiste de France* under *Jules Guesde* and the *Parti socialiste français* under *Jean Jaurès*, a party pledged to reforms and willing to assume responsibility in a Government. Both of these directions were present in the charter of the SFIO even though the emphasis was clearly on the idea of class struggle as seen by Guesde:

> Par son but, par son idéal, par les moyens qu'il emploie, le Parti socialiste, tout en poursuivant la réalisation des réformes immédiates revendiquées par la classe ouvrière, n'est pas un parti de réforme, mais un parti de lutte de classe et de révolution. (Defrasne 1975, p. 75)

One can see, then, that the tension between the left wing and the centre in the Socialist party thus has its roots far back in the past; in the end it goes all the way back to the antagonism between the revolutionaries and the revisionists in the 19th century (Ligou 1962). The conclusive schism would seem to have taken place in December 1920 at the *party congress in Tours* (cf. *Fig. 21*). At that time a majority of the delegates elected to join the Third (Communist) International, which had been formed in 1919 under the leadership of the Soviet Union. This group became the French Communist Party and thus from the very start had the opportunity to develop into a mass-based party. The party newspaper, *L'Humanité*, became the official organ of the Communist Party. Only a small group remained Socialists, a development which ran a completely different course in Germany. However, a leftist revolutionary wing (which objected only to the Soviet form of communism) and a moderate revisionist wing continued to struggle for supremacy in this minority group. One of the members of the revolutionary wing was Jules Guesde, "one of the founding fathers of French socialism, [a man] who had taken his Marxist ideology from Karl Kautsky, the German social-democratic theoretician, at the beginning of this century and who had vigorously opposed the concept of 'socialist humanism' held by Jean Jaurès". Guesde continues to have adherents amongst the French Socialists up to this day. The term *class front* "is directly attributable to him [Guesde] and tacitly implies an alliance with the Communists" (Sandoz 1985, p. 49).

The minority group of 1920 retained the party's old name, SFIO, and a predominantly Marxist platform. Similar to the programme of the German SPD between the wars, however, that of the SFIO was not based on the principle of armed overthrow but rather on social reforms aimed at improving the working and living conditions of the people. The Socialists have been shaped to a great extent by their relationship to the Communists, viewing them either as competition (especially with respect to the working class) or as partners (in joint action against conservative or fascist forces) – so much so that it is difficult to describe either of the parties by itself.

The Socialists have cooperated with the Communists three times in all since the congress in which the two groups parted company. It is, however, not only important to be aware of these three phases, one should also know about the three main reasons for their separation:

1. During the Third Republic the two parties combined forces in 1934 to organize fervent demonstrations against the fascist *Ligues*. After the anti-fascist bourgeois Radical Party joined the movement and after the three parties won the 1936 elections, this *unité d'action* led to a Government headed by the Socialist *Léon Blum*, the first Government by a *front populaire*; the role of the PCF in this arrangement was only that of supporting the Socialist and Radical Government. With the help of this majority the Government succeeded in nationalizing several enterprises (armament factories, Banque de France, creation of the French railway company SNCF) and in introducing substantial social reforms: for example, the 40-hour work week and 15 days of paid vacation were granted, wage hikes were increased by 7 to 15%, the number of mandatory school years was increased to 14. Why, then, did the popular front fall apart two years later? Historians are still not in agreement as to the answer to this question. The following points are a few factors in the problem. Despite the urges of the Communists, the Government refused to support the Republicans in the Spanish Civil War, while the fascist countries (the German Third Reich, Italy) provided massive assistance to Franco's troops. However, Stalin's show trials in Moscow, the financial problems of the Government of the Left – due in particular to the social reforms – in the same way as the ensuing

inflation (Blum called for a *pause* in new social welfare projects) and hesitation to continue with nationalization were further factors. As is to be expected, Communist historians emphasize the errors of the Socialists and the manoeuvring of the world of high finance and other moneyed groups when depicting the international and national reasons behind the breach (e.g. in Köller/Töpfer 1978, pp. 580-584). At the same time, bourgeois historians naturally point their finger at the riskiness of leftist economic policy which according to them is doomed to failure from the outset (e.g. Sieburg 1975, p. 409).

2. The SFIO, PCF and MRP formed a coalition Government lasting from the beginning of the Fourth Republic to May 1947 and headed by President de Gaulle up to 20 January 1946. The coalition was a continuation of the cooperation which had started in the French Resistance. This situation was brought to an end, again by international politics (the "Cold War" and apparently by American pressure on France) and a wage freeze (to which the PCF was opposed). – This *tripartisme* was responsible for several important innovations: planned economy upon governmental recommendation, numerous nationalizations and the introduction of statutory social security (cf. 3.5). – Following the breakup of the coalition, the SFIO cooperated alternately with the MRP and the Radicals or left-wing Gaullists.

3. During the Fifth Republic[2] the SFIO was compelled by the new system of majority vote to try to form a counterweight to the Gaullists. It was only typical for them that this meant looking to either the bourgeois block *or* to the Communists for help. Despite the efforts of presidential candidate Mitterrand, not yet a member of the SFIO, the strategy of alliance with the non-communist parties of the Left – the PCF was consulted merely as a matter of election tactics – did not meet with success (cf. Schmidt et. al. 1981, p. 286). What is more, this "bourgeois" course cost the SFIO members and voters. An attempt was then made to gain power by the opposite strategy. The *Parti socialiste* was founded as a result of a shift to the left aimed at making it possible to cooperate with the Communists – the official date is 1969, although the much more significant union with the *Convention des institutions républicaines* led by Mitterrand did not take place until June 1971.

The foundation of the PS changed the face of the French party system completely. With its clear left-wing course, the party, now under Mitterrand's leadership, set its sights on conscientiously representing the interests of the wage-earners, a group that had increased greatly in

2 Side note to the SFIO and the Fifth Republic: The majority of the SFIO had urged the population to ratify the constitution of the Fifth Republic. This led to the secession of a Marxist-oriented group in favour of *autogestion* (self-management). In 1960 this group christened itself *Parti socialiste unifié* [PSU], under which name they disbanded in 1990. Cf. Fig. 21 and Goguel/Grosser 1976, p. 110f.

number and thus also in electoral influence through the transformation of France into a modern industrial nation. It was a mass-based party aiming to subdue capitalism – arm-in-arm with the Communists.

The Communists, who at the time had more members and voters than the Socialists (they received 20% of the votes in the *élections législatives* of June 1968, the joint ballot of Socialists and Radicals attained only 16.6%), accepted the offer. The result was the famous *Programme commun de gouvernement* of 1972, a platform for the elections in the following year. This was to be the starting point of the continuous rise of the PS until its victory in 1981. The values laid down in the programme were one important factor contributing to the success: they were a signal of consensus to the people voting for the Communists (important for the second ballot) as well as words of courtship to the lower and middle social classes and to the intelligentia. The main long-term goal was to transform the country into a non-capitalistic society. This was accompanied by short-term goals seeking to nationalize large businesses and enterprises and to balance out the grave disparities which still existed in the distribution of income and in educational opportunities. In foreign policy the party was to continue the Gaullist course of independence while at the same time stressing solidarity with the Third World. Even more important, though, was how the Socialists – as opposed to the PCF with its regulatory and government-oriented views of state socialism – envisioned this structural change. The PS borrowed the basic concept of *autogestion* (self-management), a concept which had its origin in anarcho-syndicalism, from the CFDT trade union, the PSU and the student movements of May 1968. Instead of co-determination (*cogestion*), it was the principle of self-management that was supposed to dominate factories, businesses and all segments of society (e.g. communes, neighbourhoods, *départements*, schools, universities, the media, and also the women's liberation movement). Furthermore, the people were to be freed from their dependence not in the distant future, but starting then and there (cf. Jäger 1978, pp. 94-100; Schmidt et. al. 1981, pp. 70-73). This platform attracted many young people, teachers and union members of the CFDT to the PS. Even though the PS did not succeed in totally absorbing the PSU, as had been planned in 1974, it did manage to take many active members, including Rocard, the head of the party, away from the PSU to supplement its own ranks (Baron 1977, p. 84).

An additional factor was that persons voting for one of the parties of the Left in the first ballot usually gave their vote in the second ballot to the candidate of the Left who has the best chance of winning. Since this was normally the candidate from the PS, the overall upward trend for the Socialists was able to survive the dissolution of the alliance of the Left in the fall of 1977 and also the ensuing elections in 1978, in which the parties of the Left did only moderately well.

In May of 1981 came Mitterrand's sensational victory in the presidential elections; in June 1981 the Socialists (together with the MRG) achieved a record result, 37.5% in the *premier tour* (first round) of the new elections for the *Assemblée nationale* ordered by Mitterrand; thanks to the electoral system, finally, the Socialists won the final absolute majority in the *deuxième tour* (second round). All of this left its mark on France. There are numerous reasons for these victories, reasons which can only be briefly outlined here: a grave economic situation with a considerable foreign-trade deficit, high inflation and unemployment, and on the other hand Mitterrand's proposed countermeasures, meticulously calculated and thus credible for many of the voters; the attractiveness of *autogestion* and thus of the programme for decentralization in the *régions* and *départements*; Giscard d'Estaing's autocratic mode of governing which had resulted in disharmony within the right wing, this in contrast to the unity of the left wing and to the agreement that Communist voters would give their votes to Socialist candidates when the latter had better chances of winning in the second ballots. It was beneficial for the Socialists that they had not been allied with the PCF *before* the presidential elections and also that the Communists did very *poorly* in the first ballots. In this way, it was not possible for the RPR and UDF to convince the voters of a "Communist menace" or of the looming phantom of a *«régime socialo-communiste»*. Mitterrand and the Socialists became acceptable even for a number of conservative voters disillusioned by the Giscard regime. (For details see, e.g., Sandoz 1981, Reif 1981 and especially Chapsal 1984, pp. 707-713, 718-734.)

Maus 1981 contains the texts of campaign speeches, pamphlets by the presidential candidates and a complete version of the *débat télévisé* between Giscard d'Estaing and Mitterrand on 5 May 1981.
Mitterrand's highly symbolic visit to the *Panthéon*, the monument to the laicist patriotism of the whole of France, demonstrated to the world that *the Left had a greater awareness of history* than the RPR or UDF (cf. the detailed semiotic analysis by Kimmel/Poujol 1982, pp. 194-198).

The joint left-wing rule in France, asymmetric from the very start, lasted from the middle of 1981 to the middle of 1984, a mere three years. Because of the Socialists' overwhelming majority in the electorate and in Parliament, the PCF was represented with only four ministers. When this period is compared to the two other, more genuine "popular front" periods, one cannot fail to note that in all three cases it was a *combination of economic conflicts and conflicts in domestic policy in the context of an economic crisis on the one hand and basic differences in foreign policy on the other* that brought about the breakup of the alliance - despite all the differences in the three historical situations.

The *political shift* led to a course of austerity in economic policy which began in the summer of 1982 and was intensified in the spring of 1983, a policy which took recourse to almost exactly the same unpopular measures (wage freezes, dismissals, cf. 3.8) which had triggered protests from the Communists in 1937 and 1947, protests which were followed by Communist-supported strikes and finally by their withdrawal from the alliance.

In the area of *domestic affairs*, the Communists could no longer tolerate the fact that they were continuing to lose votes in communal, cantonal and European elections (in the 1979 European elections they had reached 20.5%, in 1984 only 11.18%), primarily to the Socialists, their "junior partner" of 1972. Thus in a speech delivered at the 25th party congress of the PCF Marchais (1985, p. 78) emphasized «que la réduction systématique de la vie politique nationale à un soi-disant affrontement droite-gauche conduit à une bipolarisation mutilante, qui étouffe la voix des communistes et de tous ceux qui refusent de se soumettre à la crise» and in his introductory words reminded the delegates of historical precedents and of the convention in 1920 which brought about the great split (T. 10) - he thus proved to be just as historically minded as Mitterrand, the crucial difference being that Marchais went back to 1789.

> T. 10:
> Oui, le choix historique du Congrès de Tours fut le bon! Oui, les militants qui décidèrent en 1920 de manifester leur fidélité aux combats des révolutionnaires de 1789, des insurgés de 1848, des communards et de Jean Jaurès, ces militants qui, tel Marcel Cachin, choisirent de rompre avec la politique de collaboration de classes et de fonder le Parti communiste français eurent raison! (Marchais 1985, p. 7)

Seen from the viewpoint of the French Communists, therefore, the reasons for the split could be traced back to the traditional ideological differences between the parties (class struggle vs. class collaboration).

Finally, Mitterrand's stance in *foreign policy*, a decidedly anti-Soviet strategy (for example he denounced the "suppression of Afghanistan and Poland" and sanctioned the stationing of American nuclear weapons in Europe) also played its part in bringing about the rupture. Since the Right never ceased to criticize the "Communist infiltration" in the Government of the Left, this strategy was clearly aimed at fending off the attacks from that sector. In this respect, the standpoint taken by the Socialists was dictated by domestic reasons compelling them to set themselves off from the PCF.

Conspicuous parallels can therefore be noted in the relationship of the two large parties of the Left to each other, despite the fact that their positions on world and domestic politics are so completely different. These parallels not only show that it is impossible to view or understand one or the other of the two parties in isolation, they also reveal the divergence inherent in the very "natures" of the two allies: ever since it was formed the PS has been fluctuating between its inherited reformative and revolutionary inclinations, between an *alliance à gauche* and an *alliance au centre*. At the same time it finds it difficult to enter into an alliance with a partner that is not able to relinquish its own traditional view of itself without completely losing its own identity as the "vanguard of the working class" and as the moving force behind the French part of the world-wide revolution. The PCF, however, is in danger of losing its identity anyway - in the face of increasing Socialist preponderance (cf. 2.7).

The only item of the original Socialist platform to survive past 1981 was the concept of *autogestion*. Its effects, however, were more evident in politics than in factories and businesses, namely in the decentralization and ensuing high degree of self-administration of the *communes, départements et régions*. An increase in *autogestion* was also registered in the area of culture, especially in the *départements* and *régions* in which the Socialists were able to maintain their majority. For example, theatres and museums were able to see to their own affairs for the most part and the measures of the leftist government were responsible for an initially very high number of independently run *radios libres* and for substantially more freedom in television programming than was possible before 1981 (cf. 6.2).

After 1981 the term *autogestion* (stage 1) was gradually replaced in the platform rhetoric by the concept of *modernisation*, i.e. freedom of choice for "France Inc." and strategies necessary for adapting this "company" to the European and world markets (stage 2, cf. Baier 1988 and Brauns 1988). However, with the approach of the internal European market in 1992/93 "self-determination for France" is beginning to be supplanted in the language of, in particular, the French Socialists by "self- determination for Europe": the team of France and West Germany is supposed to see to it that *l'Europe* is protected from all *extra-Européens* (cf. Schubert 1988, pp. 345-347 and also Mitterrand's «*Lettre à tous les Français*» in Libération 7 April 1988). Thus it is possible to predict the advent of a third stage, a stage in which the principles of free enterprise will hold *within* the EC, while the United States, Japan etc. will be confronted with a more protectionist attitude. The author thinks it probable that the central idea of *self-determination*, an idea which started out on the level of activities in and about factories and individual businesses (stage 1) and which was then transferred to the national level under a different name (stage 2), is now beginning to be projected onto the European level (stage 3).

After years of programmatic discussions the PS, having found back to its reformist roots (Sandoz 1985, p. 50f.; Leggewie 1986, p. 92ff.), finally agreed on a platform similar to that of the German SPD in their "Bad Godesberg Programme", which they adopted at the extraordinary party conference held in Paris in December 1991: the new platform entitled «*Horizon 2000*» turns its back on a *unilateral* tie to Marxism and propagates social market economy. But two of the essential features of "social democracy" are lacking in the PS: 1) "the existence of a well-knit membership organization with a large proportion of workers", and 2) "close ties to the trade unions" – a problem which is witnessed to by the fact that even the C.F.D.T. (cf. 4.6.3), which used to be sympathetic to the PS, has backed away from it (Bock 1988, p. 81). As flexible as it is, even the PS cannot afford to give up its own identity in front of its members and steady voters. The revolution of 1789 and the three basic, interdependent revolutionary principles continue to be the focal point of every party of the Left in France, a country so aware of its history and tradition. A party of the Left will be assessed by the measure of its success in the further, step-by-step realization of these ideals. In this era of electronics, managers and problems of energy and ecology, therefore, it may strive to be "modern", but it must never call in question the historical dynamics of the revolution.

Three strategies were tried out during the socialist minority governments until 1988, usually linked to the name of each prime minister. Reference is made here to the beginning of this chapter (before 2.1). The third government under Pierre Bérégovoy, previously minister of economy and finance, made the attempt to appear suprapartisan in character by appointing numerous experts (after both the *alliance au centre* and the *alliance à gauche* had failed).

The *membership of the PS* is dominated by the wage-earning middle classes (in particular teachers and *cadres*, i.e. management). There is a definite deficit of workers and farmers as compared to intellectuals and management. A large part of the active "new" Socialists come from bourgeois and Christian families (Jäger 1978a, p. 8). These different backgrounds alone indicate that it is possible for revolutionary and reformative factions to co-exist, with revolutionary theory on the one hand and flexible practice and tactics open to compromise on the other. Mere opportunism is counteracted, however, both by the obligation imposed on the party by its historical heritage and by the influence of the Protestants – e.g. Rocard, Mermaz, Jospin – in the party (cf. Willaime 1985, pp. 41-46). According to internal statistics, the number of members in the PS grew from 90,000 in 1971 to double that amount in 1980 and then increased to 230,000 after the successful elections of 1981 (Quid 1983, p. 787); this number was reduced somewhat following the change in economic policy: 215,000 in 1983, 210,000 in 1984 and 187,000 in 1986 (Quid 1987, p. 711; Quid 1992, p. 708). Internal political *courants* (currants) fluctuate quite a bit - as can be seen from the votes at the party conventions every two years. There is, however, a certain amount of stability to three groupings: a centre-left *courant* around Mauroy, Mermaz and Jospin, a current called *Socialisme et République* which emerged from CERES (*Centre d'Etudes, de Recherches et d'Education Socialistes*) in 1986 and which at the moment is centred around Chevènement - CERES used to include between 15 and 20% of the party members, it played a big part in swinging the party around from the SFIO to the PS after its initial, not very successful centrist course and was also a decisive factor in the *Programme commun* of 1972 - and finally various social-democratic groups on the other side, currently led by Rocard and other figures. The statutes of the party do not allow these *courants* to take on any organizational form of their own, yet the proportion of votes given to these currants determines the composition of all decision-making committees in the

- *sections* (local branches)
- *fédérations* (the next higher organizational step at the *département* level), and at the
- national level (i.e. the party executive and the executive office).

Thus the *courants* in the PS are of great importance. A *thoroughly structured* democratic system based in this manner on internal proportions is foreign to other French and German parties. With only slight exceptions, the *spectrum of PS voters* reflects the social structure of France (cf. Kempf 1989a, p. 148; for more details see *Table 2*). In this respect at least, the PS has almost become a fully-fledged catch-all party. Even the areas with a high concentration of PS voters are no longer concentrated in certain regions but instead dispersed throughout the whole country, even though it is true that certain regions were especially strong in various elections, e.g. the southwest with its growth-related problems and hopes, the regions Nord – Pas de Calais and Ile de France (the latter with a "rightist" majority, however) and several traditionally Socialist *départements* such as Bouches-du-Rhône or Nièvre (Mitterrand's home *département*). – The regional elections of 22 March 1992 (with proportional representation) ended in a disaster for the socialists (18.3%) and their allies (*majorité présidentielle, divers gauche*, 2.2%): «Ce n'est plus un échec, c'est un débâcle» (Serge July in Libération, 24 March 1992, p. 3). The ratio of socialist and UDF/RPR presidents in the 22 regions of the mother land was previously 3:19; socialists and their allies did not succeed in improving this result. After the cantonal elections of 22 and 29 March 1992 (with the majority voting system in two ballots applying in the 99 *départements* including 4 DOMs) held simultaneously, the delegates voted 75 "Conservatives" (+5) and only 22 socialists (-5) for presidents of the *conseils généraux*; both communists held their seats. The PS vote shrank in all age groups and professional sections (for details see *Table 2*).

Cf. 2.5.3 for information on the MRG, the consistent, smaller ally of the Socialists since 1972.

2.7 *The Communists (PCF)*

The main events in the history of the PCF have already been mentioned in the previous section. Since in addition the PCF no longer occupies the pivotal position that Goguel/Grosser (1976, 98) at one time gave it, this section will be primarily concerned with the significance of the party in the cultural history of France.

The French Communist Party was highly respected by numerous artists and intellectuals during the period between the wars, in the Resistance and after the World War II. From 1920 on it was *the* party of the French Left and as such claimed to be the rightful heir of the Enlightenment and of the nation's revolutionary struggles. When viewed in this manner, French history reveals a direct line running from the Jacobins through Babeuf, the revolution of 1848 and the Commune of 1871 to Leninism and the Russian October Revolution of 1917, the actual starting point of World Communism. The PCF carried on these revolutionary impulses – whose "roots" can be found in France itself – in its own country (cf. Caute 1967). This national component was complemented by committed participation in international matters, for example in the Spanish Civil War and more generally in defending democratic standards and values against "fascism" at home and abroad. The progressive forces in France allied with the Soviet Union to form a bulwark against "fascism" and to aid all suppressed peoples of the world: this was a gratifying, promising vision which was brought to an end for some by the dogmatic attitude of the PCF, for others by Stalin's show trials, for most, however, by the rude jolt of the pact signed by Hitler and Stalin on 23 August 1939 ... It was not until German troops unexpectedly marched on the Soviet Union (22 June 1941) that the forces of the PCF and its sympathizers were free to join the Resistance after having had their hands tied for nearly two years by this pact (cf. 7.1.2).

The significant part played by the Communists in the Resistance and the great number of Resistance fighters from their ranks who fell during the war have not been forgotten. In the 1950's, moreover, the PCF was the only large party opposed to the Algerian War. It was for these reasons that numerous intellectuals and artists identified themselves with the Communists.

At this point it is appropriate to mention at least a few of the prominent figures who have been associated with the PCF at certain times or over decades (T. 11).

T. 11:
The first wave of writers to join or to profess sympathy for the newly founded PCF came after 1920. Anatole France, Henri Barbusse, Georges Duhamel and Jules Romains were among the very first editors of *Clarté*, the Communist literary magazine. In 1927, the surrealists, headed by Breton, Aragon and Eluard, pledged themselves to the party, and after 1932/33 even such individualists as Gide and Malraux followed suit. A new wave of membership applications coming from intellectuals in a wide-ranging spectrum of fields followed the victory of the Popular Front; the painter Fernand Léger, the physicist Paul Langevin, the critic Julien Benda, the architect Le Corbusier and the film director Jean Renoir were some of the most prominent adherents of the PCF and thus adherents of Moscow in Paris. The last wave of new members came in 1944/45 triggered by the *Libération*. The symbolic figures in this wave were the husband and wife physicist team of Joliot and Curie for the sciences, Picasso for the arts and for literature doubtlessly Jean-Paul Sartre, who, even though he never officially joined the party, supported its policies up to the end of the 1950's with only occasional criticism. (Reichel 1984, p. 398; cf. also Caute 1967 and the magazine *Lendemains*, e.g. issues 9 [Aragon], 29 [Malraux], 33 [Résistance], 42 [Front populaire, Sartre] and 60 [Sartre].)

The influence of the party has been decreasing almost steadily ever since the PCF attained its zenith in November 1946 (at which time it was the strongest party, numbering about one million members and 5.5 million voters, i.e. 28.3% of the votes). In 1986 the number of votes it received dropped below the 10% mark for the very first time (cf. *Table 1*). There are various *reasons for the decline of the PCF* (even though it must be emphasized that Communists in France and in the Mediterranean countries continue to be common in leading positions at the communal level, in factories and businesses, in trade unions and in cultural life). These reasons are:

- De Gaulle adopted an anti-Communist stance which has been propagated by various groups and by segments of the media ever since the Cold War era. The effects were especially apparent after de Gaulle took power (cf. *Table 1* and Goguel/Grosser 1976, p. 100).
- The PCF was not forceful enough in steering a "Eurocommunist" course, a course clearly distinguishable from that followed by the Soviet Union. Unlike the Italian Communist Party, for example, it passed up a good opportunity to do so after the 20th Party Congress of the Communist Party of the Soviet Union in 1956. (Baron 1977, pp. 90-92, cf. also Marchais' "self-criticism" [1985, pp. 10-12]; for more on "Eurocommunism" see Jäger 1980, pp. 73-83.)
- The party leadership has become antiquated, as Ehrmann (1976, p. 163) observed with respect to Thorez. It is not easy for a party in this situation to adapt to new situations, especially in a strictly hierarchic organization. In other words, the fact that the committees responsible for making the important decisions are made up mostly of elderly politicians makes it more difficult to introduce innovations than when individual leaders who are advanced in years – e.g. President de Gaulle or President Mitterrand – are surrounded by a staff of selected advisers, some of which are young.

- The difficulty of adapting the theory and practice of Marxism to the altered social conditions. This problem has been proved by the fact that many members have been barred from or have left the party.
- The numbers of the industrial proletariat, the actual societal base of the party, are decreasing. Nearly one million industrial jobs were lost between 1975 and 1982 alone, primarily in the steel industry, the dockyards and in mining, the traditional strongholds of the PCF and the CGT (cf. 3.5 and Martelli 1986, Morawe 1985).
- Finally, there are the votes that go to the Socialists in the second ballots, although this phenomenon should probably be considered of secondary importance.

Thus it seems apt to compare the situation at hand with the decline of the once so important and influential Radical party, even though the PCF has not been affected nearly as much. As far as one can tell from the present situation, a comeback for the PCF would only be conceivable if social, economic and political circumstances were to change and if the party would adjust its programme, strategy and leadership.

This process is reflected by a *decline in the PCF's cultural influence* in and through intellectuals. Reichel (1984, p. 400ff.) describes in detail the various stages in the process and notes that it is related to the repeated instances of intellectuals being expelled because of differing opinions. It is highly significant that the one single "change of direction" with the most consequences for the present situation was not made back in May 1968 when the PCF joined forces with de Gaulle by behaving like a "party of law and order". It is true that by doing so the PCF forfeited its revolutionary image in the eyes of many Frenchmen – such as the important and outspoken voices of Jean-Paul Sartre and Simone de Beauvoir – but another "change of direction", namely that triggered by the French translation of Solzhenitsyn's *Gulag Archipelago*, was even more critical. There were also other Soviet dissidents at the time who gave speeches and published books in Paris, and the criticism of totalitarianism by the *nouveaux philosophes* (André Glucksmann, Bernard-Henri Lévy, Jean-Marie Benoist and others; cf. the June 1982 issue of the magazine *Dokumente*, which was dedicated to them) was influenced by these books – mainly *Gulag Archipelago* – and augmented the loss of confidence in the PCF.

It is hard to evaluate the importance of these cultural factors. At any rate, it is not the intellectuals who dominate in the membership of the PCF (as they do in the PS), but rather workers (36%), service workers and other employees (*employés*, 21%) and the retired as well as other groups designated *inactifs* in the statistics (27%) – these numbers were provided by the PCF for 1979 (Menyesch/Uterwedde 1982, p. 167). The official percentage of workers was substantially higher around 1970 (60%) while the number of *employés* was somewhat smaller (18.5%, Borella 1973, p. 177); this would mean that the proportion of workers in the party has shrunk by about one half whereas the increase in *employés* resulted in only moderate growth.

According to Ph. Robrieux, only about 200,000 of the 710,000 members quoted in 1982 – 608,543 at the end of 1984 according to Marchais 1985, p. 83 – paid their dues (Quid 1985, p. 610); Kempf also estimates the "actual" number of members at 150,000 to 200,000 (1983a, p. 35). 608,000 members, only 104,000 of which pay their dues, were claimed to have been registered in 1985 (Quid 1989, p. 709).The "revised" figures quoted by the party were 325,000 in 1985, and as many as 702,864 in 1988 ... (Quid 1992, p. 706). The party is also experiencing similar losses in voters, even in the traditional strongholds of the PCF: the industrial area of the *région du Nord*, the industrialized *ceinture rouge* around Paris (cf. the analysis of Ivry-sur-Seine by Lojkine/Viet-Depaule 1984), as well as the Mediterranean coastal regions, whose wine-growers, small farmers and farm labourers often used to vote PCF in order to voice their protest to difficulties in selling their products and dealing with the centralistic administration.

In the face of this membership and voter crisis the PCF tried to build up a greater degree of support among the *travailleurs immigrés*, the immigrant workers (cf. Marchais 1985, p. 73f.), however this goal was pursued while maintaining a *proper amount of discretion*. France's "hidden racism" and widespread reservations towards foreign workers made it impossible for the PCF to approach this subject with too much fervour. Not until 1987/88 did the PCF begin at times to stand up more fervently for the rights of the *immigrés* - either out of humanitarian duty or with the courage of the desperate who do not have much to lose after election defeats. The publicity that the movement *S.O.S. Racisme* has received in France is certainly partially responsible for this more positive attitude towards the *immigrés*.

For information on the *party organization* based on Lenin's principle of "democratic centralism" see Goguel/Grosser 1976, p. 103 and Jäger 1978, pp. 50-54. In this context one must distinguish between two things: the theoretical submission of the leadership of the party to the will of a majority determined in democratic elections (thus formulated by Marchais 1985, p. 86f.), and the practical reality that free discussion in fact does take place in the *party cells* at the community level and in factories and businesses, but that leadership and control come "from above" at each of the *higher levels of organization* (*départements*, party congresses, central committee). In other words, when all is said and done it is the 21 members of the *politburo* who regulate affairs. This group, however, has had a decade-long gerontocratic tradition – similar to the former Communist Party of the Soviet Union and the highest decision-making levels in the Roman Catholic Church in both Rome and France.

Finally, a few words should be said as to the most important reasons why the PCF, despite all its losses, continues to be a much more significant factor in France than a Communist or post-Communist party is in Germany.

– The social conflicts are greater in France – as is also the case in Spain, Portugal, Italy and Greece – because of decades of extreme disparity in income, property and taxation coupled with a process of "full industrialization" which did not start until the middle of this century (cf. Chap. 3 and 4 and Ehrmann 1976, p. 163).

- The French Communists were more important than their German counterparts from the very start since they were in the majority both at the "splitting" convention in Tours and afterwards, since they were one of the forces behind the Popular Front and also because of their involvement in the *Résistance*.
- France's geopolitical situation is different from Germany's; West Germany was located between the two blocks and had experienced strong anti-Communism sentiment since the time of Adenauer.
- France has a strong "revolutionary-democratic tradition".
- The French Communists were on good terms with the largest French trade union *CGTunitaire*before 1936 and continue to be so with the current CGT. This trade union has served as a "drive belt" for PCF policies through the years (Schmidt et. al. 1981, p. 117). It was not possible, on the other hand, for the West German Communists to have any real kind of influence on activities of the German trade unions. Aside from the reasons for this given earlier, the West German Communist party DKP was faced with the unified organizational front offered by the DGB (the German federation of trade unions) whereas the French unions are in a state of disunity.

The 1988 presidential elections brought extremely disappointing results for the PCF: its candidate, André Lajoinie, received a mere 6.76% of the votes cast on 24 April 1988. However, the PCF recovered somewhat in the next parliamentary elections and gained 11.32% of the votes in the first ballot. Despite this, some of the party's internal critics turned their backs on the PCF, gave their support in the presidential elections to one of Lajoinie's opponents, Pierre Juquin (who won 2.10% of the votes, details in Bock 1988, p. 80), and together with Trotskyites and leftist *écologistes* founded the party *Nouvelle Gauche* in December 1988. But they remained marginal. In spite of predictions as to its early demise, the PCF has (for the above reasons) even survived the collapse of communism in Eastern Europe. They now present themselves as moral force (in view of the finance and corruption scandals shaking France's political scene) and profess to pursue democratic-pluralistic aims. So far the proportion of votes for the PCF keeps constant at approximately 8% (cf. Tables 1 and 2).

2.8 *Other parties in France*

Further characteristic features of and changes in French politics come to light when one takes a look at the remaining parties of the Left, at the ecological groups that take part in elections, at the *Front National*, at the *divers droite* and at the political clubs, which play a significant role in the formation and development of certain parties and groups of parties.

2.8.1 Other leftist parties

Both the Trotskyite and the Maoist parties (cf. Schmidt et. al. 1983, p. 31f., p. 52, p. 129f., pp. 172, 238) have lost the importance they had in the years around 1968. For instance, the Trotskyite *Lutte ouvrière*, led by Arlette Laguiller, received 2.06% of the votes in the 1984 European elections and only 1.44% in the 1989 European elections. The PSU (cf. 2.6), whose ideas and concepts provoked discussions in the entire non-orthodox Left in the late sixties, disbanded in 1990 (cf. *Fig. 21*) (See 2.5.4 for the PSD, the "centrist" offspring of the PS).

2.8.2 Environmentalist parties

The environmental movements and parties in France struggled against two disadvantages. First, the large parties of the Left have long since revised their originally negative attitude towards nuclear power plants and the *force de frappe* as formulated in their *programme commun* of 1972 in favour of a positive one. This change bore in mind the goal of attaining independence in matters of energy and defense. Secondly, the leftist parties are in favour of "economical" completion of national prestige projects (e.g. large dam projects, highway construction, TGV = *trains à grande vitesse*) regardless of adverse effects on the environment. Due to the *"patriotic" heritage in all of the large French parties*, the environmentalist groups have as yet to meet with any support in these parties for their endeavours, a situation quite different from that in Germany where the SPD (and sometimes latently even the FDP and CDU) shared some of the concerns of the Greens. It was not until 1985 that the *Parti socialiste* began to reconsider its position as a result of consultations with the German Social Democrats. Furthermore, for many years, the awareness of ecological problems has not grown as much in France as it has in Germany. A poll taken by the Commission of the European Communities in March / April 1986 indicated that 84% of the German population considered ecology an important and especially urgent matter. Germany thus took second place in the E.C. after Italy (86%), where the shock caused by Chernobyl was even greater than in Germany and where only two of the four nuclear power plants switched off after the accident are back in operation under strict security precautions. The French were at the very bottom of the list with 59%. *Structural differences* are one of the reasons for this: France has both a smaller population and a greater surface area – and at the same time a smaller proportion of forests – than does West Germany (France 1986: 55.4 million inhab., 547,026 km² = 101.3 inhab. per km²; Germany 1986: 61.1 million inhab., 248,678 km² = 245.9 inhab. per km²). German reunification has changed *this* proportion very little (France 1990: 56.6 million inhabitants, 551,700 km² = 102 inhab. per km²; Germany 1990: 79.7 million inhabitants, 356,945 km² = 223 inhab. per km²).

However, further reasons for the higher degree of ecological awareness in Germany can be found in the history of *German culture and thought*. The *Naturkult*, i.e. "nature cult", shared by Goethe and German Romanticism is part of a German tradition which also influenced bourgeois and anti-bourgeois "alternative" movements from the late 19th century on - youth movements and movements advocating the return to more simple life-styles; these and similar traditions were at no time nearly as important in France. It seems that a naïve faith in progress and growth has become widespread in France following the increased industrialization of the 1960's – and that the confidence in government and its ability to overcome environmental problems with logic and reason is unshakable. The information provided by the French media on ecological problems thus strikes foreign observers as being scanty and at times even distorted (Keller 1986).The question is whether a great deal has changed. Anyone keeping an eye open on reports on this subject will be able to see or read them – but not anywhere as frequent as in the German media. Changes in education, too, progress very slowly in France (Grosse/Rappenecker 1991, p. 38).

Aside from this widespread faith in progress and government, the *traditional conflict between Right and Left* continued to be lively (despite movement towards the Centre): this left little room for environmental parties. – An additional factor is the *lack of political unity* amongst the French *écologistes.* They were, for example, unable to agree upon a joint ballot for the 1984 European elections. A ballot who was oriented to rank-and-file democracy, *Les Verts – Europe Ecologie,* received 3.37%. The "left of Centre group *Entente Radicale Ecologiste* (ERE) made up of right-wing and left-wing Liberal Democrats and environmentalists led by Olivier Stirn, François Doubin and Brice Lalonde" (Höhne 1984, p. 83) achieved a mere 3.31%. The French *écologistes* – as opposed to the German Greens – thus lost an opportunity to enter the European Parliament, which would have been possible on this occasion since the European elections are proportional. This had very harmful consequences for them. Their election results sank to 1.24% in the 1986 parliamentary elections and to 1.21% in the 1988 parliamentary elections. They had more success in the presidential elections preceding the 1988 parliamentary elections: their candidate Antoine Waechter took 3.78% of the votes in the first ballot.

The party *Les Verts* was born in 1984 as the result of a fusion. In 1988 it claimed 1800 members at the national level and 2000 to 3000 members at regional levels (Quid 1989, p. 713). Since they have very few members and since membership dues are practically their only source of income, the French Greens have serious financial difficulties. This imposes grave restrictions on their methods of attracting voters and new members. The (very restricted) political party financing laws of 1988 and 1990 have hardly improved the situation of the *Verts*, particularly since these laws only refer to the elections for the *Assemblée nationale* (majority voting system) and therefore favour the parties represented there.

In the first ballot of the *élections municipales* on 12 March 1989, the French Greens attained more than 10% of the votes in a number of cities, especially in Alsace, around Lille, in the *région parisienne* and in the west. This startling result encouraged the *écologistes* to hope for improvements in environmental awareness in France.

They reached as much as 10.6% in the European elections on 18 June 1989, which meant that they were the fourth strongest party formation in France. Thanks to proportional representation, they took nine seats at Strasbourg. But because of French centralism (v. Oppeln 1989, p. 199f.) and the differences in suffrage and law, their situation compared with the German Green Party remained incomparably more difficult (Grosse/Rappenecker 1991, p. 28f., ibid. other literature). The old problem of fragmentation of the *écologistes* again showed quite clearly during the regional elections of 22 March 1992. The *Verts* received 6.8%, i.e. 7.5% together with some *divers écologistes*, while the candidates of the rival *Génération Ecologie* (GE) led by the minister of the environment Brice Lalonde (who eventually resigned from the government) received 7.1% of the votes. 43% of the voters for the GE (founded in 1990) and 31% of the voters for the *Verts* decided on their votes only a few days/hours before the vote, however.

The *Verts*, who had until now insisted on strict rank-and-file democracy, have meanwhile created a party structure; they consider themselves outside the Left-Right antagonisms. The GE on the other hand, supported by skilled political professionals coming from other camps, tends more toward the "Left" (despite its strict rejection of *basisme*, i.e. rank- and-file democracy); they still face the task of having to establish a party organization throughout France. In view of these opposites and considering the absence of a broad-based loyal electorate, the future prospects of the *écologistes* are not exactly rosy. But as a new political force and in their capacity as "majority procurers", they are wooed both by the PS and by the moderate Right (UPF).

2.8.3 *Front national*

The far-right party *Front national* (FN), on the other hand, did succeed in entering the European Parliament in 1984. Their 10.98% and 10 seats made them the *fourth largest party* (the RPR/UDF ran on a joint ballot). In 1986 they even managed to outdo the French Communist Party (cf. *Table 1*). The spectacular success of the FN is founded on their polemic attacks on the "*foreignization*" of France, i.e. attacks on the large number of foreigners and families of "foreign workers", in particular from North Africa, during a time of rising *unemployment*.The FN has therefore a different profile from the petit-bourgeois protest movement of the *Poujadistes* (cf. Kempf 1989, p. 170), although Le Pen and many of his supporters were at one time active in their ranks (cf. *Fig. 21*).

By claiming that the "foreign workers" are taking the dwindling number of jobs away from the French, the FN made inroads not only into the group of the "right" voters but also of the "left". Their campaign against *crime*(conveniently including crimes committed by foreigners) and in favour of toughening the penalties for crimes was another effective move. For example, 88% of the voters of the Far Right are in favour of reinstating the death penalty, which was repealed under Mitterrand. Finally, the FN's attack on the *«bande des quatre»* successfully appealed to a widespread distrust of the four established "parties" (RPR – UDF – PS – PCF) and their politicians. The opinion «qu'une fois élus les hommes politiques oublient leurs promesses» is shared by many, even by people who do not vote for the *Front national*.

"Le Pen is the spell-binding new mouth-piece for the hidden racism which is more widespread in the French Republic than many would like to admit", observes Kolboom (1984, p. 230). To be sure, the FN denies all accusations of racism by claiming that it respects the foreigners' *identité nationale* and that this is precisely the reason why the FN wants to protect them by paying for their return to the lands of their origin. They, the foreigners, are allegedly in danger of being deprived of their national and cultural uniqueness in a "uniform, universal and egalitarian soup". This reveals significant parallels to the ideology of the (intellectual) *Nouvelle Droite* centred around Alain Benoist, Pierre Vial and Louis Pauwels (Weingarten 1984, p. 89f.). However, two anti-Semitic remarks that Le Pen made in September 1987 and September 1988 gave a glimpse beneath the surface of how close he actually is to Nazism. These remarks triggered off nationwide indignation and were partly responsible for a drop in the number of FN sympathizers (details in Baier 1988, pp. 69-81 and Le Monde, 6 January 1989). The proportion of votes given to Le Pen decreased sharply after the record level of 14.41% he achieved in the 1988 presidential elections (parliamentary elections: 9.2%, only a single FN candidate was awarded a seat in the second ballot; cantonal elections on 25 September 1988: 5.4%, only four seats in the *conseils généraux* were won in the second ballot, cf. 1.3).But this low point was soon overcome. Le Pen's supporters reached 11.7% in the 1989 European elections, and as much as 13.9% in the regional elections – with a particularly high proportion of white collar people and workers (cf. *Table 2*) and the highest share of regular voters of all parties (72%: vote decided for several months, 11%: vote decided a few weeks ago, cf. Libération 24 March 1992, p. 4). The fact that the FN has a stable and loyal group of supporters and meanwhile represents an integral factor in France's political landscape cannot even be denied by its harshest opponents.

According to information from the FN, the number of members rose from 7000 to about 25,000 between 1976 and 1984, and finally reached more than 100,000 in 1988 (Quid 1985, p. 607; Quid 1992, p. 702). Its strongholds can be found in big cities, which in the face of rising unemployment are greatly affected by immigration and crime (1984, for example: Paris 15%, Lyon 17%, Marseille 21%).Marseille is *the* outstanding study object in Loch's popular study (1990, [2]1991) on the FN. The FN can also claim regional concentrations in areas greatly affected by ***immigration***: along the Mediterranean coast, in the south-west and in the Ile de France. The 1986 parliamentary elections, as well, display a striking correlation between immigration statistics and high election percentages for the FN (Le Nouvel Observateur 4 April 1986, p. 28f.; see de Weck 1986 for a biography of Le Pen, the founder of the party.)

The FN reaped its first successes in rural areas (especially in Alsace where it won more than 20% of the votes) during the 1988 presidential elections. Le Pen succeeded in reaching disquieted farmers and businessmen with his warnings labelling the European internal market a *«Waterloo pour la France»*. Chirac basically lost the second ballot in these elections because of his refusal to give in to pressure from his former underdog opponent, Barre, who wanted him to clearly renounce the FN, and because Chirac also refused to comply with the demands from the FN (cf. Le Monde 26 April 1988 and Kempf 1988, p. 108). This cost him votes from both sides - more, though, from Le Pen's followers. This is an instance in which the FN played a key role, both indirectly - in the internal quarrels between the bourgeois parties - and directly. The losses of the FN in the subsequent elections spared the RPR and the UDF for the moment from having to deal with the unpleasant question of whether or not to form a coalition with the FN - in contrast to 1986, at which time the "bourgeois" parties, for example, were able to reach a majority for their candidates for ***président*** in five regional parliaments with only the help of the FN. In 1992, the RPR-UDF alliance (officially) disclaimed any suggestion of joining forces with the FN. But it seems questionable whether they can stick to this course for the 1992 *législatives* and after.

The deeper reasons behind the success of the *Front National* can be found in the common fear that society is about to collapse and the resulting longing for the legendary France of the "Good Old Days". This is borne witness to by well thought-out slogans such as «Français, libérons la France!» (Benoit/Benoit/Lech 1986, p. 210) and oratorical crusades against the ***immigrés*** or against an *Empire de l'Europe*. The FN can make use of such methods to gain protest voters. – Another factor is the growing distrust of the population in the established parties and the incapacity of the moderate Right to show its real alternatives to "socialist" policies since 1988. Mitterrand saw the FN in a particular role: to be the "troublemaker in the opponent's camp". This was shown most clearly by the introduction of proportional representation for the 1986 *législatives*, which promptly gave the FN 34 mandates in the national assembly. This is a precedence case that is quoted time and again. La Repubblica, the Italian daily, published an article that was highly interesting in this context (24 March 1992, p. 4). It referred to the results of the regional elections just closed (more precisely: the opinion polls immediately *before* the election). If the national assembly had been elected by the same *proportional representation*, the *Front National* would have reached 89 of the 555 seats in the assembly. The majority voting system, on the other hand, would have given the FN just two seats. This helps to explain why both the UPF and virtually all the socialists reject a *scrutin proportionnel* for the national assembly elections and why they also violently object to its well-dosed mixture with the *scrutin majoritaire* (occasionally thrown back into the debate by Mitterrand).

2.8.4 *Divers droite, divers gauche*

The importance of the *divers droite* is a typical feature of French politics. This term is used to designate local politicians of the "Right" who are not associated with a party but who use their reputation to run in communal, cantonal, regional and even national elections as independents. These *divédés* acquired 10.3% of the votes in the 1979 cantonal elections, 12.95% in 1982, 14.6% in 1985 and 11.5% in 1988: the closer the RPR and UDF approach one another, the greater the chances are that these people will win. This is because of their outsider status, because they provide the voters with an alternative and especially because it is possible for them to take votes away from the Left as well since they are classed as "independents". Only the administrative agencies and official statistics classify them, occasionally against their will, as *divers droite*. Their role in the *Assemblée nationale* is that of *apparenté au groupe RPR* or *apparenté au groupe UDF*.

The importance of the *divers gauche*, on the other hand, has declined. One effect of the structured party system of the Fifth Republic is that the voters of the *divers gauche* were absorbed during the 1970's, for the most part by the Socialists (also by the MRG in certain regions, cf. 2.5.3) but also by the UDF parties (e.g. the PSD, cf. 2.5.4). They thus lost votes in the cantonal elections, achieving 3.16% in 1979, 1.54% in 1982 and 1.76% in 1985. As a consequence, for example, in 1985 only 59 candidates from the *divers gauche* acquired seats in the *conseils généraux*, as opposed to 425 from the *divers droite* (Höhne 1985, p. 145). The proportion of votes in the 1992 regional election was 2.5% (div. g.) and 4.5% (div. d.).

2.8.5 Political *clubs*

The political *clubs* are yet another way of participating in politics without directly joining a party. There are *clubs* grouped around the Socialists and the *radicaux de gauche* just as there are those located relatively close to the RPR (*Club de l'Horloge, Club 89*) or the UDF (cf. 2.5.4). They are loosely organized discussion groups which can crystallize into action groups. They also sponsor training courses, working conferences, internal lectures and publish their own journals. This is a phenomenon that originated in England and France in the 18th century but whose heyday, as hinted at in one of the club names (*Club 89*), was during the *Grande Revolution*. The *clubs* are actually the predecessors of leftist dignitary parties; apart from the *Club des Jacobins*, for example, there were also other, in part more "moderate" *clubs*. The Revolution of 1848, the era of the Commune and, to a lesser extent, the years between the two world wars were periods in which the clubs flourished anew. After a relatively long break the clubs came back to life again starting in 1951, initially "because of dissatisfaction with the political course of the *Parti radical* or of the SFIO; after 1958 the clubs professed the goal of suggesting and preparing an alternative to Gaullism" (Kowalsky 1983, p. 82). Their survival is due, on the one hand, to the respect in which the republican revolutions are held (thus, for example, the name *Club des Jacobins* of a group founded in 1951 by Charles Hernu – Minister of Defence from 1981-1985), and on the other, to the possibilities they have of influencing the parties. We know, for example, that they played a significant part in Mitterrand's candidacy for president in 1965, in the foundation of the *Parti socialiste* in 1969, in its expansion in 1971, but also in the foundation of the *Parti républicain* in 1977 (Schmidt et. al. 1981, pp. 143 and 145). As is evidenced by the last example, the success of leftist *clubs* in recruiting leaders for the upper echelons of the parties and in deciding party strategy stimulated the formation of similar *clubs* around the Giscardists. Giscard d'Estaing himself, for example, had called the *Clubs Perspectives et réalités* into being in 1965/66. The last to follow suit were the Gaullists. Among other groups that they founded is the elite *Club de l'Horloge* which was officially started in 1974 by a hundred young *énarques* and *polytechniciens* (cf. 5.3.1) and which has aided in preparing ideological and strategic counteroffensives against the PS and socialist-oriented clubs. The reciprocal nature of this relationship should be emphasized at this point. The *clubs* support the parties and do the groundwork for party alliances aimed at gaining or keeping power. They serve in particular as "think-tanks" for party programmes and strategy and as instruments for recruiting political talent (Fabre-Rosane 1984, p. 53f.). At the same time, the politicians and parties support the *clubs* so as to gain a base of political power or to acquire a tool for propagating their goals in educated and influential circles.

2.9 *A tentative comparison of the party systems in France and Germany*

The previous sections have pointed out several parallels and differences between the party systems in the two countries. Due to the introductory nature of the present book, the following comparisons shall be limited to two outlines based on two separate criteria: 1) changes in the system, and 2) political affinity and cooperation in the European Parliament since its institution in 1979. For further aspects see Jäger 1980 and Grosse 1987.

2.9.1 Changes in party systems

Both countries are following a trend leading from post-war multi-party systems to concentration and reduction. This is true not with respect to the number of parties in existence but to "their realistic chances of acquiring political power" and thus to their ability to participate directly in the Government by negotiating with other parties on election strategy and coalitions (Schlangen 1977, p. 124). When seen from this *qualitative* viewpoint, the *numerous changes in the French system* depicted above are in stark contrast to an astounding degree of *continuity in (West) Germany*. This continuity is evidenced by the stability of the large parties depicted in *Fig. 22*.

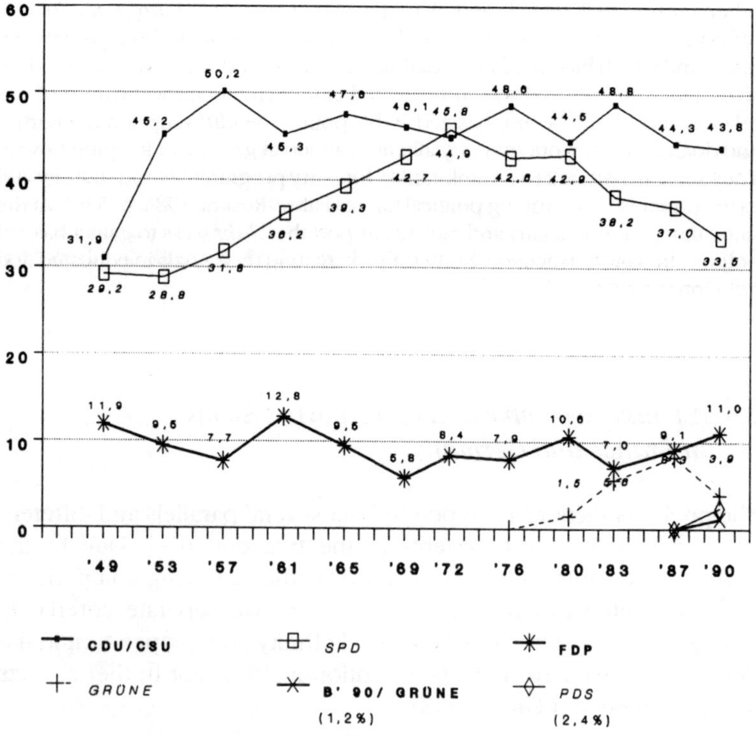

Fig. 22: The way of the parties during the *Bundestag* elections (percentages of the second votes, source: Gibowski/Kaase 1991, p. 3f.)

There are various reasons for this continuity.

The failure of the Weimar Republic and the great number of parties in the political arena of the time induced bourgeois groupings to merge into larger groups. This was the case with the CDU/CSU (Christian Democratic Union/ Christian Social Union); the word *Union* emphasizes their interdenominational nature. The CDU was rooted in the tradition of the Catholic *Zentrum* party, but it also integrated Protestant groups and absorbed increasing numbers of smaller bourgeois parties. In the same fashion, the CSU emerged to a great extent from the *Bayerische Volkspartei* (Bavarian People's Party) to attract more and more voters and adherents from the *Bayernpartei* (Bavaria[n] Party). The FDP (Free Democrat Party) as well was formed by a merger in 1948. It united the progressive left-wing liberal tradition of the *Deutsche Demokratische Partei* (German Democratic Party), based primarily in southern Germany, with more traditional liberal-conservative groupings, for the most part from northern Germany, e.g. the right-wing liberal *Deutsche Volkspartei* (German People's Party). These early mergers were the initial steps in concentrating the German parties to a few groups. The KPD (German Communist Party) was originally represented in the Bundestag but lost many votes to the SPD (Social Democratic Party) because of the Cold War and widespread anti-Communism. This strengthened the SPD's claim to being the sole representative of the workers and employees at the federal level.

Fig. 22 shows a continuous increase in votes for the SPD from 1957 to 1972. This reflects the process by which the Social Democrats came to accept the free enterprise system and West Germany's integration into the West. This process came to a head in the Bad Godesberg Programme (1959) after the clear-cut victories of the CDU/CSU in 1953 and 1957. The SPD, too, became a catch-all party with voters from the bourgeois classes. This decrease in ideological imbalance between the CDU/CSU and the Social Democrats evidenced itself in the coalitions which the SPD was part of: first the Great Coalition with the CDU/CSU (1966-69) and then the coalition with the FDP (1969-82). The CDU/ CSU, on the other hand, was able to counterbalance this majority at the federal level with a growing majority in the *Länder* and in the *Bundesrat*. This development often led to compromises involving all the parties. This "stagnation" in the face of the economic crisis, a growing national debt and other factors resulted in the SPD losing votes and in a new surge for the CDU/CSU.

The SPD membership reached a peak in 1976 (1,022,000), after which numbers of members resigned, some to join citizens' action groups and eventually the Greens. It nevertheless continued to be the party with traditionally the largest number of members. *Table 3* shows that the German parties generally have more members (as well as a somewhat greater proportion of women) than do the French parties. It also illustrates the drop in party membership – except for the CSU and the Greens.

Table 3: Membership figures of German political parties (with women's shares in %)

	1984	1987	1991
SPD	920000 (25% w.)	910063 (25,9% w.)	920618 (27,3% w.)
CDU	736000 (22% w.)	718590 (22,2% w.)	655200 (22,9% w.)
CSU	185000 (14% w.)	184565 (14,0% w.)	186197 (15,3% w.)
FDP	73000 (25% w.)	64756 (24,0% w.)	178625
Greens	32000 (30% w.)	43543	42142

(Source: Statistisches Bundesamt 1985, 12.2.2; Haefs 1988, p. 175f.; Fischer World Almanac 1992, p. 310f., containing only details on FDP *with* new federal states, ibid.: PDS approx. 250,000, Bündnis 90 [Alliance 90]/Greens (ex GDR) approx. 110,000)

One *particularly striking item* in this short outline of developments in the West German party system is the fact that the SPD did not come into power until after its "shift towards the *centre*". When one looks at the Fifth Republic, however, the success of the French Socialists increased from 1972 on because of the alliance of the *Left* and campaign strategy with the PCF. This finally resulted in them taking power in 1981 – without an alliance of this kind. This difference from Germany mirrors the greater degree of *social conflict* in France, a country which had only been fully industrialized since de Gaulle and Pompidou, and also reflects the polarized political culture in this tense situation, a polarization further nourished by the *system of majority vote* (Jäger 1980, p. 588).

After having changed its course in 1982, the PS is now pursuing a highly debated and often enough rejected "Bad Godesberg"-type course: it is going through the same process that the German SPD completed back in 1959 despite a great amount of internal resistance. In 1991 the PS officially announced the change-over (cf. 2.6). The current basic structure of the French party system can thus be represented by the following simplified diagram:

PCF – parties of the "Centre" – FN
PS | UDF – RPR

(cf. *Fig. 19*, sections 2.5 and 2.8.3). The highly insecure role of the *centristes* (cf. 2.5.2) and the *écologistes* (cf. 2.8.2) as potential coalition partners or at least as "majority procurers" must be pointed out again in this context.

The structure in Germany is somewhat more reduced. Although up to now the FDP has served as a "third force" and as a corrective factor against the political monopoly of a single party, the de facto two-party system has been tending toward an unstable two-block system ever since the Greens came on the scene and since their renewed coalition with the SPD in Hesse. In this two-block system, however, there is still a definite gap between the Greens and the established parties:

Parties of the "Centre"
Greens – SPD | FDP – CDU/CSU

Because of the presence of the *Front national*, the *relative* position of the RPR in the French political system is more clearly that of "moderate right" than is, for example, the position of the CSU in the eyes of the German Greens, Social Democrats or Free Democrats.

A new development within the Green Party is becoming apparent. At their national party convention in Duisburg on 3-5 March 1989 they declared that they are willing to enter into coalitions (with the SPD). There were three important internal factions in the Greens: the fundamentalists, the *Realpolitiker* (advocates of *Realpolitik*, i.e. pragmatic politics) and the *Grüner Aufbruch* (more or less equivalent to "Green Renewal"), unaligned Greens with the goal of overcoming block differences. The latter two of these groups joined forces, bringing to an end many years of domination by fundamentalist attitudes opposed to coalition and to collaboration in forming a Government. After the defeat suffered by the West German Green party at the 1990 Federal election, the fundamentalists left the party in 1991. The Greens continue to be outsiders but are currently on the way to becoming a left-oriented environmental bourgeois party: *the distance from the centre is decreasing*. Clear indications of this shift are the coalitions formed in various federal states with the SPD or even with the SPD and the FDP. These changes in the system (and, in general, the significant role played by the governments of the federal states in contrast to France) are reflected in *Bundesrat* majorities quite different from the previous composition (cf. for instance, Das Parlament 20 Sept. 1991, p. 15). - The gradual move of the Green party to the centre, which was, and still is, accompanied by numerous crises, was illustrated by Raschke in 1991.

It should be stressed that the very terms *centre* and *Mitte* evoke the connotation 'moderation'. This connotation is a favourite and frequent tool of the UDF, RPR, FDP and CDU/CSU, especially during election campaigns. It is important to differentiate between the term describing political position and the emotional catchword, especially since the same word is used for both meanings. People and groups (i.e. also politicians and parties) make mistakes - out of ignorance, egotism, desire for prestige, cemented rivalry, financial dependence, excessive tractability or for whatever reasons. It is quite possible for the methods or actions of a party of the Centre to lack any manner of "moderation" whatsoever and thus to be far removed from the moderate *aurea mediocritas*, the golden mean guided by reason and serving the public welfare. (It is not necessary to include a list of examples for such conduct.)

The reason behind the growing competition for the "centre" and its great number of fluctuating voters is the considerable expansion of the wage-earning middle classes consisting of employees and civil servants. Their number grew from 20.6% of the population in West Germany in 1950 to 45.6% in 1980 and even to 50.7% in 1988 (Schultze 1983, p. 9; Fischer World Almanac 1992, p. 326). France has experienced a similar, albeit somewhat smaller growth (cf. 4.5.2).

This fact also provides a reason for why the FDP has been able to maintain its position on the political stage. Its strong point used to be the traditional middle class (independent businessmen and self-employed professionals). While other parties of the traditional middle class – the DP (*Deutsche Partei*) for example – lost more and more votes and members, the FDP managed to shift its emphasis to employees and civil servants in time. The coalition with the SPD in 1969, aside from causing a stir, was also another important factor in attracting new voters (cf. Schultze 1983, p. 10). The *Parti républicain* in France was able to redefine its emphasis in the same way, something which the *Républicains indépendants* and above all the bourgeois and farmer party CNI of the 1950's did not succeed in doing (cf. Kempf 1983, p. 141ff., p. 188f. and Kempf 1983a, p. 37). Aside from unskilled and skilled workers, there is an *overproportionately large number of middle-echelon employees and civil servants* who vote for the SPD, whereas the CDU/CSU receives its votes primarily from independent businessmen, self-employed professionals, farmers and *upper-echelon employees and civil servants*, although it too has a substantial number of *middle-echelon* employees and civil servants (cf. Schultze 1983, p. 10 and also Schultze 1987 and Feist/Krieger 1987, which contain evaluations of sociological research conducted on the results of the 1987 *Bundestag* elections; according to these studies, the "ecological cleavage" and job security are becoming more and more important). These social changes have also had a very strong impact on the first all-German Federal elections in 1990, cf. Gibowski / Kaase 1991, pp. 15-19.

Thus it is possible in both countries to associate the tendency of the parties to gather in a wide Centre with the growth of the wage-earning middle classes. In addition, it was demonstrated in an earlier section (2.7) that the loss of importance suffered by the French Communists is also directly connected with social changes: the decline in the number of the industrial labourers. It is not yet possible to tell whether social changes in the *professions libérales* and the *cadres supérieurs* will also have their effects on the party system, and if they do, what these effects will be like. In any event, initial analyses by Capdevielle et. al. 1981, Grossmann 1983 and Chapsal 1984, p. 750 indicate that these processes are important and that an extremely large proportion of the votes that brought the PS to power in 1981 came from this group of voters.

2.9.2. Political affinities in the European Parliament

When comparing French and German parties on the basis of their strength and their political affinities in the European Parliament, one can note the following characteristic features (cf. Tables 4 and 5).

Tables 4 and 5: The number of representatives from the French and German parties in the various political groupings in the European Parliament.

Table 4: 2nd legislative period 1984-1989 (16 Nov 1984)

Comm.	Soc.	Rainb.	–	Lib.	EPP-CD	EDA	ER	Indep.
PCF (10)	PS (20)	–	–	PR (7) UDF (5)	UDF (7) CDS (2)	RPR (18) CNI (2)	FN (10)	–
–	SPD (33)	Greens (7)	–	–	CDU (34) CSU (7)	–	–	–

(Source: Das neue Europäische Parlament, Bonn 1984, p. 6)

Table 5: 3rd legislative period 1989-1994 (10 June 1991)

Comm.	Soc.	Rainb.	Greens	Lib.	EPP-CD	EDA	ER	Indep.
PCF (7)	PS (17) o. P. (5)	Verts- UPC (1)	Verts (8)	UDF (3) PR (4) Rad (3) o. P. (3)	CDS (5)	RPR (12) CNI (1)	FN (10)	non-a. (2)
–	SPD (31)	Greens (1)	Greens (7)	FDP (4)	CDU (25) CSU (7)	–	non-a. (3)	non-a. (2) Rep (1)

(Source: EP membership list dated 10 June 1991, Luxembourg: Office des publications officielles des Communautés europèenes 1991, pp. 3-75, and memorandum No. 155.962 Parlement Européen, March 1992)

Key to abbreviations: Rainb. = Rainbow Group, comprised various ecological, minority-oriented and pacifist parties, with the German Greens as strongest grouping; the group split in 1989: the minority-oriented parties remained in the Rainb., while the Greens (meanwhile recruited from 6 countries) formed their own parliamentarian grouping. UPC = Unione di u populu corsu, Corsican Autonomist Party. Lib. – Liberal and Democratic Group. EPP = European People's Party (CD = Christian Democrats). EDA = European Democratic Alliance; CNI = cf. 2.5.1; these include the Irish Fianna Fail Party, the Scottish National Party and a Spanish group. ER = Technical Group of the European Right; Rep. = Republicans; non-a. = non-affiliated.

1. The Communist Party is represented only in France, albeit in continuous decline. On the extreme right wing, the *Front National* maintained its numbers, strengthened by 6 Republicans from Germany. The Republicans' chairman Schönhuber soon fell out with the *Front National* within the European Right Group, believing them to be too "radical". This led to members leaving the party (except Schönhuber) and to fragmentation, as shown in *Table 5*. In any case, France is the only country represented in both extreme wings of the party spectrum. More specific, the crystallization around the French FN is counterbalanced by a fragmentation on the German extreme right wing, which can be followed back to the early days of the Federal Republic and even back to the Weimar Republic. It is now reflected even on the level of the European Parliament.
2. Similarly, it is only in France that the "Centre" exhibits such great variety. Whereas the whole of the RPR (and the CNI) belong to a single political grouping, the party federation UDF is divided. Part of it belongs to the Christian Democrats: only the CDS, the "worn-out" successor of the MRP, shares the same views on European politics as the powerful German CDU/CSU; the strength of the French Christian Democrats was equal to that of their German equivalents only in the first years following World War II. This grouping is further supplemented by various French *divers droite* (2.8.4). On the other hand, the traditional position of another segment of the UDF (including other *divers droite* and the PR) is at the side of the Liberals, with whom the representatives of the German FDP collaborated in the first European Parliament from 1979 (failing in the second election in 1984) and again from 1989. The fact that a total of 4 representatives (3 UDF, 1 non-a.) changed sides to the Christian Democrat EPP in December 1991 clearly shows the fluctuations within the French Liberals. This move was triggered by Giscard d'Estaing's intention to become president of the Parliament. He believed that the Liberal group was too weak to achieve his objective, and he succeeded in persuading three more representatives – among them the press baron Hersant (cf. 6.1.5) – to change sides. But, unexpectedly and disappointingly for Giscard, the German Christian Democrat E. Klepsch was elected into office. The tendency toward concentration among the large groups also showed in one RPR member and one non-affiliated member changing sides to the Christian Democrats, who now count 11 French representatives.

But, in 1984, UDF and RPR entered the elections on a *joint ticket.* The post-electoral separation into Liberals, Christian Democrats and Gaullists was predictable. All in all, the French Centre-Right spectrum in the European Parliament reflects, in its diversity and instability, the character of the French parties in the homeland, while the German parties CDU/CSU and FDP represent well-established forces.

3. Only the German Greens were represented in 1984. The success of the French Greens in 1989 is not only due to the more "spontaneous" electoral behaviour frequently found in European elections ("protest votes"), but it also shows (with a typical phase shift in relation to Germany) the substantial growth of environmental awareness in France. In the wake of May 1968, ecological citizens' initiatives were formed in both countries, at times with a greater resonance in France. But owing to the power of French administration (construction of nuclear power stations, etc.) and the ensuing political bipolarization, protest movements subsided in France. The successes of German citizens' initiatives against administration in courts of justice, their entry into the *Bundestag* in 1983, followed by a more vigorous response to ecological demands on the part the established parties, contributed to the growth of the Green party. When the full impact of the Chernobyl accident (1986), played down by the French government and the media, finally became known in France, and after the air and waste disposal problems in the conurbations, the greenhouse effect and the hole in the ozone layer reached public awareness, the immediate effect was in favour of the *Verts.* Incidentally, this phase shift in relation to the German Greens also applies to the other industrialized countries of continental Europe (Italy, Benelux), as shown particularly impressive during the last European elections in their capacity as a "mood indicator".
4. The most striking point is that the RPR does not belong to the EPP even though it must be classified as conservative or "moderately open to innovation". Despite concessions it made after 1978, it is impossible for the "neo-Gaullist" party to endorse the programme of the EPP: some of its demands are that the powers of the European Parliament should be expanded, that the E.C. should be made into a "United States of Europe" and that there should be a "European Government that is willing and able to assume real governmental control" (EVP 1983, p. 32). In this way, the RPR maintains its individual character – despite all the concessions it has made in its economic and defence policy to the goals propagated by the liberal-conservative parties of Western Europe.

3. France – a modern industrial nation?

(Heinz-Helmut Lüger)

France's economic development is often portrayed negatively from the West German point of view. This was especially true during the leftist government between 1981 and 1986. France – although the fourth largest trading power among the industrial nations – is still often referred to as "Europe's sick man", afflicted by economic backwardness and deficient international competitiveness (cf. the Mitterrand cartoon below).

Fig. 23: The Man in the Yellow Racing Jersey
(Die Zeit, 17 June 1983)

Criticizing such a generalized and superficial viewpoint does not at all mean belittling the difficulties of the French economy – especially its current economic policy. However, for a more accurate understanding of the situation it is first necessary to examine the unique conditions of France's development without using the West German situation as the only yardstick.

3.1 *Foreign trade deficit, inflation, unemployment*

For a long time now, France's central economic policy has been aimed at reducing the country's foreign trade deficit and fighting against inflation and unemployment. Finding solutions to these problems has not only been considered – and is still considered – a decisive criterion for economic success, it also shows the restricted political room for action. In the early 80's, for example, INSEE, the Institute of Statistics, made the following prognosis: «Entre le risque d'une reprise de l'inflation, celui d'une persistance d'un déficit extérieur élevé et celui d'une récession, la voie que peut suivre l'économie française est, à court terme, très étroite.»

In 1982, the *trade deficit* of more than 100 billion Francs was at an absolute high and unleashed a number of radical government regulations (cf. 3.8). However, the reasons for these notorious foreign trade problems are so complex that they could not simply be explained by high energy import costs or specific misjudgments in economic policy. The French economy has also suffered severe setbacks on account of its comparatively lower export activity, its weak industrial competitive margin in certain branches and the unbalanced trade exchange with the Federal Republic of Germany. These factors will be discussed later.

The *rate of inflation*, although it has ceased to be a central issue for several years now, nevertheless determined the course of discussions on economical policy for several decades. Even during the recovery period following World War II, inflation was already considered an unsolved problem of the French economy, and it remained clearly higher than in most other European industrial nations throughout the 70's and 80's. In 1981 the inflation rate even rose to 14%. Nevertheless, a wage and price freeze gradually helped to lower it and it sunk to below 3% in 1988. In 1991, the rate of price increases was for the first time actually below that in Germany. The immediate consequences of this inflationary tendency have included increased export prices – affecting, in turn, the trade balance – and a virtually permanent monetary weakness.

At the start of the world economic crisis in 1973/74, structural (and not only cyclical) unemployment increasingly turned into a central issue for all European countries. This also applied to France which reported 2.1 million unemployed in 1991 (FRG: 2.3 million in the last several years). In spite of massive efforts, it was not possible to bring about a decrease in these figures.

This brief overview shows that altogether the crisis bore consequences for France which were unlike those for Germany.
Dissimilar circumstances at the outset of this period and a different level of adjustment to the so-called "international division of labour" certainly play an important role. Though on the other hand, continuous mass unemployment, for example, shows that certain problems are not to be seen as being specifically related to one individual country but to the European industrial society on the whole.

In order to gain deeper insight into this context, i.e. in order to reveal the symptomatic nature of the phenomena mentioned above, we must elaborate on the *economic structures* of both countries (sectors, regional distribution, degree of concentration). Reference to data on *economic history* will then provide us with a further means of evaluation since many aspects can only be understood as the result of long developmental processes. This background information will then allow for a discussion on several current economic difficulties and attempted political solutions.

3.2 *Industrial lag in comparison to Germany*

A heavy import dependency and the inadequate competitiveness of important industrial branches in France are the basic causes of the country's economic problems. Such an assertion can be exemplified by selected areas:

T. 12:
France relies heavily on imports. In certain instances, this dependency is even somewhat absurd. Shoe and leather goods account for 38% of the country's imports, even though France has enjoyed a long tradition in this branch and has ample production capacity. Although the 15% share of furniture imports is a more modest percentage, it is unexplainable why the French export timber only to re-import it as furniture.

The textile sector is an especially extreme case. In 1970, the import of apparel still accounted for 6.3% of the French market. Ten years later, this figure climbed to 22.7%. This shift is indicative of the decline of an entire industrial branch characterized by massive layoffs and the economic devastation of entire regions. It is no wonder that the government refuses to stand and watch such a "sellout of national interests."

The problem in the mechanical engineering sector, in which the import share amounts to 58.4% (1970: 37.9%), is especially serious as this branch is of strategic importance. An industrial nation with the ambitions of France cannot afford to be dependent on other countries in this key technological sector if it does not want to miss out on becoming integrated in the stream of industrial development. (H.H. Bremer/K.P. Schmid, Die Zeit, 26 March 1982)

These examples draw our attention to three aspects. 1) Despite the availability of raw materials for certain consumer goods, France imports goods (e.g. lumber – furniture) which are produced abroad and whose resulting net value increases outside the country as well. In the textiles branch, consumer goods production is increasingly being relocated to countries with low wages. 2) The large share of machinery imports (machinery being an important capital-goods sector) results in a technological dependency on foreign countries. Finally, 3) these deficiencies are by no means offset by commensurate assets of other branches.

However striking these examples may seem, how little do they actually tell us about their relevance within the economic structure. Does, for instance, the small share of the textile industry bear the same significance as the low level of the lumbering industry? What function does the share of the capital-goods sector serve in general? In order to answer these types of questions, we must first look at the *sectoral economic structure* and distinguish between the three main sectors:

- agriculture and forestry, fishing (primary sector),
- industry at large (secondary sector),
- services (tertiary sector).

The general sector profile (*Table 6*) indicates several characteristic differences in levels of employment and shares of the gross domestic product.

The percentage of those employed in the French agrarian sector – 7.5% – is in itself low, but compared with Germany (as well as with other foreign countries) this figure is relatively high. The services branch is by far the largest sector. In Germany, by contrast, this sector is distinctly smaller. In terms of the secondary sector, we are dealing with a reverse situation. In 1970, the German manufacturing industry accounted for about 54% of the market (Ambrosius 1983, p. 244ff.; Baumier 1983, p. 111). Since then there has been a continual decline – although on different levels – in both countries. Several figures, for example, the comparatively high share of agricultural and low share of industrial activity in France, are definitely related to the level of economic development (Braudel/Labrousse 1982; Voss 1984). A comparison of the sectors, which then only includes relative values, would certainly be too general for drawing any accurate

Table 6: Sector Profile

	Employment profile F	Employment profile FRG	Share of gross domestic product F	Share of gross domestic product FRG
	%	%	%	%
Agriculture	7.5	5.1	3.4	1.5 (1.7)
Industry	30.1	40.5	30.7	41.1 (34.1)
Services	62.4	54.4	65.9	57.4 (64.2)

(In brackets: the new federal states)

(From: Mermet 1990, p. 265; Min. de l'Industrie 1991, p. 17ff.; BMWI 1990; Hübner/Rohlfs 1991, p. 155ff.)

conclusions. Furthermore, we would still have to consider the follo-wing:

- the way in which the individual sectors have developed in the last decades and how they have changed in importance (for a comparison of the various *developmental stages*, see 3.7) and
- the distribution of individual branches within each particular sector (*branch structure* analysis).

Table 7 provides some basic information on specific branches of French industry and their significance. Production sectors have in general been divided into the following categories: industry in the strict sense includes a) the *industries intermédiares*/semi-finished goods industry (eg, chemicals, iron and steel, paper, glass). b) the *industries d'équipement*/capital goods industry (eg, mechanical engineering, ship and aircraft building, the electrical and the automobile industry; as can be seen from *Table 7*, some capital goods sectors have been listed separately in recent statistics), c) the *industries de biens de consommation*/consumer goods industry (eg, textiles, clothing, leather, lumber and paper processing, pharmaceutical products sectors). Beyond this there are d) the *industries agricoles et alimentaires*/ farming and foods industries, e) the *énergie* (eg, mining, electricity, petroleum, gas) and f) *the bâtiment*/construction sectors. It is only possible to a limited extent to make any direct comparison of these figures with German statistics since the categories used and distinctions drawn do not match and often have a different basis. The comparison attempted below is therefore to be regarded with some reservation.

In France, capital goods hold a leading position in the industrial sector (accounting for approx. 24% of national product). The emphasis is in particular on the electrical industry, motor vehicle construction and mechanical engineering, i.e. for the most part growth industries, and strongly indicative of France's relatively "modern" industrial structure. Due to the chemical industry, the *biens intermédiares* sector has also risen slightly. In contrast, the share of the foods and consumer goods industries has dropped slightly - as it has also done in Germany (cf. *Table 8*). Nevertheless, there are several essential differences between France and Germany:

- The industrial sector on the whole carries comparatively little weight, especially in the capital-goods sector; rates of growth in particular are significantly lower (cf. *Table 7*). In several branches there is not even enough capacity to cover domestic demand.
- The structural handicap is worsened by the fact that France is in a rather weak position as compared with its competitors in those consumer and capital-goods sectors which are ripe for development and for which a heavy demand in the future has been predicted (e.g. tools, mechanical engineering, electrical and electronics branches). Indeed, one might say that the "French industry is not adapting to the developmental prospects of universal demand" (Lebas 1981, p. 91). This assertion does not dismiss the fact that France has clearly reached a top position in several fields of technology. One need only consider its atomic technology, locomotive and tramcar industry (TGV, Métro), defense and space industries or areas of its chemical industry.
- By contrast, declining (and thus *depressed*) branches such as textile/apparel, leather, and steel (cf. Capul/Meurs 1988, p. 174ff.) still enjoy a relatively important position. In Germany, the percentage of people employed in these areas is already considerably lower. These sectors of the French economy will probably have to rely on further "adaptive measures," i.e. company shut-downs and massive layoffs, even with the large number of governmental subsidies attempting to delay this development.

In times of economic growth the above mentioned structural deficits have virtually no significant consequences. However, the more expensive energy imports (due to the oil crises of 1973 and 1979), the heightened international competition and the development of new rationalization techniques have aggravated to an even greater extent the weaknesses of the French industry, its disadvantageous specialization and the related dependency in key technological sectors.

Table 7: Industrial Branches in France

	Share of Total Employment Figures for Industry (in %)				Share of National Product (in %)			
	1959	1972	1980	1989	1959	1972	1980	1989
Industries agricoles et alimentaires	8,5	8,0	7,8	9,2	11,2	10,2	9,3	9,5
Energie	5,7	4,2	3,6	3,9	11,2	15,6	11,6	12,7
Bâtiment	21,9	24,8	24,9	25,2	22,6	17,1	20,5	18,2
Industrie au sens strict:	(63,9)	(63,0)	(63,7)	(61,7)	(55,0)	(57,1)	(58,6)	(59,6)
– Biens intermédiaires	20,4	11,6	20,3	19,4	21,2	14,3	20,6	21,0
– Biens d'équipement professionnel			16,2	16,7			16,9	17,0
– Biens d'équipement ménager	18,8	28,7	1,1	1,0	17,7	27,7	0,8	0,6
– Matériels de transport terrestre			6,8	5,9			5,8	6,2
– Biens de consommation courante	24,7	22,7	19,3	18,7	16,1	15,1	15,5	14,8
	100	100	100	100	100	100	100	100

(Calculated on the basis of: Min de l'Industrie 1982ff.; INSEE 1980ff.; Ferrandon/Waquet 1979)

Table 8: Industrial Branches in Germany

	Share of Total Employment Figures for Industry (in %)					Share of National Product (in %)				
	1950	1960	1970	1980	1989	1950	1960	1970	1980	1989
Mining	12,1	7,9	3,4	3,0	2,8	5,6	4,5	2,7	2,4	1,7
Primary industry	22,9	21,9	21,0	20,2	19,0	28,0	31,1	30,5	31,8	27,3
Capital goods industry	29,9	38,8	45,5	49,6	53,9	22,8	32,6	38,1	39,4	46,0
Consumer goods industry	27,8	24,9	23,7	20,8	18,2	25,2	18,3	16,2	14,5	13,9
Foods and luxuries industry	7,3	6,5	6,4	6,4	6,1	18,4	13,5	12,5	11,9	11,1
	100	100	100	100	100	100	100	100	100	100

(Compiled from: Ambrosius 1983, 261; BMWI 1990, 38f.; Inst. der deutschen Wirtschaft 1990, 61ff.)

3.3 *Regional imbalance: «Paris et le désert français?»*

If we examine the sector and branch structure of France, we find a highly developed industrial production apparatus still in need of modernization. *Regional structure* also helps to describe economic development and output since the balance between the various markets depends on how uniformly the various regions develop, the extent to which the standard of living within the population diverges and how possible crises are handled.

3.3.1 Distribution of urban centres

The industrial map of France shows the following urban centres (*Fig. 24*):

- The *Région Parisienne*, which produces about 28% of the gross domestic product and in which approximately one fifth of the French population lives, is the most important centre. The electrical, automobile, airplane and chemical industries in particular are concentrated in this region. The service sector is highly centralized (administration, research, universities) and most of the largest corporations, banks and insurance companies have their headquarters here.
- The other urban areas contribute considerably less to the country's economic output: the *Région Nord* in the north, 6% (coal, iron and steel, textiles, motor vehicles), *Alsace* and *Lorraine* in the east, 6.5% (coal, iron and steel, textiles, mechanical engineering), *Rhône-Alpes* in the south, 9% (metalworking, chemicals, energy, textiles, food) and *Provence-Côte d'Azur* 7% (chemicals, energy, shipbuilding, steel), whereby the similar gross domestic product figures result from branches with different levels of output. In terms of their location, the main centres are virtually restricted to the section of France north of *a line between Le Havre and Marseille.* The entire western and southwestern areas – disregarding several sub-centres such as Nantes, Bordeaux or Toulouse – have for the most part retained their agrarian structure and have very little industry.

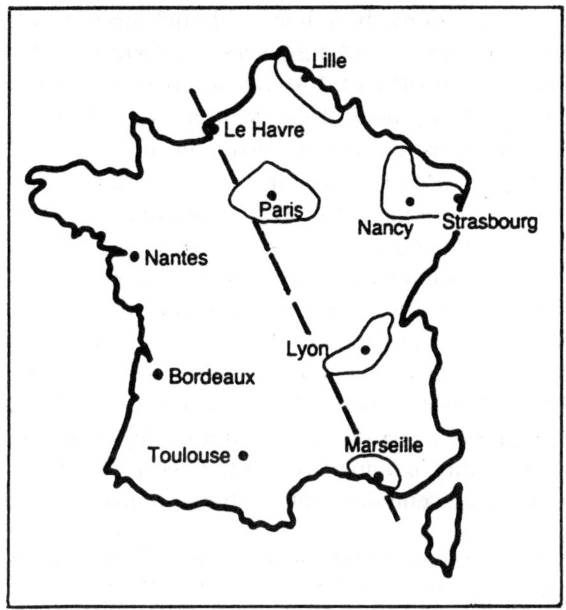

Fig. 24: Distribution of industrial centres

By contrast, there is no single dominant commercial centre in Germany comparable to that of the Région Parisienne. One of the characteristics of Germany is the existence of many urban areas of equal standing and thus a more decentralized distribution of economic activity. For this reason – apart from the transitional problems of the new federal states – non- industrial areas are of less consequence from the start.

The absolute economic pre-eminence of the region around Paris has considerable consequences for the French economy. This economic and administrative concentration not only brings about numerous transportation, housing and environmental problems, but is also responsible for widely *blocking the development of other regions*: "The...maelstrom which reaches out to the surrounding countryside and all of France, the continuous flux of people and business establishments are the main obstacles for a harmonious regional distribution of the industrial potential, thus working counter to the uniform development of all regions. This is one of the major drawbacks generally common to centrally organized political systems. Only a vigorous and extensive regionalisation could remedy this situation" (Kuntze 1978, p. 41). In the last few decades there have been numerous attempts precisely along these lines, although up to now only a few have been successful. The *Aménagement du Territoire*, a federal regional plan launched in 1963 (cf. 1.3), intended, for example, to promote the economic development of the western and southern regions by creating specific jobs in industry. However, the imbalance between Paris and the province remained virtually unaltered. Neither a real decentralization of the region around Paris nor the creation of an industrial counterbalance in the west/southwest regions of France was effected. The reforms implemented by the leftist government since 1982 were in particular directed towards shifting jurisdiction to the regional level. At least the initial effects of this shift can be noted: The various regions now enjoy greater policy autonomy, have independent financial resources at their disposal and – most importantly – are able to develop programs to modernise economic structure (cf. Neumann 1989; critical to this: Becquart-Leclercq 1989, p. 193ff.). Despite this progress, however, centralism still continues to make its presence felt.

Moreover, the transportation network (airways, railways, highways) exclusively serving Paris has a stabilizing effect on centralisation, all the more considering that new routes seem to be primarily geared towards *connecting the province to the centre.* The following statement was made on the occasion of the T.G.V. Atlantique (= train à grande vitesse): "Enfin, en rapprochant l'Aquitaine et la Bretagne du centre de la France, c'est une grande opération d'aménagement du territoire qui est lancée et qui concerne neuf millions d'habitants" (Le Monde, 17 September 1983). In view of such measures it is indeed possible to claim that the notion of centralism has taken on a life of its own and continues to carry more weight than real economic necessities: "Since the communication network, like the spokes of a wheel with Paris at the hub, is being reinforced even today – i.e., with the high-velocity train (TGV) network at the end of the 20th Century virtually identical to the postal network of the 18th Century – we must ask ourselves if this centralised structure can really be explained by the dictates of necessity alone. Are we not viewing an attitude which regards centralism as a necessity?" (Ammon 1989, p. 139; cf. *Fig. 25*)

The disparities discussed above can become drastically worse in the event structural problems affecting regions and branches merge, i.e. in the case of industrial monostructure. In such an instance, the crisis of one branch can easily lead to an overall regional crisis if there are no other industrial branches to absorb laid-off workers. A migrational tendency ("*exode industriel*") within the population is yet another consequence (cf. Todd 1988, p. 189ff.). Depressed industries of this kind include, above all, the textile and iron/steel sectors concentrated in northern France.

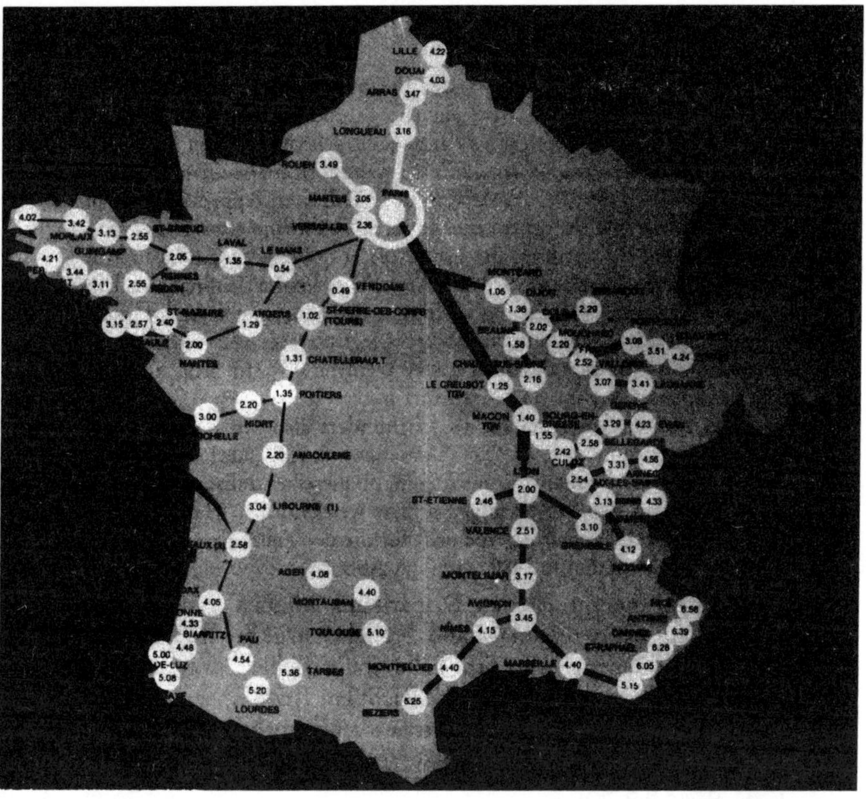

Fig. 25: French TGV Network
(From: Les Echos 57/1990)

T. 13:
SIDÉRURGIE
De désastre en désastre

A Denain, les cheminées des hauts fourneaux ne fument plus. Seul le panneau «sidérurgie» planté sur le bord de l'autoroute signale encore aux voyageurs qui traversent la plaine froide du Nord la vocation de Denain. Usinor, qui faisait vivre hier 10000 ouvriers, a fermé depuis 1976 ses immenses ateliers, et aujourd'hui la dernière aciérie est condamnée. Le gouvernement a décidé de l'arrêter le 1er janvier 1984.

Le 26 novembre, M. Pierre Mauroy est venu annoncer les premières mesures de son plan de sauvetage industriel pour la région. Un plan mal accueilli par les quelques centaines de sidérurgistes massés devant l'hôtel de ville, qui n'en ont retenu qu'une chose: le gros des investissements sidérurgiques ira ailleurs, à Dunkerque et en Lorraine. Eux auront droit à des emplois de remplacement: un centre de recherche et une unité de

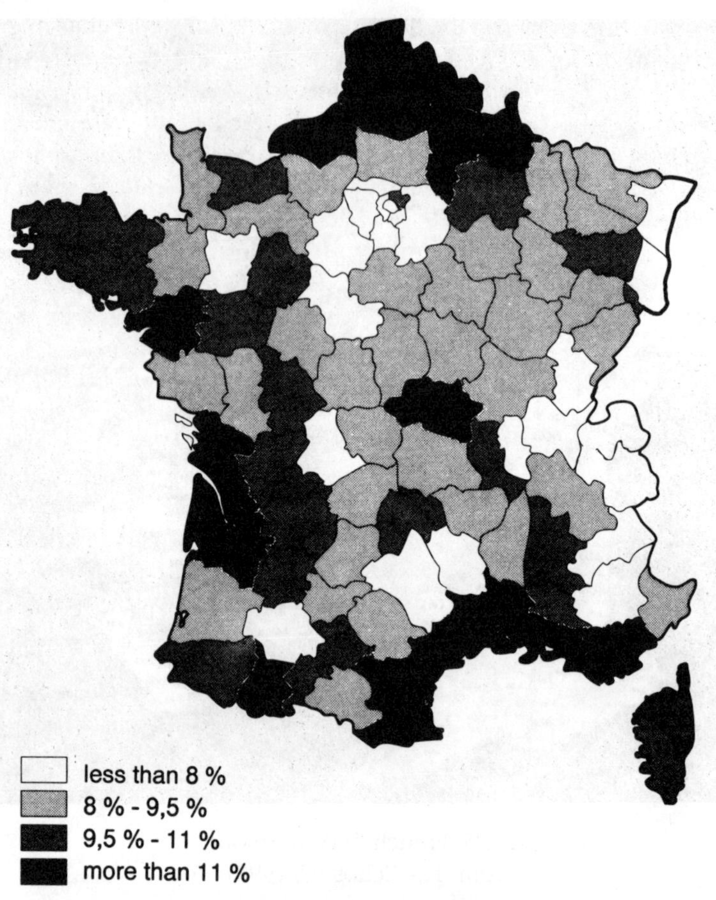

Fig. 26: Unemployment Rates
(From: CF 246/1990)

robotique de Renault, des heures de sous-traitance de Thomson, un laboratoire de matériels de la SNCF, etc....

Après sept ans de chute spectaculaire de la production et des effectifs, la sidérurgie européenne n'a jamais été plus mal en point. En octobre, la production est tombée au plus bas niveau depuis 1973: 8,4 millions de tonnes, 24 % de moins qu'il y a un an. Au total, selon la commission, l'Europe des Neuf ne peut plus espérer produire et vendre, à l'horizon 1985, que 120 millions de tonnes d'acier. Pour une utilisation correcte des usines, une capacité de production européenne de 142 millions de tonnes suffirait largement: 35 % de moins qu'aujourd'hui ... (C. Bunodière, Le Nouvel Economiste, 6 Dec. 1982)

The situation in Denain in the Région Nord is typical of the adjustment crisis within the entire metalworking industry. Wherever there is a lack of a diversified production structure there are far-reaching repercussions. Similar problems exist in Lorraine where the mining, steel and textile industries have been forced to drastically reduce their capacity. The same applies to the coastal areas which support a large share of the shipping industry. Long-term effective solutions are found above all in the establishment of new growth industries. Certain regions which are under-industrialized or depend on depressed branches are susceptible to crisis situations. Such crises are then reflected by high rates of unemployment (as shown by the overview in *Fig. 26*).

Recently there seems to have been a balancing out of regional differences in Southern and Southwestern regions of France. In the 50's, industrial activity was more or less concentrated in the area north of the Le Havre – Marseille line. The 60's, however, saw a series of fairly large industrial settlements in the West, particularly in the Basse-Normandie, Pays de la Loire and Poitou-Charentes regions. A further shift resulted from the industrial crisis which began in 1973/4 and led to a relative decline of this sector. Hardest hit were the old peak regions (the North, Lorraine). As already discussed above, it was particularly the traditional branches, the textile and steel industries and mining, that suffered setbacks. In contrast, the West and Southwest were able to assert themselves with relative success. This success is in part accounted for by the high-tech branches settled in these regions (motor vehicles, electronics, metalworking) being less susceptible to the crisis and by the high percentage of small and medium-sized companies, which were more flexible in their response to altered conditions (Uhrich 1987, p. 13ff.; Ammon 1989, p. 187ff.). Moreover, there was distinct growth in the tertiary sector, particularly in several regions in the Southwest – a development which still continues today. A comparison of the Gross Domestic Product per Inhabitant for the various regions (*Fig. 27*) make these changes apparent. While the map confirms the imbalances we have been discussing – the majority of "wealthier" regions are still found north of the Le Havre-Marseille line –, there is no longer a wide separation in all areas. This impression becomes more distinct upon bringing figures from the 70's into the picture: it is then apparent that, apart from the absolute exception, the Paris metropolitan area, figures for most Northern regions are on the decline while those for Southern regions are predominantly on the rise (Uhrich 1987, p. 57); i.e. regional structural weaknesses and the resulting imbalances are tending to decrease.

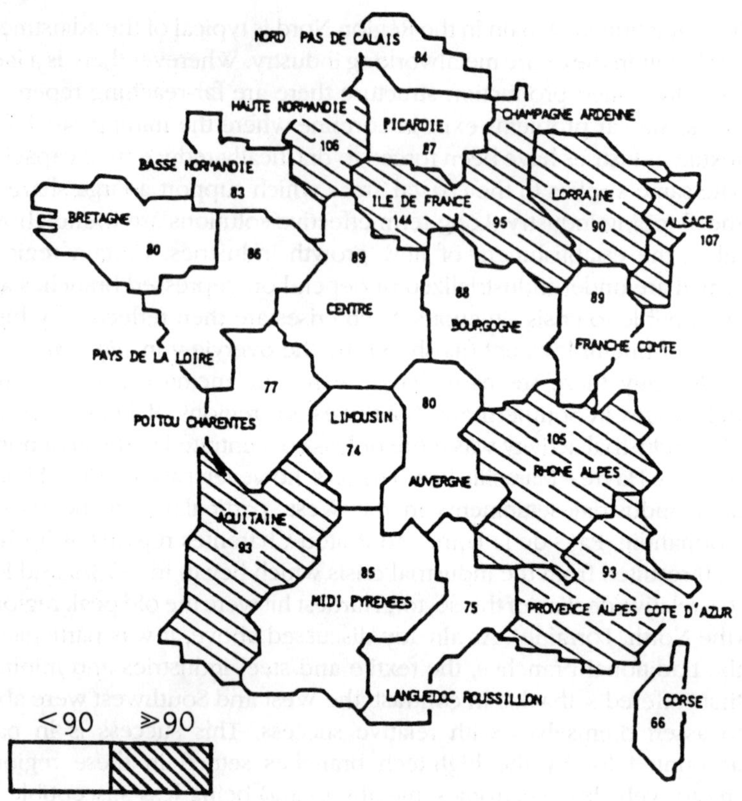

Fig. 27: Gross Domestic Product per Inhabitant by Region
(Average index for all France = 100)
(From: Uhrich 1987, p. 56)

3.3.2 Regional Structural Weaknesses in the Federal Republic of Germany

The economic gap between individual regions within the old federal states in Germany is by no means as large as in France. However, there are still several regional structural problems in Germany:

- A number of predominantly agricultural regions with little industry (Emsland, East Friesland, East Bavaria) continue to suffer from a lack of long-term desirable employment opportunities.
- Massive restructuring efforts have been launched in the Ruhr area and Saarland as a result of the decline in the mining, iron and steel

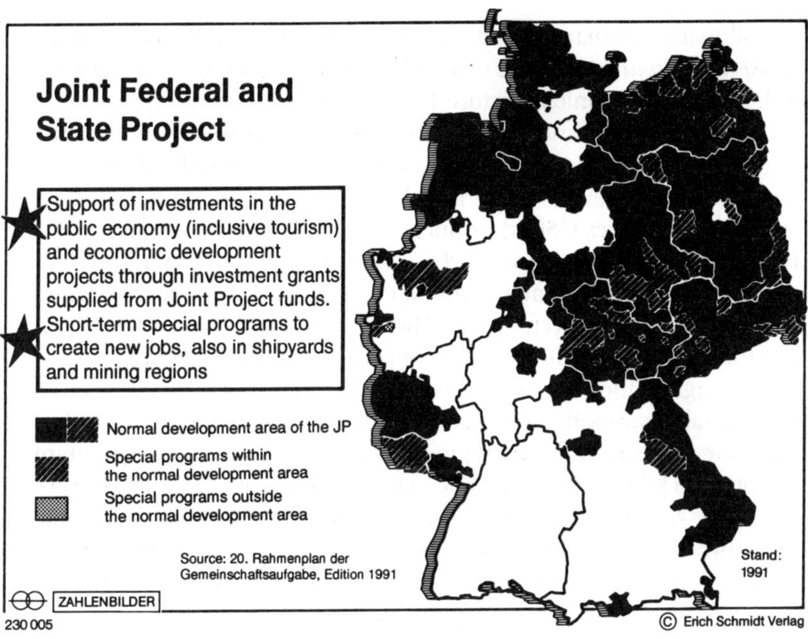

Fig. 28: Regional Structural Policy

industries. All of this has resulted in a loss of jobs and an increase in demographic migration, but also to some extent in the establishment of new industrial branches. This process began with the coal mining crisis in the 50's and is still continuing.

- Up until 1990, the areas bordering on the GDR also qualified as structurally weak and susceptible to crises because of their isolated position (and the transport links, cut off after 1945). Since 1990, they have profited from German re-unification, particularly in consumer goods trade.

Without a doubt, the regional problems discussed here have contributed to an escalation of the differences often cryptically termed the "North-South divide". Far from insignificant is the impact of these economic imbalances on unemployment figures in the regions concerned. Nonetheless, regional differences on the whole are less serious in Germany than in France. Furthermore, economic activity in Germany is based on a greater number of urban centres. At the same time, its political federalism prevents a high degree of centralization.

Following German re-unification, we can now also speak of an "*East-West divide*". After the near collapse of production in the Eastern federal states, the initial picture here is extremely grim: the national product lies significantly below 1989 levels in all sectors and entire regions are threatened with an unparalleled de-industrialisation. Unemployment levels were initially held within certain limits by statistical cosmetics ("Short hours zero"), early retirement rulings and job market policy measures such as continuing education, re-training and job creation (1991: an unemployment rate of 11.8%) and are likely to escalate drastically (cf. Priewe/Hickel 1991; Christ/Neubauer 1991). For this reason the entire region comprising the new federal states has been assigned the status of industrial development zone and receives considerable support, particularly for industrial investment and infrastructure projects, from the regional economic development program maintained jointly by federal and state governments. (*Fig. 28* gives an overview of the Joint Project, "Improvement of Regional Economic Structure".) Prognoses concerning any end to the East German transformational crisis or the possibility of a "second German economic miracle" seem, however, premature.

3.4 *Two economies side-by-side*

3.4.1 Government promotion of economic concentration

Company mergers in Germany are subject to control by the German Federal Trade Commission (*Bundeskartellamt*). The antitrust legislation (laws governing fair competition) can cause mergers of certain dimensions to be stopped or even revoked. Even though the effectiveness of such laws must not be overestimated (since they only have a minimal influence on economic concentration), the contrast they offer to corresponding political priorities in France is noteworthy. In order to improve competitiveness, the Fifth Economic Plan (1966-70), for example, required that a small number of enterprises or groups of enterprises should be created in every branch within a certain dimensional category so that they would be able to stand up to international competition. The sixth plan (1971-75) continued this *systematic promotion of economic concentration* by encouraging a fundamental restructuring of the industrial sector through public intervention (tax measures, loans). One typical example: the 1974 publicly "aided" merger of the private automobile companies Citroën and Peugeot.

The reason for these measures is that for a long time French businesses were run by small and medium-scale (family-owned) enterprises (Jetter 1979, p. 83f.; Uterwedde 1979, p. 32ff.). It is precisely this in part anachronistic structural defect that is one of the main weaknesses of the French economy:

T. 14:
Only 1,100 out of a total of 1.6 million businesses, i.e. merely 7 out of 10,000, were responsible for more than one third of the total volume of sales of all businesses; another 1,300, i.e. 8 out of 10,000, produced about 7% of this global turnover. In summary, *15 out of a total of 10,000 businesses produce altogether 42,2% of overall sales in industry and trade* ... Conversely, more than 1.5 million companies (93%) contribute less than one sixth (15.9%) to the total volume of sales! This means that virtually 1,540,000 businesses control a market equivalent to less than one half of the market dominated by the 2,400 giants. In other words, 1,300 small-sized businesses produce less than one large enterprise. These figures are additionally substantiated by the distribution of employees: 39% of all employed persons work in 0.3% of the businesses, i.e. in those with more than 500 employees; *90% of all firms have less than 10 workers* and 80% of all businesses in the trade sector do not have a single employee. More than one third of all those employed work in companies with a staff of 1-50 persons, another 30% work in firms with 51-500 employees. (Kempf 1980, p. 277f.; italics by H.H.L.)

The situation today is not quite the same as the one depicted in T. 14, which is based on data from 1972. The reason for this is that the number of small craftsman's establishments, farms and retail businesses has dropped considerably as a result of progressive concentration and monopolization. This is part of a trend which developed at the end of the nineteenth century, heavily disrupting the position of the traditional French middle class (*farmers, craftsmen, businessmen*) (cf. Kolboom 1975). Nevertheless, despite intensive efforts in France to attain the level of economic concentration found in other countries (especially in Germany), certain structural aspects have not disappeared. Small-scale enterprises are still of great importance (approximately 90% have less than 10 employees). Nearly 68% of industrial enterprises operate with less than 50 employees (see *Table 9*; small infant businesses have been left out). However, their share of the turnover is a mere 12%. (By comparison, the small-scale industrial operators in Germany, although fewer, produce a larger share of the turnover.)

Table 9: Company Size in Industry

Size	Number of Establishments		Employees	Turnover
		(%)	(%)	(%)
10- 19	22,163	35.7	5.9	3.6
20- 49	22,411	36.1	12.8	8.7
50- 99	8,008	12.9	10.1	7.3
100-199	3,973	6.4	9.9	7.8
200-499	2,669	4.3	14.4	13.5
500 and up	1,490	2.4	46.0	56.8
other establishments	1,366	2.2	0.9	2.3
		100.0	100.0	100.0

(From: Min. de l'Industrie 1991, p. 15ff.)

On the other hand, a very small number of large establishments (0.8%) produce nearly 50% of the total volume of sales and employ about 40% of the labour force. (For further details, see Morvan 1972, p. 275ff.; Jewineney 1989; Min. de l'Industrie 1991, p. 13ff.).

3.4.2 The traditional middle class

The export activity of medium and small-scale businesses is even of greater relevance than these figures. One can see that export activity in France, unlike in Germany, is almost exclusively dominated by the larger establishments. By contrast, the share of *petites et moyennes entreprises* (PME) is extremely minimal. This is above all due to their "traditional" production and management techniques. This contrast is reminiscent of the concept of "non-simultaneity" which has occasionally given rise to critical remarks: "In France there are two economies that uneasily co-exist: a modern one, most of it implanted since the war by the technocrats and a few big State and private firms; and below it, an old, creaking infrastructure, based on artisanship, low turnover with high profits, and the ideal of the small family business." (Ardagh 1968, p. 7f.). Even today there is still much truth to this highly quoted statement.

The "side-by-side existence of two national economies under tension" is further characterized by heavy conflicts and the way they are provoked by the resistance of the traditional middle-class to structural changes.

Voie ferrée arrachée par les producteurs de scaroles, près du Boulou (P.-O.)

Fig. 29
(From: L'Express, 12 February 1982)

The first culminating point was in the 50's. *Poujadism*, named after its founder Pierre Poujade, was basically an "anti-parliamentary, anti-governmental protest movement" against the "transformation process in France which was leading to an industrialized, capitalistic oligopoly" (Bock 1975, p. 54; cf. Haupt/Koch 1978; Weisenfeld 1982, p. 112ff.). The demand for protective measures against the increasing spread of consumer markets (*supermarchés, hypermarchés*) marked the first step of action. However, the movement soon ended up as a "tamed" parliamentary organization with a general restoration program. Under the leadership of Gérard Nicoud, this movement was re-radicalized in 1968/69, once again due to the worsening social position of the *petit commerce*. The conflict was characterized by very militant forms of resistance which not only included demonstrations, sales and tax strikes, but also spectacular illegal actions (such as street blockades, the occupation of tax offices, the destruction of tax files etc.). In terms of its organization, the movement was united at a national level in the CID-UNATI (Comité d'Information et de Défense – Union Nationale des Travailleurs Indépendants), independent of the Federation of Medium and Small-scale Businesses (CGPME) and the more large-scale industrial CNPF (cf. 4.6.4). Its ideology was founded on the traditional values of the lower middle class, the "dernières libertés" (Nicoud 1972). It pleaded for the family business (criticizing the conspiracy of powerful syndicates), the importance of individual responsibility and chances for social advancement based solely on individual ability and performance. Finally, the political success resulted in the *loi d'orientation du commerce et de l'artisanat*, which was passed in 1973 and named *Loi Royer* after the former Minister of Commerce and Small Trade. This law, which is still in force today, ensures French small-scale operators important tax benefits and, above all, extensive protection against the new, so-called *grandes surfaces.* The *grandes surfaces* are regulated by the *commissions d'urbanisation* in which both trade representatives and representatives of area municipalities make decisions regarding the establishment of large-scale enterprises. However, it is obvious that such protective measures are not suitable for combatting the forces threatening the existence of many small-scale businesses. It is therefore not too surprising that the French middle class, including the farmers, repeatedly draw attention to themselves by spectacular acts of protest (cf. *Fig. 29*). Slogans such as "Désossez Mitterrand!", "Socialistes, chienlit!", "Contrôle des prix, KGB" (Le Point, 9 May 1983) are no rarity.

3.5 *Nationalization and indicative planning*

Descriptions of the French economic system usually emphasize the high degree of governmental influence. It is sometimes even referred to as an uninterrupted tradition of state dirigisme. However, it is questionable whether one can regard France as having a central planned economy which is basically in opposition to the economic system of the Federal Republic of Germany. The reason for this is that even the West German "free enterprise system" does not function without federal intervention (consider the long-term structural and research policies, price subsidies for agriculture or the socialization of money-losing branches) and the concept of market and competition has not been fully abandoned in France.

The *nationalization issue* in particular has given rise to controversial opinions. Although West German constitutional law expressly permits the nationalization of capital goods (Article 15), such proposals are virtually tabu in economic discussions. (Despite the fact that several important branches such as the postal system or the waterworks and electric power industries are under governmental control.)

In France there have been roughly four different phases during which large-scale nationalizations took place or the public sector played a vital role in realizing certain economic objectives.

3.5.1 Expansion of the public sector since 1936

Several armament and aircraft industries were already nationalized under the *Popular Front government* in 1936. In 1937, following Léon Blum's resignation, the railways were united to form the SNCF and placed under governmental supervision.

An extensive reorganization of the French economy took place after the *Libération* between 1944 and 1946. The public sector in particular was expanded.

In 1944 the parties and unions which were united in the *Conseil National de la Résistance* (CNR) demanded the elimination of the "féodalités économiques", which had been accused of the debacle of 1940 as well as collaboration with the Nazis, and called for public takeover of the large monopolies ("retour à la nation de tous les grands moyens de production monopolisés"). The provisional government under de Gaulle endorsed this position. The preamble to the 1946 constitution thus read as follows: "Tout bien, toute entreprise dont l'exploitation a ou acquiert les caractères d'un service public national ou d'un monopole de fait doit devenir la propriété de la collectivité."

These measures – supported by all important political powers – were intended to create the conditions necessary for a quick recovery and facilitate a specific federal economic policy with investment plans for particular key sectors. Those institutions affected in particular by the nationalization program included the coal mining industry, the Banque de France, several depositary banks (including Crédit Lyonnais, Société Générale), the power supply industry and gasworks (founding of EDF/GDF), the largest insurance companies and the aircraft and automobile industries (Gnome et Rhône, Renault) whose management had collaborated with the Nazi regime.

The *planification* was introduced between 1946 and 1947 as a means of implementing the new economic priorities in France. This is a type of intermediate-term economic plan which prescribes specific investment goals and interests for the entire industrial sector or individual branches. These goals are set up by a planning commissariat (*Commissariat général au plan*) which is subordinate to the prime minister. Concrete detailing is then carried out in various committees made up of representatives from the trade unions and employers' associations. The plan covers a period of several years, but is not binding for private industry. Its sole purpose is to act as a recommendation guideline for private industry (*indicative planning*) even though the government does have certain means of control, for example, by granting loans and contracts. Thus, the French *planification* has very little in common with the forms of a central planned economy.

The First Plan (1947-53) attempted to coordinate programs for stimulating the economy (recovery, use of Marshall plan funds) and upgrading the productive apparatus. It concentrated on helping the raw materials industries and improving the industrial infrastructure (especially of the transportation network). State intervention was alleviated to some degree since several important branches were already nationalized.

The third essential phase of government economic policy began in 1957 with the founding of the *European Economic Community* (EEC). This event forced France to fully reorient its foreign trade relations. Up until then, France had primarily traded with countries belonging to the franc zone (thus removing part of the pressure of international competition). By opening its doors to the European Market, France had to lift its customs barriers. It was thus necessary to stimulate economic growth, speed up industrial modernization, reorganize certain branches (for example, by creating larger entrepreneurial groups), adapt new fields of specialization (e.g. in agriculture) and regulate foreign direct investments (in order to limit the inflow of foreign funds in vital branches). If it had not been for federal programs and government intervention, such a fundamental economic transformation process would have hardly been possible.

Although the success of national economic planning in the phases described above cannot be denied, the *planification* began losing its weight in the late 60's. This became obvious in 1968 when the large unions started to withdraw from the planning commissions. The planification was further weakened by the oil crisis of 1973/74. This not only made the energy problem apparent but also made the highly ambitious aims of the fourth plan (elimination of the structural weaknesses in industry, annual economic growth of 5.8 - 6%) turn into an illusion. National economic planning was then officially and completely abrogated by the administration under Giscard d'Estaing and his prime minister Raymond Barre (1976-81). The individual institutions survived, but in reality the firm liberal course (which promoted rigorous "streamlining" of certain branches, increased unemployment and cutbacks in social services) precluded the realization of the resolved plans.

3.5.2 Nationalization programme of 1981

A reorientation in French national economic policy followed the *election of Mitterrand in 1981*. One of the first structural reforms carried out by the socialist-communist government was a nationalization program which was much more comprehensive in comparison to the earlier phases. (In 1977 the nationalization issue contributed to the break in the leftist alliance; cf. Leithäuser 1978). The result was that the majority of the private banks, two steel concerns (in actuality already state-run due to many years of subsidies) as well as a number of other industrial concerns went under government control. These entrepreneurial groups belonged to:

a) the industrial sector

- *La Compagnie générale d'électricité* (the fourth largest entrepreneurial group; electric goods, electrical engineering, computers; total volume of sales in 1980: 46.5 billion francs),
- *Saint-Gobain* (glass, building materials, electronics; total volume of sales: 43.5 billion francs),
  Péchiney-Ugine-Kuhlmann (metalworking, chemicals; total volume of sales: 38.1 billion francs),
- *Rhône-Poulenc* (chemicals, textiles; total volume of sales: 30.2 billion francs),
- *Thomas-Brandt* (electric goods, electronics; total volume of sales: 36.5 billion francs),
- *Usinor* and *Sacilor* (iron, steel: total volume of sales: 22.0 billion francs and 16.8 billion francs, resp.),
- *Dassault-Bréguet* (aircraft and armament industries; total volume of sales: 10.7 billion francs),
- *Matra* (armament industry, electronics; total volume of sales: 6.8 billion francs).

b) banks and financing

A total of 39 banks became nationalized. Among them were *Crédit du Nord*, the *Crédit Commercial de France*, and the *Banque de Paris et des Pays-Bas*. By consequence, nearly the entire finance sector was under government control. (For exact figures, see: Regards sur l'actualité 79/ 1982, p. 35ff.).

As a result, 13 of the 20 largest groups of concerns belonging to the industrial sector became public-owned. This affected the entire steel industry, the majority of aluminum production, the chemical producing branches and the armament industry, 50% of glass production as well as a large share of the pharmaceutical branches. Overall turnover of the nationalized sector accounted for about 30% of the total volume of sales of the French industry.

The costs incurred by the nationalization activities, especially the indemnity owed to the shareholders, amounted to around 40 billion francs. (Originally, the government had assessed the amount of compensation much lower. However, the opposition appealed to the *Conseil constitutionnel* to examine the constitutionality of the assessment. Due to the protest lodged by the Conseil

Fig. 30
(From: L'Aurore, 18 February 1982)

constitutionnel, the amount of compensation was then raised by 15%). The disparity between financial expenditure and economic profit then became the target of public criticism (*Fig. 30*). The government was especially accused of not having been content with majority ownerships of 51%.

By way of the nationalizations the government began pursuing several politico-social and economic goals. One more or less classical justification was the *control of entrepreneurial groups which had become market-dominating in production* whose influence on other important economic branches was to be limited. This was the predominant motive, for example, behind the nationalization plans of 1944 and the later joint federal program of 1972:

T. 15:
En cette année 1981, plus d'un siècle et demi après le développement du capitalisme en France, les phénomènes d'accumulation et de concentration du capital, de la multinationalisation du capital dans le monde, me conduisent à considérer comme juste et nécessaire qu'un certain nombre d'entreprises devenues des monopoles ou tendant au monopole et fabriquant des produits nécessaires à la nation soient nationalisées, fassent corps avec la nation; qu'elles ne disposent pas d'un pouvoir économique, et donc politique, qui leur permette de prévaloir sur les décisions de l'intérêt général, et pas davantage, ayant aboli toute concurrence nationale au-dessous d'elles, d'être maîtresses du marché... (François Mitterrand at a press conference on 26 September 1981)

Moreover, the expansion of the public sector was supposed to create blanket conditions which allowed for a better coordination of industrial priorities. This especially applied to the promotion of international competitiveness, the development of new technologies etc. Pierre Dreyfus, the Minister of Industry at the time, once observed:

> L'enjeu est donc de créer les conditions permettant de construire un outil industriel novateur capable de prendre l'offensive dans deux directions: le progrès technologique, facteur de progrès social, et le face-à-face avec les multinationales. Objectif ambitieux dont il est clair que seule la nation peut l'accomplir.

Since nationalization efforts mainly affected branches and entrepreneurial groups of future significance, federal plans for long-term policies in technology were easier to put through in France than in Germany. The same applied on a European level to the solution of more complex research and developmental tasks which required the coordination of national resources (cf. Neumann 1983). Finally, it was hoped that the nationalization activity would allow France to deal with the world recession more efficiently and bring about an upturn in business.

Without wanting to draw any general conclusions, one can say that the results of the program lag behind the aims envisioned. A short-term economic revival proved impossible and the nationalized concerns did not fulfil the pacemaker role assigned to them. The problems connected with the job market remained unchanged and the structural deficiencies, together with their negative effects on the balance of trade, could not be eliminated from one day to the next. In such a situation, the model of a socialist and free market economy remained largely illusory. This was especially true in view of the fact that no decisive changes had occurred in company management or in terms of codetermination at the workplace. Moreover, it has become clear that a purely national economic policy independent of international power structures is, in view of trans-national economic inter-dependencies, no longer possible.

In 1986 the new conservative government under Chirac announced a fundamental policy re-orientation by renouncing *state-controlled economic policies.* 65 state-owned groups of enterprises were immediately denationalized. At first, the French public did not aim their criticism so much at the new privately-owned enterprises as such. What they actually disapproved of was the fact that the concerns nationalized after 1945 were passed into private hands and that French firms could then become controlled by foreign capital.

However, after the New York Stock Exchange crash in October 1987, the denationalization program had to be stopped. Up until then, the government had sold about 20 groups of enterprises in the form of stocks. This included such concerns as Saint-Gobain, the Compagnie Générale d'Électricité and the media concern Havas. Each individual enterprise was denationalized one hundred percent (as opposed to a step-by-step increase of capital by private capital). Foreign capital stock was limited to a maximum of 20 percent. 10 percent was reserved for company employees. 70 percent of the shares could be sold at the Paris Stock Exchange. The proceeds of the denationalized enterprises amounted to more than 90 billion francs. This was welcome relief for the national budget (cf. Uterwedde 1987; Capul/Mews 1988, p. 243ff.).

According to official reports, the purpose of these measures was to liberalize the economy (thus rendering it more competitive), break with the tradition of national dirigisme and transform state capitalism into popular capitalism by a wide dispersal of stock ownership. Nonetheless, the government did not endorse a total rejection of old traditional colbertistic practices. First, mandatory public approval allowed the government to retain a certain degree of influence on the composition of investor groups in the case of larger ownership shares. Second, the announced liberalization became grotesquely dubious when *Balladur*, Minister of Economic Affairs and Finances, introduced the so-called "hard core" in the denationalized concerns. Each "hard core", made up of financially strong shareholders (*groupes d'actionnaires stables*), was to be authoritative in determining corporate policy. It soon turned out that this circle of privileged shareholders mainly consisted of friends and patrons of the Gaullist party. Consequently, the government was accused of not having denationalized the concerns but in reality of having "chiracisized" them. In any event, the one-sided selection of principal shareholders made it possible for vital instruments of control to remain in the hands of the government.

The denationalization which had been planned since 1986 were not revoked in 1988 by the centre-left coalition government. It was the dissolution of the "hard cores" of stockholders which was under discussion, but not a total waiver of government influence.

In spite of its policy of liberalization and denationalization, it must be noted that the French State continues to play an important role in economic life. Steering manoeuvres, whether in the form of promotion of auxiliary conditions or direct action, targeted investment activities or the financing of various research projects, are the order of the day. Apparently the tradition of French economic style includes – beyond party boundaries – an ordering and steering function on the part of the French State: "Even today, the State and its administrators have a sacred character. Often people expect the State to enter the stage as an enterprise, filling an ordering function and acting as a controller, because they themselves lack faith in private initiative and believe that unencumbered negotiation of individual interests only gives rise to inequalities. The State - in keeping with age-old tradition – slipped into this role during the difficult times following the Second World War and has since tended to strengthen its position during periods of growth. The important role of the State in the French economy is only superficially linked to the political orientation of the government." (Ammon 1989, p. 157)

State economic policy swings back and forth between these attitudes and expectations on the one hand and various liberalizing measures geared to the EC single market and international competitive capacity on the other; apparently there is no continuous policy being pursed over successive election periods.

3.6 *Permanent problems in foreign trade*

Although the French economy has been increasing its participation in the international market, it has not yet succeeded in solving one problem: the elimination of its chronic foreign trade deficit. Apart from several brief periods, its exports – in contrast to Germany – have mostly lagged behind its imports. This development goes back to the 60's (*Fig. 31*). Up until 1982, foreign trade problems increased drastically. It was only after this that the deficit gradually started to recede, finally remaining for certain periods in a kind of "équilibre dans le déséquilibre." Since 1988, however, it has experienced further decline as a result of weakness in industrial production (cf. 3.2).

The most prevalent explanation for the negative trade deficit in France is the country's *dependency on foreign energy imports*. This is correct inasmuch as energy imports in 1984 were recorded at 25%, still the largest share of total imports. (In the same time period, the share of energy imports in Germany was reported to be 18%). However, the depreciation of the dollar and the drop in oil prices after 1986 caused energy imports to decrease by approximately 100 billion francs to a share of 10.1%. This is the reason for the virtually redressed balance of trade at that time. In 1973 the French economy experienced a decisive turning point. At this point, while Germany was importing only 55%, France was importing 78% of its energy needs (especially crude oil) in order to meet the requirements of its energy consumption and the drastic oil price hikes by the producing countries made the heavy dependency on imports more obvious than ever before. Since then, France, which is especially poor in raw materials, has been trying to radically lower its crude oil needs and achieve greater independence of the oil-producing countries in the long-term. Under Giscard d'Estaing the focus of these efforts was the adamant promotion of its atomic energy industry. Within a few years, the government carried out a massive nuclear program (virtually unaffected by public protest and

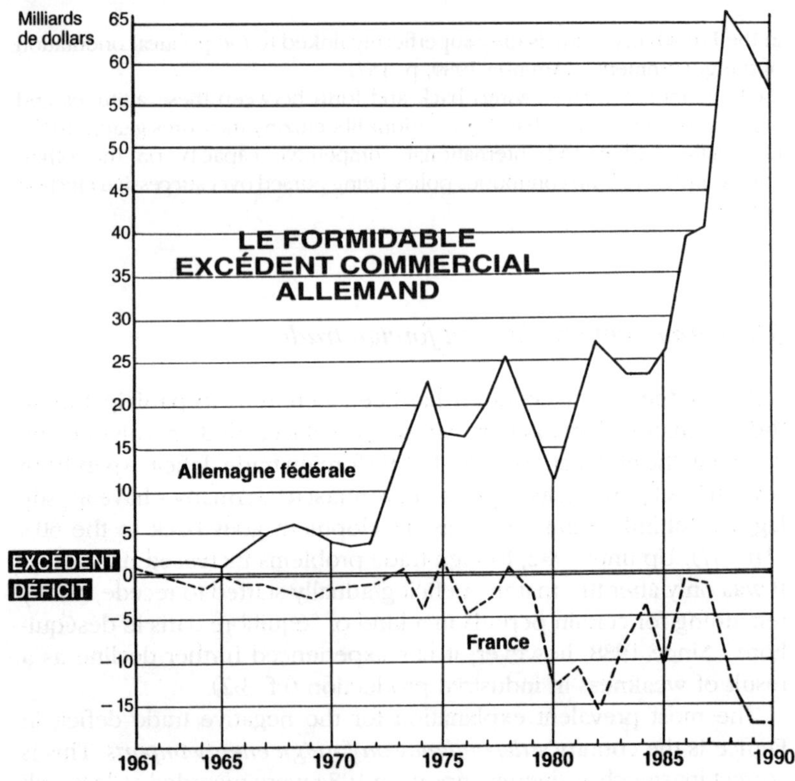

Fig. 31: Developments in the Balance of Trade
(From: Le Monde 1979, p. 19; INSEE 1991, p. 155ff.; Inst. der deutschen Wirtschaft 1992, p. 71ff.)

ecological considerations). The result is that France now has more than twice as many atomic energy plants as Germany and meets about 75% of its power requirements by means of this energy source (cf. *Fig. 32*). Due to the country's deficit and the overcapacity of *Electricité de France*, France therefore hopes to increase the volume of atomic energy exports to its neighbouring countries. France is aiming at the European domestic market in particular.

Measured against total imports, the percentage of crude oil imports is still high, but is clearly on the decline. Therefore, this cannot be the sole explanation for the foreign trade deficit in France. It seems to be of greater significance that *imports cannot be counterbalanced by export activity equal in magnitude.* An examination of the trade structure provides more detailed information (*Table 10*).

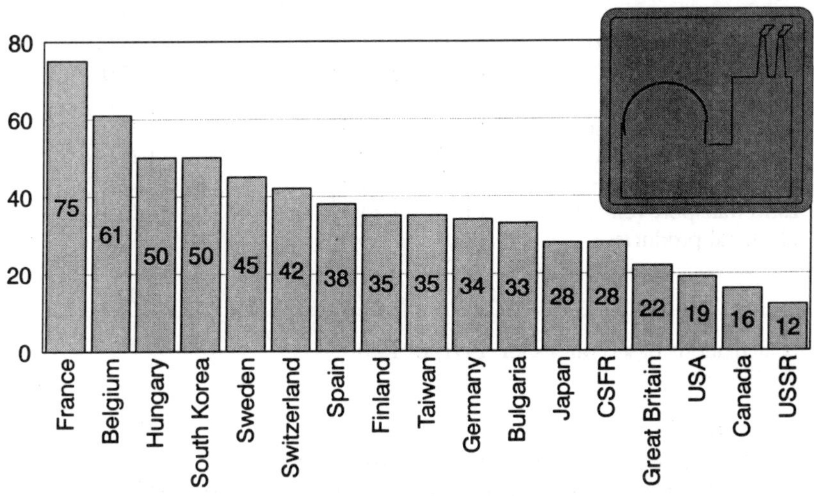

Fig. 32: Meeting the Power Requirements with Atomic Energy. (Share of current generation in % (as of 1989))

The export industry roughly reflects the weaknesses peculiar to the French production structure. France produces a relatively high percentage of agricultural and food products (16.2%) and, in comparison to Germany, a considerably lower percentage of capital-goods (41.6% versus 55.7%; cf. *Table 11*). With such an export structure, import costs are naturally of greater consequence. This is one of the most crucial adjustment inadequacies of French industry (see Plihon 1987, p. 52ff.; Verdié 1987, p. 226ff.; Unterwedde 1988, p. 38ff.; Capul/Meurs 1988, p. 65ff. as well as excerpts from an interview with Edith Cresson, previously European Minister and then Prime Minister, in T. 16).

Table 10: France and its Foreign Trade

	Exports (bill. f)	Exports (%)	Imports (bill. f)	Imports (%)
Agriculture, forestry, fishing	85.0	7.0	50.6	4.0
Agricultural and food products	105.6	9.0	88.9	7.0
Energy	31.2	2.7	123.8	9.8
Semifinished products	287.3	24.5	330.0	25.9
Professional equipment	312.4	26.5	306.0	24.0
Household appliances	19.7	1.7	33.8	2.7
Land transport vehicles	157.3	13.4	132.0	10.4
Electrical products	175.6	15.0	207.8	16.2
	1174.1	100.0	1272.9	100.0

(Calculations based on: INSEE 1991, p. 155)

T. 16:
Le coup de colère du ministre des Affaires européennes
Edith Cresson: “La dégradation de nos échanges est spectaculaire”
Les Français n’ont toujours pas la fibre industrielle. Pour Edith Cresson, ils risquent de le payer cher.
L’Evénement du jeudi: Le mark s’envole, et notre déficit commercial se creuse. La France n’est-elle pas en train de prendre un retard dangereux par rapport à l’Allemagne, juste au moment où celle-ci est portée par la situation internationale?
Edith Cresson: C’est un événement sans précédent! La dégradation de nos échanges industrielles est spectaculaire... Il n’y a jamais eu un tel effondrement. En 1984, nous avions un solde positif de cent milliards de francs. Cette année, le déficit dépassera les soixante milliards de francs. Je ressens cette situation comme une faiblesse dans certaines négociations. (...) Nous ne pourrons être crédibles face à nos partenaires, pour entraîner l’Europe, qu’avec une situation de notre balance industrielle en redressement.

Mais l’économie française n’est-elle pas en plein boom?
– Quand le matin, à la radio, j’entends déclarer que la situation économique est brillante et que maintenant on peut se consacrer au social, j’en avale mon café de travers. On ne peut faire réellement du social qu’en redistribuant des excédents industriels. C’est ce que fait l’Allemagne qui, ainsi, peut rémunérer plus cher ses ouvriers et ses cadres avec les marges prises sur son énorme excédent industriel.

> La France néglige ses ouvriers et son industrie?
> – C'est l'une des explications de notre faiblesse. En France, on a toujours davantage poussé les jeunes vers l'administration que vers l'industrie. Aujourd'hui, le secteur public attire moins, mais ce sont les activités financières qui ont pris le relais, pas l'industrie. Or sans base industrielle, la finance et les activités de services en général ne peuvent que faciliter l'introduction de produits étrangers. Autre déficience: le mode d'organisation des entreprises. Les sructures d'encadrement sont obsolètes, les méthodes de promotion reposent sur les diplômes et non sur l'efficacité... Il y a pléthore de cadres intermédiaires, beaucoup plus qu'en Allemagne. (...)
> Prêchez-vous pour un retour du dirigisme?
> – Pas du tout. Les pages des journaux sont pleines du débat sur le "ni-ni" (ni privatisation ni nationalisation), ou des arbitrages sur les dotations aux entreprises publiques ... Ce n'est pas le problème essentiel. Ce qui l'est, c'est d'inciter les entreprises à mieux se mobiliser et à bien définir leurs stratégies dans la construction européenne et l'environnement mondial. (...)
> (From: L'Evénement du jeudi, 30 Nov. 1989)

Neither the shortcomings in its industrial structure nor the country's competitive disadvantages have improved in the last several years. In fact, since 1984 it has become more and more obvious that the French export industry has been suffering losses in markets of their most important trade partners. On the one hand, this is related to the *area-specific distribution of exports.* A large part of France's export commodities go to third-world and oil-producing countries whose buying power has significantly shrunk due to their heavy burden of debts and the increases in oil prices. On the other hand, the most crucial reason may be the *insufficient supply of goods.* In comparison to other industrial nations, the French economy is often not able to react appropriately or adequately to market demand (as well as changes in demand). This is especially true of the chemical industry in which export surpluses are on the decline and even deficits have been reported since 1987.

> Contrairement au Japon et à la RFA, qui ont su se spécialiser et constituer des pôles de compétitivité dans des secteurs porteurs (comme l'industrie chimique et mécanique en RFA), la France a gardé une *structure industrielle peu spécialisée avec des points forts* (industries du nucléaire, de l'aéronautique et de l'équipement militaire) *moins nombreux et plus limités* que ces deux pays. (Plihon 1987, p. 54; italics by H.H.L.)

Table 11: Foreign trade and the Federal Republic of Germany

	Exports (%)	Imports (%)
Agriculture, forestry and hunting	1.2	7.4
Food and semi-luxuries	4.2	6.3
Mining, energy	0.7	6.7
Raw materials and manufacturing	23.9	26.0
Capital-goods (and automobiles)	55.7	32.2
Consumer goods	12.1	17.5
Others	2.2	3.9

(From: Institut der deutschen Wirtschaft 1988, p. 112)

These competitive weaknesses become much more apparent in terms of the specific ***trade exchange between Germany and France.*** Most striking is the quantitative imbalance since Germany exports considerably more to France than vice versa. In 1987 France recorded a record trade deficit; Germany's trade surplus has meanwhile reached DM 8.6 billion (Illust. 32; for further details: Lasserre 1986, Nivollet 1987). In the last couple of years French trade has continued to suffer deficits. Industrial commodities, especially capital-goods (e.g. machines), durable goods (e.g. household appliances), vehicles and day-to-day consumer goods (e.g. textiles) account for the largest share of these deficits. These branches reveal the weaknesses of the French industry and the strengths of the German industry (see the development curve in *Fig. 34*).

There is also a ***structural deficit*** in France which in turn stems from the trade exchange in the capital-goods sector: "In this sector the internationalization process led to the adjustment of production techniques. Since the French capital-goods industry did not comprise enough modern and highly specialized branches and, furthermore, lacked adequate production capacity, it had to import the machines necessary for modernizing its productive apparatus, above all from Germany" (Deubner et al. 1978, p. 108f.). The result was a clear dependency relationship (despite the partially reduced deficits since 1982) which still exists today. If France requires, for example, technically advanced equipment for modernizing its industry, the German export industry reaps the benefits. Moreover, when such capital-goods are imported, the adaptation of certain norms and procedures adds to the perpetuation of this technological dependency. In other words, the

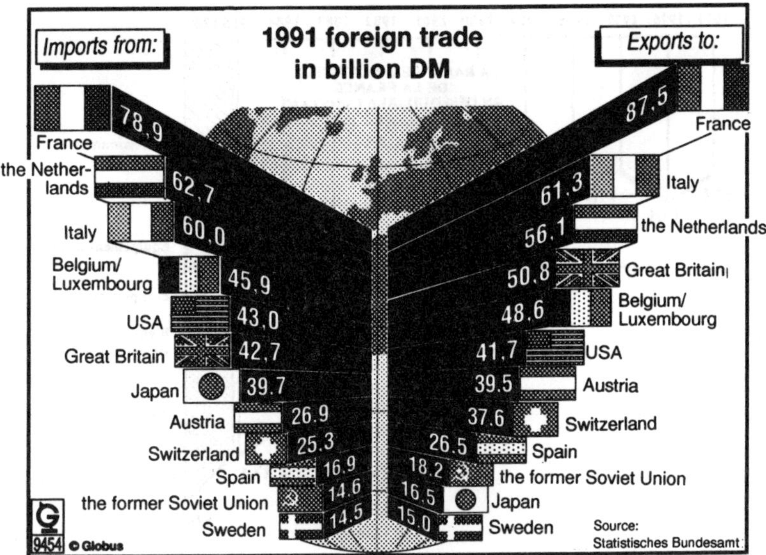

Fig. 33: Germany's Most Important Trading Partners

structural dominance of Germany – owing to its specialization in highly developed and processed commodities – contributes significantly to the difficulties of French foreign trade.

Another factor contributing to France's low export activity is its *marketing problems.* In this context, it is symptomatic that the study of foreign languages in France is, generally speaking, still of relatively subordinate importance. This deficiency, along with other inadequacies (insufficient professional schooling, the image of poor product quality, delayed deliveries etc), compounds the problems facing the country's export situation.

T. 17:
French entrepreneurs make especially heavy weather of marketing their products abroad. The Paris Chamber of Industry and Commerce conducted a survey in which the German, Italian, British, Belgian and American trading partners were asked to evaluate French competitiveness. The results were devastating. These countries unanimously complained of the French "weaknesses in both organization of trade and adaptability to market demand."

As an old colonial power, France is more used to a convenient system of distribution rather than aggressive sales techniques. Thus, its export endeavours often end up as failures as soon as the language barriers are reached. The French are only slowly learning that their motto "Do as all others do, speak French", is no longer very up-to-date.

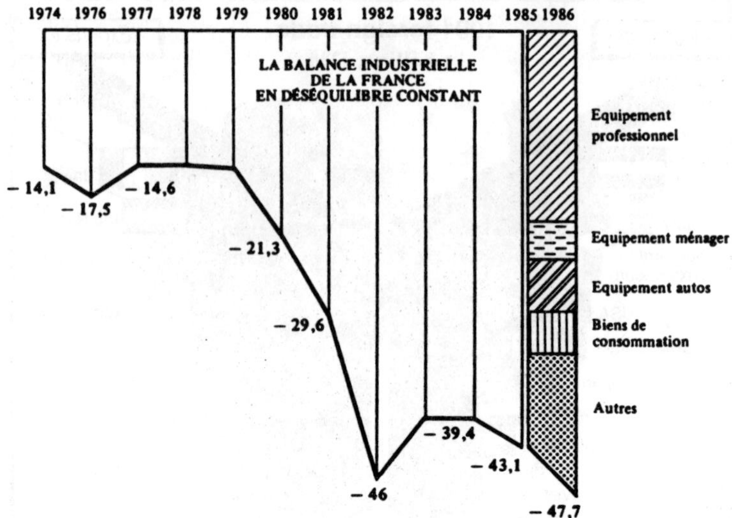

Fig. 34: French Import Surpluses in the Industrial Commodity Exchange between France and the Federal Republic of Germany (in billions of francs) (From: Le Monde, 11 Jan. 1987).

(...)
In the meantime, the government is trying everything in its power to stimulate the competitiveness of the French economy. At present, the Ministry of Industry is trying to heighten the French awareness of quality workmanship by engaging in a large-scale marketing campaign. Huge bill posters – which are even found in the Paris metro – are supposed to teach the public what "quality" is by conjugating such thoughts as "I avoid failures. You avoid deficiencies. He avoids delayed deliveries..."
(M.L. Hauch/M. Fleck, Die Zeit, 3 July 1987)

The differences between the economic structures of France and Germany, which are presented in greater detail in sections 3.2 to 3.6, are summarized in *Table 12.*

The reasons for the difficulties experienced by the French economy in general and by French foreign trade in particular are very complex and cannot be eliminated from one day to the next. This is why large-scale proposals and radical measures, as they have been discussed in public up to now, are usually oversimplified. At first glance, one might thus well conceive of a connection between the *reduction of work hours* and economic competitiveness. In his well-received book, *La France paresseuse* (1987, p. 11), Victor Scherrer observes, "Nos industries sont malades du temps de travail. Et c'est la France qui s'affaiblit...". In a somewhat less pathetic manner, the author adds the following in more concrete terms:

> Si l'on quitte les statistiques, on découvre une réalité bien vivante, ancrée dans nos habitudes et nos schémas mentaux: une France égoïste, indolente, une France de petits ponts et de grands week-ends, de champions du temps libre, de stakhanovistes des repos compensateurs et des congés maladie, de combinards du calendries. Une France qui déifie les avantages acquis aux dépens des autres. (1987, p. 14)

Nevertheless, the demand for longer work hours soon turns out to be a poorly disguised new version of the old stereotype of work ethic and quality. Of course, one must concede the accuracy of some of Scherrer's observations. However, his criticism does not at all touch upon the main reasons for what he calls *«déclin»* or *«décadence»*. Moreover, this hypothesis is easily refuted by comparative figures from other countries, for example, Germany. The author also responds positively to the argument repeatedly put forth by big business that *excessive payload and fringe benefits* impair French export ability. Even on this point, a comparison on an international level produces a totally different picture. With its undoubtedly higher wage level, Germany ranks higher than France in the category of fringe benefits. With regard to payload, France does not even belong to the top ten (Germany ranks second after Switzerland).

The real weaknesses of France's competitive position cannot be explained in this way. However viable the demand for longer work hours and a reduction of fringe benefits might be as an anti-union strategy, the structural causes remain vague. In order to close the obvious gaps in production, raise general productivity and improve economic adaptiveness to international market demands, a fundamental modernization of the production apparatus will be of greater necessity. Only in this way will France be able to reduce the imbalance in foreign trade in the long run.

Table 12: Economic Structure of France and the Federal Republic of Germany

	France	Germany
Economic system:	Market economy with government indicative planning	Model of a "social market economy"
	Nationalization of numerous branches and groups of enterprises	
	Prescribed medium-term objectives (planification)	Rejection of investment control, only "global control"
Economic sectors in general:	Dominance of services, relatively high degree of agriculture, comparatively small degree of industry	Dominance of services, comparatively high degree of industry
Industry:	Lower share of capital-goods	Pre-eminence of capital-goods sector
	A generally smaller percentage of growth industries	Comparatively advanced adjustment to international market
	Continued high degree of depressed branches	
	Dependency on imports in key sectors of technology	
Regional structure:	Urban centres north of the dividing line between Le Havre and Marseille	No dominant centre
	Paris region most important centre	Decentralized distribution of urban centres
	Under-industrialisation of the west and southwest	Aside from the new federal states, fewer problem areas, and these scattered across the country
Business concentration:	Government promotion of concentration	High degree of concentration already achieved earlier.
	Large proportion of (non-exporting) small and middle-sized businesses	Export-oriented small and middle-sized businesses
	Severe social conflicts (neopoujadism)	
Foreign trade:	Foreign trade deficit	Export surplus, especially in terms of capital goods
	Low export volume	
	Structural dependency on Germany	France most important trade partner

3.7 *Protectionism, retarded industrialization, dynamic post-war development*

The above discussion on the economic tendencies in France might easily convey an incorrect picture if one disregards the different initial conditions and developmental processes within both countries. For this purpose, we turn to a brief historical overview.

3.7.1 Population growth and economic development

France was for the most part an agricultural country in the nineteenth century. Around 45-50% of its workforce was engaged in farming, the industrialization process was making very slow progress and all in all economic growth was at a low level. This stagnating development continued virtually through the Third Republic. It was especially characteristic of the industrial lag which France, unlike other European countries, experienced after this period.

By contrast, Germany went through a heavy industrialization period in the second half of the nineteenth century. By 1900 there were already more people working in the secondary than in the primary sector. (In France, this was not a fact until after the second World War). Furthermore, the modern industrial branches in particular (chemicals, mechanical engineering, optics, electronics) played a large role in this development. They facilitated intensive foreign trade activity, i.e. the export of industrial finished goods and the import of raw materials. On the average, economic growth was considerably higher in Germany than in France (cf. *Table 13*).

One of the main reasons for the very divergent industrialization processes was the particular *demographic development* of each country. While the population of both countries was about the same around 1800, the opposite tendency began to evolve during the following decades. In Germany, there was a population explosion accompanied by heavy urbanization (1800: 24.5 million; 1850: 35.0 million; 1900: 56.3 million inhabitants). By contrast, population growth in France lagged far behind all the way up to the mid-twentieth century. From 1850 to 1950 the population only grew by about 16%. (In the exact same period the rate of growth in Germany, i.e. that part now known as the Federal Republic, was 179%). The rapid population growth in Germany led to an immense increase in the demand for goods. This necessitated an expansion of industrial production for which a greater workforce was available.

Table 13: Average Annual Economic Growth
(measured in terms of gross domestic product) 1870 - 1990

	France	Germany (as of 1950: FRG)
1870/71 - 1913	1.6 %	2.9 %
1914 - 1949	0.7 %	1.2 %
1950 - 1960	4.8 %	8.5 %
1961 - 1970	5.8 %	4.8 %
1971 - 1980	3.6 %	2.7 %
1981 - 1990	2.1 %	2.1 %

(From: OCDE 1974, p. 14; Frankreich-Jahrbuch 1991, p. 262)

Consequently, the transformation of Germany's economic structure was characterized by a high rate of industrialization, increasing business concentration and high rates of growth. In France, the effects of its demographic development were more negative. "There was no population growth which could have stimulated economic production. The propensity to invest did not increase due to the absence of mass buying power. The economy was unable to create more jobs since the number of employed stagnated" (Menyesch 1978, p. 34). This situation was ultimately brought about by the slow-paced industrial development and the general politico-social immobility of French society during the Third Republic.

3.7.2 Protectionism in the past

The faulty dynamics of the French economy were coupled with a certain leaning towards *protectionist measures* which primarily aimed at shielding French merchandise. The drastic tariff hike ordered in 1892 by Jules *Méline* is a classic example. Its goal was to improve the sales of the domestic economy (particularly of the agricultural sector) and help a whole group of depressed branches reach an upturn (though limited) by making imports more expensive.

T. 18:
Toute l'industrie ne progresse pas au même rythme. Certains secteurs sont à la traîne: les cuirs et peaux, l'habillement, le textile, dont la production passe de l'indice 85 en 1900 à l'indice 100 seulement en 1913. Or ces

> secteurs emploient de nombreux ouvriers: 2465000 dans le textile et l'habillement, 704000 dans le bois et l'ameublement, contre 828000 pour l'ensemble de la sidérurgie, de la métallurgie et des constructions mécaniques.
>
> D'autre part, l'agriculture piétine, avec des rendements faibles (13,6 quintaux à l'hectare pour le blé en moyenne, de 1901 à 1910). Or elle représente 40 % du produit physique de l'économie française en 1910.
>
> Le protectionnisme (Méline, 1892) est donc nécessaire, non seulement pour défendre les produits agricoles français contre la concurrence des pays neufs qui provoque une baisse des prix depuis 1882-1885, mais aussi pour réserver le marché intérieur et colonial aux industries cotonnières et même métallurgiques. Encore qu'on ne puisse le dire de toute l'économie, dans l'ensemble, la mentalité dominante est davantage celle du rentier que de l'entrepreneur. (Prost 1979, p. 9)

Such protectionist measures had enjoyed a tradition in France. Beginning in the seventeenth century, they were already characteristic of *French mercantilism.* Jean-Baptiste *Colbert,* the economic and financial expert of Louis XIV, insisted on intensive government promotion of industry and foreign commerce in order to secure an active trade balance. Apart from a considerable reinforcement of central supreme power, these measures also led to the expansion of existing manufactures, the founding of numerous state-owned establishments which were subject to precise production regulations, the development of new industries, the improvement of the infrastructure (roads, rivers) and the abolishment of inland customs duties. Parallel to the promotion of the domestic market, an import ban on finished goods as well as high protective tariffs were intended to provide the economy with the necessary margin for an upturn. Even though Colbertism failed to be a sweeping success in the end (most of all due to the high war expenditures under Louis XIV), a similar attitude of mind seems to have remained intact up into the twentieth century: "Protectionism means rapid growth, foreign competition means danger" (Lebas 1981, p. 83; cf. also Ammon 1989, p.66). This may be prooved by the recurrent tendency in France to create import bans on foreign commodities and exercise price and exchange controls. One cannot seriously claim that on account of national dirigisme and investment controls the French economy smoothly fits into the Colbertist tradition and that "market economy in France has virtually remained a foreign word" (cf. Schmid 1983). There are simply too many structural similarities between France and other industrial nations.

For a long time, the economic relations to its *colonies* provided France with relative protection against international market conditions. After 1945, this was also true of those countries belonging to the *franc zone.* It is symptomatic, for example, that even in the early 50's more than 40% of France's foreign trade was transacted within the franc zone, i.e. mainly with African nations. By comparison, only 15% of its foreign trade was carried out with other European industrialized countries. The privileged mercantile conditions (and the resulting delay in industrial modernization) are one more reason for the inadequate adjustment to international competition (cf. Caron 1981, Cameron 1971).

3.7.3 Turning to the European Market

The fundamental structural transformation of the French economy can only be understood in terms of its protectionist past, its low level of industrialization and comparatively antiquated production apparatus. This transition became necessary after the signing of the *Rome Agreements* in 1957. The integration of France into the international and, above all, European commodity exchange required a radical reorientation. This meant increasing the share of industry and decreasing the share of agriculture in particular. The consequence was that France underwent an extremely dynamic development in the 60's. Some of the most significant indicators included:

- high rates of growth (cf. *Table 13*) which, owing to the backlog demand between 1960 and 1970, exceeded those rates reported for Germany,
- an adjustment of the level of industrialization in France to that of the other EEC partners,
- shifts in foreign trade (for example, if exports to EEC countries nearly doubled, the importance of the franc zone decreased significantly).

As mentioned before, government control and coordination played a large role in effectuating economic upheaval (see 3.5). Despite the incontestable positive outcome of this period, several problems have remained unchanged. These problems ultimately become apparent in France's permanent foreign trade difficulties. They also indicate the depressed state of various branches as well as more general competitive weaknesses.

With the creation of the *European domestic market in 1993*, the *grand marché*, France will have to prove its export power once again, above all against that of other developed industrialized nations. For this reason, its production framework will require basic improvements (cf. 3.6; cf. also T. 16). The development of suitable marketing strategies will be of equal importance. The adjustment and approximation of value-added tax rates are still unsolved issues. Compared with the VAT of most other EC countries, the French TVA (*taxe sur la valeur ajoutée*) is appreciably higher. Individual rates range from 2.1% to 33.3%. The standard rate equals 18.6% (in Germany it is 7%; the standard rate 14%, beginning 1993, 15%). If France maintains a very high rate, competitiveness will be at risk. Likewise, a drastic decrease would result in an extreme drop in takings for the national budget. The proposed lifting of tariff customs is at least receiving wide journalistic coverage in France. Whether the new European euphoria will in fact be connected with an improvement of economic conditions or whether it will actually turn out to be a "huge bluff" (Baier 1988, p. 21) remains to be seen in the next following years.

3.8 *Change of economic policy*

In 1981 the socialist-communist government was primarily concerned with revitalizing its economy as well as getting over the world crisis which followed the second "oil shock" in 1979. Prior to this, the Giscard/Barre administration had unsuccessfully attempted to find a way out of the crisis. Of key importance was their anti-inflation program (which forced France to accept a higher rate of unemployment). The government also raised fixed resale prices, brought down wages and cut back on social services. The economic situation continued to worsen through 1981. The number of unemployed had risen to 1.8 million and the rate of inflation was at an all-time high at 13.6% (the highest ever recorded in the Fifth Republic). Export problems, especially in the capital-goods sector, aggravated the foreign trade deficit and economic growth fell radically short of expectations.

In this situation, the economic recovery program was specifically geared towards increasing the purchasing power of the lower income classes (by raising annuities and the legal minimum wage by 10%, and by improving a number of social services). The purpose of these measures was to bring about an *increase in domestic demand* and a pick-up in the consumer goods industry. Parallel to this "reconquête du marché intérieur", the *fight against unemployment* was top priority.

ÇA MANQUE D'ÉLAN...
— On m'appelle la navette spatiale du pauvre...

Fig. 35a
(From: Le hérisson, 19 Nov. 1981)

As many as 200,000 new positions were approved of in the public service sector. With "solidarity contracts" the government appealed to businesses and communities to create more jobs. Weekly working hours were lowered to 39 (originally, the 35-hour work week was to become effective by 1985) and the age of retirement was lowered to 60. Furthermore, the government tried to bring on a decisive change in the investment climate and implement a variety of structural reforms by nationalizing large parts of finance and industry. In turn, these nationalizations made direct intervention possible.

Nevertheless, these measures did not fulfil the goals set by the Mauroy administration. There was neither a lasting boost in the economy nor a radical change in the labour market. At first, the number of jobless continued to rise, later becoming stable at an estimated 2 million. Altogether, increased mass consumption helped by no means overcome the crisis. Though domestic demand did rise considerably, it was mainly the foreign companies which profited. This was once again an indication of the structural weaknesses of French industry. French producers were not able to adequately respond to the increased domestic demand. Consequently, the foreign trade deficit worsened, prices sky-rocketed and the value of the franc became increasingly unstable (the franc was devaluated a number of times within a relatively short period). As a result, the government was finally forced to adapt a radical change of policy.

The *turnabout from a socially oriented labour policy to a more conservative stabilizing policy* took place in several stages. The first change in priorities became apparent in June 1982 when the government enacted a subsequent program to help curb inflation and the foreign trade deficit. In addition to a number of budget cutbacks, this program was to introduce a four month wage and price freeze. Moreover, the planned reduction of working hours was to be stopped indefinitely. The most decisive step was effected in March 1983. With the third devaluation of the franc, the government announced an austerity plan which aimed at a reduction in purchasing power. Greater efforts were to be employed in halting the unaltered high rate of inflation and in balancing deficits of the budget. Even though the fight against unemployment was still the primary issue of public concern (cf. T. 19), the change of policy was apparent.

T. 19:

Mais maintenant nous avons plus que jamais à vaincre sur trois fronts: le chômage, l'inflation, le commerce extérieur ...

En un an, exactement quatorze mois, le chômage s'est accru de 29 % en Allemagne, de 22 % aux Etats-Unis, en France: 4%. Mais, la limitation de la croissance du chômage a entraîné pour nous un effort financier qui n'a pas permis de réduire l'inflation aussi rapidement que chez d'autres.

Quant à cette inflation, c'est une triste histoire qui a commencé avec le choc pétrolier en 1973. Ceux qui gouvernaient à l'époque ont vu le franc perdre en sept ans 40 % de sa valeur par rapport au mark et nous, nous avons dû, à notre tour, dévaluer trois fois. C'est la loi à laquelle nul n'échappe: un pays dont la hausse des prix dépasse celle de ses voisins est condamné à dévaluer d'une façon ou d'une autre.

Telle est la vérité. Je devais vous la dire sans chercher d'excuses trompeuses.

Mais elle nous dicte notre devoir.

Il est temps, grand temps, d'arrêter la machine infernale. Combattre l'inflation, c'est sauver la monnaie et le pouvoir d'achat.

Voilà pourquoi je lutterai, et le gouvernement avec moi, de toutes nos forces, contre ce mal, et mobiliserai le pays à cette fin. (François Mitterrand, in a televised address to the nation on 23 March 1983)

Under the direction of the Minister of Economic Affairs at that time, *Delors*, concrete steps were taken toward the absorption of excess buying power: compulsory loans at a 10% income tax rate, special levies at a rate of 1% of taxable income for reorganizing the Sécurité

Sociale (excluded from these levies were lower income classes), an 8% increase in rates and taxes and additional incentives for long-term savings opportunities. Furthermore, restrictions were placed on the outflow of currency (2000 francs per person annually). The effect of this measure was uncertain from the outset. Nonetheless, this measure was widely discussed in the media.

The savings program and the continued austerity policy under *Fabius* (1984-86) made the trend away from the initial social welfare policy clear. The intended socialist reforms were no longer a point of discussion. This change in direction did not only mean adapting the stabilizing policy of the other social democratic or conservative European countries. It also purported a remarkable approach to the measures contained in the *Plan Barre* introduced in 1976. This course of action naturally did not put an end to the notorious competitive weaknesses of the French economy, for example with regards to the production structure or the trade exchange imbalance between France and West Germany. Only long-term restructuring programs and an improved adjustment to international competitive conditions (cf. Rehfeldt 1986) were able to accomplish this. The Ninth Plan (1984-89), which made the *modernization of the production apparatus* top priority, was to be the first step in this direction.

Even after the political reorientation in 1986, the same economic problems were on the agenda. Price stability had to be secured, growth stimulated, competitiveness promoted and mass unemployment reduced. The *Chirac* Administration (1986-88) attempted to find a solution by means of a large-scale liberalization program which, among other things, included

- the denationalization of state-owned entrepreneurial groups (see 3.5.2),
- complete price decontrol,
- the relaxation of foreign trade controls as well as the introduction of tax shelters for big business,
- the lifting of restrictions on discharge (the so-called "flexibilization", cf. Bue et al. 1987).

Several of these plans were in effect a continuation of the liberalization policies initiated by the previous administration (above all the measures aimed at improving the blanket conditions for big business). The termination of this program was set for the presidential elections in the spring of 1988. Obviously, an overall evaluation is only possible within limits as much of the program's impact will only become noticeable on a medium or long-term basis.

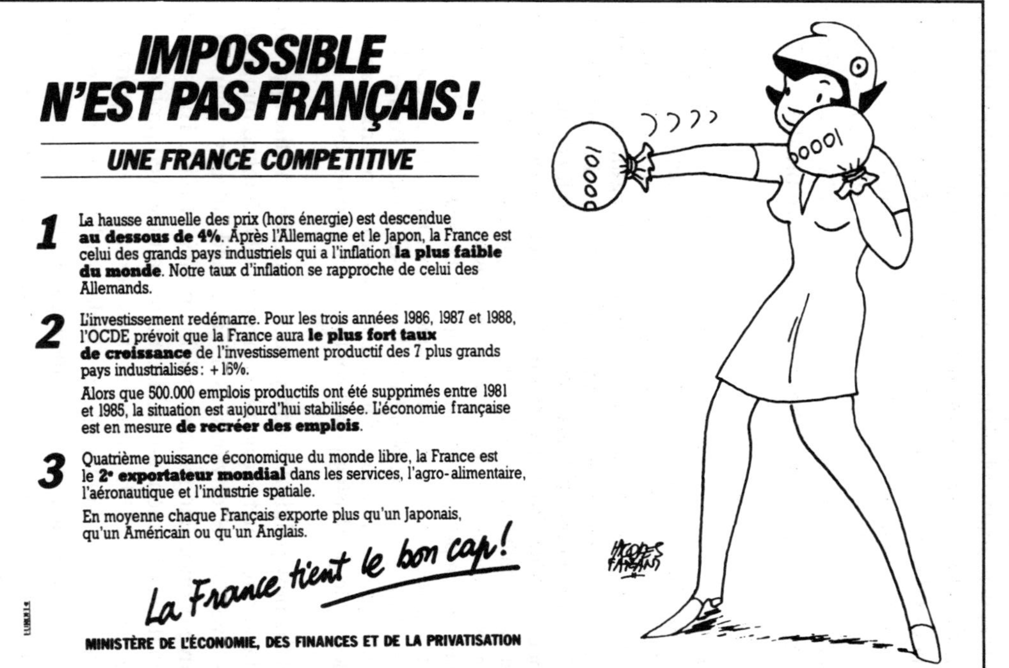

Fig. 35b: Advertisement from a Publicity Campaign of the Chirac Administration (5 Nov. 1987)

There was no total break in continuity. The liberal "turnaround" was limited in comparison to the program originally proclaimed. This administration was able to chalk up the success of having lowered the rate of inflation to below 4% (even though this was ultimately the consequence of the austerity policy in effect since 1982/83). Moreover, extensive wage stabilization and improvements in the investment climate were the result of tax incentives and the repeal of government regulations. Nonetheless, business investments neither reached the forecasted record high nor did they make a decisive breakthrough in the export sector.

The success stories in *Fig. 35b* specifically omit mention of the aspects relevant to this situation. Thus, the national self-esteem might feel flattered to have a leading position in the export of services, agricultural products and high-level technology, but this suffices by no means in adjusting the negative foreign trade balance (see the remarks on the German-French exchange of commodities in 3.6 and 7.2.1). Whenever references are made to a stabilized employment situation, one is talking about an extremely high level of unemployment, i.e. approximately 2.7 million jobless. Besides, the majority of all newly created jobs belong to the category of the so-called *emplois précaires* (part-time jobs, limited contracts, temporary work, internships; cf. Delarue 1987). The liberalization policy made sure that labour became less expensive – once again a continuation of the policies implemented by Minister Fabius. Further drawbacks include the redistribution of income in favour of top earners and the resulting decline in purchasing power for the lower income classes.

In spite of the new political majority elected in 1988 and the approach towards the centre, chief economic concerns only changed minimally. This was even more obvious as France had already adapted a conservative economizing and stabilizing policy in 1983. The sinking of the high unemployment rate still remains an unsolved problem (cf. Uterwedde 1989, p. 233ff.; Pruniaux/Tresmontant 1990). Apart from this and in view of the European single market, there is now a consensus transcending party boundaries as to the necessity for dynamic transition and modernisation of the production apparatus as the means for achieving a *France compétitive.*

4. Social Change – Social Conflicts

(Heinz-Helmut Lüger)

Starting in 1945, France went through an industrialization process which had taken over 100 years in Germany. This development was accompanied by radical social changes. The *structural transformation of the individual economic sectors* deserve special attention as these changes reveal some of the most significant causes and effects of this transition.

4.1 *Shifting Among the Sectors*

Up until the first half of the twentieth century the French economy was predominantly agrarian. *By the end of World War II 37% of the labour force was still engaged in agriculture.* (In Germany, not even 25% of its workers were in agriculture). Nevertheless, this percentage dropped drastically – especially in terms of the gross domestic product. Between 1946 and 1962 alone, the number of employed persons in agriculture decreased by nearly 50%. The shrinking agrarian sector – a widely embraced trend toward the development of a modern industrial society – meant on a large scale the migration of a great many farm workers to industrial regions and the ruin of numerous small-sized agricultural businesses in particular. Such small enterprises were neither able to meet the necessity of greater mechanization nor to set up larger production units. It was especially a problem in the case of smaller production units because adjustments affecting operational methods and the system of sales and distribution had been widely neglected in the agricultural sector prior to 1940.

"The agrarian community experienced only minimal progress and, to a large extent, continued to follow the traditions of its forefathers. It had a low standard of living and was subject to a rough working environment, characterized by little mechanization. Living conditions were poor, and water and electricity a rarity. The type of organization and state of modernization of this sector resulted in a large share of the agricultural product being put towards *immediate living expenses.* At the beginning of the Twentieth century, there were still only 45,000 businesses with more than 6 employed compared with over 3 million businesses with less than 6 employed. Only 250 estates had more than 50 employed. This discrepancy basically remained up to World War II." (Menyesch 1978, p. 34; see Mendras 1970 and Klatzmann 1980, p.11ff.)

This is why the social consequences of the economic structural transformation had, on the whole, an even greater lasting impact on the agrarian sector. Since this developmental tendency in Germany set in much earlier and was spread out over a longer period of time, the effects were less drastic. The number of employed did continue to drop after the war, but these figures were comparatively lower at the outset. Between 1945 and 1975 approximately an additional 2 million people in France had to give up earning their livelihood in agriculture.

The decline in the primary sector was advantageous to industry and services. In these sectors, however, considerable social "adjustment problems" arose. The traditional middle class, i.e. the *craftsmen and small businessmen*, was hit the hardest. The most common types of enterprises – similar to those in the French agrarian sector – were the small-scale and family businesses. The percentage of *self-employed persons* was thus exceptionally high. In 1900 they made up altogether more than 40% of the total workforce. In 1955 they comprised a mere 34%. Within two decades the number of self-employed had fallen to below 16%. This trend which, moreover, was a perpetual source of conflict, was primarily a result of the continuous concentration process forced under the de Gaulle and Pompidou administrations. The trend was aggravated by outdated production methods, a minimal share of turnover and a lack of small export-oriented businesses (see 3.4).

Parallel to this was the growth of the *wage-earning groups* within the same period of time, which was mainly linked to the increasing size of the service sector (from 36% to more than 50% of the labour force). This development was essentially a consequence of the expansion of the industrial sector: "Cette *explosion* du tertiaire est étroitement liée au développement industriel dont il est à la fois la conséquence induite et le moteur. C'est ainsi que depuis 1954 la population employée dans le commerce a augmenté de 35%, celle employée dans les banques et les assurances de 70%, celle employée dans le secteur des services rendus aux entreprises de 250%"(Lasserre 1977, p. 244). Since the mid-70's, however, these figures have been partially on the decline or have remained stagnant. (For a more precise description of the individual social classes and occupational groups, see 4.5).

Germany went through similar developments as those in the French agrarian sector. The shifting among the economic sectors, however, was not as pronounced and occurred within another type of economic structure. Especially owing to the advanced stage of concentration in Germany, the number of self-employed persons was much less (*Table 14*) and, in comparison to France, the fluctuating numbers did not bring about such radical consequences.

Table 14: Self-employed and Salary/Wage Earners in Germany

	1950	1960	1970	1980	1989
Self-employed persons (without contributing family members)	14.5%	12.0%	10.5%	9.0%	8.9%
Salary/wage earners	70.9%	71.6%	83.5%	87.4%	89.1%

(From: Fürstenberg 1978, p. 40f.; Claessens et al. 1985, p. 216; BMWI 1990, p. 11)

4.2 *Intensification of regional differences*

4.2.1 Trend of concentration in urban areas

The outlined socio-economic transformation has also resulted in regional regroupings, namely

- in the *migration from rural, economically disadvantaged areas* on the one hand and
- in the *growing population concentration in certain urban areas* on the other hand.

Fig. 36 shows the extent to which the quantitative relation between rural and urban populations has changed since 1945. According to the chart, by 1982 only one out of four Frenchmen lived in rural areas, i.e. in communities with populations of less than 2000 inhabitants. The main cause of this trend commonly referred to as the "rural exodus" (*exode rural*) is the decline of the agrarian sector. Not only farm workers but also many self-employed felt intimidated by the high investments necessary to strengthen their competitive position. Consequently, they were forced to give up their professions and, for the most part, migrated to urban regions with job opportunities in industry. Other reasons for the migration trend such as working

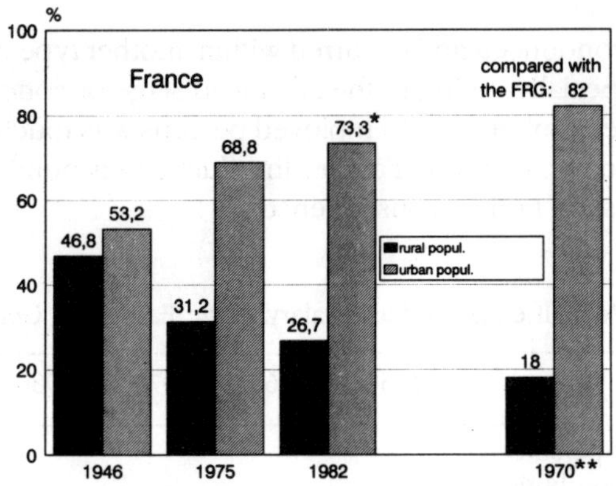

* The percentage here appears rather high since the INSEE no longer employs the same criterion in distinguishing between the *communes rurales* and the *unités urbaines*; since 1982, the relationship between these figures has remained virtually constant.
** Percentages for the following years are not represented here due to the fact that incorporations resulting from local government reforms have placed limits on the comparability of the figures.

Fig. 36: Distribution of Rural and Urban Population.
(From: Armengaud/Fine 1983, p. 109; INSEE 1984a, p. 60; 1991, p. 16; Statist. Bundesamt 1983, p. 50)

conditions, opportunities to advance etc. are more secondary in importance. This domestic migration did not lead to a general urbanization in France but rather intensified the demographic density of several economic centres (cf. *Fig. 37*). One big exception is the region around Paris. The *agglomération parisienne* (often referred to as the "phénomène unique et monstrueux") has a population of about 10 million people, which represents 18.5% of the total population of France. Nevertheless, in the last few years population growth in this region seems to have stagnated, a development that can be traced back to diverse tendencies:

- since the middle of the 1950s, the Paris municipal area has experienced a drop in population of approx. 700,000 inhabitants;
- growth in the *Petite Couronne* (with the Départements Hauts-de-Seine, Seine-St.Denis, Val-de-Marne) has slowed since the end of the 1960s, particularly as a result of a restrictive residential policy;
- in the Départements of the *Grande Couronne* (Seine-et-Marne, Yvelines, Val d'Oise), where numerous new residential settlements, the

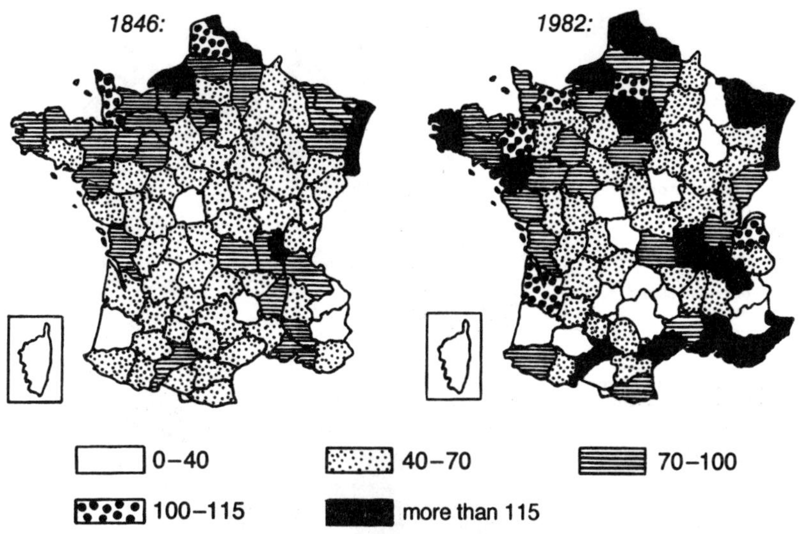

Fig. 37: Population Density of France (inhabitants/km²) in 1846 and 1982. (From: Armengaud 1976, p. 9; INSEE 1984b, p. 11)

so-called *Villes Nouvelles* are being established, on the other hand, there is a relatively large increase in population, with approx. detailed information on this complex re-location process and on changes in the economic structure, cf.: Limouzin 1986, Pletsch 1991.)

The other urban areas in France are continuing to experience significant growth in population. In general, however, it can be seen that there is a tendency similar to the development in Paris. Provided that a certain degree of saturation is reached in urban areas and worsening living conditions progress, the population in the centres of large cities tends to drop, in particular to the advantage of surrounding towns and rural communities:

> Les villes s'installent à la campagne ... Tandis que les grands centres urbains se vident et que les banlieues stagnent, voici que les communes rurales, à la périphérie des villes, se mettent à champignonner. Dans la région parisienne, par exemple, c'est la ruée vers l'Oise. En Provence-Côte d'Azur, la population des communes de moins de deux cents habitants a augmenté de 15 %. Bref, le mouvement d'urbanisation vieux de plus de cent ans a été stoppé net ...
>
> C'est ainsi que le terroir français se repeuple. (F. O. Giesbert, Le Nouvel Observateur, 17 Feb. 1984)

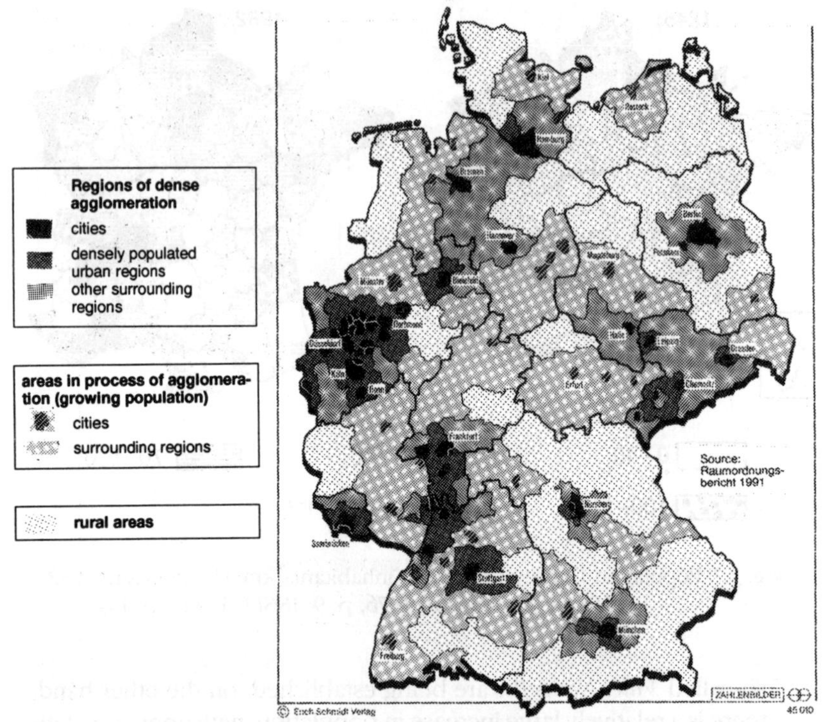

Fig. 38: Population density in the Federal Republic of Germany

Whether or not the results of the 1982 census point to the beginning of a *rurbanisation* in France, a trend towards the urbanization of rural regions, remains doubtful since these changes have only affected the outskirts of large cities up till now.

4.2.2 High population density and decentral urban areas in the Federal Republic of Germany

Germany's particular economic development allowed the country to go through an earlier "reversal of the pre-industrial urban-rural population distribution". Afterwards, as in France, the trend in Germany toward urbanization continued, i.e. particularly the growing concentration of a number of densely populated areas and, ultimately, the decreasing population of central cities. However, there are two major differences between the trends in both countries:

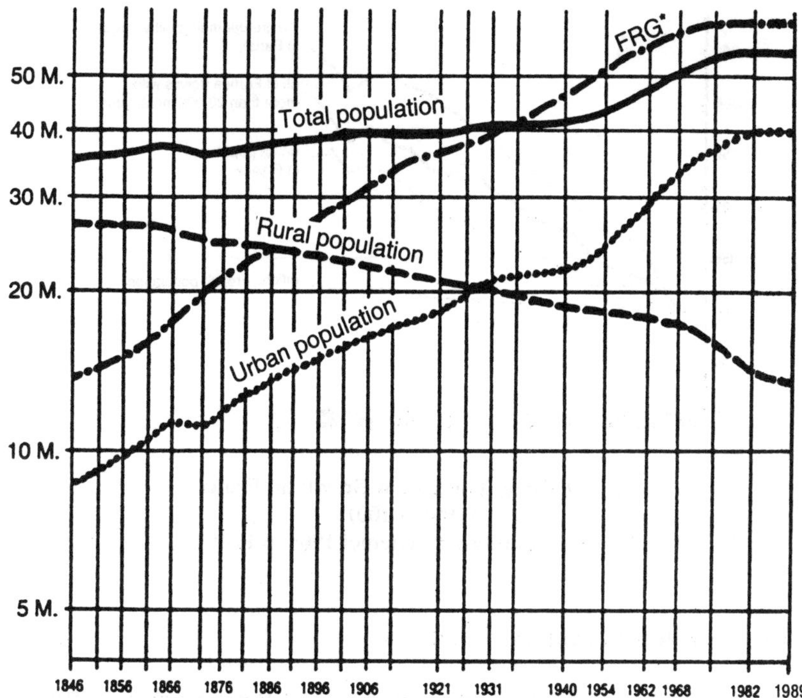

* prior to 1949: territory belonging to the Federal Republic

Fig. 39: Demographic Development.
(From: Dupeux 1982, p. 20; INSEE 1984a, p. 60; Mermit 1991; Statist. Bundesamt 1983, p. 45ff.; 1989, p. 28ff.)

a) The mean *population density* in Germany, 252 inhabitants per square kilometre (153 inhabitants/km² in the new federal states), is *considerably higher* than in France; in fact, it is one of the highest in Europe (following the Netherlands and Belgium; France has 103 inhabitants/km²).

b) The *densely populated areas* (see *Fig. 38*), which at the same time are also industrial centres, have a more *decentral distribution of population*; nearly half of the population lives in one of the urban areas with a density of more than 2000 inhabitants/km². The Rhine-Ruhr region is certainly one of the most densely populated areas in Germany, but due to the structural crisis in the Ruhr area (mining and heavy industry, population migration) it is by no means of such central importance as the region around Paris is for France.

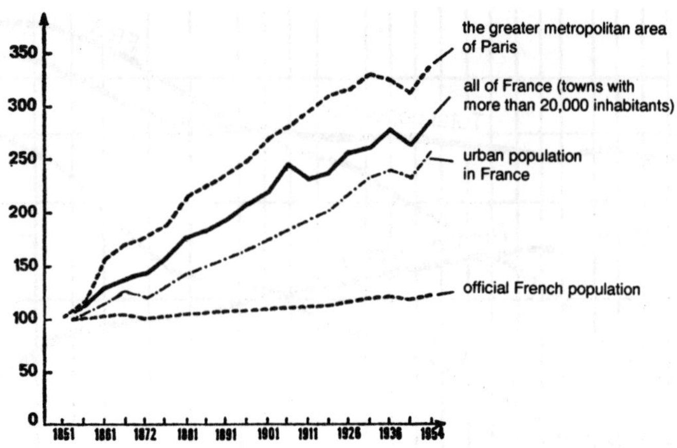

Fig. 40: Urban Population Growth in France.
(1851 = 100)
(From: Carrière/Pinchemel 1963, p.120)

4.2.3 Nineteenth century conditions

It was not just the urbanization trends and the decrease in rural population which were responsible for post-war development in France, but also the increasing industrialization which had set in in the mid-nineteenth century. The first demographic survey of this type began with the 1846 census. *Fig. 39* graphs the population changes in both France and Germany since 1846. Those who profited from the domestic migration, as depicted by *Fig. 40*, were, above all, the region around Paris and other cities containing more than 20,000 inhabitants.

The depopulation of the rural areas is generally attributed to the *worsening situation in the agricultural sector.* This sector has been hit not only by the various *crises agricoles* (crop failures, low grain prices, competition of foreign products etc.), especially between 1850 and 1914, but also by the effects of technological progress. The use of machines and the changes in cultivation methods both increased earnings and, at the same time, ousted a great many *ouvriers agricoles* out of agricultural production.

T. 20:
Surtout, cette époque est celle où l'action de la «révolution agricole» se fit pleinement sentir. Elle se traduisit par un accroissement des rendements,

> et donc des quantités produites. L'on cite toujours, à cet égard, l'emploi des machines, parce que son effet sur la quantité de main-d'oeuvre employée est très apparent. Mais d'autres progrès – assolements complexes, semences sélectionnées, engrais artificiels, etc. – contribuèrent aussi à accroître les rendements. Autrement dit, on put produire davantage avec une main d'oeuvre moindre: dès lors, une partie des travailleurs ruraux, devenue excédentaire, se trouva privée d'emploi. (Armengaud 1976, 68)

On the other hand, the need for a greater labour force came about as a result of larger industrial colonies, an increase in trade and, above all, the expansion of the railway network in each individual region. In turn, the need for labour put even more pressure on the *exode rural.* Altogether, this caused a sweeping regional redistribution of the population. This development continued up into the 1970's and just recently has seemed to come to a standstill. The extent of the migrational trend is shown by a demographic comparison of the years 1846 and 1982 (*Fig. 37*). The migrational trend also affected the distribution of different age groups in that continuous migration to industrialized areas reinforced a certain disproportion between the age groups of many regions. This situation is exemplified by the differences in the population of Northern and Southern France. Generally speaking, there are more people living in the southern départements who are above the age of 65, while the number of young people is comparably higher in the northern parts of France. (For further details and a more precise breakdown of age distribution in France, see INSEE 1984a, p. 88ff.)

4.3 *Problems of population growth*

Despite basic regional changes, it can be seen that, with the exception of the Ile-de-France region, urbanization in France has taken much longer than in several of its neighbouring countries. In England, for instance, city population exceeded rural population as early as 1850. In Germany, this had already been the case since 1890. Only after World War II could France attain such a population distribution.

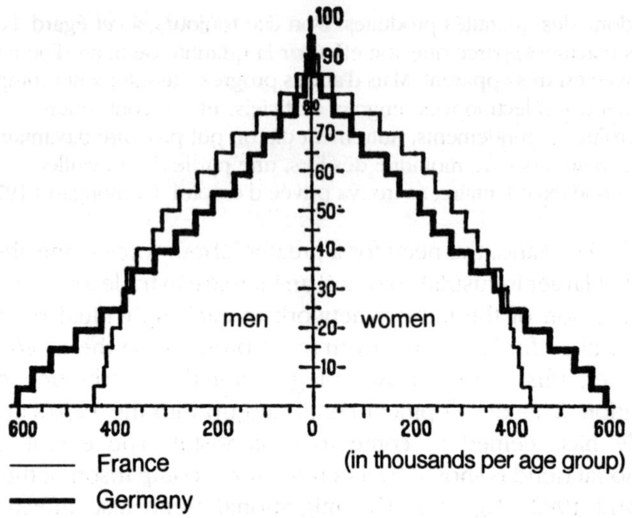

Fig. 41: Age Scale Comparison between France and Germany (1911). (From: Armengaud/Fine 1983, p.7)

The demographic differences between France and its neighbours are based on varying growth patterns. For approximately one century, namely from 1845 to 1945 (cf. *Fig. 39*), France experienced only minimal population growth. Between 1934 and 1936 there was even a drop in population. This not only brought about the existing regional differences in population on a broad scale, but also effected a *disadvantageous age distribution* (a comparably smaller proportion of 0-20 year olds, increased proportion of older age groups). *Fig. 41* shows the age scale in 1911.

Above and beyond that, the demographic stagnation had considerable economic consequences – little increase in demand of goods, retarded industrialization, modest economic growth – and was partially responsible for the basic economic lag in France after World War II. One of the contributing factors to the modest increase in population was the ideal of the small family and, in connection with this, the widespread fear that a high birth rate would endanger the level of wealth already attained. Alain Peyrefitte regards this as a decisive aspect of the *mal français* which still has repercussions today: «Pourtant, les Français n'ont pas encore admis la corrélation entre la croissance démographique et la croissance économique ... Au contraire, dans les pays qui ont effectué leur décollage économique, l'accroissement de la population stimule l'activité économique ... L'inconscient des Français refuse ces réalités. Il conserve, profondément enracinée, la certitude que la croissance démographique entraîne le chômage et la misère. "Plus il y a de bouches à nourrir, moins on se nourrit." *A la fin du XXe siècle, nous réagissons comme nos aïeux au XVIIIe. Nous n'avons toujours pas assimilé les règles du développement économique. Nous gardons la mentalité d'un pays sous-développé, surpeuplé par rapport à ses ressources. Notre malthusianisme remonte à ses propres sources, en provoquant un malthusianisme démographique, dont il se nourrit.*» (Peyrefitte 1976, p.125)

The founder of Malthusianism was the English social researcher Th. R. *Malthus* (1766-1834). The main hypothesis of his *Essay on the Principle of Population* was that population growth increases more rapidly than crop yield, thus inevitably giving rise to the misery of the human race. (Today, the concept of "Malthusianism" mainly stands for an obsolete, historically refuted way of thinking.)

It is questionable, on the other hand, whether or not it is still possible to think exclusively in terms of the relationship between population and economic growth (as Peyrefitte does) in a period characterized by unemployment and the destruction of natural resources.

Only after the end of World War II did France experience another growth in population. Within just two decades the French population increased by approximately 10 million people (more than in previous century). It was not only the general improvement of external conditions which helped stimulate the economy during the period of recovery. Governmental demographic policies also played a decisive role. Such measures were the result of lengthy discussions on the *crise démographique* (cf. Trotignon 1968, p. 119ff.) which specifically dealt with improving the financial situation of families and providing grants and infrastructure facilities for child care. As in other European countries, however, this trend only lasted up to the beginning of the 60's. Since 1964, the population growth rate has been on the decline, once again bringing criticism into the arena: "On retourne au malthusianisme, au suicide collectif" (Peyrefitte 1976, p. 123).

Its 1982 census reported that France had around 54.3 million inhabitants. Although these numbers have slightly increased in the last couple of years (especially due to the foreign immigration to France), the excess of births over deaths has steadily decreased. The graph above (*Fig. 42*) provides an overview of the age group structure and the most recent demographic history. Most striking is the distribution

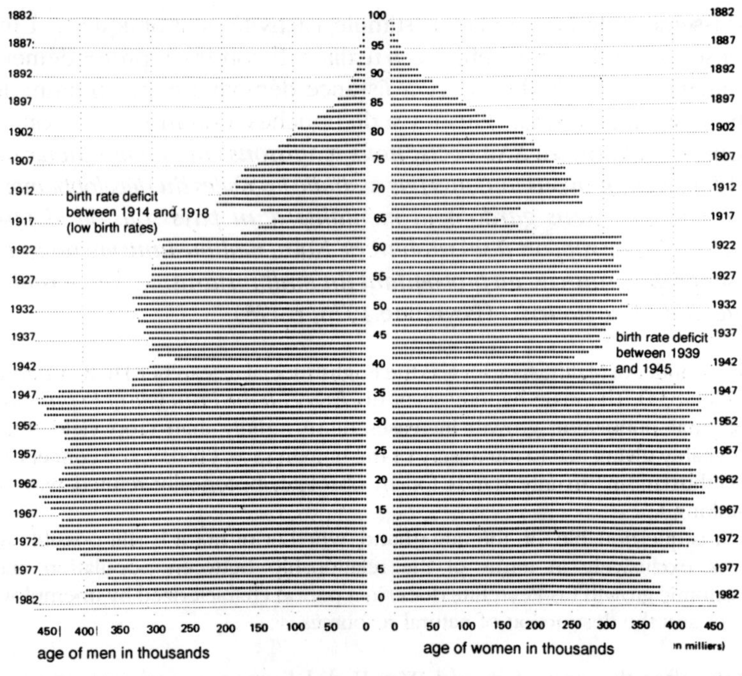

Fig. 42: Age Scale in France.
(From: INSEE 1984a, p. 87)

of the age groups (in comparison to the post-war period, a low ratio of youth under 20 (28.7%) and a relatively high ratio of those above 65 (13.9%)) as well as the demographic effects of both world wars.

As a result of the birth-rate deficit in Germany since 1974, there has been a slight drop in population (1974: 62.1 million, 1978: 61.3 million, 1988: 61.1 million inhabitants). For a long time the low birth-rate had been concealed by the flow of immigration, especially of displaced persons, refugees from East Germany (more than 3 m. by 1961) as well as foreign workers. A new wave of immigration has been under way since the end of the 1980s. Not including those moving from the GDR (1989: 330,000), there were nearly 1 m. immigrants to the Federal Republic of Germany from Eastern Europe between 1989 and 1991 (primarily from Poland, Rumania and the Soviet Union). In legal terms, according to the provisions of the German refugee law, this group of "immigrants of German origin" enjoyed the same status as did refugees; considerable funding was made available by the federal

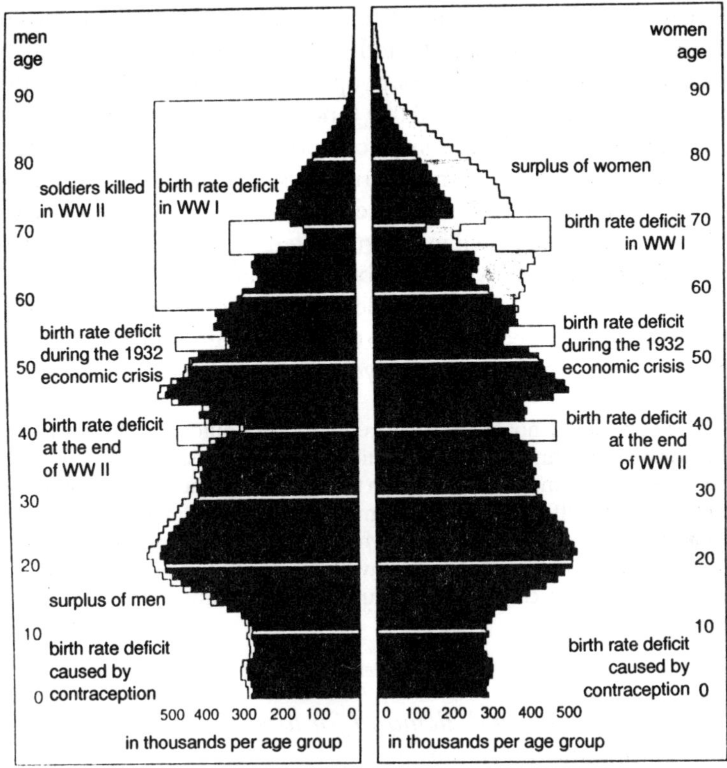

Fig. 43: Age Scale in Germany.
(From: Bulka/Lücking 1989, p. 19; cf. Cornelius 1988, p. 23)

government to pave the way for their integration into society (eg, language instruction, unemployment payments, higher and continuing education). In view of the favourable age distribution among these immigrants (with two thirds being of employable age), people hoped for a reduction in average population among the resident population and – long-term – an improvement in "employable potential". Unfortunately, the preference given these immigrants in their search for housing accommodation resulted in an almost total collapse of the housing market.

The social tension arising in response to this situation vented itself primarily on another group of immigrants, those seeking asylum. Certainly not the least important factor here was a carefully directed campaign on the part of the Christian people's parties opposing "asylum seekers" and unrestricted right to asylum (liberal asylum laws). And in fact the number of people seeking asylum in the period from 1989-91 was approx. 570,000 (and on the rise), with a considerable number of so-called economic or poverty refugees among them, particularly from countries in Eastern and Southern Europe. In spite of this, it is clear that the asylum debate is all too often motivated by party politics and little interested in the true extent of the immigration wave (cf. the figures cited above). It can be seen from the age scale for West Germany overall (*Fig. 43*) that the demographic problems here (higher ratio of older-aged persons, low birth-rate) are very similar to those in France and, to some extent, are even more obvious.

Relatively speaking, however, such trends do not automatically mean problems caused in connection with annuity payments – just to name one of the most common arguments. Especially in terms of the financial aspect of welfare benefits, it is the effect of the employment ratio, i.e. the ratio of those in the labour force to the total population, which is of greater significance. Up until now, no pioneer solution seems to have been found for containing the continuing employment crises in both France and Germany.

4.4 *Population trend, demand for labour,* immigration étrangère

4.4.1 Early deficits in the job market

The population trend and foreign population size are indirectly related. Beginning in the mid-nineteenth century, the stagnating birth-rate and the higher ratio of older-aged people continued to bring about situations in which the increasing demand for labour could no longer be met. France required an especially large number of unskilled workers as industrialization progressed in certain regions and businesses began employing machinery and switching over to mass production. In this particular situation, there were not enough people who had left the agricultural sector to constitute an adequate workforce.

This is why French industry started recruiting on a large- scale basis foreign workers from Belgium, Germany, Switzerland, Italy and Spain. They were mainly employed in Paris and several départements near the border (Nord, Moselle, Bas/Haut-Rhin, Var, Bouches-du-Rhône).

Beginning in 1880, the number of foreigners totalled more than one million, representing 7-8% of the total workforce. By the turn of the century, the shortage of labour was so great that the French industry had to intensify its foreign labour recruitment program. For the coal mining industry alone, tens of thousands of Italians had been brought into the country within a short period of time. Since much of the available labour was absorbed by key industrial areas (ultimately due to higher wages), a precarious situation emerged for the agricultural sector. The deficit in the agricultural workforce could no longer be remedied by recruiting more seasonal workers from neighbouring countries. Consequently, France concluded labour recruitment agreements with Poland and in 1913 more than 20,000 polish workers were employed in the French agrarian sector.

Prior to the First World War aliens in France comprised 3% of the total population (not including naturalizations). On the one hand, this pointed to the economic necessity of the so-called "importations de main-d'oeuvre" and the impediment of industrial development by stagnating population growth. On the other hand, foreign immigration has not only been an important economic factor but also an important demographic one despite xenophobic reactions beginning in the nineteenth century (cf. Gaspard/Servan-Schreiber 1984, p. 70ff.).

The *recruitment of foreign labour during the World Wars* served an entirely different function. During both World Wars (but also as early as 1870/71), France fell heavily back on its colonies, particularly the Maghreb countries Algeria, Morocco, and Tunesia, in order to replace the French workers who had been conscripted.

> La guerre (de 1914-18) fut l'occasion d'une déportation de travailleurs maghrébins vers la France pour remplacer les soldats et les travailleurs français absents. 132000 Maghrébins sont alors recrutés pour travailler dans les fermes et les usines d'armement ... Lorsque éclata le deuxième conflit mondial, la France puisa de nouveau dans ses colonies du Maghreb pour renforcer ses effectifs. (Benchenane 1984, 209f.)

The author then adds with embitterment:

> Pour la troisième fois en moins d'un siècle, les Maghrébins musulmans allaient verser leur sang pour défendre la France qui, par ailleurs, les colonisait, les dominait, les exploitait et les humiliait. Plus même, on peut affirmer – et l'Histoire est là pour l'attester – que les Maghrébins firent plus pour libérer la France que beaucoup de Français eux-mêmes dont le gouvernement officiel avait choisi la voie de la collaboration, alors que la majorité des citoyens français optaient pour le désarmement moral et l'attentisme.

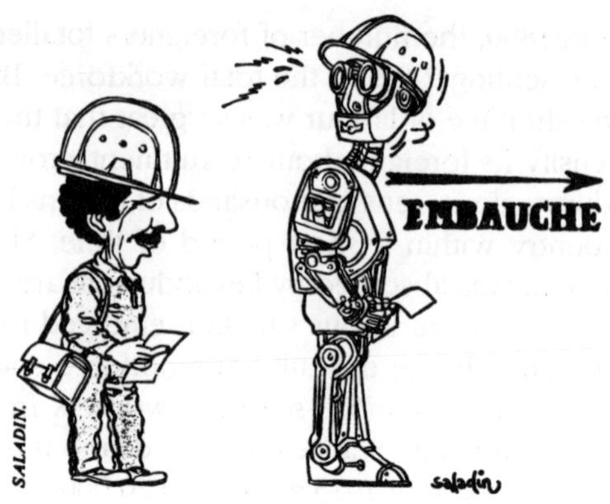

Fig. 44
(From: Le Monde 1984, p.12)

After 1918 the underhanded French economy lacked about 3 million labourers so that in the years that followed the number of foreigners climbed rapidly from 1.1 to 2.7 million. In 1931, the number of foreigners made up 6.6% of the total population, a percentage which is almost equivalent to that of the 80's (cf. *Table 15*; cf. Lebon 1990, p. 25f.). The only real difference between the foreign population then and now is the new composition of nationalities.

Once again, a similar situation emerged after 1945. The losses caused by the war, the country's economic recovery and the minimal excess of births over deaths in the interim between the wars gave rise to another continuous wave of immigration. The peak of immigration was reached in the 60's during the economic boom. Furthermore, more than 1 million so-called "rapatriés" immigrated from Algeria which had won its independence.

When the recession began in 1974, the French government ordered an immigration bar. Ever since then, the immigration quota has basically only changed as a result of family reunification. The extent of illegal immigration (*immigration clandestine*) is for the most part overestimated. *Table 15* provides a specific breakdown of the alien population in France (the values have scarcely changed since). The *Maghrébins* (above all Algerians and Moroccans) constitute the largest group. They are also the primary target of xenophobic attacks. The regional distribution of the foreign population is also important to note. Nearly two-thirds live in the regions Ile-de-France, Rhône-Alpes and Provence-Côte d'Azur. In these areas foreigners often comprise more than 20% of the population.

Table 15: Foreign Residential Population in France (in millions of inhabitants)

	1931		1975		1982	
Total population	41.23		52.60		54.27	
Foreigners	2.71	(=6.6%)	3.44	(=6.5%)*	3.68	(=6.8%)
Origin:						
– Europe	2.46	(=90.5%)	2.10	(=61.1%)	1.76	(=47.8%)
Belgium	0.25		0.06		0.05	
Germany/FRG	0.07		0.04		0.04	
Italy	0.81		0.46		0.33	
Poland	0.51		0.09		0.06	
Portugal	0.05		0.76		0.76	
Spain	0.35		0.50		0.32	
– Africa	0.11	(=3.9%)	1.19	(=34.6%)	1.57	(=42.8%)
Algeria }			0.71		0.80	
Morocco }	0.09		0.26		0.43	
Tunesia }			0.14		0.19	
– Other countries	0.14		0.15		0.35	

* INSEE estimates are approx. 10-15% below the figures released by the Department of the Interior.

(From: INSEE 1984a, p.90; cf. Mermet 1986, p.171)

The *travailleurs immigrés* are hit worse by unemployment than the native workers as they are largely hired for unskilled jobs and are the first victims of rationalization measures (cf. *Fig. 44*).

Although it has not yet been possible to point to a displacement of native labour by foreign workers (as it has been suggested by extremists and various right-wing groups: "2 millions d'immigrés – 2 millions de chômeurs"), competition does seem to have become more intense even for less appealing jobs. For instance, more and more native Frenchmen are seeking jobs normally filled by foreigners.

In addition to ethnic and social factors, this development might be of greater significance in explaining xenophobic tendencies than certain tolerance limits which are commonly referred to. The so-called *tipping-point* research, which postulates definite limits for the influx of foreigners, is partially based on inapplicable prerequisites (cf. Gaspard/Servan-Schreiber 1984, p. 149ff.; Tsiakalos 1983, p. 78ff.).

4.4.2 Foreign labour in the German economy

Immigration to France has had a long tradition connected with demographic problems which virtually go back to the beginning of the country's industrialization period. By contrast, foreign immigration to Germany took place against the background of mass emigration resulting from the population explosion in the nineteenth century. It was only around the turn of the century when Germany began to experience a gradual transition from emigration to immigration (Bade 1983, p. 29ff). Thus, in several regions there arose a need for labour which no longer could be met by native recruitment. The sectors affected included agriculture (due to rural exodus), industry and construction (due to the continuous booming economy). This was especially a problem for the mining industry in Upper Silesia and the Ruhr area as well as for the agricultural industry in East Prussia. In 1910 the number of foreigners totalled more than one million, out of which 800,000 alone came from Poland. At the same time (and contrary to economic interests) the Prussian administration made efforts to curb the flow of immigration both in terms of the numbers of immigrants and the regions to which they immigrated. This policy primarily purported to counteract the danger of a further "polonization". Above and beyond this, restrictive measures (mandatory departure, prohibition of family reunification) were intended to preclude *seasonal migrant workers* from becoming permanent resident workers.

In the Weimar Republic, this system of foreign labour continued up to the economic depression. Then with the beginning of World War II, the *national socialist government in Germany* adopted a *new foreign labour policy*. Essentially, this policy involved compulsory recruitment in the occupied territories in order to provide the armament and agricultural industries with the workforce they were lacking. During this time, about 2 million forced labourers were deported from Poland alone. Altogether, the number of displaced persons totalled around 7.5 million.

At the end of the 1950's, a labour situation similar to the one in France emerged in Germany. A massive recruitment of additional labour became necessary in order to ensure economic growth (cf. McRae 1980, p.11f; Knight/Kowalsky 1991, p.43ff.). Consequently, all available means were employed in promoting the "import of labour", the majority of the foreigners coming from the agrarian regions of the Mediterranean countries, especially Turkey. The immigration bar in 1973 brought this development to a temporary halt. In 1989, about 4.8

Table 16: Foreign residential population in Germany

	1961 (%)	1970 (%)	1980 (%)	1986 (in 1000)	(%)
Turks	1.0	15.8	32.8	1435	1.8
Yugoslavians	2.4	17.3	14.2	591	13.1
Italians	28.7	19.3	13.9	537	11.9
Greeks	6.1	11.5	6.7	280	6.2
Spaniards	6.4	8.2	4.0	149	3.3
Others	55.4	27.9	28.4	1521	33.7

(From: Hübner/Rohlfs 1988, p.61ff.)

million foreigners were living in West Germany (1.7 million of which belonged to the labour force), thus comprising 7.7% of the total population. *Table 16* provides an overview of the immigrant population in Germany.

In the eastern federal states, on the other hand, the percentage of foreigners is significantly lower. At the end of 1989 the were approx. 191,000 foreigners (primarily Vietnamese and Poles) residing in the GDR, i.e. not even 1.2% of the total population. In spite of this minimal percentage of foreigners, there was a marked increase in anti-foreigner sentiment in the new federal states after re-unification. Figure 45 provides an overview of the regional distribution of the foreign population.

The recruitment of foreign labour, which for many years brought considerable economic advantages, is now meeting with growing criticism in Germany as it has in France. This is not only reflected by increasing xenophobic tendencies but also by restrictive government action (limits on family reunification, constraints on the issuing of alien's residence permits, encouraging alien departure). In fact, it seems as if "a considerable percentage of the foreign population is becoming redundant from an economic point of view" (Manfrass 1984a, p. 62; cf. Gautier 1983). These foreigners are now subject to the consequences of a lack of long-term alien policies. This situation is even graver in light of the fact that the widely segmented job market, i.e. the division of work done by foreigners and by natives, is becoming less important as crisis and mass unemployment progress (cf. Dohse 1983).

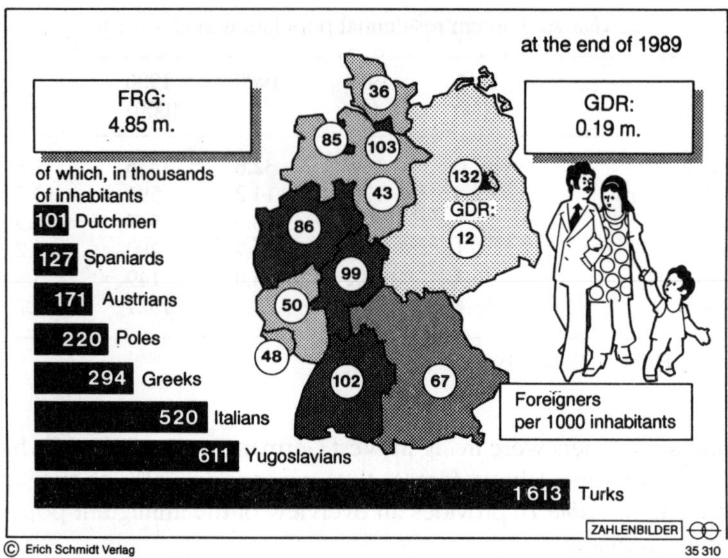

Fig. 45: Regional Distribution of the Foreign Population

4.5 *Work force structure and social classes*

We have already seen how the conditions of industrialization in France are closely related to the country's social structure. The reciprocal relationship between economic and demographic developments is a good example of this. An overview of the social structures will further illustrate the interdependency of economic and social factors.

4.5.1 Facts on gainful occupation

As a rule, information on *gainful occupation* is particularly important for social research. What does this mean in terms of the different economic sectors? What is the distribution of the various occupational groups and what developmental trends are discernable? Section 4.1 dealt with the general shifts and processes of transition among agriculture, industry and services. The following section will now focus its attention on the individual social groups.

Table 17a: Distribution of the Different Occupational Groups in France

catégorie socioprofessionnelles	(milliers)	(% des actifs)
1. Agriculteurs exploitants	1475	6,4
2. Artisans, commerçants, chefs d'entreprise	1835	7,9
3. Cadres, professions intellectuelles supérieures	1895	8,2
4. Professions intermédiaires	3971	17,1
5. Employés	6247	27,0
6. Ouvriers (y compris agricoles)	7749	33,4
7. Retraités	7436	
8. Autres sans activité professionnelle	23665	
Total	54273	
dont actifs (postes 1 à 6)	23172	100

(From: INSEE 1984a, p. 61; 1991, p. 33)

In France it is usual for occupational groups to be statisticised according to a standard framework which contains 8, 24 or 42 *catégories socioprofessionelles* depending upon the level of differentiation. On a more specific level a further 489 *professions* are differentiated (or 455 if the statistics are solely limited to employed persons). In these categories data is compiled according to occupation, qualifications, function, company size and economic sector. At the same time, such data also serves as the basis of assessment for the national census (*rencensements*) which is taken every six to eight years. Naturally, the categorical breakdown is influenced by certain presuppositions and interpretations. The definability of certain sizes as well as the classification and homogeneity of various groups have repeatedly been a problem. Nevertheless, the data which is broken down into occupational/social categories seems to lend itself to further social research (of a different theoretical provenance as well). The 1982 census was slightly revised and adapted to new occupational designations (cf. INSEE 1984a, p. 30f.; Desrosières et al. 1983). However, in order to warrant a basis of comparison with less recent data, the older classification scheme was not changed. *Table 17a* lists the *catégories socioprofessionelles* for level 8 and *Table 17b* lists those for levels 24 and 42.

Before we take a closer look at the data, a general remark concerning employment figures should be made. For the past several years, the ratio of the working population (employed and unemployed) in France to the country's total population has been about 43%, only slightly below that in Germany. At the same time, the percentage of working women (43%) is still noticeably lower than that of working men (57%). The discrepancy becomes even more apparent when the ratio of women to the total population is taken into account: out of

Table 17b: Profession by Groups in France

catégories socioprofessionnelles niveaux 8 et 24	niveaux 42	hommes (milliers)	femmes (milliers)
1. *Agriculteurs exploitants*		*927*	*548*
10. Agriculteurs exploitants	11. Agriculteurs sur petite exploitation	419	270
	12. Agriculteurs sur moyenne exploitation	290	161
	13. Agriculteurs sur grande exploitation	218	117
2. *Artisans, commerçants, chefs d'entreprise*		*1218*	*616*
21. Artisans	21. Artisans	685	219
22. Commerçants et assimilés	22. Commerçants et assimilés	422	375
23. Chefs d'entreprise 10 salariés et plus	23. Chefs d'entreprise 10 salariés et plus	111	22
3. *Cadres, professions intellectuelles supérieures*		*1425*	*470*
31. Professions libérales	31. Professions libérales	173	66
32. Cadres de la fonction publique, professions intellectuelles et artistiques	33. Cadres de la fonction publique	186	59
	34. Professeurs, professions scientifiques	193	160
	35. Professions de l'information, des arts et des spectacles	70	47
36. Cadres d'entreprise	37. Cadres administratifs et commerciaux d'entreprise	444	114
	38. Ingénieurs et cadres techniques d'entreprise	359	24
4. *Professions intermédiaires*		*2369*	*1602*
41. Professions intermédiaires de l'enseignement, de la santé, de la fonction publique et assimilés	42. Instituteurs et assimilés	283	493
	43. Professions intermédiaires de la santé et du travail social	157	457

	44. Clergé, religieux	33	26
	45. Professions intermédiaires administratives de la fonction publique	148	130
46. Professions intermédiaires administratives et commercial des entreprises	46. Professions intermédiaires administratives et commerciales des entreprises	597	399
47. Techniciens	47. Techniciens	615	62
48. Contremaîtres, agents de maîtrise	48. Contremaîtres, agents de maîtrise	536	35
5. *Employés*		*1725*	*4522*
51. Employés de la fonction publique	52. Employés civils et agents de service de la fonction publique	418	1285
	53. Policiers et militaires	359	21
54. Employés administratifs d'entreprise	54. Employés administratifs d'entreprise	639	1892
55. Employés de commerce	55. Employés de commerce	157	585
56. Personnels des services directs aux particuliers	56. Personnels des services directs aus particuliers	152	739
6. *Ouvriers*		*6148*	*1601*
6. Ouvriers qualifiés	62. Ouvriers qualifiés de type industriel	1428	175
	63. Ouvriers qualifiés de type artisanal	1371	138
	64. Chauffeurs	556	10
	65. Ouvriers qualifiés de la manutention, du magasinage et du transport	383	33
66. Ouvriers non qualifiés	67. Ouvriers non qualifiés de type industriel	1451	902
	68. Ouvriers non qualifiés de type artisanal	710	297
69. Ouvriers agricoles	69. Ouvriers agricoles	249	46

catégories socioprofessionnelles niveaux 8 et 24	niveaux 42	hommes (milliers)	femmes
7. *Retraités*		*3620*	*3816*
71. Anciens agriculteurs exploitants	71. Anciens agriculteurs exploitants	583	763
72. Anciens artisans, commerçants, chefs d'entreprise	72. Anciens artisans, commerçants, chefs d'entreprise	332	423
73. Anciens cadres et professions intermédiaires	74. Anciens cadres	248	96
	75. Anciennes professions intermédiaires	383	339
76. Ancienes employés et ouvriers	77. Ancienes employés	729	1247
	78. Ancienes ouvriers	1345	948
8. *Autres personnes sans activité professionnelle*		*9061*	*14605*
81. Chômeurs n'ayant jamais travaillé	81. Chômeurs n'ayant jamais travaillé	128	225
82. Inactifs divers (autres que retraités)	83. Militaires du contingent	251	–
	84. Elèves, étudiants (de 15 ans ou plus)	2109	2169
	85. Personnes diverses sans activité professionnelle de moins de 60 ans	6444	10363
	86. Personnes diverses sans activitě professionnelle de 60 ans et plus	129	1848
	Total	*26493*	*27780*
	dont actifs (postes 1 à 6)	*13812*	*9359*

(From: INSEE 1984a, p. 61; 1991, p. 33)

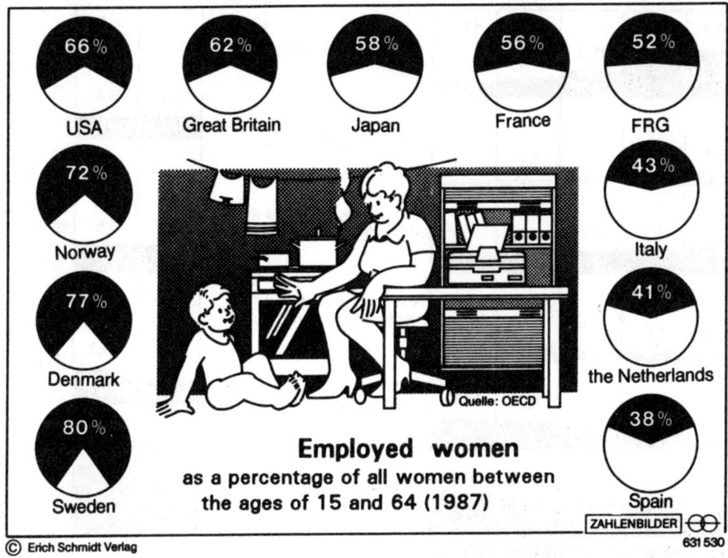

Fig. 46: An International Comparison of Women in Employment

every 100 women of employable age (15 - 64 years old), only about 56 are employed, while the figure for men is around 76%. It should be noted, however, that there is scarcely any difference between employment figures for men and women in the 17 - 25 year-old range (cf. *Fig. 46* for an international comparison of female employment percentages).

Contrary to other conclusions, the ratio of working women to the total population in France is actually no greater than in Germany, where the ratio is nearly identical. (The statistics are only different for working mothers with children under 18. In this case the ratio in France is over 50%, while in Germany it is barely 35%). In both France and Germany the occupations of women seem to be limited to relatively few areas. Apart from a few *professions intermédiaires* in the educational, health and administrative fields, most women work as clerks or unskilled workers and perform jobs which require fewer professional qualifications. Such occupations are characterized by lower pay and a greater possibility of job loss (cf. *Table 18*). Consequently, the female workforce is more vulnerable to rationalization measures in the service sectors and especially in the production branches. Although the rate of unemployment for women is not yet as high as it is for foreigners,

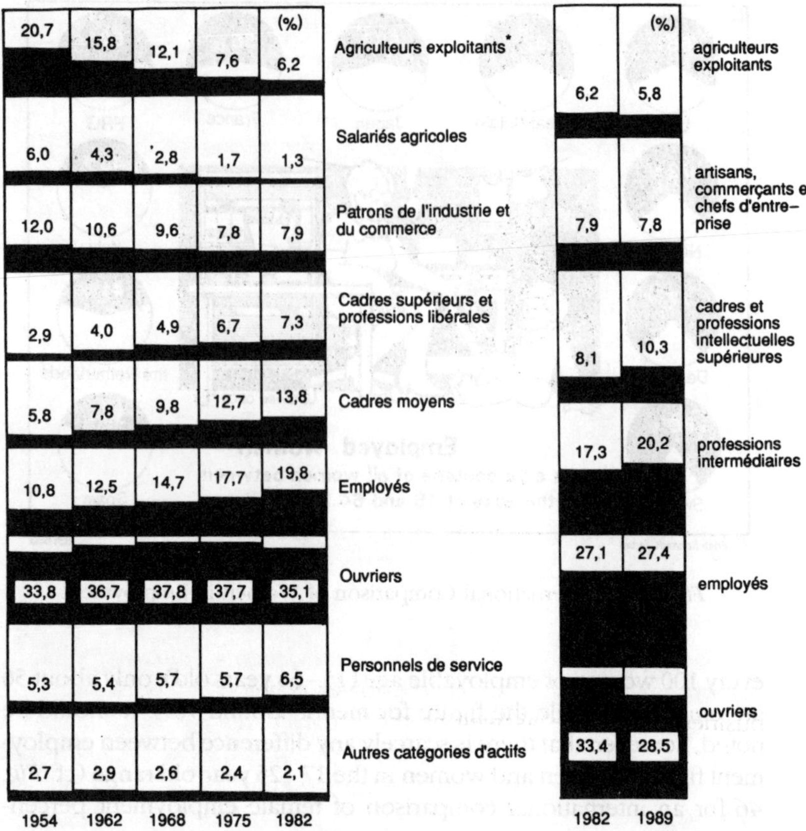

* categories according to the old nomenclature (as compared with *Table 17a*, deviating percentages are a result of different categorizations)

Fig. 47: Development of the Various Occupational Groups in France. (From: Armengaud/Fine 1983, p.116; INSEE 1984a, 1990)

it is clearly higher than the rate of unemployment for men. This fact holds true for both France and Germany (cf. Reichel 1984, p. 333; Commission 1990, p. 87ff.).

4.5.2 Distribution of occupational groups

Within the scheme of occupational groups and their related social structure in France, workers still comprise by far the largest group. They make up approximately 30% of the labour force. Within this group, the percentage of skilled workers (*ouvriers qualifiés*) in industry and crafts is the highest. The number of unskilled workers (*ouvriers non qualifés*, previously known as *ouvriers spécialisés* and *manoeuvres*), who are mostly engaged in industrial production, is also surprisingly high. In this category there is a large proportion of foreigners and women. By contrast, as a result of the decreased importance of the agrarian sector there are very few agricultural workers (*ouvriers agricoles*).

A look at the development within the last couple of decades shows that the absolute number of workers has been stagnating and that the relative number of workers has even been on the decline (*Fig. 47*). While the ratio of workers is slowly declining as a result of the structural transformation of the economy, the ratio of the *employés* in particular (roughly translated to mean employees and low-ranking civil servants) is steadily increasing. Since 1954 this ratio has more than doubled. It is important to note that the category *employés* primarily comprises those who are in the lower echelons of public service, business and trade as well as those considered to be service staff (domestic help etc.) according to the latest INSEE nomenclature. It sometimes appears difficult to precisely define the working classes. Moreover, the rapid growth of this occupational category is characterized by an extraordinarily high percentage of women (72.4%). Conversely, men dominate 79.8% of the middle and senior managerial positions (in *Table 17b* these are classified as *professions intermédiaires* and *cadres* under 33, 37-38, 46-48).

The *professions intermédiaires*, the third largest occupational group in France, has become even more significant since it now comprises 17.1% of the total workforce. This rather heterogenous category includes primary school teachers, clergymen, middle-management staff in administration, business and the social service area as well as technicians and master craftsmen. The high growth rates of middle management and technical occupational groups etc. are a result of the altered qualification demands described above and are an indication of the industrial progress in France. The *professions intermédiaires* together with some groups of employees are generally classed under the category *couche moyenne salariée*, to which about one third of the labour force belongs.

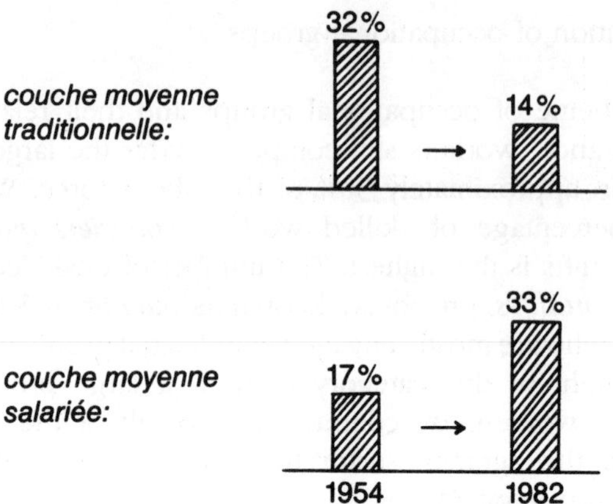

Fig. 48: Transformation of the French Middle Class

In contrast to the expanding middle class wage and salary earners, the "traditional" self-employed middle class is in the process of shrinking:

- From 1954 to 1990 the number of self-employed farmers (*agriculteurs exploitants*) dropped to less than a quarter of what it was before,
- In the same period of time, the percentage of independent contractors, especially skilled tradesmen and merchants (*petits artisans* and *commerçants*), significantly decreased from 12% to 7.2%. In terms of the ratio of middle class self-employed to wage and salary earners, a reversal has to a certain extent been taking place since the 1950s (*Fig. 48*).

These figures are indicative of two fundamental trends. The *proportion of wage and salary earners* began to *increase* and the *agricultural, retail and skilled trade sectors* (the smaller industrial establishments to a lesser extent) began to *lose* their *functional relevance* in an economic system based on concentration and centralization. The decline of the traditional middle class, which at one point was not only the backbone of the Third Republic but was also largely shielded from economic competition by protectionist measures, is still the cause of a great number conflicts (cf. 3.4.2). These conflicts have been additionally aggravated by the fact that the renouncement of individual independence and the taking up of factory work are deemed as a form of unacceptable social degradation according to petty bourgeois morals (for a description of the resulting political radicalization up to fascist

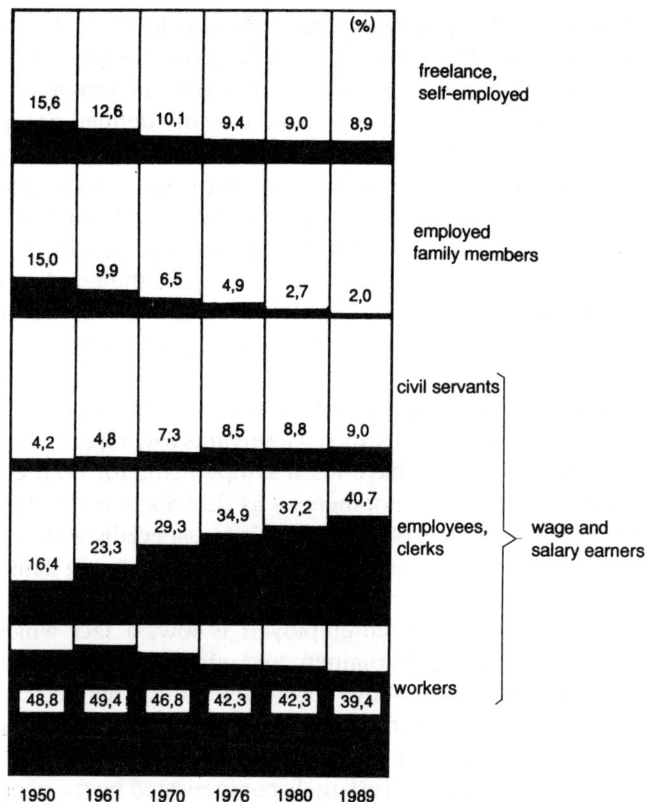

Fig. 49: Development of Gainful Employment in Germany. (From: BMWI 1990, p. 11; Inst. der deutschen Wirtschaft 1990, p. 11; the categories selected here do not correspond to the categories used for France)

tendencies, see Kühnl 1979, p.80ff.). Toward the close of the nineteenth century, the livelihood of the small industries started to become threatened. During this time small-scale operators, especially in such economically dynamic areas as metalworking, mining and textiles, were forced to give way to technologically advanced large-scale enterprises (Haupt 1976, p. 75). Not until half a century later did retail tradesmen experience a comparable crisis as new forms of distribution such as the *centres commerciaux* emerged.

The *cadres* and the *professions intellectuelles supérieures* make up another heterogenous group. This category includes all professionals (the *professions libérales*) such as doctors, pharmacists, lawyers etc. as well as the growing group of high school and college instructors and, finally, the *cadres* in the narrower sense. In its revised usage, this term, which only partially coincides with the category of senior or top executives in English, does not represent a clearly defined group of employed persons. It includes executive corporate managers as well as scientific staff, engineers and high-ranking employees in public service. Those people who belong to this category have typically graduated from a *Grande Ecole* and earn above-average salaries.

Only in certain respects is it possible to compare the employment structure of France and Germany since the statistical categories differ much too greatly. Therefore, the overview in *Fig. 49* provides only a few points of comparison.

For the most part, the relative decline in the working classes and the increased number of employees and civil servants (owing to the growing significance of services) have been symptomatic for both countries. Nonetheless, these developments – as described in chapter 3 – have taken place in different economic settings, especially with regard to the specific distribution of sectors and branches. Thus, any statistical parallels are not necessarily indicative of equivalent conditions. It is significant that the ratio of self-employed is low, a fact which is attributed to the absence of a prominent "old middle class". The radical shrinking process, which has above all affected the agrarian sector, has led to fewer social conflicts in France. This is probably because the development there took place over a longer period of time, thus in a less abrupt manner, and could be largely compensated by the expanding industrial sector. The ratio of wage and salary earners rose steadily up to 1990 and since then it has changed only minimally. In Germany, salary and wage workers now make up nearly 90% of the workforce.

4.5.3 Models and criteria of social classes

Obviously, the "occupational position" criterion does not even designate a roughly unified social group. For this reason, a variety of models have been developed, which, with the inclusion of other distinguishing characteristics, aim at establishing a coherent social classification system. The most decisive criteria in the *social class model* are income, education, property and also occupational position. Other class analyses are based on self- or outside appraisals within a given range. The social structure of the population and its breakdown into classes (e.g. upper class, upper/middle/lower middle class, upper/lower lower class as well as the extreme déclassé) can also vary to a considerable degree (Claessens et al. 1985, p. 290ff., see also Glass/König 1968).

In connection with the marxist analysis the *class analytical approach* is, by contrast, based on the ownership of capital goods. The distribution of wealth, income and consumption as well as the opposing interests of individuals, societal groups and classes are derived from this factor (Leisewitz 1980, p. 92). The working class and the bourgeois form the two basic classes of common society and are analogous to the opposition between capital proprietorship and paid labour. Then there are the intermediary or middle classes which are heterogenous in themselves and comprise the self-employed middle classes (farmers, skilled tradesmen and retailers), the intelligence (experts) and the middle class wage earners (supervisory and managerial staff).

These approaches are by no means so contrary as one tends to believe and definitely do contain parallels. However, they could be made even more specific with regard to their premises, indicators and classifications according to rank and class. Due to the constraints of this text book, only related specialized literature can be referred to (cf. Bischoff 1976, Leisewitz 1980. For a brief overview of France, see Menyesch/ Uterwedde 1982, p. 98ff.; also Fossaert 1980). Both models have in common the fact that they distinctly oppose the theory of a levelled out middle class society which has broken down the social ranks through "universal consumption of industrial and journalistic mass production" (Schelsky 1979, p. 328). How little this is true of France and Germany may be shown by a brief glance at the distribution of income.

The actual rise in the standard of living and income in the decades following World War II is indisputable. However, not all groups profited to the same extent. Particularly during the 50's and 60's, the income brackets in France diverged substantially (as has again been the case since 1984) because the upper income classes experienced considerably higher growth rates than the lower income classes (professionals earned on the average eight times as much as farm workers; the income gap becomes even more obvious when extreme values are compared). In 1968, the *Accords de Grenelle* caused a temporary change in trend with a 35% increase in the SMIG, the guaranteed legal minimum wage rate (which, since 1970, has been known as the SMIC, *salaire minimum interprofessionel de croissance*). However, this measure proved to be insufficient – just as later cost-of-living adjustments as well as the 10% increase in 1981 – in effecting a fundamental income redistribution and in eliminating some serious discrepancies.

The following chart is arranged according to socio- professional categories (*Table 18*) and shows the incomes of wage and salary earners.

Table 18: Average Earnings (1000 francs/year)

Socio-professional categories	Earnings men	women	both
Managerial staff, top executives	248,4	176,0	232,1
Technicians	128,0	108,7	125,4
other professions intermédiares	137,4	110,0	124,3
Employees	91,0	80,0	83,1
Skilled workers	89,0	73,6	87,0
Non-skilled workers	79,1	63,8	74,3
Combined average	*119,9*	*90,7*	*109,3*

(From: INSEE 1991, p.83)

The *table 18* demonstrates continued high earnings margins as well as the large wage differentials between men and women. On the average, the earnings for men are almost a third higher (for a further breakdown according to income class, cf. Le Monde 1986a, p. 52, Mermet 1990, p. 295ff. and CERC 1987, p. 23ff.; 1989, p. 25ff.). If earnings margins are compared between certain branches and sectors, for example between industry and agriculture, or different regions, for example between Paris and the French Provence, large discrepancies can be observed. There are also substantial differences within the individual occupational categories mentioned above. The result is a classification according to income groups (*Fig. 50*).

Since the data in *Fig. 50* relates to income before taxes, slight shifts should be presumed. Exact data is available virtually only for wage and salary earners. The earnings of self-employed and professionals often have to be roughly estimated. Not to be forgotten is the high rate of tax evasion. Moreover, it also appears to be of significance that inequalities are only partially balanced out by tax progressions. Direct taxation (*impôt sur le revenu*), if compared on an international level, is relatively low. A more important source of federal revenue is indirect taxation, especially the value added tax (*taxe sur la valeur ajoutée*, T.V.A.). In the past, the French tax system had often been criticized as being antisocial since it heavily burdened those in the lower income brackets. Nonetheless, in 1984 the socialist government decided to lower income taxes and at the same time raise general tariffs and various value-added tax rates for consumer goods. (For information on the possible change in the French value-added tax rates with regard to the European domestic market, see 3.7.3.)

Several international studies have shown that the *inégalités sociales*, particularly as a result of income distribution, are much more critical in France than in comparable countries (for example, they are twice as great as in

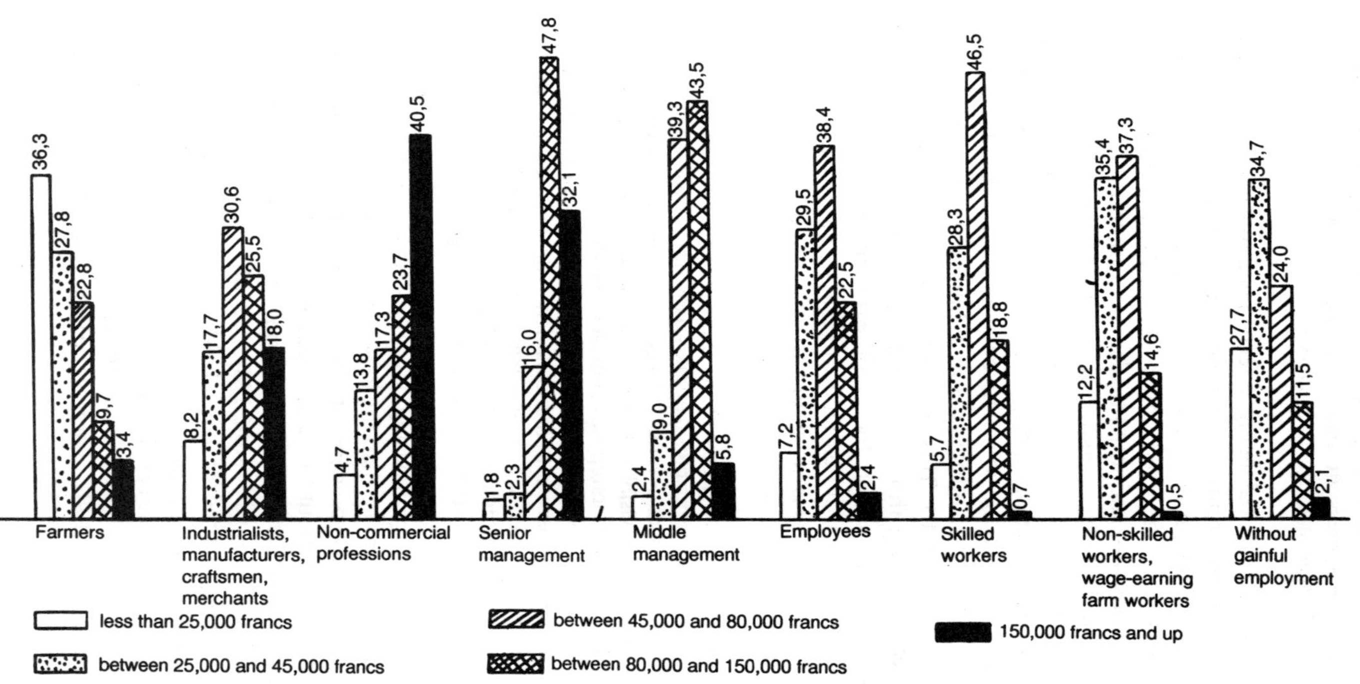

Fig. 50: Distribution of Annual Earnings According to Occupational Category (based on Canceill 1984, p. 45)

Germany, three times as great as in neighbouring countries etc.). However, since these surveys are based on different criteria their results cannot be summed up as mathematic equations.

Nonetheless, balancing effects resulting from tax measures and social services remain relatively modest. At the bottom of the social hierarchy, the proportion of those who no longer have ample income is growing. (One need only consider the phenomenon of the *nouveaux pauvres*, and in particular the long-term unemployed and the aged, without means and increasingly driven to the fringe of society). Continuing mass unemployment and the segmentation of the employment market into numerous unsecured occupational forms (cf. 3.8) have cemented the so-called imbalances. In 1988, the Rocard government voted to introduce for a limited time a *revenu minimum d'insertion* (RMI). This programme was to relieve the extremes of poverty among those excluded from the employment market and, above all, to promote their re-integration into that market. However, such legislation did as little to combat the structural causes of the occupational crisis as it did to overcome the enduring tendency towards a "dualistic society":

> Avec la montée irrésistible du chômage de longue durée, et la diminution des vieilles solidarités familiales dans une société où le déracinement et la solitude sont devenus le lot de beaucoup, la pauvreté fait des dégâts de plus en plus visibles dans nos pays riches. L'immobilier flambe à Paris et les profits des entreprises s'envolent, tandis que les "restaus du coeur" ont bien du mal à servir tous ceux qui frappent à leur porte: le RMI permet au moins d'apaiser la bonne conscience de ceux qui sont du bon côté du manche. ... Ainsi, le revenu minimum peut-il déboucher sur une société durablement dualiste, où le minimum accordé aux uns permet de gérer l'exclusion ... (D. Clerc, in: Verdié 1989, p.366ff.)

The increase in purchasing power has also favoured the upper income classes much more than the lower income classes in the last couple of years. Twenty percent of those in the highest income brackets benefited by about 45% of the gain, whereas 20% of those in the lowest income brackets could enjoy only 8.7% of the newly distributed purchasing power (Verdié 1987, p. 238ff.; for a more exact breakdown according to type of household, see CERC 1987, p. 117ff.). Such inequalities appear much more extreme when other advantages and privileges (such as special premiums, job security, low retirement ages, special social services etc.) are taken into account. In his bestseller *Toujours plus!* (1982), François de Closets analyzed the extent to which

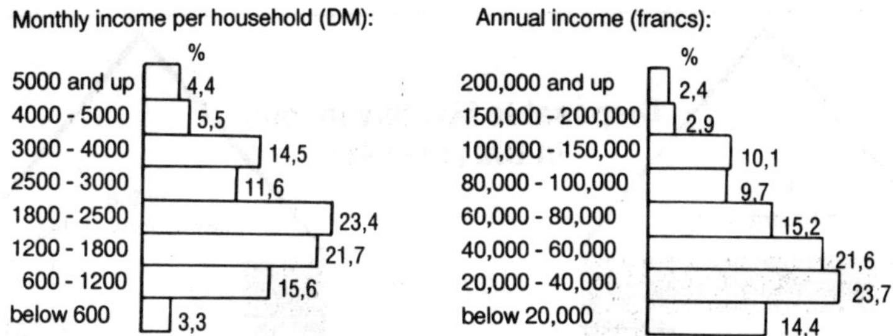

Fig. 51: Distribution of Income in % of Households (comparison of Germany and France). (From: Statist. Bundesamt 1983, p. 100; Canceill 1984, p. 45; INSEE 1984b, p. 85)

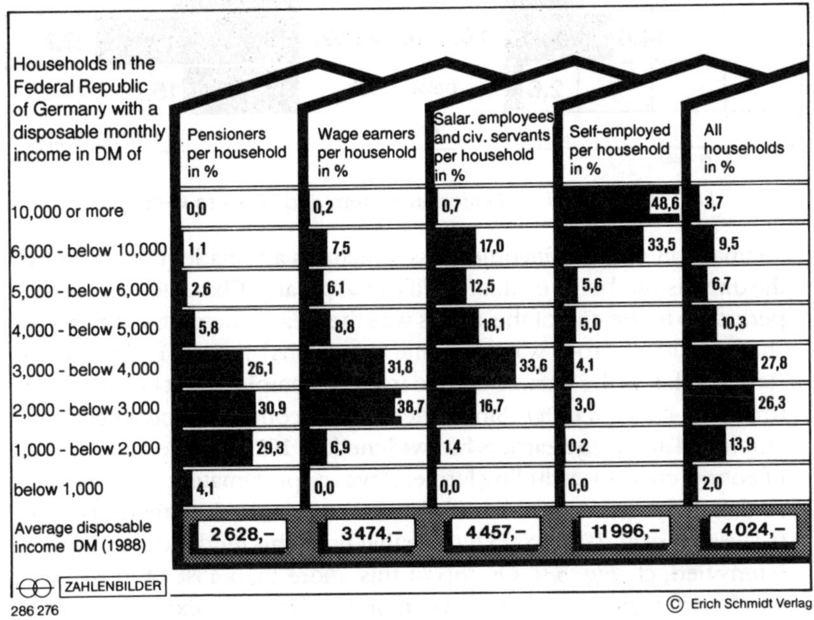

Households in the Federal Republic of Germany with a disposable monthly income in DM of
Pensioners per household in %
Wage earners per household in %
Salar. employees and civ. servants per household in %
Self-employed per household in %
All households in %
10,000 or more 0,0 0,2 0,7 48,6 3,7
6,000 - below 10,000 1,1 7,5 17,0 33,5 9,5
5,000 - below 6,000 2,6 6,1 12,5 5,6 6,7
4,000 - below 5,000 5,8 8,8 18,1 5,0 10,3
3,000 - below 4,000 26,1 31,8 33,6 4,1 27,8
2,000 - below 3,000 30,9 38,7 16,7 3,0 26,3
1,000 - below 2,000 29,3 6,9 1,4 0,2 13,9
below 1,000 4,1 0,0 0,0 0,0 2,0
Average disposable income DM (1988) 2628,– 3474,– 4457,– 11996,– 4024,–
ZAHLENBILDER
286 276
© Erich Schmidt Verlag

Fig. 52: Distribution of Average Annual Income in Germany

such *facteurs non monétaires* have furthered existing discrepancies. The distribution of wealth also poses great inequalities.

In some respects, the distribution of income in Germany is similar, although there seems to be a greater proportion of lower income classes in France (cf. *Fig. 51*). Available statistical data for a direct

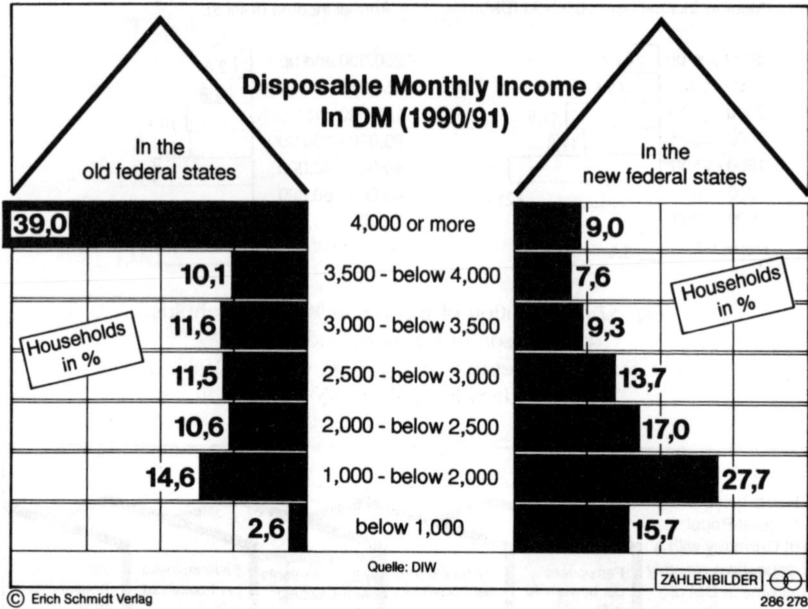

Fig. 53: Income Distribution in Eastern and Western Germany.

comparison of these income class structures are inadequate because the dimensions being evaluated differ too greatly. Characteristic for the period up to the end of the 1970's was the steady increase in the wage share (ratio of gross wage income to national income) which then started to fall as the income earned from self-employment began to rise (from 73.4% to 65.7%). Since then, the income gap between self-employed and wage earners has widened. In 1970 the average income of entrepreneurs (excluding farmers) was approximately twice as high as that of wage earners. In 1978 it was two and a half times as high (Claessens et al. 1985, p. 232; since that time, this tendency has further intensified, cf. *Fig. 53*). On top of this, more than 45% of those self-employed were found to have monthly incomes exceeding 6000 German marks. Barely 10% of the civil servants and less than 4% of the workers had incomes greater than this amount.

Income figures for employed females are similar to those in France, with earnings significantly below those for men (down by approx. 30%). It would be an oversimplification, however, to trace this inequality back to discriminating treatment on the job; the causes are sooner to be found in differing qualifications and career-mindedness and the distribution in various branches of the economy. On the whole, inequalities between the individual classes are growing. The escalation of the problem of the “new poor” in recent years testifies to this fact (cf. Werth 1991). Since 1990 there has been a further problem area, the consequences of which cannot yet be foreseen, i.e. the disparity between incomes in Eastern and Western Germany (cf. *Fig. 53*).

4.6 *Industrial conflicts and representation of interests*

The material conditions and inequalities outlined above are continually changing. The share of the national product as well as related living conditions and the balance of power are the source of frequent conflict among different groups in society. Such opposing interests inevitably give rise to problems which are more or less approached in every society by particular institutionalized means. The social environment in France, especially in terms of the relationship between entrepreneurs and workers, is widely regarded as being shaped more by conflict than by the meeting of the minds. This is typically reflected by the high number of industrial conflicts, the widespread lack of national collective bargaining and the militancy of politically oriented unions. It is difficult to evaluate such situations just by themselves. Quite often they can only be understood when compared with equivalent situations in other countries. This point can be illustrated with the following newspaper excerpts:

T. 22:

E.G.F. : GRÈVES
LA SEMAINE PROCHAINE

● La C.G.T. Electricité-Gaz de France a appelé, hier, à des grèves les 27, 28 et 29 novembre successivement dans trois grands groupes de régions. Ces arrêts de travail « en principe » de vingt-quatre heures pour chacune des régions se traduiront par une baisse de la production

Au cours d'une conférence de presse au siège de la Fédération C.G.T. de l'E.G.F., à Pantin (Seine-Saint-Denis), François Duteil, secrétaire général, a précisé que le 27 seront concernées les régions Ouest, Centre et Sud-Ouest ; le 28, l'Est, Rhône-Alpes et le Sud-Est ; le 29, le Nord, la Normandie et la région Ile-de-France.

(23. 11. 1984)

T2C : GRÈVE DE DEUX FOIS DEUX HEURES AUJOURD'HUI

La société T2C informe sa clientèle qu'elle est saisie d'un nouveau préavis de grève déposé pour la journée du 6 décembre, aux heures suivantes : de 7 heures à 9 heures et de 16 h. 30 à 18 h. 30.

Elle ne peut donc garantir aucun service aux jours et heures indiqués.

(6. 12. 1984)

ÉTAT DES ROUTES

L'ensemble des réseaux est enneigé et glissant. Les équipements spéciaux sont recommandés. Sont fermés : les cols du pas de Peyrol, de la Croix-Saint-Robert, les départementales 149 de Besse à Picherande et 15 entre Le Puy et Valence.

Dans certains secteurs de la Haute-Loire, en raison d'une grève des agents, le déneigement ne sera pas assuré entre 17 heures le 14 janvier et 7 h. 30 le 15 janvier.

(15. 1. 1985)

(From: La Montagne)

Actually, there is nothing exceptional about strike actions. They often take place spontaneously without any broad union support and sometimes affect only certain professions or industries, enterprises or just relatively small occupational groups (for example, one group of the E.G.F. workers and the street cleaners in Haute-Loire or the bus drivers in the city of Clermont-Ferrand). By contrast, nationwide actions which are centrally organized are much less frequent. The splitting up of the unions into different fractions often precludes them from having a common strategy.

4.6.1 Traditional union pluralism

The *union pluralism* typical of France goes back to the nineteenth century. Even prior to 1884 when professional organizations were finally legalized under the *Loi Waldeck- Rousseau* (named after the former Minister of the Interior Waldeck-Rousseau), there had already existed approximately 500 different trade unions (*chambres syndicales*). As the labour movement grew and the legal situation improved, the trend towards forming federations also took an upward turn. An example of this trend was the founding of the *Fédération Nationale des Syndicats* and the *Fédération des Bourses du Travail.* Nevertheless, controversial political notions influenced by revolutionary *marxists*, *reformists* and *anarchist syndicalism*, inspired by Proudhon, were still adhered to (for details, see Lefranc 1967, Goldschmidt 1974; Schüter, 1989).

In comparison with other countries in which a large class of wage earners emerged at an early point in time, the union movement in France experienced a slow start and for a long time was hindered by restrictive legislation. The *Loi Le Chapelier*, enacted in 1791, was of great consequence. This law not only banned trade guilds but associations in general:

> L'anéantissement de toutes espèces de corporations des citoyens du même état ou profession étant une des bases fondamentales de la constitution française, il est défendu de les rétablir de fait, sous quelque prétexte et quelque forme que ce soit. (Dupeux 1982, p.98; see also Kolboom 1984a)

The Loi Le Chapelier, which was based on liberal, individual-oriented economic concepts, proscribed any type of professional association and was even exacerbated to the disadvantage of the working classes in the *Code Napoléon*. Later, this law was progressively weakened: in 1864 there was a partial lift of the ban against associations and in 1884 professional organizations were officially recognized. Consequences of it still continued to have an effect up until 1936.

The first attempt at unifying different union movements was made in *1895* when the National Federation of Labour Associations merged with sections of the National Federation of Unions and founded the *Confédération Générale du Travail.* Although this was at first nothing more than a loose unification of existing ideological movements led by adherents of anarchist syndicalism (cf. Moissonnier 1977, p. 46ff.), this merger went through an organizational consolidation in the years thereafter.

The anarchist syndicalism movement also determined the *Charta von Amiens* in 1906: the C.G.T. decided upon a strategy of *action directe* (with wildcat strikes and factory occupation) as the means to achieve its goals and adopted a policy of strict independence from political parties. Even today these same principles continue to characterize by and large the way the French unions view themselves. They also account for the propensity to certain forms of action, as discussed above, and the unions' reservations concerning any form of assimilation (e.g., any co-determination modelled on the German system). Further development was, in short, essentially influenced by disunion and rapprochement of the individual trade unions (Reynaud 1975, Goldschmidt 1974, Droz 1977; cf. *Fig. 54*). Following the disunion of socialists and communists at the *national convention in Tours*, the C.G.T. split into a communist-oriented union and a reformist-socialist union. The threat of fascism in 1936 then caused the unions to rejoin. However, with the end of the Popular Front and the Russo-German Pact of 1939 the union split apart from the communists. During World War II under the 1943 *Perreux Agreement* the unions were reunited. In 1947 in the wake of the Cold War and the conflict over the Marshall Plan, this group was again at odds with itself. Finally, the union was divided into the *C.G.T.* and the *F.O.* which still exist today.

Parallel to the marxist and reformist movements, there was also a third group, the *Christian union movement*, which established itself as a union in 1919. Starting in the 1950's, however, advocates of a laicistic, left-wing course gained more and more clout. In 1964 they succeeded in putting through a non- denominational program and renamed the union the C.F.D.T. In 1965 the traditional line became known as the *C.F.T.C.-Maintenue.*

Other fundamental union movements in France include the *professional organizations* (the C.G.C. represents high-level and middle management) and the *independent professional associations*, for example, the F.E.N. is the teachers' union.

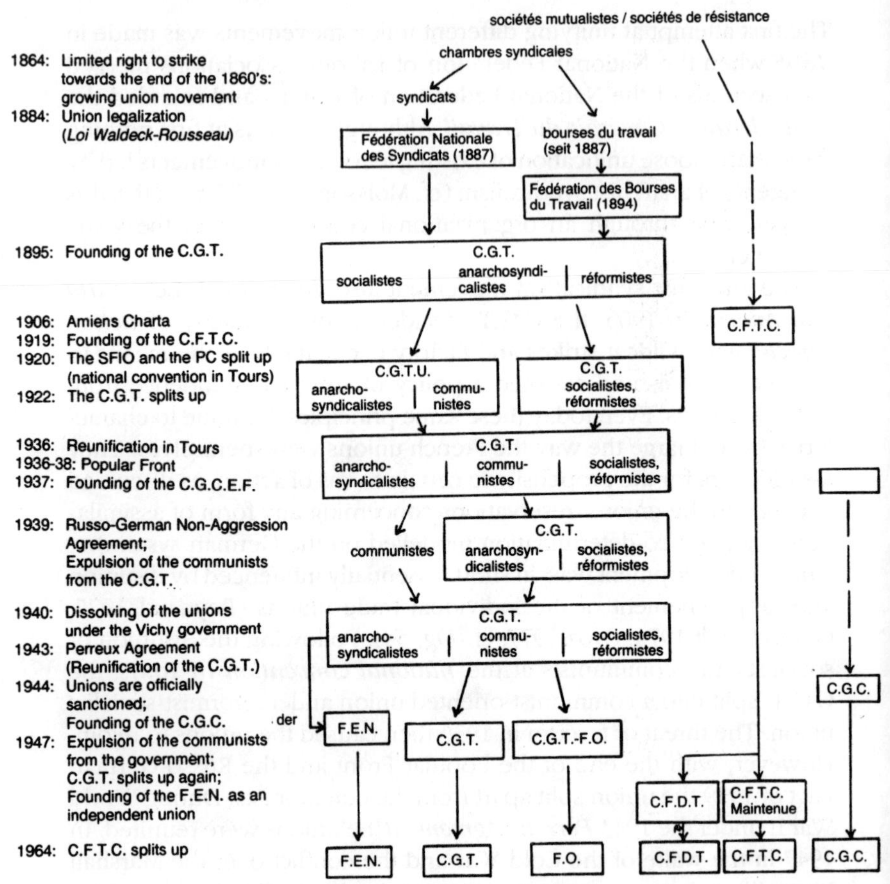

Fig. 54: The French Union Movement.
(From: Capdevielle/Mouriaux 1976, p. 28f.;
Menyesch/Uterwedde 1982, p. 114f.)

The development of the *German trade-union movement* was also closely connected to the struggle for freedom of association in the nineteenth century. Since this right was granted only in few states (in 1871 for the entire German Empire) while the prohibition of regional political organizations remained in force, union activities in particular were subject to heavy restrictions. Nevertheless, as a result of the aggravated social conditions in the first half of the nineteenth century, a number of associations were founded aside from the traditional trade guilds. The 1848 Revolution brought about a short-term upswing and eventually led to the founding of the first professional unions. Even though the defeat of the revolution caused these unions to be dissolved and restrictive legislation to be enacted, the response thereafter was the establishment of numerous union- like organizations on a local level. In 1863 Ferdinand Lassalle founded the *Allgemeinen deutschen Arbeiterverein* (General German Labour Association) whose counterpart was the *Verband deutscher Arbeitervereine* (German Federation of Labour Associations). Later on, other groups such as the *Allgemeine Deutsche Arbeiterschaftsverband* (General German Labour Federation) and the pro-business *Hirsch-Dunckerschen Gewerkvereine* (labour associations) were founded. All in all, the union movement was so splintered that by the 1870's great efforts were launched towards organizational concentration. A good example of these endeavours was the *Allgemeine Deutsche Metallarbeiterverband* (General German Federation of Metalworkers), set up in 1874, in which both social democrats and Lassalle followers joined forces. Despite efforts towards unifying these divergent ideological movements, the ideological differences between the groups remained until the establishment of the Weimar Republic. There were the free socialist-oriented unions, an anti-socialist Christian union movement and the Hirsch-Duncker Labour Associations. Compared to France, Germany experienced neither a pronounced anarchist nor a significant communist union movement. The cleavage among the unions did not begin to disappear until the end of World War II when the *Deutscher Gewerkschaftsbund* (Confederation of German Trade Unions) was formed. This federation combines a number of unions and represents the majority of all union members. (For more on the history of the union movement, see Deppe et al. 1981, Klönne/Reese 1984, Schuster 1974; for an overview of the various types of unions in other countries, see v. Beyme 1980, p. 75ff.)

4.6.2 Weak organization

Participation in the many trade union associations in France is not particularly high. The average union membership of wage earners (now approx. 10%) is clearly lower than in Germany (36%) and in other comparable countries (Peter 1985, Kowalsky 1986, Noblecourt 1990).

Union membership structure is particularly significant: only 7% of female employees and only 1% of all employees between the ages of 18 and 21 are organized into unions. This situation is – from union perspective – all the more alarming when viewed in the light of most recent developments: During the 1970's, union membership figures were still at 25%, but since then the numbers have been dropping off steadily (Mermet 1990, p. 275ff.; Rehfeldt 1991, p. 95ff.). Moreover, there are often considerable differences between branches, sectors and professional groups (e.g., union membership in the public sector is approx. three times as high as in the private sector).

Table 19: Works Committee Elections (percentages of votes)

	1984	1986	1988	1990
CGT	29,3	27,1	26,7	24,9
CFDT	21,0	21,2	20,7	19,9
CFTC	3,8	3,8	3,7	3,6
CGT-FO	13,9	14,4	13,7	12,8
CFE-CGC	7,1	7,5	6,8	6,5
autres syndicats	4,8	5,0	4,8	5,6
non syndiqués	19,7	21,1	23,5	26,6

(From: Libération 27 July 1991)

Membership figures are, however, not the sole criterion required to determine the weight exerted by the French unions. Various "social elections", eg for works committees (*Comités d'entreprise*), industrial arbitration (*Conseils de Prud'hommes*), and for social security (*Sécurité sociale*), continue to play a significant role. The results of the last works committee elections are shown in *Table 19*.

The social elections continue to comprise an importance basis for union legitimation and the unions obviously enjoy strong support here: in the most recent works committee elections, all of the unions together were at least able to secure 70% of the votes (in the other elections the results were even clearer; cf. Verdié 1989, p. 386ff.). These impressive figures should nevertheless not be allowed to conceal the fact that the overall share of the unions has dropped drastically. It was the non-organized representatives who were able to profit from this and were the leading group in 1990 with 26.6% of the votes (though receiving only 19.7% in 1984 and in 1966 a mere 12%). Moreover, election participation is steadily on the decrease and often there is no list of candidates, so that no employee's representative is elected. All of these developments go to indicate that France's unions are in the midst of a serious crisis, possibly threatening their very existence.

The causes of this decline are of a very complex nature. Weak labour organization might well be the result of the few instances of company codetermination and the high degree of legislation which dominates social welfare policy. Moreover, weak organization is ultimately a reflection of the certain types of union objectives and conflict-oriented nature of their activities. According to opinion polls, the rivalry that exists between individual unions is also finding less and less support.

Fig. 55
(From: Le Nouvel Observateur, 3 November 1988)

Thus, the number of union members has continued to decrease in the last few years. Unfavourable job market conditions and dwindling political influence have caused various union programmes (such as the right to self-determination demanded by the C.F.D.T.) to lose their appeal. "The last several years of experience...have clearly revealed the contradiction between a program of social change and reformist activity and have also cast doubts on union competence to come up with a firm concept for realizing their far-reaching goals. In this respect, the leftist government has added to the crisis of the French unions - unintentionally and, for many, surprisingly - which to a large extent is an identity crisis" (Wurm 1985, p. 60).

Two further causes of a general nature should also be mentioned:

- the continuing mass unemployment, which has had demobilizing effects on union activities.
- changes in the employment structure resulting from the tertiarizing process (cf. 4.5.1) and the far-reaching technological transformation: "(This transformation) promotes the rise of high-tech sectors with their traditionally low level of union organization while making traditional branches obsolete. It is thus provoking the crisis and the demise of both old industrial regions and the bastions of union strength established in them." (Rehfeldt 1991, p. 102; cf. Noblecourt 1990, p. 147ff.)

The degree to which the unions have lost their appeal and ability to mobilize became apparent when in 1977 the railway strikes and then above all the *grèves des infirmières* in the autumn of 1988 took place with virtually no union participation. The strikes were organized by ad hoc committees, i.e. the so-called "coordinations". The unions were ruthlessly steamrollered by these actions (cf. *Fig. 55*). It is an open question whether the *crise syndicale*, marked by the drop in union membership and a lack of confidence in the unions, will continue or whether the unions will be able to regain their previous power by implementing new strategies and goals and possibly by undergoing re-structuring as well. A radical re-orientation might be possible in connection with the European domestic market (cf. Rose 1989, Lecher 1989, Partikel 1989).

4.6.3 "Representative" Unions

The C.G.T., C.F.D.T., F.O., C.F.T.C., F.E.N., and C.G.C. are unions at the national level and are thus the bargaining partners of the state and industry. In collective bargaining contracts the signature of at least one representative union is required.

Despite its recent heavy membership losses, the C.G.T. (*Confédération générale du travail*) is still the most powerful union with 800,000 active members (as is true of statistics for all the other unions, these figures are to be regarded with a degree of scepticism since they vary a great deal, depending on the source). Nevertheless, in employee elections its membership interest fell from over 55% to around 25%. The reasons for this decline do not only seem to be related to current trends but also to the progressing shrinkage of the "traditional" working classes, the stronghold of the C.G.T.. This has left the C.G.T. with many unsolved structural problems. Historically, this union began in 1895 as a unifier of different political movements (cf. *Fig. 54*). Today, with its distinct anti-capitalist goals the C.G.T. represents a political line very close to that of the PCF (even though only 20% of its members belong to the communist party). (The C.G.T.'s close affiliation to the communist party – which is also in the midst of a crisis situation – is another reason for the unions' significant drop in membership; see Leggewie 1986, p. 83ff.). In labour disputes the C.G.T. is frequently more unyielding and less willing to compromise than other trade unions.

The C.G.T. has often cooperated with the more socialist-oriented

C.F.D.T. (*Confédération française démocratique du travail*) in the past. However, the cooperation became a less frequent occurrence under the austerity policy of the socialist government. The C.F.D.T. was not able to profit from the dwindling membership of the C.G.T. and in 1984 had less than one million members (1989: 500,000). The main goal of the C.F.D.T., which emerged from the former Christian union C.F.T.C. in 1964, is the democratization of labour conditions (*socialisme autogestionnaire*). For this reason, the union is very receptive to spontaneous grass roots actions (for example, intervention at the LIP clock factory in Besançon in 1973 followed by later production takeover). The support lost by the C.F.D.T. and the C.G.T. in social elections shows the general disappointment over the public welfare policies the leftist government has introduced since 1982.

The trade union *Force ouvrière (C.G.T.-F.O.)* received greater support in the 1980's. During this time it has emerged as the second most powerful organization both in terms of works committee elections and general membership. In 1947/48 the F.O. split from the communist-oriented C.G.T. pretending to be its sole legitimate successor (thus, the abbreviation C.G.T.-F.O.). The F.O. based its separation on the *Amiens Charta* (1906) and the strict separation from political parties decreed by it. This union regards itself as reformist and distinguishes itself through its rigid anti-communist course, its forbearance of extensive sociopolitical goals (clearly separating political from union mandate) and its support of concerted action with government and industry. There is close contact between the C.G.T.-F.O and the DGB (Confederation of German Trade Unions) on a European level.

The C.F.T.C. (*Confédération française des travailleurs chrétiens*) plays a much smaller role than the above three federations. Even though the majority organized a laicistic union with the C.F.D.T. in 1964, the C.F.T.C. still remains loyal to catholic doctrine and propagates concerted cooperative efforts which avoid traditional union combative measures. In social elections this union usually does not win more than 5% of the votes (except in traditionally catholic regions).

When the F.O. withdrew from the umbrella organization C.G.T. in 1947, the F.E.N. *(Fédération de l'éducation nationale)* remained the sole representative organ for the body of teachers in France. The F.E.N. represents various political movements and has united a number of branch associations (organized according to primary school teachers, high school teachers etc.). The F.E.N. follows the laicistic tradition and took an active part in discussions on governmental promotion of private denominational schools (the *querelle scolaire* is discussed in

5.1.4). Branch associations normally represent professional interests. French civil servants were given the right to strike in 1946.

The C.G.C. (*Confédération générale des cadres*, which since 1981 has been officially known as the C.F.E.-C.G.C., *Conféderation française de l'encadrement* – C.G.C.) basically comprises management, engineers, technicians as well as master craftsmen and commercial agents. Notwithstanding this, the majority of those who belong to these professional groups are organized in the C.G.T., C.F.D.T. and F.O. The C.G.C., often referred to as "moderate" by the German press, was founded in 1944 when it disassociated from the workers' union C.G.T. The C.G.C. supports concerted cooperative action and rejects the combative measures of other unions due to their class struggle character. (For more detailed information on the French unions, see Caire 1971, Lefranc 1969, Reynaud 1975, Steiert 1978, Peter 1985, Noblecourt 1990, Haensch/Tümmers 1991, p.288ff.)

4.6.4 Employers' associations

The *C.N.P.F. (Conseil national du patronat français)* is the most important umbrella organization for employers. It acts as a central, closed lobby when dealing with the various unions. Branch and regional associations are responsible for membership. Business associations in France have been in existence since the beginning of the nineteenth century. While the working classes were prohibited from organizing their own interest groups, entrepreneurial organizations were tacitly tolerated. The *Confédération générale de la production française* emerged in 1919 as the first central trade association. After World War II, the patronage reorganized itself as the C.N.P.F. Since French entrepreneurship had largely compromised itself during the war through its close collaboration with the Vichy government and the Nazis, it was forced to make concessions after the country's liberation (*planification, sécurité sociale*). But altogether, French management has adopted a generally conservative attitude by adamantly resisting social progress and the extension of union rights (cf. Brizay 1975, Lefranc 1976, Weber 1988, Kowalsky 1991).

Limited interest on the part of the entrepreneurs in cooperating with the unions is the object of the caricature in *Fig. 56*. The rejection of the *Lois Auroux*, which modestly extended employees' representation rights, and the *Accords Matignon*, which introduced the 40-hour week, collective bargaining and paid

Fig. 56
(From: Laurent-Atthalin 1983, p. 18)

vacation in 1936, are some examples of the hostile attitude employers have displayed towards employees.

The large-scale enterprises set the tone in the C.N.P.F. The small and middle-sized businesses with less than 500 employees, though officially members of the same association, are united in their own organization called the C.G.P.M.E. (*Conféderation général des petites et moyennes entreprises*). This organization mainly seeks to secure protectionist measures, tax benefits and loan privileges. The small enterprises are subject to immense pressure due to the concentration of and competition with the larger groups of enterprises. Thus, the C.N.P.F. supports a common lobby and underscores the *liberté d'entreprendre* which they claim is threatened by the left-wing parties (for more on the line of the C.N.P.F., see Kolboom 1978). There have also been increasing approaches by the C.N.P.F. toward the C.G.C. and the F.O.

The most important agrarian trade association is the F.N.S.E.A. (*Fédération nationale des syndicats d'exploitants agricoles*) which has organized approximately two-thirds of all self-employed farmers. Just as in the C.N.P.F., there are also various interest groups in this organization. For example, the interests of the dominant, export-oriented large-scale enterprises (*grands exploitants*) are different than those of small family businesses struggling for their survival.

4.6.5 Organizational representation in the Federal Republic of Germany

Unlike in France, where the C.N.P.F. is virtually the only organization representing the interests of the country's employers, there exist in Germany various central federations which have separate functions. The *Bundesvereinigung der Deutschen Arbeitgeberverbände* (BDA) (National Federation of German Employers' Associations) represents the 46 united employers' associations in union contract negotiations. The *Bundesverband der Deutschen Industrie* (BDI) (National Federation of German Industries) is also a combination of both trade organizations and regional associations but is concerned with political-economical issues and represents the industry in its dealings with political bodies and institutions. Finally, at federal level, the chambers of industry and commerce (as public legal institutions) are united in the *Deutschen Industrie und Handelstag* (DIHT) (Federation of German Chambers of Industry and Commerce) and the chambers of skilled trades are united in the *Zentralverband des deutschen Handwerks* (ZVDH) (Central Association of German Chambers of Crafts). In addition, the associations have various unofficial means of representing their interests, whether it be their access to press coverage and their connections to political parties or to the "many representatives of capital in the network of advisory boards, boards of trustees and brain trusts etc. which exert such great influence on government will and policy" (Claessens et al. 1985, p. 238).

There are several characteristic differences between *German* and French *unionism*. In Germany there is neither a comparable cleavage among the trade unions nor the phenomenon of politically opposed unions. The *Confederation of German Trade Unions* (DGB), organized in 1949 as a parent union, represents more than 80% of all union members with its membership of nearly 8 million people. This percentage is even higher in work council elections. In Germany the unions are more rigidly organized. The DGB combines 16 individual trade unions (cf. *Fig. 57*); a re-structuring with the fusion of certain individual unions is, however, under discussion. Sixty-six per cent of all DGB members are workers, 23% are employees and 11% civil servants. The DGB is regarded as a financially powerful union with its own establishments and educational facilities. However, in the last few years, mismanagement within the DGB has caused it to suffer a considerable loss of economic power. Although the DGB is independent in terms of its ideological outlook and party affiliation, its Social democrat slant is unmistakable.

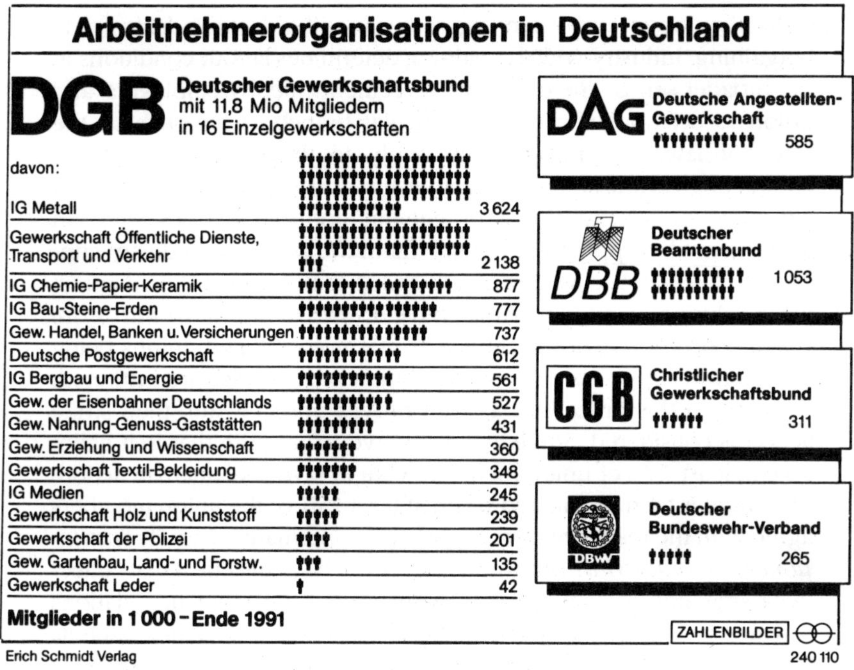

Arbeitnehmerorganisationen in Deutschland
DGB
Deutscher Gewerkschaftsbund
mit 11,8 Mio Mitgliedern
in 16 Einzelgewerkschaften
davon:
IG Metall 3 624
Gewerkschaft Öffentliche Dienste, Transport und Verkehr 2 138
IG Chemie-Papier-Keramik 877
IG Bau-Steine-Erden 777
Gew. Handel, Banken u. Versicherungen 737
Deutsche Postgewerkschaft 612
IG Bergbau und Energie 561
Gew. der Eisenbahner Deutschlands 527
Gew. Nahrung-Genuss-Gaststätten 431
Gew. Erziehung und Wissenschaft 360
Gewerkschaft Textil-Bekleidung 348
IG Medien 245
Gewerkschaft Holz und Kunststoff 239
Gewerkschaft der Polizei 201
Gew. Gartenbau, Land- und Forstw. 135
Gewerkschaft Leder 42
Mitglieder in 1 000 – Ende 1991
DAG
Deutsche Angestellten-Gewerkschaft 585
DBB
Deutscher Beamtenbund 1 053
CGB
Christlicher Gewerkschaftsbund 311
DBwV
Deutscher Bundeswehr-Verband 265
ZAHLENBILDER
Erich Schmidt Verlag
240 110

Fig. 57: German Trade Unions

In addition to the DGB, there are also the following union organizations: the *Deutsche Beamtenbund* (DBB) (German Civil Servants Association) with around 794,000 members, the *Deutsche Angestellten Gewerkschaft* (DAG) (Union of German Salaried Employees) with around 504,000 members, the *Christliche Gewerkschaftsbund Deutschlands* (CGB) (Christian Federation of German Trade Unions) with about 305,000 members as well as the *Bundeswehrverband* (Association of German Federal Armed Forces) with approximately 265,000 members.

4.6.6 Labour conditions and collective bargaining

In Germany, labour conditions are not subject to government regulation. Wage and work conditions are negotiated autonomously by the trade associations and the respective unions without government interference. *Bargaining power autonomy* is guaranteed by Article 9 of the German constitution and the Collective Agreement Act of 1952.

Collective wage and salary agreements differ from industry-wide bargaining. Industry-wide bargaining determines labour conditions in the broader sense. The collective agreements met by employers' and union associations affecting a particular branch or region have the force of law, but initially only apply to those members of the contracting organizations. Only after the government has declared a collective agreement to be of general application does such an agreement also apply to nonmembers in the particular industry concerned. Every collective agreement specifies the terms of the contract period during which the parties have a *duty to maintain industrial peace (Friedenspflicht)*. In the event of employers and unions being unable to reach an agreement, arbitration proceedings are instituted. Only when this procedure as well proves unsuccessful, then strike action is considered. Strike actions, however, require that in a ballot vote at least 75% of union members vote in favour of such an action. The strike is then terminated when at least 25% of the union members agree with the results of new negotiations. Germany's heavily *institutionalized industrial arbitration procedures* have the effect that collective bargaining agreements are usually arrived at through negotiations – without state-enforced conciliation – and industrial action such as strikes and lockouts are comparatively rare (cf. Neumann 1981; for greater detail, see Kißler/Lasserre 1987).

Bargaining power autonomy, however, does not mean that the state does not have any means of intervention at its disposal. Apart from the regulation of general outline conditions (for example, through tax legislation, foreign trade policy etc.), the state also has direct means of influence. For instance, the government has an interest in adhering to certain wage-price guideposts in order to secure its own economic priorities. This includes appealing to the unions during wage negotiations to moderate their demands and calling attention to the export dependency of the German economy. (For more on the tradition of such "recommendations" from Bismarck to Kohl, see Kessler 1984). Examples of government intervention in negotiations between the industry and the unions include the 1984 conflict over the reduction of working hours and the 1985/86 talks on government neutrality during labour disputes (amendment of 116 of the Arbeitsförderungsgesetz).

In France, collective bargaining agreements (*conventions collectives*) are of less importance in regulating labour conditions. There are two major differences with respect to the system in Germany. *Labour disputes carry significantly more weight than wage/salary negotiations* and *government continuously interferes in arbitration of such disputes* (Adam/Reynaud 1978, Lasserre 1981, Kißler/ Lasserre 1987). Although there have been several attempts since 1936 to establish a system of collective bargaining, there still exists no unified bargaining process for the various economic branches. Even if there are union agreements in a particular sector, they are not automatically binding on the employers. The nature of such agreements can also be not binding from the outset. Employees of small-sized businesses in particular are not protected by any collective bargaining agreements: «il y a encore des vides conventionnels qui ressemblent à des déserts. C'est très sensible quand on descend de la branche à l'entreprise: seulement près de 10 % des établissements de dix salariés et plus déclarent appliquer une convention ou un accord propre à l'entreprise ou à l'établissement» (Laurent-Atthalin 1983, p. 57). And yet, resistance against collective contractual commitments stems from both the employers and the unions. Due to their distinct patriarchal, authoritative attitude, many employers are basically wary of bilateral trade agreements. In this sense, the significance of family holdings in the French economy is still very substantial (for certain changes, see Kowalsky 1988). French employers tend only to accept global agreements at national level which at most minimally restrict entrepreneurial latitude. For the unions, the danger of gradually becoming integrated in the existing economic system through cooperative behaviour is to the fore. Moreover, union pluralism (along with the thus implied competitive relationship) makes the meeting of minds more difficult. Another impedance results from the fact that union federations only represent a relatively small portion of workers and that the activities of nonunion members play a more important role.

The institutionalization of arbitration procedures, as in Germany, is often criticized from the French point of view as being bureaucratic as well as an obstacle for spontaneous action (cf. Lasserre 1983, p. 269). On the other hand, it is precisely the lack of such arbitration regulations in France which frequently obstructs the defusing of labour disputes and brings government intervention into the arena. In this context, strikes have priority over negotiations. They demonstrate the respective balance of power and the support of concrete demands.

And yet, whether or not the demands of workers can be pushed through often does not essentially turn on the justification of such demands, but rather on the types of pressure an occupational group might exercise in asserting these demands. Some examples of this include the walk-outs of the *centres de tri*, the *conducteurs de métro* or the *éboueurs parisiens*. «La grève est l'arme des forts et non des faibles», «pour se faire rendre justice, il faut au moins tenir Paris» (de Closets, 1982, p. 55ff.). This statement of facts is no doubt closely related

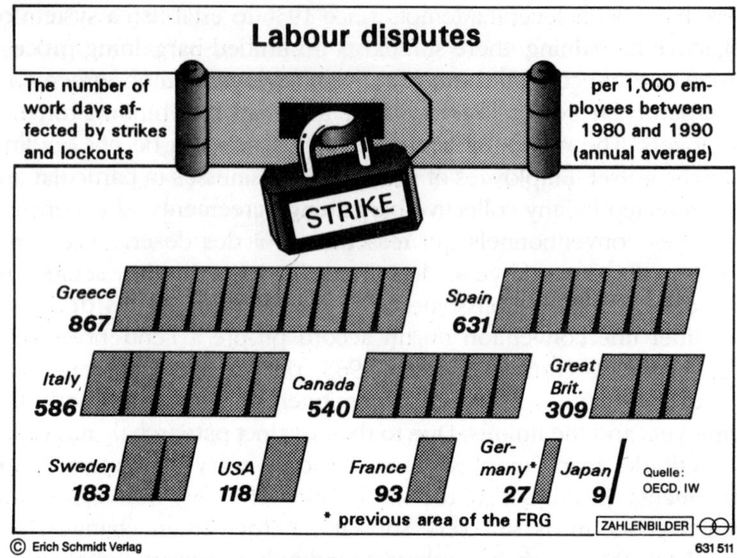

Fig. 58: A Comparison of Strike Frequency

to the still very distinct corporatistic structures, i.e. limited representation of professional interests. However, union activities cannot be reduced to the promotion of egotistical interests of specific groups, as de Closets implied in 1985 when speaking against the French unions.

For the reasons mentioned above, it appears by no means unusual that France ranks ahead of Germany in the statistics on strike frequency (*Fig. 58*). However, such numerical comparisons have little bearing since the function of strike action differs according to the particular labour conditions in question. The figures for France also become much more relative when compared on an international level. Furthermore, the frequency of strikes in France has steadily decreased in the last several years.

4.6.7 Codetermination

The institutionalized arbitration procedures on the one hand and the extensive lack of fixed negotiating steps on the other hand are reflected by the regulation of *workers' participation and codetermination.* The regulations in German industry are more strongly geared towards the mediation of opposing interests than in France.

At an in-company level, the German Works Council Constitution Act provides for the safeguarding of employee interests by a *works council.* Businesses with more than five employees have such councils which consist of elected staff representatives (the number of works councils depends on the size of the establishment). The works council has the right to be informed of financial issues, participates in decisions affecting personnel regulations and has a say in matters of social relevance. Though their rights are very limited (this is why the Act was also rejected by the unions in 1952), the powers of the works councils in Germany go beyond those of the *comité d'entreprise* in France, which has to be formed in companies with at least 50 employees. This latter is more like a works committee than a workers' representative. Either the head of the enterprise or a representative appointed by him presides over the chair. Then, depending on the size of the company, there are also 3 to 11 elected members of the staff and (in companies with at least 300 employees) one or more *représentants syndicaux* who are elected by the represented unions.

Roughly speaking, the *comité d'entreprise* has access to information on company finances (business annual report), and must be consulted with on issues concerning company restructuring, work hours and work conditions. The committee's main function is the organization of social and cultural activities (such as further vocational training, management of sports facilities, vacation homes etc.) which may also be the result of autonomous initiatives. The *comité d'entreprise* receives 0.2% of the company's gross wages for the financing of such activities. Although such committees are only set up in establishments with at least 50 employees and even then hardly limit the power of company stockholders (even the 1982 *Lois Auroux* have not changed this), they still encounter heavy resistance from the entrepreneurs. In many instances, either committee work is hindered or the meetings are altogether prevented from taking place. In 1981, this was the case in 18% of French enterprises. (For a more detailed analysis, see Laurent-Atthalin 1983, Bachy 1981; for more on the Auroux reform, see Kißler 1986, Kißler/Lasserre 1987, p. 68ff., Schüter, 1989).

In companies with at least 16 employees *délégués du personnel* are elected annually. Their function is to represent staff interests concerning pay, work conditions and the enforcement of collective bargaining agreements. They must also be consulted in cases of notice of dismissal.

Parallel to staff representation, employees have also been able to organize *sections syndicales* since 1968 (and since 1982 this has even been independent of company size). If a business has a minimum of 50 employees, it is possible for each section of a representative union to elect a *délégué syndical* (trade-union representative). In contrast to shop stewards in Germany who primarily act as the liaison between union and workers, the *délégué syndical* represents the particular union in management and to some extent takes over the tasks of the staff representative. In companies with 300 or more employees, this delegate automatically participates as a trade union representative in the *comité d'entreprise*.

There exist various forms of codetermination in Germany with regards to the overseeing of company decisions and participation in supervisory committees. The most extensive form of workers' participation is guaranteed by the *Montan-Mitbestimmungsgesetz von 1951* (*Codetermination Law of 1951*, with the coal and steel industry as the only field of application). This law was the result of the belief harboured by all the political parties at the time of the founding of the Federal Republic of Germany that an economic concentration of power could easily threaten political stability. This law provides for an equal representation of stockholders and workers in mining, iron and steel concerns (with more than 100 employees), i.e. both sides delegate the same number of representatives to the supervisory board in addition to a so-called neutral member who has been elected by both parties. This form of codetermination was also advocated by the trade-unions – as a step towards promoting the equality of rights between those on the side of capital and those on the side of labour. However, management's increased resistance against codetermination precluded the unions from getting codetermination on a basis of parity enforced by subsequent legislative acts. As a result of the *Betriebsverfassungsgesetz von 1952* (*Works Council Constitution Act of 1952*) companies with between 500 and 2000 employees had to have a one-third participation of workers' representatives on their supervisory boards. The *Mitbestimmungsgesetz of 1976* (which applied to stock corporations with more than 2000 employees) provides for equal representation of stockholders and employees on the supervisory board. However, this parity is virtually obviated by the fact that an executive manager must be among the labour representatives and, in the event of a tie-vote, the chairman of the supervisory board who is elected by the stockholders has a double vote. (This is explained in greater detail in Barthel/Dikau 1980, Nutzinger 1981).

Approximately 26% of all salary/wage earners are affected by such codetermination legislation. Sixty percent are only affected by in-plant codetermination regulations (through works and staff councils). Finally, the remaining 14% do not have the right to codetermination.

Even though institutional codetermination for labour has in actuality only given rise to very limited participation in company decision-making processes (only 2.8% of the labour force is affected by the ECSS modal of equality in participation), there is once again a growing tendency to defuse conflicts of interest through negotiations and legal redress. "Cooperation is superseding conflict" (Nutzinger 1981, p. 211). This becomes even more apparent when compared with France where codetermination virtually does not exist in the sense described above. Delegates to the *comités d'entreprises* are only permitted as nonvoting *observateurs* in supervisory committees. As depicted above, most trade unions prefer other forms of interest representation. Any changes in existing structures are additionally hindered by the fact that French entrepreneurs are very cautious about losing any domain of autonomy. In this context, the following quote should be kept in mind, even though the author, a former Gaullist minister, drew his conclusions entirely from superficial phenomena:

> T. 23:
> Dans les pays de tradition romaine, le progrès social, comme la démocratie, est né de la violence. Il a été une conquête sanglante arrachée à l'ordre immuable. Les ouvriers, faute d'avoir été traités en véritables partenaires, sont toujours tentés de s'emparer de vive force de ce qui, ailleurs, est accordé comme un droit. Ils se persuadent que, sans la lutte des classes, et sans des actions violentes, leurs intérêts ne seraient pas défendus. Ils ne veulent pas savoir que les pays où les ouvriers ont le plus haut niveau de vie, comme la Suisse, l'Allemagne occidentale, les Pays-Bas ou la Suède, sont précisément ceux où la grève a disparu à peu près complètement de l'arsenal syndical et la «lutte des classes» de l'idéologie ouvrière.
>
> Chacun s'enferme dans cette logique absurde. Les patrons ont raison de se défier des syndicats, qui ont raison de se défier des patrons; c'est pourquoi chacun continue. (Peyrefitte 1976, p.421)

5. The education system: traditions and reforms

(Ernst Ulrich Grosse)

In 1985, the faculty of the *Collège de France*, the oldest and highest ranking educational institution in France, drew up proposals for the reform of educational structures and methods. The French president himself had appointed them to work out such recommendations. The chief demand was that pupils and students finally be conceded greater freedom and more opportunities for self-discovery and self-determination. Such proposals had a good deal in common with the alternative pedagogical notions of Rabelais, Rousseau and Freinet, Comenius, Pestalozzi and numerous other reformers who had criticized the prevailing educational modes of their day. The committee emphasized that the quintessence of these alternative methods was based on «les vertus de l'apprentissage par l'expérience, inlassablement exaltées, depuis Rousseau et Pestalozzi, par tous les réformateurs» (Collège de France 1985, p. 49).

Dozens of similar recommendations – as well as the innovations based on them which for the most part were quickly abandoned – can be found in French and German educational history of the twentieth century. For example, in the 70's one tenth (*les 10%*) of the curriculum in French schools was supposed to be left to the discretion of the pupils, i.e. their *activités personelles librement agréés et poursuivies.* Many children who had become de-motivated by the same old transfer of knowledge and learning by rote responded very positively to this reform (refer to the caricature of Plantu, *Fig. 59*). In practice, however, this measure was largely ignored and, in the meantime, there is nothing to be heard about the "10%", as is the case with most of the recommendations made by the *Collège de France* (apart from the technical innovations which even prior to 1985 were already being introduced in primary and secondary schools and universities; the opinion is that the future of France will depend on the preparedness of the nation's youth to become integrated into the electronic age).

In 1981 the *projets d'action éducative* purported to displace the "10%" reform by stimulating the motivation among pupils and making the schools more open

Fig. 59: The Response to Curriculum-oriented and Self-determined Learning. (From: ME, Feb. 1978, p. 46)

to the environment surrounding them. Between 1983 and 1984 a great deal of idealism and dedication helped bring about 12,283 such projects throughout France. Later on, it was precisely these projects which received a new orientation: the introduction to business and technology. Their scope became smaller (ME, Feb. 1988, p. 23).

It seems as though the tradition as it has existed (learning as *piochage* or "memorization, cramming", better known as *bachotage* on the *lycée* level, which means "swotting for the *bachot*", i.e. the school-leaving examination) has once again won out over the alternative tradition of the great pedagogical utopias and reform initiatives. The right *combination* between teaching sense of duty (ultimately heteronomous, but acceptable), discipline and responsibility, on the one hand, and, on the other hand, educating growing children to make their own decisions and act maturely has not yet been found. Therefore, although the majority of 18-year old adolescents are legally considered to be of age, they are not by any means mature – contrary to how it may appear on the surface. Due to the shortcomings of the educational system this ambivalence is then perpetuated in consequent university studies and professional careers. The eloquent complaints of many adolescents, parents and teachers (e.g. in Vincent 1974, a documentation which has remained up-to-date on account of the tradition-oriented education system in France) have adequately verified these assertions.

The opposition between heteronomous and self-determined learning also applies *mutatis mutandis* to the situation in Germany. In the meantime, the educational systems of both countries have developed a great deal in common. However, there are also deep-rooted, historically evolved structural differences which have remained intact. The following section is intended as an introduction to both the similarities and main differences.

5.1 *Common problems and principal differences*

Three common, related problems (quantity, contents and access with regard to the educational system) and five principal differences (key words: *éducation, centralisation, querelle scolaire, collège jésuite* and *système binaire* of higher learning) will be covered.

5.1.1 Common problems

Since the 1950's, schools in both countries – and since the 1960's the universities – have felt the pressure of high post-war birth-rates. *Table 18* exemplifies this based on three school/academic years in France, where the quantitative and qualitative problems in the educational system became apparent approx. 5 years earlier than they did in Germany.

Table 20: Enrolment in Secondary Schools (S II) and Institutions of Higher Learning in France

1963/64	2,9 m. S II	383 500 Stud.
1967/68	3,5 m. S II	645 300 Stud.
1972/73	4,6 m. S II	910 000 Stud.

(From: Nieser 1977, p. 21)

At the same time, economic growth and technological progress caused an increase in the demand for more "mobile", adaptable employees as well as faculty competent in scientific and technological areas. This created a demand for changes in the curriculum, especially in terms of maths, natural sciences and technical subjects. Due to restrictions placed on school hours and learning capacity, this change actually debased philological and historical subjects, perhaps with the exception of English as the leading international language for commercial and general communication purposes (within this framework, one can note within France – which is indeed centralistic – a broader range of choices for 1st and 2nd foreign languages than in Germany).

The changeover in France to liberal/capitalistic Giscardism and in Germany to the social democratic/liberal coalition (Brandt administration, Schmidt administration) provided the necessary response to demands for equal opportunity in education. Public revenue resulting from the economic upswing allowed for the necessary financial assistance.

Both nations were faced with the same problems concerning quantity, content and "social" structure of their educational systems and both had to try to solve them. Both countries "succeeded" (?) in expanding and reorienting their educational systems to a considerable degree.

However, economic impetus was followed by recession. After the years characterized by high birth-rates came the birth-rate slump, caused in part by the "pill". The validity of the accusation must be judged as to whether responsible politicians, recognizing these trends in good time, closed their eyes to them for tactical reasons involving their constituency and elections. In any event, when the period of euphoria and educational enhancement had been over for a long time, both governments were superseded by conservative administrations, Germany in 1983 and France in 1986. The joint effect of three factors, namely economy, demography and politics, led in turn to a new trend. Once again, educational content and access were at stake. The improvements of the schools and universities, which the "liberal" administrations had already slowed down on account of the recession and the decreasing birth-rate, were finally "stopped". Unaffected by these measures were certain technical or medical schools with a promising future. Shrinking school enrolment (beginning in 1973/74) and stagnating or, at best, modest economic growth (and thus the tight financial situation of all those institutions maintaining schools) had *five serious consequences*:

1. There were very few vacant positions for teachers. As a result of massive hiring up to around the mid-70's and the subsequent hiring

restrictions, teaching positions were blocked. They became sought-after rarities in both countries. (The changing trend now affecting France [cf. 5.3.2] will also become visible in Germany within a few years.)

2. Therefore, teacher education programs at universities had to be reoriented. Now, France seems to have had better fortune than Germany (see 5.3 and 5.3.2; cf. also 5.3.5)

3. Some schools (especially elementary schools and high schools or *lycées*) had to shut down. Owing to the internal *competition* in schools of one district and possibly even the new social *composition* of the school population following the expansion phase, requirements were *lowered* and grades were *inflated*. These changes are still going on today. They also seem to be encouraged by higher educational and professional prospects. Every school seems to want to make it easier for their pupils to reach the most desirable educational goals. This includes not only acceptance into programs with *restricted entry* at German universities, French *classes préparatoires* as well as *Grandes Ecoles*, and acceptance at medical, professional and technical schools in France, but also simply obtaining jobs and trainee positions in the service sector (banks, insurance companies, trade, hospitals, public offices etc.). The German schools (*Hauptschulen, Realschulen* and *Gymnasien*) as well as the French *collèges* and *lycées* are opening their doors as wide as possible in order to be able to survive the competition. Their *graduates* are given optimal grades so that they may stand a chance in the competition they then face when applying to colleges and universities and ultimately for jobs. There is confidence that "verbal propaganda" is still the best means of advertisement, even for schools...

4. All this has an immediate effect on the *educational content*. Since only knowledge and knowledge-based skills are easy to evaluate and can therefore be quantified, the curriculum is divided into relatively easily consumable and reproducible mini-series. Students who are *creative* and are able to reflect upon themselves and *make decisions* are not in demand; nor is the *socially outgoing* personality geared towards help and cooperation ("teamwork"). The result is that in this system it is mostly the swift reproducer, the one with the memory filled to the brim, the conforming "mnemo-technician" who is more "competitive" than "cooperative", who is successful but hardly the independent thinker – to the dismay of many teachers. Even with differences in degree between France and Germany (see 5.4.2), the tendency in both countries is the same. All welcome countermeasures proposed by

committed educators (for example, school concerts, field trips, foreign exchange programs, extra-curricular activities, invitations, weekend seminars) are only a drop in the bucket under such learning conditions. The well-known reversal holds true more than ever for the degenerated education system of the present: *non vitae, sed scholae discimus.*

5. If one seeks to counteract "grade inflation" in schools by implementing stricter standardization and control (as is at least the case with the *baccalauréat* in France and the *Zentralabitur* in Baden-Württemberg), the only results in such instances are raised performance standards and a greater selection of "competitive mnemo-technicians". In other words, the creative and innovative, self-determining and social abilities of talented and highly talented students are choked off to an even larger extent. If good grades have lost the value they had twenty years ago and the hard-working, conforming, knowledge-hording and -reproducing mould of youth is bred and even celebrated by the systems of "education," then the calls for the formation of a true elite in the interest of the nation, for a more highly-skilled and sovereign elite capable of decision-making and commitment are actually a consequence of the deficiencies of the respective systems of education. The "conservative" governments, however, want to make *admission* to institutions of higher "learning" more difficult, i.e. they want to make schools and vocational training more appealing and promote the more professionally oriented technical schools to an even greater degree than the universities. In this way they intend to lower the number of unemployed with such academic degrees as the *licence/maîtrise* and the *Staatsexamen/Magisterexamen.* In lieu of such graduates, a *"new elite"* more suited for national leadership is supposed to take over. This elite group is expected to be familiar with modern technology, commercial law, personnel management, negotiating skills and be loyal to its country and *conservative* (but *innovative* in terms of international economic competition and national export interests). In other words, this group is supposed to represent the new civil servant or manager nobility. Of course, no one would describe the "new elite" so blatantly. The transition from an egalitarian to an elitist education will be carried out very carefully and with the necessary tact, i.e with consideration of constituencies and lobbies, and the necessary concessions to non-business related-technical subjects, experts and institutions of learning. The traditional *Gymnasien* and *lycées* as well as both traditional and modern universities still provide "semi-education" without immediate utility. Parallel to this,

institutions of learning are being designed for the "new elite". France is much more advanced with its *Grandes Ecoles* than Germany which at present is still experiencing great difficulties in setting up elitist universities and programs of study. It is no wonder. If schools prepared mature high school (Abitur) and college graduates to be able to deal with current problems and to solve them, elitist schools and education would no longer be necessary. This, of course, would require a reevaluation of the entire education system: a change in educational objectives, the inclusion of creative experience, autonomous decision-making and teamwork in the curriculum, the expansion of history as a school subject as well as the integration of subjects such as technology, business, psychology and applied psychology (in terms of the practical experience described above). The various levels of difficulty from junior high school to the university programs in dire need of reform would be affected by these changes. In France similar desiderata have been announced. For example, François Périgot, president of the CNPF, has deemed the «faculté d'adaption, créativité, capacité de travailler en commun» (ME, Oct. 1988, p.11) necessary «aptitudes que l'école ne développe guère».

The former Minister of Education in Hesse, Ludwig von Friedeburg, likened the transition from an egalitarian to an elitist education - which also took place in France – to "the swing of the pendulum between change and restauration". His evaluation of the situation was:

> "Phases of societal enhancement and increased opportunities in education and career are followed by reactionary periods. When resources have become scarce and the better spots at the universities rare, it is a question of holding onto attained positions while throttling the rush from below. In times of economic prosperity, *Gymnasien* and universities were opened. The rule of thumb was push instead of selection. A rigid selection process has now begun. The economic downswing has reawakened the discussion on the formation of the elite." (Die Zeit, 6 April 1984)

Influenced by the growing enrolment in schools and universities as well as the economic upswing, both countries have accordingly a) built up and b) democratized their education systems. At present, they must face the question of whether and how these structures can be maintained or, if need be, reorganized in view of the altered economic and demographic situations. Until it is realized that, in addition to functional unemployment and the helplessness of many parents, competition among schools also directly opposes high cultural ideals of performance, a lot of water will have flowed under the bridge.

5.1.2 Various educational concepts

The fundamental concepts of the French education system are *éducation* and *enseignement*. They presuppose an *educator* who leads the "pupil" to certain norms, values and abilities which are in accordance with interests of either the nation or some national group. In other words, there is a duality consisting of a knowledgable and guiding educator and pupils who are entrusted to this educator and taught by him or her. Within the German education system, the concept of *Bildung* still predominantly implies "self-maturation". The educator only gives the "plant", the evolving personality, support. It can only develop and learn about itself by means of its character, decisions and commitment to its studies. Thus, *éducation* is regarded as a dual and transitive process determined by society, whereas *Bildung* is considered to be an individual, "monadic" and intransitive developmental process leading to an individual personality, career and existence. This is no different than the process of blossoming or the formation of crystals. In this respect, the concept of *éducation* is related to a community-oriented, societal ideology, while the concept of *Bildung* refers to an individualistic, monadic and ultimately biologically oriented one (as is the case with the concept of *Reife* [maturity] and the previous term *Reifeprüfung* [school-leaving exam]. For more on this subject, see 5.4.2. Unfortunately, the scope of this discussion does not allow for a further analysis of the difference in meaning between the French *éducation* and its English equivalent.

In today's world of education, the various forms of learning in the *lycée*, in the reformed last three years of German secondary school and in the universities of both countries contain *remnants* of these two fundamentally different concepts. These remnants have been able to survive on both sides of the Rhine in spite of the problematic developments discussed here (cf. Rappenecker 1990, p. 357). In conclusion, it might be added that, from a philosophical point of view, *éducation* and *Bildung* do not end with the beginning of a career. "Being shaped" and "shaping oneself " are also in actuality life-long processes. However, if one disregards adult education centres, *éducation permanente* and re-education courses (both public and on an internal company basis), continuing education seminars and the newly begun senior citizen study programs, this truth has barely begun to be recognized on an institutional level. The awareness of these new tasks exists in all political parties. There are considerable difficulties in realizing the appropriate plans, however. Adult education will primarily have economic and social tasks. If the trend toward a reduction in the working week ("the 35-hour week") and an increase in leisure time continues, then the so-called *quaternary sector* of institutionalized adult education might also become differentiated and larger in scope.

5.1.3 Centralism and federalism

In the Federal Republic of Germany the Länder (states) have the power to make decisions relating to education. In practice, only the Conference of the State Ministries of Education serves as a counterbalance. In France, the education system already began to undergo a step-by-step centralization process in the nineteenth century. Under Napoleon, a unified and hierarchical administrative structure was created in *secondary and tertiary education* (*lycées, facultés, Grandes Ecoles*) and the state monopoly on education was implemented. Strict supervision and discipline were enforced in these institutions to educate future administrative and military leaders (for further details, cf. Green 1990, pp. 146-154). By contrast, *the primary schools* remained de facto in the hands of the *Frères des Ecoles Chrétiennes*, a catholic monastic order. It was not until the Third Republic that the primary schools became a part of the centralized education and school administrative structure. In the struggle against the monarchy and "clericalism", laws were passed in 1881/82 which made general primary schools mandatory for all children (for more details, cf. 5.2).

A very particular organization underlies the *administrative structure*. The Minister of Education stands at the top. He is in charge of 25 (previously 21) *académies*, i.e. regional administrative entities of the education system (cf. *Fig. 60*). To a large extent, the bounds of the *académies* coincide with those of the administrative *régions* (e.g. académie de Rennes: région Bretagne). Every *académie* is headed by a *recteur* (principal) who is answerable to the minister for all schools in his district. Up until 1968, he was also the head of the respective universities. Since then, this has been the responsibility of the university president; the function of the *recteur* in this area is limited to a supervisory role. In each département of an *académie* the teachers are supervised by an *inspecteur d'académie* (in the *lycées* and *collèges*) or an *inspecteur départemental* (in the *écoles primaires*), both who answer to the *recteur*. The *inspecteur* is responsible for teacher evaluation (important for their career opportunities) as well as educational planning and supervision. This centralized system dating back to Napoleon is characterized by the following aspects:

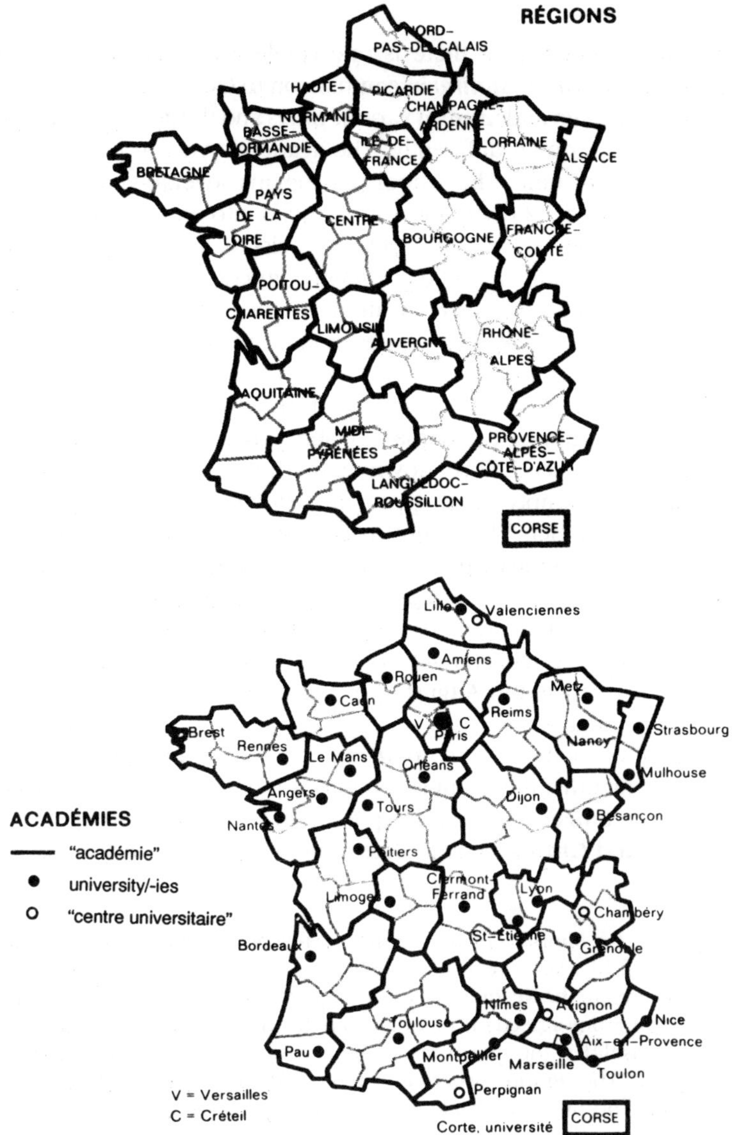

Fig. 60: Régions and *académies* in France
(From: Petit Larousse illustré 1981, p. 1801)

The *centres universitaires* in the above map have since been transformed into *universités*. In some of the larger cities, "the" university has been split into three according to disciplines; Paris has 13 universities. The *Université 2000* plan calls for seven new universities: four in the Ile-de-France region, two in the Département Nord and one in La Rochelle.

1. Throughout France there is one single academic year (*année scolaire, année universitaire*) in comparison to Germany in which the school years begin and finish at various times and the academic semesters are broken down differently. The academic year in France goes from October to June. The school year begins several weeks earlier. On a trial basis, a 7:2 rhythm was introduced into schools throughout France from 1990/91 on: with every 7 weeks of instruction followed by two weeks of holidays. The *grandes vacances*, however, remain an exception to this. Summer vacation in the schools (*les grandes vacances/vacances d'été*) lasts longer in France than in Germany: eight to nine weeks in comparison to the German average of six weeks. The summer vacation does not only determine the rhythm of school life but also – and to a greater extent than in Germany – economic life. Many factories and offices close down with the beginning of summer vacation. Cities empty since approximately 25 million French go on vacation in summer. The return to school life is a similar event: *la rentrée* is made visible by the appropriate decoration of all department store display windows. Throughout France, the first day of school is on the same day in September. While all business activity (not just in terms of larger establishments but also, for example, shops and libraries) is restricted in August, the start of the school year sets it in motion once again.

2. The level of the *baccalauréat* is standardized throughout France due to the fact that the exam is centrally administered. (This does not apply to the universities. In principle, it is up to the discretion of each *université* and *Grande Ecole* to determine what is to be instructed and tested.)

In Germany, the Ministers of Education have reached a compromise regarding the *Oberstufe* (the last 3 years of Gymnasium) and the *Abitur* (school-leaving exam). There are, however, no standard regulations as in France. In October 1987, the Ministers agreed on a list of joint regulations by means of which they hope to consolidate the spectrum of general education starting in the 1989/90 school year. The *mutual recognition of the Abitur* among the individual German states – no more and no less – thereby remains safeguarded.

The process of re-unification in Germany has given rise to a further problem: the *Abitur* requires 12 years of school in the *new* federal states but, up to now, 13 years in the *old* ones. This has flamed a new discussion which is still far from settled. These differences serve to illustrate further the autonomy of the *Land* in education policy and the difficulty in achieving a consensus at the Ministers of Education Conference.

3. The French *éducation nationale* may be designated as the world's largest centrally directed establishment. The ministry in Paris directs and pays more than one million employees. (A recent tendency, which could be termed a cautious policy of de-centralisation, does not necessarily stand in contradiction to the existing system. The new policy is indeed a concession to accommodate the wishes of the regions and départements, but remains nevertheless centrally directed.)

In Germany, there are some similarities (as in the case of the *Abitur*) owing to the educational jurisdiction of the states, but no such uniform regulations. Apart from the federal government's right of co-determination in matters concerning vocational training, fundamental political decisions regarding the educational system are closely related to party representation and plurality. For example, this includes the issue pertaining to the comprehensive or subdivided school system.

The socialist-liberal coalition (see 2.9.1), supported by the Confederation of German Trade Unions, had planned to establish the comprehensive schools as standard institutions, as well as the comprehensive universities in tertiary education. This was foreseen in the overall educational plan which was drawn up beginning in the mid-70's and then passed into law in 1973. Later on, several SPD-FDP bulwarks fell one after the other. The states and respective Ministries of Education which had remained predominantly SPD-governed took extremely bitter rearguard action in favour of the *Gesamtschule*. What is the situation like today? If calculations are based on official figures, integrated comprehensive schools (in comparison to cooperative comprehensive schools which unite several types of schools "under one roof") represent about 8.9% of the schools and 5% of the pupils at schools providing general education (see Bundesministerium für Bildung und Wissenschaft 1985, pp.24 and 26). And in 1989 the *Gesamtschulen* (integrated comprehensive schools) could lay claim to only 0.273 m. of the total 6.734 m. pupils attending schools providing general education (i.e., 4.05%). Therefore, it is hardly possible to talk about Germany falling into "two educational scenes". However this conflict on the front is evaluated, it does elucidate the contrast between the situations in the individual German states (even with considerable differences of degree in the way the Christian-Democratic Ministries of Education approach the comprehensive school issue) and the uniform regulations in France.

5.1.4 *"Séparation des Eglises et de L'Etat"* vs. *Staatskirchen und Staat* (Separation of Church and State vs. "State Churches" and the State)

In Germany, religious instruction is typically taught at school and theology is a commonly offered major at the universities. In addition, two-thirds of all kindergartens are directed and financed, either fully or in part, by both the Protestant and Catholic churches. Church and State do not stand in opposition to one another. Pursuant to the concordats concluded between individual federal states and the Vatican (Bavaria 1924, Prussia 1929, Baden 1932) and still in force in the FRG, and pursuant to the concordat concluded between the State and the Vatican in 1933 (cf. Lill 1990, p. 468f.; for a more differentiated account: Nobécourt 1977), which has since been applied to other confessions by way of analogy, the State collects church taxes from every employed person belonging to a religious denomination. Even today, the church tax remains the most important source of revenue for German churches. In this respect, they are "state churches" (not officially, of course, since Article 4 of the constitution guarantees freedom of worship and since other religious communities, e.g. the Jewish community, enjoy the same rights). The representatives of the Church play a role in public life which by no means is to be underestimated. In accordance with the norm of active, Christian commitment, they are very involved in the political parties, lobbies, the peace movement and the broadcasting councils (even as official delegates of the Church) which make decisions concerning radio and television programs.

In France, the situation is different (excepting the special case of Alsace-Lorraine). In 1905, Church and State were fully separated owing to the victory of the *républicains*, especially the *radicaux* (cf. 2.5.3) and the Freemasons, who were extremely influential in the Third Republic. Ever since then, there have been two systems. On the one hand, there is the public school system (*école publique*) which does not have any religious instruction and, on the other hand, the so-called private school system (*école privée*, referred to by its advocates as the *école libre*). Approximately 2.2 million pupils, (i.e. currently 17% of all pupils) attend private schools, 90% of whom are Catholic. Striking is the high percentage of private schools (between 25 and 30%) on secondary school level (*collèges, lycées, lycées professionnels*). This might be related to the widespread and, at the same time, controversial view that private schools are more concerned with the discipline and performance of their pupils. Another decisive factor is the fact that the children of foreign workers are mostly excluded from attending private schools due to the high tuition, while children from middle and upper-class families more or less remain among "their own kind". This is particularly true of those regions containing a well-developed private school system of *recent* origin. In this respect it is also necessary to distinguish between "new" and "old" *écoles privées* regions (Rouault 1990).

The age-old *querelle scolaire* between the anticlerical supporters of the uniform public school (*«laïcs»*) and the advocates of publicly funded private schools (*«cathos» = catholiques*) dates back to the French Revolution and the nineteenth century. The clergy was on the side of the monarchy and, therefore, the republicans were anticlerical. Ever since then, the *querelle scolaire* flares up time and again. Rightist administrations seek to promote private schools, while leftist administrations seek to restrict them (see Schmidt et al. 1981, p. 263; 1983, pp. 13-16). Leftist governments have continuously tried – and up to now without success – to realize the egalitarian claim of the constitutions of 1948 and 1958 in the face of all increases in state subsidies put through by the rightists and protested by the leftists. (The preamble of 1958 thus says: «La Nation garantit l'égal accès de l'enfant et de l'adulte à l'instruction, à la formation professionnelle et à la culture.») The last attempt of the government to influence massively the private school system and the mediation efforts of the former Minister of Education, Savary, led to fierce reactions on both sides (cf. *Fig. 61*). The minister's resignation and, soon thereafter, the resignation of the entire Mauroy cabinet in July 1984 were directly related to Catholic-led mass demonstrations. This was probably also connected to the strategic errors of the socialists who had not anticipated such resistance (and consequently such a massive anti-campaign carried out by political opponents among their own constituency).

Naturally, the *querelle scolaire* seems – from a German perspective, at least – to be outdated since there are other weighty problems in France (discipline, motivation, quality of performance, integration of the children of foreign workers, inclusion of modern technology) which should come to the forefront of debate.

However, as long as the indisputable social privileges of private schools and their pupils exist – privileges which contradict the immortal spirit of the Great Revolution in France – the *querelle scolaire* will virtually remain alive. This dispute could even flare up again tomorrow.

(Dessin de PLANTU.)

Fig. 61: Caricature of the *Querelle Scolaire.*
(From: Le Monde, 29 Nov. 1983)

The "Thursday holiday" (*jeudi libre*), which was introduced in 1882, began as a compromise between the republican camp and the church (since 1972, there is a "Wednesday holiday" (*mercredi libre*) for *primary schools* and *collèges*, but on the *lycée* level only for part of the day). In 1882, the republican camp did not have so much power as to be able to effect a total separation of Church and State. It was only powerful enough to enforce compulsory education at public schools (*enseignement primaire: gratuit, obligatoire et laïque*: primary education: free, mandatory and secular). One day a week was reserved for religious instruction outside normal instruction. This compromise remained in effect even after the final separation of Church and State in 1905. However, the public schools (*écoles publiques*) are increasingly breaking this resolution – to the annoyance of the Church – in favour of the Saturday holiday and catechism postponed until that day. (Nevertheless, there is no total separation of Church and State. This is not only evident in the state subsidies awarded to private schools but also, for example, in the continued validity of the concordat between Napoleon and Pius VII (1801) for the benefit of Alsace and Moselle as well as the different religious television broadcasts on Sunday mornings). In accordance with the separation of Church and State, Catholic clergymen receive their education at different *universités libres* which are officially termed *Instituts catholiques.*

The three *départements* Haut-Rhin, Bas-Rhin and Moselle (at that time comprising German Alsace-Lorraine [Elsaß- Lothringen]) are excluded from the separation of Church and State taking effect in 1905. These *départements* still have religious education at state schools, their clerics are still paid through the State, and they each have a Protestant and a Catholic Faculty at one of Strassbourg's three state universities. The churches in these *départements* are faring better than those in other parts of France, and they are more firmly anchored in the population.

5.1.5 The spirit of the Jesuit college vs. the influence of Protestantism

French children attend *all-day schools,* starting with the *école maternelle* on up to the *lycée.* Instruction begins at 8 o'clock (in some preschools at 9 o'clock) and generally continues until 4:30 in the afternoon (with a lunch break from 12 to 2 o'clock). Each instruction period lasts 50 or 55 minutes (and not just 45 minutes as in Germany). Thus, the day at school is long. Being young means going to school – to a greater extent than in Germany. Moreover, a large number of pupils (in rural areas almost 50%) attend *boarding schools* which belong to nearly every *lycée.* These pupils are called *«internes»* (the others are *«externes»*). In this way, those from rural areas are spared the long trips to school. Moreover, in contrast to the usually elite German boarding schools, the French boarding schools also accept children coming from low-income families. Considering the facilities of the *école maternelle,* the all-day school and the *boarding school* as a whole and then the resulting minimal parental influence, the following conclusions are compelling. In France, usually as soon as a child reaches the age of three, school becomes the *primary* education authority. A child must become accustomed to school at a young age. With respect to the long school days and instruction periods on the one hand and the greater number of holidays (compared with other countries) including summer vacation (France has an average of only 180 schooldays, Germany between 200 and 226) on the other hand, the criticism of the *«malmenage scolaire»* ("too short a school year, school days too long") is by no means anything new. (ME, Jan. 1983, p. 9; see also ME, Dec. 1988, pp. 17-22).

Psychological research shows that the ability of children to absorb information begins slacking off after 40 minutes at the latest, especially on Friday afternoons and Saturdays. In addition, long summer vacations are said to lead to a *«perte rapide de connaissances et d'attitudes scolaires»* ("rapid loss of knowledge and school attitude") (ME, Jan. 1983, pp. 8-9). The evaluation of the 55-minute instruction periods should be more differentiated. These time slots should not be condemned a priori as they can prove to be of great advantage for certain types of instruction (e.g. course work requiring intensive in-class exercise of materials) as well as particular classes (e.g. "shop" courses and physical education), especially when compared with the German 45-minute system. Neither the "longer" nor the "shorter" instruction period is representative of a didactic optimum. It is much more the subjects and the contents and organization of the syllabus which are the deciding factors. The possibility of a thorough and *in-depth acquisition* of *related* knowledge and skills is of special importance, however. Particularly the *rigid* 55 and 45-minute systems, still dominant on both sides of the Rhine, clearly show how little most public and private schools have been open to impulses from pedagogical reform movements (e.g. Ecole Freinet, Waldorf school, Montessori school) – despite various important changes in the educational system.

By contrast, the long summer vacation in France is criticized almost everywhere. The reduction of summer vacation has failed in part due to the resistance of the teachers' unions and in part due to the vacation plans of parents as well as the usual adjustment of companies to this school rhythm (ME, Jan. 1983, pp. 8-9). On the 7:2 rhythm introduced elsewhere cf. 5.1.3.

All-day schools and boarding schools both go back to the *Jesuit schools* of the seventeenth and eighteenth centuries, originating in the counter-reformation (Contre-Réforme) and the *Ratio atque institutio studiorum* which was enacted in 1599 and, with modifications, is still valid today in all Jesuit schools throughout the world (see Dolch 1959, pp. 238-242). However, the function of these all-day schools with boarding facilities was vastly different from the one today: "Children were supposed to grow up behind school walls in a world free of sin with its own perfect organization of societal living. The means of achieving this included the total disappearance of the individual within the group, the supervision of all by all, discipline and strict formalism" (Stephan 1978, p. 148). When the public *lycée* replaced the previously dominant *collège jésuite* during Napolean's rule, Jesuit organizational and disciplinary forms were adapted. Even the spirit of the Jesuit school continued and still continues to exist in the principle of *aemulatio* (*émulation*, driving competition among pupils), the promotion of the intellect and, especially, the underscoring of systematic and logical written expression.

The Jesuit schools, which gave instruction only in Latin, placed great emphasis on the importance of rhetoric, the techniques of effective argumentation, and cultivated linguistic norms (for an evaluation, cf. Green 1990, p. 160). These ideals were passed on to the French language as it was and still is taught in schools today. The construct of thought and the characteristic style of speech of Jaurès, de Gaulle, Pompidou or Mitterrand – just to name a few examples – would be inconceivable without this educational background. *These forms and goals - in actuality intended for the Jesuit schools and then the lycées - became later generalized, starting with the primary schools up to the Grandes Ecoles.* This is but one of many examples, especially characteristic of France, illustrating the phenomenon of the *"fall"* (or rather the democratization) of advanced culture: from the various forms of address (*Madame, Mademoiselle, Monsieur*), to standard language as such, to gastronomy (including white bread and red wine "for all") as well as to the popular traditions of hunting and horse race. In fact, the Jesuit schools began with the "democratization" of educational curricula and formal *politesse* (literally: "polishing", i.e. the finishing or rounding off). The urban middle-class retained its privileged status in the Jesuit schools, however, talented children from the lower classes also received the opportunity of social advancement, especially within the clergy (Frijhoff/Julia 1975). The Bonaparte regime continued this trend, thereby forging links to the educational institutions of the Third, Fourth and Fifth Republics. The conservative turnaround already started to become apparent in French education policy under the leftist government's Minister of Education Chevènement (after the Savary era). The question remains as to whether the return to greater selection, more work and discipline, a solid, well-structured *exposé* and correct language use with well-defined orthography will be carried out or if this is at all possible. Would this even include the reintroduction of the *distribution des prix* and *tableaux d'honneur* (award and honour roll system, i.e. *the "emulation" principle*) which used to be common? It also remains to be seen whether conservative school and university critics will be able to put through their distinctly, often at times vehemently expressed demands (see e.g. Nouvel Observateur, 2 March 1984, p. 24). In any case, a radical, irreversible transition has taken place from the *humanistic Jesuit school* to *mass education* with its new dominant maths-science-technology component. Jesuit "democratization" tried to assimilate the lower tiers into the upper levels, i.e. talented lower class pupils to the elite level. Modern "democratization" tends to assimilate from the upper tiers to the lower levels, i.e. creating a lowering of the general level. This structural change is so radical that all counter-currents (see 5.1.1 and 5.1.4) cannot alter the overall picture.

This process is similar to the one which can be observed in Germany.

If many features of the education system in France can be traced back to the *Jesuit school system* (which was involved in the *counter-reformation* and its dogmatic propaganda), then the origins of the education systems of the Weimar Republic and the Federal Republic of Germany are to be found in the *Protestant high schools* and the *Protestant-influenced universities* pursuant to the Neo-Hellenism of W. v. Humboldt. The Lutheran and Calvinist conception of mercy centres around the individual rather than a group to be won over by *propaganda fide* (propagating the faith). If religious salvation is a sign of God's mercy, then – and in recollection of Max Weber's well-known essay on capitalism – diligence, persistence, thrift, self-discipline and the thereby acquired earthly success are proof of God's influence and effect on the individual. The Protestant merchant's son from long ago has become the career-striving child of the employee or civil servant in affluent West German society. The former Lutheran and Calvinist ethic of the glory of God and Prussia on earth (translator's note: "Prussia's Gloria" was the title of a well-known German military march until 1945), which had already been bred in classroom and vicarage, has been transformed into the glance of pure material status symbols. Nevertheless, a little bit of this idealistic eagerness to improve one's mind has been well preserved in German classrooms and lecture halls. It is simply not to be erased from the minds of many teachers and students (especially female students). An undeniable protestant work and educational ethic has survived generation after generation even in families in which the grandparents rarely went to church. The norms governing behaviour and lifestyle, especially in terms of *upbringing and education*, seem to be more persistent than the philosophy, the great ideologies and goals which once created and justified these norms. This is true of the situations in both France and Germany. Nevertheless, there is a negative aspect connected with the situation in Germany which is described in greater detail in section 5.4.2. The alliance between Protestantism and Neo-Hellenism in the German educational ideal, which no doubt had once led to world-renown high schools, universities and research institutes, also has a highly fatal side. This "dark side" has shown its face whenever secular profanities such as the glory of Prussia or the eternal Fatherland of the Third Reich or even the Michael-Kohlhaas mentality of the Spartacists, the world revolutionists or the RAF (*Rote Armee Fraktion*) have taken the place of either God or the platonic qualities of goodness, truth and beauty, strived for by the seeking and learning individual.

5.1.6 "Dual" vs. "a More Uniform" system of higher learning

Compared with the fundamental dualities within the tertiary education system in France (*Grandes Ecoles* vs. *universités*), the German university system has a "monocultural" tradition (which will probably cause the failure of more recent efforts – with only few exceptions – towards the establishment of elite colleges and courses of studies. See 5.1.1). At the same time, the French tendency to separate research and instruction can be contrasted with the unification of both activities in Germany, a concept still influenced by the ideals of W. v. Humboldt. (Ideally, teachers at German *Gymnasien* and institutions of higher education provide their pupils and students with enough freedom to dedicate themselves to "learning by research", for example in terms of source research for the subject history, in regional studies of the philologies, in biochemistry and in computer technology). A qualitative comparison between the overall achievement of the *Grandes Ecoles* and *universités* and that of the German *Universitäten* is difficult, if not impossible. If the achievements of the French system of separated research and instruction were compared to those of the German system of combined research and instruction, France would unfortunately get a devastating rating. Whoever is familiar with the realities of both systems of higher education can confirm this, even if he or she is able to point out exceptions in France and Germany. (For example, the Max-Planck-Institute and the Fraunhofer Institute are both pure research institutes in the Federal Republic of Germany. In May 1968, a much more *active link* between research and instruction, especially in the field of German studies, began to emerge in France, e.g. at the *Institut d'Allemand d'Asnières*, which is part of the *Université de Paris III*. For an analysis of this combination from the French point of view, see Bertraux 1973, in particular pp. 55 and 66f.).

As a background to the distinctions discussed here lies the fact that research in France is predominantly organised by the state-run CNRS (*Centre National de la Recherche Scientifique*). The CNRS is a centrally directed institution, independent of the *universités* and the *Grandes Ecoles*. It arose out of the state-run *Caisse des recherches scientifiques* (1901); the actual founding took place in 1939. Its successes include work in atomic physics and "applied atomic energy", in oceanography, in aeronautics and in medicine – though less so (at least internationally) in the *sciences humaines.* Even Frenchmen with no affiliation therefore draw attention to the low salaries paid to many of the employees; teachers in higher education earn far more. In any case, the concentration of research (and funding for research) within the CNRS organism has lamed the *universités* for decades. Certainly a quite different factor has also contributed to this laming: the particularly long period of time required for the *thèse d'Etat.* Often eight to ten years are needed for its preparation, i.e. far longer than the German *Habilitation* (cf. 5.3.2). By completion, the author's appetite for research had often been satiated. Or else he dedicated himself to publishing – more or less exclusively in his *spécialité.* Now, however, new independent forces are arising, and not only at the *universités* but also at the *Grandes Ecoles,* which until now have been almost exclusively "practice-oriented".

For a comparison of vocational high schools and the *Grandes Ecoles,* refer to 5.3.4.

5.1.7 Conclusion: different traditions – different systems

If the education systems of both countries are subject to the pressure of party policy to a certain degree, then *older traditions* are indeed decisive for the scope of both systems. (Other important factors include changing current demands and efforts as regards quantity, content and social aspects which, depending on the government, are interpreted and influenced in a "liberal-conservative" or "socialist-social democratic" manner). In France, these traditions primarily concern centralism, the Jesuit schools of the Counter-reformation and the conflict between the egalitarian-revolutionary and elitist-conservative traditions. The *querelle scolaire* is demonstrative of the conflict between these two traditions. Especially in the twentieth century, this conflict has found a new expression in the duality between the *universités* and the (elitist) *Grandes Ecoles* which have been expanded, become more influential and greater in number. For a long time, a particular type of Grande Ecole was considered the most typical embodiment of the French education system: the *Ecole Normale Supérieure* in Paris' rue d'Ulm (see 5.3.1). In terms of prestige, the E.N.S. (which is currently more restricted to its traditional domain: teaching professions of high standing) no longer takes first place, but rather the *E.N.A.* (see ibid., cf. Bourdieu 1989, p. 188). – Federalism,

Protestantism and Neo-Hellenism, which at that time had a Protestant bias (both primarily influenced by Prussia), have shaped the traditions of the education system in Germany. Even the opposition between old elitist and old egalitarian efforts continues to exist.

On an organizational level, for example, there is the Association of Philologists (pro-Gymnasium) on the one hand and, on the other hand, the GEW, the *Gewerkschaft Erziehung und Wissenschaft*, a part of the DGB (see 4.6.5), which supports comprehensive schools. On a party level, this opposition is not as rigid due to the trend of the mass parties. This opposition, however, reflects a mere *tendency*. On the one hand, there is the educational policy of Christian-democratic governed *Länder*: in these states there is a preference for a structured school system whose advocates have rejected the designation "elitist", but not the idea of elitist courses of studies. In addition, professors have attained greater influence in university committees. On the other hand, there is the educational policy of social-democratic governed *Länder* which are more in favour of comprehensive schools (and likewise, more unfavourable towards elitist courses of studies and a "power monopoly" of the professors). Nonetheless, it must be emphasized that these fronts draw our attention away from the more essential problems and issues and abstract from them just as much as the fronts in the French *querelle scolaire* (see 5.1.4).

The most obvious manifestation of the depicted traditions in the German education system and a good example of its diversity is the expanding *Waldorf School movement* (see Leber 1985). The fundamental characteristics of this movement include: a *federalistic* structure with loose connections (each Waldorf school has its own "complexion", its own areas of experimentation - although limited), an *individualistic educational ideal* clearly influenced by *Goethe*'s body of thought (not only by Steiner's) and *Neo-Hellenism*, and certain aspects of the *Protestant educational ethic*, which are still to be researched (the appeal to the individual's own efforts, i.e. an individual learning ethic; the inclusion of impulses from educational reformists prior to 1933; Württemberg-pietistic influence of the Stuttgart movement launched in 1919). The Waldorf schools have gone through a sociological transition. They, too, were affected by the regrouping processes. Thus, the difficult attempt was made to reconcile the older, middle-class elitist tendencies with the more recent social-egalitarian or even Green-alternative ones, which have led to considerable changes in staff and students, but which have not yet been seen by the general public. If, compared with the 146 German Waldorf schools, there are now more than 582 Waldorf schools (figures from 1992) throughout Europe and the rest of the world (including 10 in France), the spirit and fundamental principles of this movement must indeed be seen as "typically German". Among the institutions of higher education, Witten-Herdecke, a more innovative private university, is comparable to the Waldorf system. Other types of schools with similar "German" characteristics enrich Germany's truly diverse educational scene. Its curricular diversity owes itself to the federalistic structure and to a private school system which, compared with France and

French Catholic private schools, reacts to changes and new educational demands and requirements in a more flexible manner.

5.2 *An overview of the school systems in France and the Federal Republic of Germany*

The following remaining differences between the systems can be seen in *Fig. 62*:

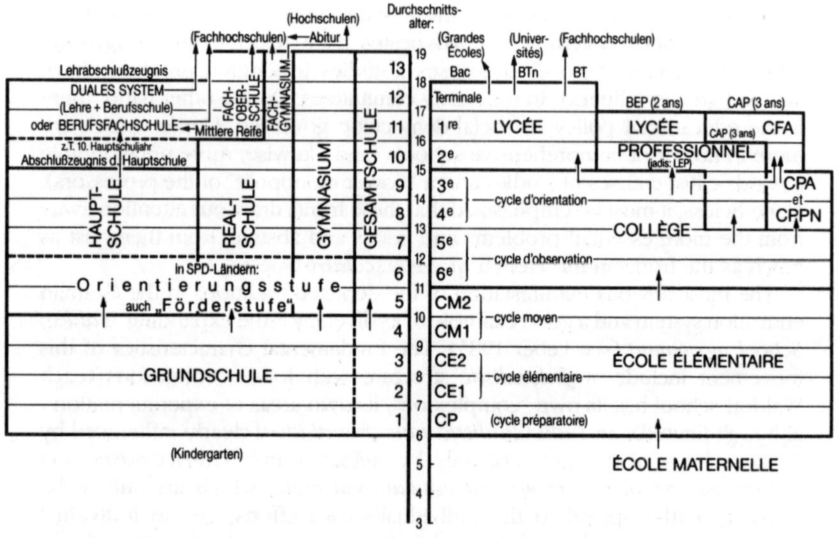

Fig. 62: The School Systems of the Federal Republic of Germany and France.

1. Unlike the German *Kindergärten*, the *écoles maternelles* are considered *part of the school system*; for this reason, teachers working at these schools (almost all of whom are women) have been trained at the *Ecoles Normales* (teacher's colleges) and are paid as primary school teachers. This has been in force since 1 January 1887 when the status of the *école maternelle* and the *école primaire* in terms of education and salaries of the *institutrices* was decreed equal. It is also for this reason that they now have to complete a three-year course of study followed by two years at an IUFM (cf. 5.3.5). Every small village has its *école maternelle* as well as its *école élémentaire*. 39% of the two-year old, 92% of the three-year old and 100% of the four and five-year

old children receive pre-school education in the école maternelle. This type of education, which served as the model for similar efforts in other countries, especially between the world wars, can be regarded very critically today in terms of the problem of early schooling as well as the *garderie* effect (both parents can work, but have less influence on their children's upbringing). French and German assessments of this situation differ (see ME, Nov. 1982, p. 21ff. and Doll in: Schmidt et al. 1981, p. 236).

2. The German four-year primary school is followed by a two-year orientation level (mixed ability classes intended to foster the particular talents of each pupil) in the states currently and, in part previously, governed by the Social Democrats. Its counterpart is the five-year *école élémentaire.*

For structure and development, cf. Gilsoul-Bézier 1989, p. 48f.; ME, Sept. 1991, p. 20-34; BO 3 Oct. 1991.

In more general terms, all pupils in France have an equal status (at least theoretically) up to and including the ninth grade (when translated into the German school system) since the *école élémentaire* is followed by the four-year *collège unique.* Its predecessor, the *Collège d'Enseignement Secondaire* (CES), was already designed after the *Réforme Fouchet* in 1963 as the school for all 11- to 15-year old children. After the *Réforme Haby,* which was passed in June 1975 and became gradually enforced in 1977, the *collège* turned into a regular school for all children in these age groups. It was also during this time that the *lycée* was finally restricted to the three upper grades (against the bitter resistance of many parents, but with the support of the former conservative president Giscard d'Estaing and his followers).

The laicistic elementary school, compulsory for children between the ages of 6 and 13, was introduced in the laws of 1881/82 by the Minister of Education, Jules Ferry. The purpose of the *école primaire* was the education of young citizens of the Republic and its teachers were intended as missionaries of the Republic. They received their training at the *Ecoles normales.* The *collège* was also founded on the egalitarian-republican tradition, with its historical origin in the leftist party program of a comprehensive school (*école unitaire*) for the youth of France (see Curtius 1931, p. 149). It can be assumed that the *collège Haby* was – among other things – established in order to take the wind out of the sails of the left-wing parties after the close election victory of Giscard d'Estaing against Mitterrand in 1974. It was namely Haby, the former Minister of Education, who presented this main part of his reform together with the primary school as the *«école commune à tous»*, at the same time making use of the equal opportunity slogan: «l'égalité des chances doit y être toujours recherchée» (Haby 1975, p. 18). The *collège* is though the biggest headache of the French education system. The ordained *enseignement commun* is difficult to realize in view of the still inadequate basic training and continuing education of its teachers as well as the differences in niveaus of the students. This is the reason why more than 6% of all school children quit as soon as the fifth grade to enter prevocational training (CPPN: *classe préprofessionelle de niveau*, followed by a CPA: *classe préparatoire à l'apprentissage*, see *Fig. 62*). Thus, the *mobilisation contre l'échec* (mobilization against failure), by means of level differentiation and counselling for pupils who might have to repeat a year, is currently in the fore of discussion (ME, May 1988, pp. 27-52 and Dec. 1991, p. 15f.).

The situation is particularly difficult in the *banlieues* in many of the major cities. Particularly in these, therefore, 554 *Zones d'Education Prioritaires* (Z.E.P.) have been established since 1981. They comprise 5,500 *écoles élémentaire*, 800 *collèges*, 130 *lycées professionnels* and 30 *lycées*. In keeping with the maxim made popular by Alain Savary, «donner plus à ceux qui ont moins», attempts are being made to provide more intensive care for 12% of France's school children. There are more teachers than usual and various other benefits have been added. In the *mal-vivre des banlieues*, the state schools are supposed to serve as centres for the radiation of hope. With this in mind, particular emphasis is also placed on adult education (cf. the *enquête* in ME, Dec. 1991, p. 18-35 and Gilsoul-Bézier 1989, p. 133).

In contrast to the *collège* or the *Z.E.P.*, it is the *Hauptschule* (not the *Gesamtschule*, cf. 5.1.3) that can be considered the most serious crisis area or the weakest link in the German education system. Because of the three-tier school system, however, the basic problem is of a different kind: this school is suffering from increasing depletion. At the beginning of the 1970s, 70% of the children attended *Hauptschule*; today the figure has dropped to a mere 31.5% throughout all of Germany, with every second school regarded as endangered (Badische Zeitung, 21 Feb. 1992). "The scientific and technological advances affecting every aspect of working life and the everyday world together with the rapidly accelerating increase in accumulated knowledge have led to increased demand for higher levels of education" is the diagnosis arrived at by the Education Specialist W. Heldmann (Die Welt, 14 Dec. 1991, p. 23). For this reason, the approach in the new federal state of Saxony is very much under discussion. In Saxony, *Hauptschule* and *Realschule* have been combined into the *Mittelschule*, after completion of which pupils can attend either a technical or an economics *Gymnasium*. The three-tier school system would thus be replaced by the *"Two-pillar Model"*, i.e. the Saxony model, which Thuringia and Saxony-Anhalt have in essence already adopted. A restructuring of this kind would require, however, considerable rethinking on the part of the old federal states – which is hard to imagine happening... Changes in two *Länder* constitutions in which the *Hauptschule* is anchored would also require political consensus. In France, on the other hand, it is the "unitary" *collège*, steeped in egalitarian tradition, that is having the greatest problems – though with respect to the same age group. Thus both school systems are paradigm expressions of differing traditions (and the difficulties involved in maintaining them in the contemporary world): the *Hauptschule* within the three-tier system is suffering from dwindling attendance and, as a result, a drop in effectiveness in performing its assigned task, while the problems of the *collège* within the French system remain unsolved. If we pursue the comparison further, however, prospects for the future are seen to diverge. Given continued growth of the "new middle classes" and further decreases in attendance, the *Hauptschule* problem could almost take care of itself someday. The *collège*, however, will remain a burning issue as long as France's deep-rooted social conflicts (cf. Chpt. 4) exist. An extreme case illustrates this point. A report from a student doing her practice teaching at a *collège* presents the following analysis: «Laure a constaté que les classes de sixième, théoriquement hétérogènes, étaient parfois très homogènes, les unes regroupant les enfants des milieux aisés, d'autres étant "de véritables classes ethniques composés exclusivement d'élèves maghrébins"» (ME Dec. 1991, p. 49).

In conclusion, the school systems on either side of the Rhine have no choice but to adapt to social (and economic) changes more than they have done up to now. This holds true for all children between 6/7 and for youths between 14/15 years, i.e. during the second decisive period in career orientation, following the first in early childhood. Every system (political party systems, languages and national economy included) has to adapt, continuously and promptly, to the larger systems within which it exists. This is the lesson of Life.

3. After the *collège*, pupils either enter the three-year *lycée* or the two-year *lycée professionnel* (up until the RPR-UDF election victory in 1986: *L.E.P.* = *lycée d'enseignement professionnel*). Pupils in the

reformed upper levels of German Gymnasien (in all Länder as of 1977 following a resolution passed by the Ministry of Education in 1972) as well as in the three-year *lycées* (gradually realized between 1973 and 1975) have the option of selecting subject concentrations according to ability and interest. This tendency, which is mostly accounted for by the growth of scientific knowledge and material as well as the choice of occupation "according to one's inclinations", is also related to the high goal of teaching children to be independent and take responsibility. This is due to the fact that in France and Germany the age of majority has been lowered to 18. Various groups have pointed out that this goal is being degenerated by knowledge portioning, grade calculations and more pressure to excel (fewer available jobs, in France: preparation for future competitions already on a lycée level, e.g. on the elitist *série C* [level C], in Germany: importance of the overall Abitur grade for the university studies with restricted entrance requirements). The *lycées* are marked by progressive specialization: from the *seconde* to the *première* and from the *première* to the *terminale*, core subjects decrease in number while elective subjects in course systems increase. The French grades or levels (*séries* with corresponding *baccalauréat*) can be summarized as follows:

A 1-3	(philosophy - literature - languages),	in future: L (*littéraire*)
B	(economics and social sciences),	in future: ES (*écon. et soc.*)
C	(major subjects: math and physics)	C-E, in future: S (*scientifique*)
D	(math, physics, biology)	
E	(math and technology)	

Compared with Germany, nearly one third of all pupils in France graduate from a technical high school (with a *baccalauréat de technicien*). Their curriculum covers:

F 1-10	(industrial sciences, inclusive F8: social-medical sciences)	in future: STI (*industr.*), STT (*tertiaires*) and STL (*laborat.*)
G 1-3	(economics)	
H	(computer science)	

STI/STT/STL stand for: *sciences et techniques industrielles/ tertiaires/ de laboratoire.*

The structural reform, which also finds expression in the names for the new levels as listed above, is intended to combat the excessive priority given to the *série C*; the change is, in addition, fuelled by the hope of attracting more future teachers – particularly from what was previously the A-levels. Today then, there are only six major levels. This is made up for by the fact that they contain, in addition to the compulsory subjects (*matières dominantes*), more "compulsory options" (*matières complémentaires de formation générale*), optional subjects (*options*) and, as part of the reform, additional hours in small groups (*modules*). Both systems are to "co-exist" as it were until 1994/ 95. In 1992/ 93 the new system will be introduced into the *seconde* and finally in 1994/95 into the *terminale*. For further details, refer to ME, Sept. 1991, p. 38-40 and the information bulletin published by the Ministry of Education, *«La rénovation pédagogique du lycée»* (*March 1992*). On the historical development, cf. Melde 1989. Rappenecker, 1990 provides a graphic account of the experiences of a German exchange teacher, in all three classes and particularly in the subject *allemand*.

Pupils of all programs already take a part of the *baccalauréat* exam at the end of the *première*: in the subject French (*épreuve anticipée de français*) this is designed to take the load off the *terminale*. The written and oral parts of the *baccalauréat* are strictly anonymous: The teachers correcting the exams do not know which test belongs to which pupil. The programs up to the *baccalauréat* are uniform throughout the country. The preparation for the exam leads to a pontificating style of instruction and consequently to a very distanced teacher/pupil relationship; even more so than would be conceivable in German schools. (Meanwhile, several Länder in Germany have adapted a standardized Abitur. However, the Abitur teacher is the first corrector for the written and the co-examiner for the oral examination of his own students). By contrast, pupils in France are neither allowed nor able to adapt themselves to the "idiosyncrasies or predilections of their teachers" (Kodron 1980, p. 13). The principle of anonymity is intended to warrant fair and equal treatment of all examinees. It is derived from the demand for equality during the French Revolution and in this formalized fashion is still fundamental for most examinations in France, especially with regards to the *concours* (the admissions competition in numerous institutions).

4. There are also many differences between the *vocational schooling* in both countries. In Germany, generally speaking, on-the-job training is supplemented by just eight to twelve class hours a week (part-time school). But there are other possibilities: on-the-job training and classroom instruction can alternate (periodic full-time school). By contrast, vocational full-time schools (training and technical colleges) are in the minority (Stooß 1981, p. 287). Since school in Germany is compulsory up to the age of 18, approximately 60-65% of all sixteen to eighteen year olds receive vocational training in this *dual system* (Aurin 1978, p. 153). Due to the fact that factories and businesses play

a vital part in this system, the search for a sufficient number of *apprenticeships* was a central objective in the federal, regional and community governments' struggle against youth unemployment (the federal government also has the power to act on such issues). The search was relatively successful. Even though in 1987 there were approximately 128,000 unemployed young adults below the age of twenty (1983: 192,000), statistics did show a surplus of apprenticeships (Haefs 1989, pp.192 and 203). The excess supply has increased because of the general thronging to obtain higher educational certificates; for this reason many professions are now experiencing serious problems in attracting trainees (for figures, cf. Fischer-Weltalmanach 1992, p. 342). In fact there were for the first time in 1991 more students than trainees in the old federal states (Die Welt, 14 Dec. 1991, p. 23); this is a tendency that educational policy will have to counteract. The French vocational school is officially called *«lycée professionnel»* (the terminology is strikingly similar to *lycée*). This is a two-year full-time school with 31 to 36 hours of weekly instruction. Since unemployment in France affected about 30% (!) of young adults below the age of 25, with the figure still at 20% in 1989, great efforts have been aimed towards improving the contact between businesses and young people who will be seeking employment later on. In 1987 the number of *jumelages école-entreprise* increased to around 12,000 contacts. These school-business partnerships involve both the *lycées professionnels* and the *collèges* (refer to 2). For at least some of the vocational pupils, industrial training has become a regular part of their education (ME, Feb. 1988, p. 29). Two-thirds of all French pupils attend full-time schools; only one-third graduate from a dual apprentice training (*apprentissage*) in an enterprise and a C.F.A. (*Centre de Formation d'Apprentis*). According to a French government plan of 25 Sept. 1991, this dual system is to be expanded greatly within the next five years – patterned on the German model. Precisely because the majority attends a full-time *lycée professionnel*, the big problem of many young adults in France up to now has been not the "apprenticeship" but rather the job-hunting *after* the completion of vocational training. The opportunities depend on the degree awarded.

The most preferred degree was the *CAP* (Certificat d'aptitude professionnelle) which could be earned in three years. It certified the educational level required for carrying out one out of 500 special occupations and received wide acceptance among employers. The two-year *BEP* (Brevet d'études professionnelles) concentrated on professional training for an entire field, making future job-hunters more flexible, but was recognized to a much smaller degree by employers. This did not change until 1986/87. The more comprehensive BEP, which embraced 2/3 of the service sector and only 1/3 of the industrial sector, clearly outstripped the specialized CAP which drew from a reversal of these proportions (ME, April 1988, p. 63). Slowly but surely the heavy growth of the service sector (see 3.2) and its demands for flexibility are having an effect on the relationship between vocationally oriented schooling and their degrees awarded. A supreme coordinating authority, which has been in existence since 1984 and also consists of employers and trade unions, intends to extend the BEP to an even greater extent at the expense of the CAP which, «pour certaines branches du secteur industriel», should only take two years to complete in the future (Haut Comité Education – Economie 1988, p. 28).

The differences between French and German professional education can be traced back historically. Owing to a very extensive period of industrialization period commencing in the nineteenth century, Germany has had a *longer* tradition of vocational schooling. In this way, cooperative efforts between the State and its entrepreneurs were able to go through a long process of maturation. According to Stooß (1981, p. 282), this form of cooperation, apparent in the dual system, ultimately goes back to the arrangements of the craft and merchant guilds. France, on the other hand, did not become industrialized until after the Second World War (see chapter 3). For this reason, the development of a modern vocational education system occurred very slowly and relatively late. Moreover, this development was in the hands of a centralized government from the very start, just as the modernization and concentration reforms in industry were under the control of the state and its *planification*. This explains the predominantly public full-time and all-day vocational schools in France.

5. In Germany, the school grades are *numbered in increasing order*. In France, this order is reversed, i.e. *from a greater to a lower number*, just as was the case in the former German high school system (*Prima, Sekunda, Tertia*, but with the differentiations *Oberprima* and *Unterprima* etc.). Only the French senior grade, i.e. the year of the *baccalauréat*, is called *«terminale»*.

5.3 *Institutions of higher learning in France and Germany*

One basic question must be asked due to the considerable increases in student enrollment in both countries (in France the number doubled between 1976/77 and 1981/82 alone, in the same period of time the number of students in Germany exceeded one million). How will so many university graduates be able to find employment when, in all probability, new technology will cause the job market to shrink in the

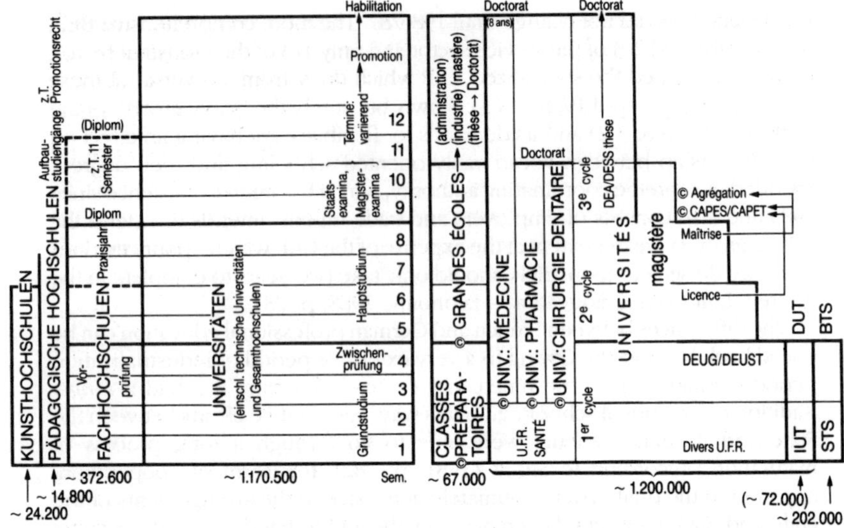

Fig. 63: The Higher Education Systems in France and the Federal Republic of Germany.

(The figures for Germany are from the Wintersemester 1990/ 91: Fischer-Weltalmanach 1992, p. 342. Only the old federal states are considered here. The figures for France are for the *année universitaire* 1990/ 91: ME, Nov. 1991, pp. 21 and 86. This includes the *premier cycle* (DEUG): 503,000. In addition, there are approx. 58,000 graduates of the *Grandes Ecoles.*)

long term? The answer is that the job market will be subject to excessive demands even if new possibilities are discovered and realized in different areas. Therefore, something has to be done about the number of graduates. The solution could be actuated *prior to* university studies (scholarship policies, whether restricted entry in Germany should be extended to different fields of study, whether it should be introduced in France where it was discussed in 1983 but later rejected). The solution could also be implemented *during* university studies by means of selection and then "reorientation" or "re-education" of those who do not pass certain test requirements (but what does one do with them then?). One attempt made by the Chirac administration – in terms of pre-university solution – was a bill (*loi Devaquet*) which was supposed to give the universities the right of *direct* restriction on admissions for their courses of study. However, this proposal was wiped as a result of mass demonstrations by pupils and students in December 1986. The problems are nonetheless increasing. In France it is estimated that the number of students will have doubled to two million or more by the year 2000 (with a lower base population). In 1988 Germany reported nearly 1.5 million students. By the year 2000, it could be dealing with an increase of more than 100% (Der Spiegel, 21 November 1988, pp. 81 and 98). Despite these urgent problems, Germany has not yet made any decisions whatsoever regarding this issue, which affects philology, law and economics, but is simply attempting to counteract them with restricted entry regulations. After their final examinations, students are abandoned to their "own devices" as well as to the overtaxed state *employment agencies*... Neither the social democrats nor the conservatives have ventured a solution since neither of the parties wants to risk a loss of votes by introducing measures in the period before or during university studies. Many students would first refer to "undemocratic measures". However, it is the *expansion of the professional colleges* which should be their real interest as well as the nation's, for example, fields ranging from the training of nurses and physical therapists to the social therapeutical and commercial fields. Unlike Germany, the system of higher education in France employs a method of *sélection.* Many candidates are forced to drop out after having failed to meet test requirements during admission competition for the *Grandes Ecoles*, the I.U.T. or the S.T.S. (see 5.3.3). The competition is also felt *during* one's studies (especially noticeable after the first year of medical school, but also during the two-year preparation for the *DEUG: Diplôme d'Études universitaires générales*, an examination equivalent in function – though broader in scope – to the German *Zwischenprüfung*). Afterwards, those who do not make it to graduation must deal with any problems on their own, as in Germany after the first and second state examinations; the exception confirms the rule. – Since the late sixties, there have been attempts in both countries to create *conformity between university education and the job market* by offering more vocationally-oriented alternatives to the standard university education at *vocational schools* (which have been up-graded to professional colleges). Welcome approaches to this expansion of the system of higher learning have been slowed down by a variety of factors:

- pupils at *lycées* and *Gymnasien* are inadequately oriented towards and informed about these colleges,
- there is a lack of financial support for a further need-based consolidation of these institutions and
- it is possible for unemployment figures to be artificially lowered (and politically exploited) by the omission of the large number of university students.

In general, the French higher education system offers more opportunities to transfer from one institution to another than are offered or usual in Germany. They are termed *passerelles*, i.e. foot crossings or little bridges. If a student can demonstrate a certain level of performance, he can switch, for example, from the IUT or STS (cf. 5.3.3) to an *université* or even get into a *Grande Ecole* after participating in an admissions competition. The term "horizontal mobility" often used in this connection means the same as the metaphor *passerelles*, which likewise emphasises the horizontal dimension. However, such transfers are normally in the interest of higher qualifications; they are linked with a vertical mobility condoned by the system. It would therefore be simpler and more accurate to speak of greater mobility in French higher education.

5.3.1 The *Grandes Ecoles*

The university system in France is characterized by the outstanding reputation of the *Grandes Ecoles*. It usually takes five years to graduate – taking into account the two-year preparatory classes (*classes préparatoires*) which are mostly offered at *lycées*. Out of the existing 306 *Grandes Ecoles*, 155 alone are *écoles d'ingénieurs*. It is thus possible to refer to *"specialized universities"*. However, they do not exist for all fields. Law and medicine, for example, have remained university domain. Instead of "specialized university", the term *"elitist university"* would also be correct since the majority of those in leading positions in nearly all fields (administration, politics, military, commerce and trade, technology) have received their education at a *Grande Ecole* (Bourdieu 1989). A considerable number of *Grandes Ecoles* come under the jurisdiction of the Ministry of Education. In addition, nearly every ministry is in charge of "its" *Grande(s) Ecole(s)*, supervising and thus controlling the education of top-level executives in its field. This is shown by *Fig. 64*.

After the usual two years of preparation, only about 10% of the applicants reach their goal in the admissions competition (*concours d'entrée, concours d'admission*). This is the result of a very tough admissions policy as is typical for every type of competition in France (for details, cf. ME, March 1992, pp. 95-129). Those who are successful have thus cleared the most important hurdle. The state-run *Grandes Ecoles* provide their students with a free education (the students receive a salary). The other *Grandes Ecoles* give their students partial

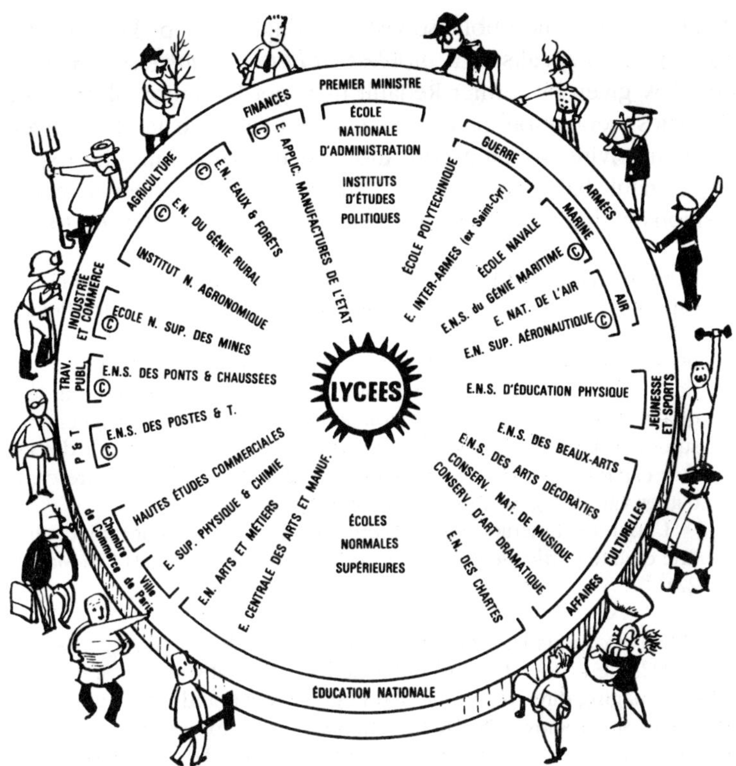

Fig. 64: Grandes Ecoles in France.
(From: Michaud/Torrès 1978, p. 173)

financial support, for instance by means of the *taxe d'apprentissage.* This tax must be paid by every company in France towards the promotion of vocational schooling. Its distribution can also be decided upon by them (Henry-Gréard 1982, p. 328). After being admitted, the students first learn theory and then get involved in more practice-related, vocationally-oriented training, furthering flexibility and creativity by means of problem-solving in small groups. After the final examination, the graduates of a class (*promotion*) are ranked according to their performance. Those with the best achievements can find well-paid positions in business or administration. "Although the old-boy network of some *Ecoles* is encrusted with favouritism and arrogance, this has created a unified and efficient élite, frequently able to join hands across the restricting barriers of French public life, both in private industry and public service." (Ardagh 1968, p. 333). Bourdieu (1989, p. 159) speaks of a *«noblesse d'Etat»* or *«noblesse d'école»*. An interview given by former Renault manager B. Hanon illustrates the graduates' reputation of intellectual mobility due to their diverse, problem-solving-oriented education. At the same time, he explains why Renault has preferred for many years to fill upper managerial positions with graduates of the *Grandes Ecoles* – in fact, up to 75%:

> Nous avons surtout besoin de généralistes, des gens qui ont à la fois la capacité d'apprendre ce qui se passe autour d'eux, qui ont une flexibilité d'esprit et qui savent communiquer. Les grandes écoles nous fournissent des individus à peu près convenablement calibrés, possédant un minimum de connaissances garanti, sachant travailler ... On peut dire tout le mal qu'on veut des classes préparatoires dont le contenu d'enseignement est sûrement à revoir, mais les élèves apprennent à se dépasser, à se défoncer. Etre capable de passer un concours de grande école, c'est être capable d'aller vite. Les gens très forts vont très vite.
>
> L'aptitude à manier des problèmes difficiles et à réagir rapidement est une qualité particulièrement appréciée dans l'industrie.» (CEN, Mai 1983, 22)

The irony: two years later Mr. Hanon had to pack his bags...

In 1992, the CNRS (cf. 5.1.6) published a comparative study of the careers of the managing directors in the 200 largest French and 200 largest German firms. This study shows clearly the eminent – and, in view of its exclusivity, questionable – role played by the *Grandes Ecoles*. For a concise but very instructive summary, cf. Die Welt, 18 Jan. 1992, p. 5.

The first schools of engineering were founded in the eighteenth century in order to provide the nation with specialized manpower for the building of bridges, streets, the mining industry etc. The obsolete university system was not able to train such a group of specialists. In the nineteenth century and the first half of the twentieth century there was a balance between the *Grandes Ecoles* and the ***universités***, i.e. a type of "division of labour". The ***héritiers***, or those coming from wealthy families, usually studied law or medicine at the universities, while the ***boursiers***, or those belonging to the poorer classes, were offered the possibility of social advancement by means of full scholarships from the *Grandes Ecoles* (Curtius 1931, p. 136). Among the graduates of the *Ecole Normale Supérieure (rue d'Ulm)*, who were supposed to be educated as teachers or professors according to the actual purpose of the ENS, have been e.g. many authors (Péguy, Romains, Giraudoux, Sartre, Simone Weil), scientists (Taine, Bergson, Fustel de Coulanges) and politicians (Jaurès, Herriot, L. Blum, Pompidou,). Not until after the Second World War did the *Grandes Ecoles* attain a clearly higher degree of prestige. On the one hand, this was the result of the unaltered highly selective competitive examinations and the transition from the traditional universities to a mass university system (without restricted entry). On the other hand, the model of the humanistically educated had been transformed to the flexible, adaptable (and "forever young", sporty, jogging) technocrat who still had a good taste for literature and the arts... (see CEN, May 1983, p. 24). This model transformation is just as clearly exhibited by the distinct preference for the C-concentration over the A-concentration in the *lycées* (Melde 1989) and now, despite reform of the *lycée*, the apparent preference for the S-concentration over the L-concentration.

The most well-known *Grandes Ecoles* are:
Ecole des Ponts et Chausées (founded in 1747)
Ecole des Mines (1783)
Ecole Polytechnique (1794, in the press referred to as *«l'X»* for the school, *«les X»* for their graduates, from the mathematical variable X)
Ecole Normale Supérieure (ENS, 1794)
Ecole Centrale (1829, industry)
Ecole Nationale Supérieure des Télécommunications (ENST, 1878, new name since 1942)
Ecole des Hautes Etudes Commerciales (HEC, 1881, private)
ENS de garçons de Saint-Cloud (1880) and the
ENS de jeunes filles (1881/82), which have now been merged into one ENS
Ecole Supérieure d'Electricité (1891)
Ecole Supérieure d'Aéronautique (1909)
ENS de l'enseignement technique (1912)
Ecole Nationale d'Administration (ENA, 1945, the press refers to the graduates as *«les énarques»* because they rule France like monarchs; well-known ENA graduates include e.g. Chirac, Giscard d'Estaing, Peyrefitte, Rocard, Chevènement, Fabius and Jospin).

The 7 *instituts d'études politiques* (IEP, *«sciences-po»*) are considered a kind of preliminary to the ENA, i.e. comprise the actual educational and research centres for political science in France. The most important is the IEP in Paris.

There are in the meantime four ENS locations: rue d'Ulm- Sèvres, Fontenay-Saint Cloud, Cachan and, the most recent, the ENS in Lyon.

The places at economics institutes (*Grandes Ecoles de Commerce et de Gestion*) are becoming more and more sought after. In addition to the HEC in Paris and similar institutions in the centre, there are now some very reputable institutes of this kind in the Province. The *Grandes Ecoles* have also initiated cautious steps towards decentralization.

5.3.2 The university diploma and competitive examinations

In France, students mostly have *one* major combined with one or more minors. For instance, German combined with e.g. English and French literature. This traditional concentration on a single, but "extended", major is object of discussion. Another contrast to the Federal Republic of Germany is the strict regimentation of university studies. French universities have by far more mandatory classes, for example, lectures (*cours magistraux*), "seminars" (*travaux dirigés*) and exercises (*travaux pratiques*). The outer organizational framework is also more rigid. It comprises three cycles which have been exemplified by the humanities, natural sciences and law and economics (see *Fig. 63*).

The DEUG was above all introduced so that many students could at least obtain a state-registered diploma in view of the high percentage of drop-outs. More than 50% of university students in France still quit their studies prematurely, i.e. especially after the first one or two years. This has a variety of reasons (ME, April 1984, p. 15; Quid 1984, p. 1381). The *licence* (equivalent to the German *Staatsexamen*, the first university degree required for the teaching profession) and the *maîtrise* (equivalent to the German *Magister*, Master of Arts/Sciences) are required before taking certain competitive examinations (*concours*): The *CAPES* or *CAPET* (see *Fig. 63*) and the *agrégation* (examination required for obtaining the best paid and most respected professorship in the French lycées) which stems from the Napoleonic era. The *licence* is required for the *CAPES*. The *maîtrise*, which consists of a written *mémoire* (dissertation) and an oral defense (including the answering of various questions), is the prerequisite for the *agrégation*. The number of positions which are contingent upon these degrees have increased considerably. Moreover, in 1988 the *CAPES* was divided into an *internal* examination (for those who already hold teaching positions, including *collège* instructors) and an *external* examination (for all other applicants) in order to obtain more *lycée* teachers in view of the growing numbers of *lycée* graduates. A similar arrangement was effectuated for the *agrégation*. There are even ambitious plans in existence for the year 2000 which foresee the graduation of 57% of all students from lycées and – through an extended period of time at school – the completion of a not yet specified *niveau bac* by altogether 80% of this generation of students (cf. ME, Oct. 1988, p. 37). In France, this goal has to be viewed against the background of the dialectic between the egalitarian tendencies in force since the French Revolution ("mass education" as responsibility of the State and "a national obsession in France", cf. Green 1990, pp. 146 and 161) and elitist tendencies (with the *Grandes Ecoles* and their obvious clout in the education sector). – A graduate with pedagogical training after the CAPES receives the title of *professeur certifié*. After one obtains the *agrégation*, one year of training is sufficient to become a *professeur agrégé*, earning a higher salary and responsible for fewer courses. The *Société des Agrégés* is dedicated to safeguarding the privileges of the *agrégés.* The study programs for both competitive examinations (many candidates take both) vary from year to year. They are announced approximately one year prior to the examination dates and covered in special preparatory courses organized by the Ecoles Normales Supérieures (in which case they are privileged since the examiners are amongst these ranks to a large extent) and the universities. The list of topics for the subject English (*session de 1987*) is provided here in order to illustrate the degree of specialization particular to these competitive examinations:

CAPES
1. Shakespeare: *Othello*
2. Goldsmith: *The Vicar of Wakefield* (written examination)
3. Dashiell Hammett: *The Glass Key* in: The Four Great Novels, (written examination)
4. Civilisation: *La Grande-Bretagne et l'Europe 1945-1975* (oral examination)

Agrégation
Literature for all applicants:
1. Shakespeare: *Othello*
2. Tennyson: *In Memoriam*
3. Evelyn Waugh: *A Handful of Dust*
4. Dashiell Hammett: *The Glass Key*
5. Walker Percy: *The Moviegoer*

Option A:
6. Donne: *The Complete English Poems*
7. Goldsmith: *The Vicar of Wakefield*
8. G.B. Shaw: *Man and Superman*
9. Seamus Heaney: *Selected Poems*, 1965-1975
10. V.S. Naipaul: *A House for Mr. Biswas*

Option B:
6. Mary Wollstonecraft: *A Vindication of the Rights of Woman*
7. Civilisation: *Les immigrations européennes aux Etats-Unis 1880-1910*
8. Civilisation: *L'idée européenne en Grande-Bretagne depuis 1945*

Option C:
«Cette option ne comporte pas de programme limitatif.»
(From: BO, 8 May 1986, p. 1529 and 12 June 1986, p. 1755)

The list of topics for the subject German (*session de 1987*) is also included to convey an impression of both examinations:

1. Hartmann von Aue: *Gregorius* (only *agrégation*)
2. Fr. Hölderlin: *Poésies* (both examinations)
3. G. Büchner: *Dantons Tod* (both examinations)

4. Fr. Nietzsche: *Die Geburt der Tragödie* (both examinations)
5. French-German relations between the First and Second World Wars (*CAPES*: «cette question n'est pas exclue, à l'écrit, de l'épreuve de commentaire dirigé»: *agrégation*: without an explanation of the text in the oral examination)
6. Th. Bernhard: *Verstörung* (only *agrégation*)

Option linguisitics (only *agrégation*):
1) comparative
2) subjunctive II
(From: BO, 8 May 1986, p. 1529 and 12 June 1986, p. 1755)

The *CAPES* and *agrégation* do not only differ in the scope of topics but also in the requirements of the written and oral sections. Just in terms of the *requirements*, the *CAPES* would be comparable to the German *Staatsexamen* (first degree required for the teaching profession) and the *agrégation* would be comparable to a Staatsexamen for especially motivated and gifted students (whereby the official equivalences are not to be taken too seriously). Note: In France, German studies are a part of university studies and the competitive examinations. No one would maintain that Middle High German and German studies are mutually exclusive... The third cycle of university studies only concerns a minority of students. The DEA year (*Diplôme d'Etudes Approfondies*) is an introduction to research methods and approaches (!) and acts as a necessary intermediary degree prior to the *thèse* (between the dissertation and German *Habilitation*, the postdoctoral lecturing qualification) which replaced the former *thèses* (the *thèse de 3e cycle* = the German *Dissertation*, the *thèse d'Etat* = the German *Habilitation*) by decree on 5 July 1984. Preparation for the *thèse* is only supposed to take two to four years. The doctorate is awarded after the oral defense (*soutenance*). The terms *licence*, *maîtrise* and *doctorat*, similar to the German *Magister* and *Doktor*, go back to scolasticism: the defense of the *thèse* is derived from the Middle-Age disputation procedures. The *thèse d'Etat*, equivalent to the German *Habilitation*, was abolished in order to encourage future scientists to engage in more diversified research activities rather than have them be involved in specialized research often taking ten years to complete.

By means of *professionnalisation*, the universities in France are making efforts to set up more vocationally-oriented programs of study in order to give students greater opportunities in the job market and to assert themselves against the dominance of the *Grandes Ecoles*. The more practice-oriented DEUST (*Diplôme d'Etudes Universitaires Scientifiques et Techniques*) was established along with the DEUG. Substantial improvements modified the *Maîtrises de Sciences et Techniques* (MST) and the professionally-oriented research study programs towards the *Diplôme d'Etudes Supérieures Specialisées* (DESS), whose percentage of graduates annually increases by 10% (ME, July 1987, p. 57). These developments also included the three-year *magistères*, the next highly selective and particularly achievement-oriented degree programs after the DEUG. Modelled after the *Grandes Ecoles*, they were introduced in 1985 and in the meantime enjoy a good reputation with big business (Bernard 1988). The *Grandes Ecoles* reacted to this challenge in 1986 by setting up a one-year specialized research program called «*mastère*». This course of study is reserved for the "elite of the elite". To date, the *magistères* have awakened little response from students. The exclusive *mastères*, on the other hand, are prospering (Quid 1992, p. 1259), as is also shown by increased advertising for it in the press.

A comparison of the relationship between universities and ministries in France and Germany (illustrated through the decision-making process when defining courses of study) is offered by Beckmeier 1991, esp. p. 145.

5.3.3 Alternatives to the university: I.U.T., S.T.S. and professional colleges

In Germany, professional colleges started coming into being in 1969 as a result of a transformation of the schools of engineering and, among others, the former colleges of social work and education and business administration. The name *Fachhochschule* (professional college) together with the usual three-year study program (four years with the practical training year; some programs even requiring five and a half years) magnify the standing of the professional colleges. It is perfectly possible for engineers who have received their education at such professional colleges to attain high posts or even managerial positions in enterprises. In France, this prospect is normally a privilege of the graduates of the *Grandes Ecoles.* Their partial functional equivalence, the parallels in course of study, the practically oriented and closely guided approach to learning and their mutual interest – which latter has increased dramatically as 1993 and the European single market draw closer – have resulted in more contact and sometimes lively interest in exchange programs between German *Fachhochschulen* and French *Grandes Ecoles* (for examples and a discus

Fig. 65: Professional School Graduates in France.
(From: ME, Jan. 1983, p. 13)

sion of the problems, cf. Meyer-Kalkus 1990, pp. 508-510; cf. ibid., relations between *Grandes Ecoles* and German universities).

German three and four-year *Fachhochschulen* can scarcely be compared to the two-year professional training institutions in France, the I.U.T. and the S.T.S. The *Instituts Universitaires de Technologie* (I.U.T.), which have been in existence since 1965, train middle-management candidates (*cadres moyens*). Originally, these schools were supposed to admit 1/4 of the lycée graduates, offering them a professionally useful alternative to a university education which would facilitate the job-hunting process later on. However, the current 96 I.U.T.s and 350 related programs at universities, also leading to the D.U.T. (D = diplôme), soon had to tighten their admissions policies. It is not a competitive examination, but rather grade assessment and an interview with a reviewing committee, by means of which only one-eighth to one-tenth of all applicants (depending on year and location) receive admission to a "professional college". The 1620 S.T.S.s (*sections de techniciens supérieurs*) have similar two-year training programs at present. However, these programs are offered locally at schools, mostly at a *lycée technique*, which are in the vicinity of the plants. As a comparison: in 1984, 57,400 students were enroled at an I.U.T., 83,000 at an S.T.S., 44,000 in a *classe préparatoire aux Grandes Ecoles*, 21,000 at an *Ecole Normale* or a collège for pedagogical training, 40,400 at a state-run *Grande Ecole*, 24,600 at an *Ecole supérieure de commerce et de gestion* (mostly private) – but 884,000 at an *université* (INSEE 1985).

Education at the S.T.S. is more specialized, now leading to 135 BTSs (Brevets de Technicien Supérieur). The I.U.T.s are more polyvalent: Their students are now able to choose from courses of study leading to 19 DUTs (Diplômes universitaires de Technologie). Many BTS and DUT recipients now prefer to pursue supplementary studies at a *université* or even at a *Grande Ecole*. The higher qualifications hold the promise of a better salary (Le Nouvel Observateur, 10 Oct. 1991, p. 172). This example is characteristic of the *passerelles* (cf. 5.3).

The competition between both types of "professional colleges" as well as their isolated existences, which offer a certain amount of security in an era marked by growing unemployment, are caricatured in *Fig. 65*.

In a nutshell, this is why the French universities even appear to be a gathering place for all those who did not make it into an I.U.T., an S.T.S. or even into a preparatory course for a *Grande Ecole*: «il (le lycéen) s'inscrit dans un établissement universitaire parce qu'il n'a pas pu se faire accepter dans une classe préparatoire aux grandes écoles, ou a été écarté d'un I.U.T. [...] ou d'une classe de techniciens supérieurs» (Le Monde hebdomadaire, 21-27 Oct. 1982, p. 10). This has not changed (ME, Oct. 1988, p. 3). In comparison to the (fully public) I.U.T., the number of those graduating from (approx. 60%, 40% private) S.T.S.s, which have been vigorously consolidated to meet demand, has increased two-fold (see *Fig. 63*). Both institutions have «une image de marque positive auprès des entreprises» (Haut Conseil Education – Economie 1988, p. 41).

5.3.4 *«Université 2000»*

In May 1991, the current Minister of Education, the socialist Lionel Jospin, presented his plan *«Université 2000»* (after initial drafts in 1990) to the Cabinet Council. This plan provides for an entire package of measures to upgrade and expand the *universités*. Certain duties are also relegated to the regions, *départements* and cities. The *collectivités locales* – under which term the regions are also included - have now agreed to the development plans up to 1995; in some areas they will even bear more of the costs than the central government. (The best overview of details and background is provided by: Le Monde, dossiers et documents n° 192, Oct. 1991: «L'explosion scolaire et universitaire», pp. 12-16. It is not possible here to attempt a comparison with the extensive study, *«Bildung 2000»*, by the *Bundestags-Enquête-*

kommission – cf. the «Themenausgabe» of: Das Parlament, 21 Dec. 1990, pp. 1-16). When the new Bérégovoy government took power (early in 1992) – with Jack Lang as Minister of Culture and now as Minister of Education – some parts of this plan were repealed, while others were not. L. Jospin wanted to sink the high drop-out rate during the first two years (the *DEUG* years) through a number of innovative measures and to make the *premier cycle* more profession-oriented. This proposal met with heated resistance, and not only from students but also from faculty. The faculty criticised stricter regulation of studies from the *Rue de Grenelle*, i.e. by the Ministry of Education. As a result, J. Lang gave way to the pressure. (The restriction of admissions at the beginning seems to be an equally implausible approach in France; this is made clear by the fate of the *loi Devaquet* in 1986, cf. 5.3). So the problem, already in existence for several decades, remains unsolved. Other measures provided for by the «*Université 2000*» plan, however, can either be expected to be implemented in the future because of consensus among those affected and among all the parties (the building of five new universities, cf. *Fig. 60*, and the expansion of the I.U.T. belong to this category) – or have already been put into effect, sometimes in the face of heated resistance. The measures already in effect should now be examined. These involve the creation of two new professional training institutions at the universities; they too comprise part of the face-lift to be given the *universités* under the rubric *professionnalisation*.

5.3.5 New university institutes for professional training

Regardless of whether 36% (1988), 57% (projected for the year 2000, cf. Quid 1992, p. 1272) or even 80% of a given generation (cf. 5.3.2) are to be educated to university entrance level: the demand for teachers in France is already considerable. At the same time, it is necessary to intensify specialised didactic training for future pedagogues. Following three pilot projects in 1990/91, the Ministry of Education introduced 28 *Instituts universitaires de formation des maîtres* (I.U.F.M.) across the country for the 1991/92 university year. Up until now, only primary school teachers were termed *maîtres*; in future, all teachers are to become pedagogical "masters". The teaching staff at the I.U.F.M. consists mainly of university faculty. The pre-requisite for admission is the *licence*. Within the two-year programme with obligatory practice teaching, candidates can choose between two *concours* after the first year. The first *concours* is intended to prepare primary school teachers, "educators" at the *école maternelle* included. This I.U.F.M programme thus provides the training that used to be the responsibility of the *Ecole normale.* The other *concours* is aimed at future *professeurs de collège et de lycée,* leading up to the familiar CAPES or CAPET. It is, however, possible to acquire this credential without taking the first year of the I.U.F.M. programme (for details, cf. ME, Dec. 1991, p. 48f. and L'Etudiant, Jan. 1992, p. 54f.)

In the 1991/92 academic year, i.e. at the same time as the I.U.F.M. was introduced, an effort was also made to establish a counterpart to the professional colleges in Germany and other countries: the *Institut universitaire professionnel* (I.U.P.). This institute – also in keeping with the *«Université 2000»* plan – will therefore be an accomplished fact by 1993 when new elections are going to be held and, as far as can be judged, a conservative government formed. There are now institutes at 27 of France's universities (map: ME, Nov. 1991, p. 24) providing training in one of five areas (*ingéniérie, communication, administration, commerce, gestion financière*), depending on the location. The graduates selected *sur dossier* complete a three-year programme including six months of practical training. To begin studies at an I.U.P., students must have completed one year of specialized studies, whence the new formula *bac+1+3.* Many of the candidates in 1991 already had the IUT or STS diploma (i.e., were already *bac+2*). The new institutes seem, then, to be drawing well. This can be explained by the fact that the *Grandes Ecoles,* to whose domain the above-named subjects have traditionally belonged, are already unable to satisfy the need for *ingénieurs* in France, to say nothing of projected demand for the year 2000 (ME, Nov. 1991, p. 22). I.U.P.'s prospects are therefore better than might be imagined without knowledge of the circumstances. Instruction (also tutorials and work on projects) and faculty structure (with half of the faculty drawn from industry) are very clearly modelled on the *Grandes Ecoles* or even more so on the *écoles d'ingénieurs.*

Of course there are great differences between the I.U.F.M, which transcends differences in type of school, and German seminars and practical training. The I.U.P.s are also integrated into the *universités* both physically and in terms of curriculum, while German *Fachhochschulen* are independent institutions. There are also parallels. It is nevertheless too soon to make any comparison; first it is necessary to follow the further development of the I.U.F.M. and the I.U.P.

It is evident from the above discussion that the innovations in France clearly reflect the tendency towards egalitarianism on the one hand (I.U.F.M.) and towards elitism on the other (I.U.P.). The characteristically French manner of playing off these opposing approaches manifests itself again and again. In Germany, however, the contrast lies in a tendency towards centralization and a strong opposing tendency towards separatism. As the most recent developments have shown, the various areas of education in each nation provide an exemplary model for the different operative tensions.

5.3.6 State-run colleges with special status

The *collège de France*, founded in 1530 by Francis I, is with its prestigious staff of instructors the top-rated college in France. The *Ecole Pratique des Hautes Etudes* (E.P.H.E., founded in 1868 and modeled after its German predecessors) and the *Ecole des Hautes Etudes en Sciences Sociales* (E.H.E.S.S., which split off from the E.P.H.E. in 1974), are both research-oriented institutes which rank higher than German universities. French "structuralism" (a.o. Barthes, Greimas) and the structural history of the «*Annales*» school both come from the E.H.E.S.S.. Several schools for architecture, translation, art and music might be considered just as elitist as the *Grandes Ecoles*.

The greatest honor for a scientist or an artist is - disregarding the *Collège de France* - the acceptance into the *institut*. What is meant is the *Institut de France* in Paris which, aside from the *Académie française* (1635), comprises four other academies: *Inscriptions et Belles-Lettres* (1663), *Sciences* (1666), *Beaux-Arts* (1795) and *Sciences morales et politiques* (1795).

5.4 *Closing remarks*

It is not possible to understand an education system by means of pure factual information on its institutions. In order to attain a grasp of a particular system, one must try to look at it in terms of the overall context of its country with all its historical transitions and requirements. This is simply because each system tries to educate every new generation in accordance with the norms, attitudes and expectations of the country to which it belongs. The greatest dangers and most frequent misunderstandings arise from *faux amis* (false friends) and spontaneous word parallels.

5.4.1 False friends

Ecole does not only mean "school" because it also implies the *Grande Ecole*. We have intentionally referred to the *université* when speaking about France on account of the French "dual" college and university system (see 5.1.6). The categories *instituteur/professeur* differ from the German *Lehrer/Professor* - disregarding the categories particular to Austria. *Le président* is the selected head of the *université*, as the *Rektor* in the German *Universität*. In every *académie* the *recteur* is responsible for *state* supervision (see 5.1.3), while in Germany it is the *Kanzler* who upholds this function. *Collège (jésuite, unique, de France)* has many different meanings which date back to scolasticism and the Jesuit school. However, there is one thing *collège* does not mean: the German *Kolleg* (cours). The French *dissertation* (consisting of an introduction, a thesis subdivided into two or three different points, and a conclusion) and the German *Dissertation* (doctoral thesis) are now worlds apart, although they have a common origin. This also holds true for the French *thèse* (in actuality an extensive thesis construction supported by an argumentative basis) and the German *These* (a mere assertion). The *baccalauréat*, the *D.E.U.G.*, *licence*, *maîtrise*, *D.E.A.* and the *doctorat* make up the *diplômes nationaux*. However, they are not equivalent to the German *Diplom* (for engineering etc.). Just like the general German term *Wissenschaft(en)*, the terms *lettres* and *sciences* ultimately contain an entire philosophy and a different ethos which cannot be illustrated here.

5.4.2 *Education* vs. *Bildung*

There are no coincidences when we are dealing with key words. From the semantic fields *apprentissage, culture, éducation, enseignement, formation, initiation, (institution), instruction* referred to by Saussure, *éducation* was selected as the term to set the tone. Nevertheless, there are two other words which are competing for its leading position: *enseignement* and *instruction*. Today's leading position can be clearly seen – at least in official linguistic usage – from the designations *é. nationale, Ministère de l'é. nationale, Fédération de l'é. nationale, é. artistique/civique/physique/professionnelle* etc. There are also idioms such as *avoir de l'é., recevoir une bonne é., manquer d'é.* and numerous members of the same word family: *éduquer, in-/éducable, éducateur, éducatif, rééduquer, rééducation*.

Nonetheless, we have: *enseignement public ou privé, enseignement primaire, secondaire et supérieur.* In the nineteenth century, Jules Ferry was *ministre de l'Instruction publique.* Under discussion was the change to *instruction civique* – in contrast to *instruction religieuse* – as well as the problems pertaining to *instruction primaire, secondaire* and *professionnelle.* – The concept of *éducation* widely replaced that of *instruction,* while the scholarly word *éducation* (first instance of use: 1495) and the noun *enseignement,* derived from *enseigner,* were endowed with a new distribution of their functions, (whereby the centralized-hierarchical system is predominantly designated by *éducation* and a person's "up-bringing" is exclusively referred to in terms of this word). The dominance of *éducation* has its roots in the French Revolution, the strong influence of Rousseau (*Emile ou de l'Education,* «On façonne les plantes par la culture, et les hommes par l'éducation») and – if one digs even deeper – the effects of Port-Royal, Pascal and Fénelon put together. In this respect, the word *éducation* reveals a longing, an ideal – not the reality. Moreover, it is vital to note that the three main concepts of *éducation, enseignement* and *instruction* imply transitivity. Historically and etymologically seen, *éducation* refers to an "ex-traction", a "raising", a cultivating transformation as it would be with the positive blossoms of fruit-bearing plants. «Aucune éducation ne transforme un être: elle l'éveille» (Barrès, quoted from Robert under *éducation*). The historical background of this term is derived from the *cultura* concept of an agrarian society which is also mirrored by the quote from Rousseau. In comparison to the term *éducation, enseignement* (etymology: *in-* + *sign*(are) + *-mentum* [*in-* + *sign*(are): the "act of signing", the "act of indicating", is derived from *in-* and *signum*], meaning: "putting a sign in one's soul") and *instruction* (etymology: *in-* + *struere,* "to build in", "to prepare or furnish with") emphasize the transfer of knowledge, views and authority from educator to pupil. This involves complementary, continually transitive aspects of the educational process.

The concept of *Bildung* was chosen to be the dominant term from the semantic field *Ausbildung, Bildung, Erziehung, Kultur, Lehre,* (*Lernen*), *Schulung, Unterweisung, Unterricht* in the Federal Republic of Germany. (In the Third Reich, *Erziehung* was the dominant term.) Just think of: *Bildungswesen, Bildungsminister/-in, berufliche Bildung, Allgemeinbildung, Bildungspolitik, eine große/höhere/nicht die geringste Bildung haben*). «Bilde Dich selbst und wirke auf andere durch das, was Du bist» were the words of Wilhelm von Humboldt (i.e. "Broaden your mind and influence the others in the way you are"). The German language does not contain the transitive verb *jdn. bilden,* i.e. "to broaden someone else's mind", but rather *jdn. ausbilden, erziehen* etc. A person can only broaden his/her own mind, i.e. in German: *sich bilden.* The concept of *Bildung,* derived from the verb *bilden,* contains a "reflexive notion".

The concept of *Bildung* goes back to – apparently – "German" traditions: the mysticism of late scolasticism, first of all, with Meister Eckhart (Magister at the University of Paris!) and his pupils Johannes Tauler and Heinrich Seuse. The Old High German *bildunga* and the Middle High German *bildunge* originally meant both 'creation, production', i.e. processes of creation and moulding, and 'portrait, form', i.e. the formed results of such processes. The Old High German *biliden* (to give a thing form) and *bilidon* (to reproduce a thing) coalesced in the Middle High German *bilden*, the starting point for *bildunge* which is filled with connotations concerning the history of civilization. It contains the Aristotelian pair "moulding force" and "material" (the sculptor e.g. creates a portrait or form out of wood or stone) as well as the Aristotelian concept of mimesis, according to which the created form is modelled after the "real" thing in artistic transformation. (It is possible that Latin influence: *formare, plasmare, imprimere,* plays a role here; according to the Grimmsches Wörterbuch [II, p. 14f.], however, such influence has first been demonstrated for the time of Luther.) As a result of mystic influence, *bildunge* came to mean 'the shaping of the mind': the divine spark or seed in one's soul – as *morphé*, the moulding force – creates from the *hýlē* (the material, here: the soul and mind of the individual) a character striving towards God, created in his image. The individualistic concept of mercy in Lutheran Protestanism and later the *Sturm und Drang* movement, the Protestant and Neo-Hellenistic Classical Period and the Age of Romanticism (which also included Catholicism, esoteric doctrines and a patriotism with sacred roots) continued to shape the mystic concept of *Bildung*. With this full background, the concept of *Bildung* ended up in the hands of Wilhelm von Humboldt. Humboldt reinforced the widespread impact of *Bildung* by reforming the *Gymnasium* and *Universität* system. Later on, this concept was disseminated with the introduction of compulsory school attendance for all children.

Bildung, phonetically shorter than the other three-syllable terms, combines vividness (i.e. crystal, icicle and cloud formation = Bildung) and profundity. In this respect, this word could be compared with a symbol in a Goethean sense. However, it contains a dangerous void: society. Neither Anglo-Saxon social nor French instructive characteristics are a part of it (at least two actors belong to *éducation*). The word *Bildung* is based on the Aristotelian concept of *entelechy*, i.e. of a self-developing organism which has its aim or its *telos* in itself, which excludes the *homo politicus*. It does not matter whether we assume the linguistic concept of Wilhelm von Humboldt, Weisgerber and Whorf or the Marxist theory of language as a superstructure and mirroring phenomenon of socio-historical developmental processes: *Bildung* – as a category which is by no means innocent or as the epitome of a complex of behaviourial and educational traditions – can produce a "monad society". Such a society – and particularly in the age of technology – has been late in receiving the necessary vaccine against totalitarianism and the degeneration of the monad to an underling.

Of course, these linguistic aspects must not be overrated; approaches and parallels have been repeatedly pointed out. But, by the same token, they should not be underrated either. Words are the vehicles of civilization. They point out differing features of the education systems of both countries following a more or less common Middle-Age tradition. They also imply different traditions which are now gradually merging in the age of the European Community and technology.

6. Developmental tendencies in mass media

There is hardly any other area that is as continuously subject to change as is the mass media. It is therefore difficult to make any definitive statements concerning its structure, especially since there are a number of technological innovations which are just now beginning to reshape the media sector from top to bottom. The audiovisual media seem to be affected most by this development, but its effects can also be observed in the press. The struggle for economic survival and security evidenced, for example, by vigorous campaigns aimed at bringing in new readers, listeners and viewers, has in part reached new levels of intensity, and it is no longer possible to foresee what the consequences will be.

The following sections present some of the data and background information in this matter and are intended to provide an initial impression of the trends in press, radio, television and film.

6.1 *The press – apparent freedom and economic dependency*

(Heinz-Helmut Lüger)

6.1.1 Stability or crisis?

Depending on one's viewpoint it is possible to arrive at very different conclusions as to the situation of the French press:

- "On the whole, one does not get the impression that the French press of today is limited by finances or the government, or that its freedom of expression is restricted. This is ensured by the mere existence of a wide variety of publications ranging politically from communist to Gaullist, each of which monitors the others with extreme acuity so as to bring any and all irregularities zealously to the public eye." (Röper 1977, p. 246).

- "The French press is in the midst of a phase which is so troubled and difficult that it has become common to speak of a crisis. This sector has indeed gone through a far-reaching development fraught with changes. This is especially true of the process of structural modernization, which now appears all the more difficult since it has continuously been put off ..." (Rozenblum 1980, p. 283)

The difference between the two above evaluations reflects two basic aspects of the press: a journalistic aspect (which tendencies are representative, how pluralistic is the spectrum of opinion?) and an economic aspect (how high are the proceeds from sales and advertising, what are the production and distribution structures like?). The situation being the way it is, the press is organized along the lines of private enterprise and operates on a two-market basis. The object of a publication is to disseminate information and to reach a certain group of buyers and readers. At the same time, these activities serve the additional purpose of opening up a channel to the lucrative market of advertisers. Virtually all products of the press are bound to a greater or lesser degree by this *two-fold nature of their merchandise.* The development of the French daily newspaper *Libération* and of the so-called alternative press in West Germany are examples of how difficult it is to escape the influence of the mentioned conditions (cf. Hirt 1984, Seul 1981, Beywl/Brombach 1982, p. 555ff.).

Consequently, a description of the French press cannot be limited to a mere inventory of news publications currently in existence but must at the same time also take into account a number of economic factors, such as circulation, degree of concentration, advertising volume, and how these factors influence journalistic content. In order to put the whole matter in perspective, the current situation in France will be compared to earlier stages of development and also to information on the West German press.

6.1.2 Increase in periodical circulation

The circulation statistics of the French press as a whole are in a phase of stagnancy. This stagnation, however, is a result of two developments which run counter to each other: a) the continuing *decline of the daily press*, b) a distinct *rise in the presse périodique*, i.e. periodicals and magazines. Furthermore, this upward trend in the latter group is for the most part attributable not to news magazines covering political affairs (*magazines d'actualité, presse hebdomadaire d'informations géné-*

Table 21: Comparison of periodicals circulation

magazines d'actualité, magazines illustrés...		***Magazines, illustrated weeklies etc.***	
1. Femme Actuelle	(1811)	1. Bild der Frau	(1967)
2. Prisma	(1267)	2. Neue Post	(1686)
3. Notre Temps	(1118)	3. Tina	(1554)
4. Messages du Secours Catholique	(1104)	4. Das Beste	(1329)
5. Sélection	(1100)	5. Stern	(1320)
6. Bonheur	(1065)	6. Freizeit Revue	(1320)
7. Modes et Travaux	(1002)	7. Das Neue Blatt	(1222)
8. Paris-Match	(876)	8. Brigitte	(1090)
⋮		9. Der Spiegel	(1087)
15. L'Express	(580)	10. Bravo	(1001)
18. Le Canard enchaîné	(423)	11. Bunte	(983)
20. Le Nouvel Observateur	(403)	12. Neue Revue	(903)
⋮		⋮	
31. Le Point	(316)	28. Die Zeit	(487)
⋮		⋮	
50. L'Evénement du jeudi	(180)		
presse de radio-télévision		***Television and radio program guides***	
1. Télé 7 jours	(3096)	1. Hör zu	(3139)
2. Télé-Star	(1873)	2. TV Hören und Sehen	(2581)
3. Télé Poche	(1731)	3. Auf einen Blick	(2555)
4. Télé Z	(1209)	4. Fernsehwoche	(2457)
5. Télé Loisirs	(1109)	5. Funk-Uhr	(1955)

(Information compiled from: Ducarroir 1900; Albert 1991, p. 88ff.; Medien Jahrbuch '91, Vol. 1, p. 32f.)

rales) but rather to television and radio program guides, illustrated weeklies (*presse de radio-télévision, magazines illustrés*) and leisure periodicals (*presse des sports et des loisirs*). In general, readers are continuing to turn more and more to easy-to-understand, highly illustrated reading material: «L'évolution récente de la presse magazine se caractérise en effet par une modification de son contenu général. La part de l'image et de la photo couleur est beaucoup plus importante dans tous les nouveaux magazines lancés depuis 1975 ...» (Boulnois 1984, p. 43). A similar development can be noted for West German periodicals, even though circulation is still greater than in France. In Germany, however, competition appears to have been intensified in the last few years as a result of overall stagnating sales. Up until now,

Fig. 66
(L'Express, Le Nouv. Obs., Le Point)

there have been no East German periodicals among the circulation leaders. The two largest, *Super Illu* and *Super TV*, are owned by West German publishing firms (Burda and Gong, each with a 50% share). *Table 21* shows the French and German periodicals with the highest circulation (the numbers in parentheses multiplied by 1000 indicate the number of copies sold in Germany or the *diffusion* in France, i.e. the number of copies in circulation).

Professional periodicals and magazines published by various associations are not included in the list. Another category missing in the list are the *Sunday newspapers* (*quotidiens du septième jour*). The circulation of these publications varies from 3.5 to 4 million copies in both countries. The high sales in France, especially compared to the daily newspapers, is usually attributed to the high demand for information on the horse races; «n'était le tiercé, les journaux du dimanche français ne trouveraient guère de lecteurs» (Albert/Leteinturier 1979, p. 110).

At any rate, the overview in *Table 21* clearly illustrates the modest role of the news magazines among the *presse périodique*. In France they account for less than 5% of a total circulation of around 50 million copies. Nonetheless they are a very important primary source of information for foreigners wishing to learn about France, for which reason the most important of them shall be described in the following paragraphs.

The magazine *L'Express* was founded in 1953 by Jean-Jacques Servan-Schreiber and Françoise Giroud and may be said to be the grandfather of all French news magazines. When it first came out, it appeared as a leftist liberal weekly newspaper. Under the influence of Pierre Mendès-France it spoke out against

CHINE: LE CHOC GORBATCHEV
L'EVENEMENT du jeudi
N° 237/20 F
Semaine du 18 au 24 mai 1989
LA GROSSE TETE TRICOLORE
Les Français sont-ils intelligents ?
La culture française est-elle encore universelle ?
Siné

Abb. 67

Fig. 67
(L'Evénement du jeudi)

the war in Indochina and later in Algeria. At an early date it became an advocate of complete structural modernization of the French economy. *L'Express* was given its current appearance in 1964, a format and layout similar to that of *Time* or the German magazine *Der Spiegel.* Its transformation into a news magazine was accompanied by a political shift to the right (anticommunism, criticism of the SFIO, but also criticism of Gaullism). In 1977, the *Express* was bought by the British Goldsmith Group; in 1987 the magazine passed into the hands of the C.G.E., the Compagnie Générale d'Electricité. Today *L'Express* is the magazine with by far the largest circulation and a large portion of its revenues comes from advertising; more than 50% of its readers come from the (well-to-do) new middle classes. *L'Express* is in favour of a liberal economic policy (in 1974 F. Giroud became a member in Giscard d'Estaing's Cabinet) and is generally classified as being affiliated with the "moderate Right" (Jamet 1983, p. 75) – although one should keep in mind the dangers of such generalized labels.

The second largest news magazine, *Le Nouvel Observateur*, came into existence in 1964 as the result of a change of ownership in the weekly magazine *France-Observateur* and of a decision to counteract circulation losses by publishing a magazine in a completely new layout patterned after *L'Express.* Jean Daniel, one of a group of politically active journalists who had left *L'Express* after it changed its course, became the new editor-in-chief. The political stance of the *Nouvel Observateur* was much more reserved than that of its predecessors *L'Observateur* (from 1950 to 1954) and *France-Observateur* (from 1954 on) – thus attracting a wider range of readers and more advertisers. An important goal of the magazine for a long time was to help bring about a leftist alliance capable of attaining a majority in government under the leadership of the PS; today its dominant stance is sooner critical of the government. Similar to *L'Express*, *Le Nouvel Observateur* is read primarily by members of the middle classes with university degrees.

Another magazine whose formation was closely linked to *L'Express* is *Le Point*. It was founded by former staff members of *L'Express* in 1971/72 following disputes concerning journalistic objectives and editorial independence; the crucial financial support for the project came from the Hachette publishing company. The governing idea behind the publication called for a politically independent news magazine which was supposed to draw subscribers away from the two existing magazines, *L'Express* in particular, and to attract new groups of readers with "unpredictable" journalism, new approaches to analyzing happenings and new sections (e.g. *ville et environnement*). *Le Point* quickly gained a circulation of more than 200,000 copies and also reported considerable advertising profits. During the campaign for the 1974 presidential elections the magazine spoke out clearly in favour of the Gaullist candidate, Chaban-Delmas, and his *nouvelle société* program. Later, however, *Le Point* decided not to settle on any one single direction but to maintain an open, right-wing liberal orientation. Differences in position from *L'Express* are in most cases only slight.

Although the news magazine market was already considered saturated, a further magazine, *L'Evénement du jeudi* was founded in 1984 through an initiative of Jean-François Kahn. The endeavour was not financed by any large publishing house, but rather through the issuing of share certificates; this measure, making the reader a stock-holder, met with astonishing response. The editor promised a complete break with traditional modes of thinking and forms of presentation: impartial and critical reporting, straight-forward and vivid discussion and, above all, an end to the polarisation of right and left wings. «Nous avons donc appelé de nos voeux non pas un consensus général et mou, mais la redéfinition de nouvelles alliances susceptibles de faire sauter les verrous conservateurs que la coupure de la France en deux camps antagonistes et d'égale force ne faisait que renforcer», states Kahn on the 5-year anniversary of the founding of his magazine (L'Evénement du jeudi, 9 Nov. 1989). This approach clearly satisfied an existing demand among readers and circulation figures rose sharply (in 1991, circulation reached a new high, actually exceeding the 200,000 mark). The unconventional presentation, often dramatic headlines and a style reminiscent of a tabloid newspaper may well have contributed to this success. The "files" on social topics contained in each issue have also gained renown.

Le Canard enchaîné occupies a unique position in the *presse périodique*. (The word *canard* is slang for both "newspaper" and "false news".) It cannot be considered a news magazine in the same sense as the three magazines dealt with above; instead it is – and is intended to be – a satirical weekly newspaper. Its importance is due to its wide circulation and its relative economic independence (*Le Canard enchaîné* contains no advertising, stocks in the controlling corporation may not be sold to anyone other than employees of the publication). Even more important, however, is the explosive nature of its political articles, which for the most part are well researched. It specializes in uncovering scandals and divulging background information not mentioned in

QU'EST-CE QUI FAIT VENDRE LES HEBDOS ?

Les sous, Chantal Nobel, le sexe, Grégory, les maladies, Delon, Caroline ?

(page 4)

70e ANNÉE – N° 3 377 – LE N° 4,50 F – 10 juillet 1985

Le Canard enchaîné

Journal satirique paraissant le mercredi

Maurice et Jeanne MARECHAL, fondateurs. R. TRENO, ancien directeur.

Drame du Heysel : le gouvernement belge n'a pas pu...

... écraser

« PAS DE SUITE A CHÂTEAUVALLON »

Mais le feuilletonton continue

PATÈRE AUSTÈRE

– Passez-moi la Constitution et un escabeau !

Mais qu'est-ce donc qui le chatouille ?

Un petit sourire, svp, M. le Président !

Le mur du çon

Ton rock, Tonton ?

Francohabitation

La République vendue par appartements

L'ACADÉMIE ROULE

LA FAR EN VEDETTE

ÇA N'ARRIVE QU'AUX AUTRES

ROCK RACKET

Fig. 68
(Le Canard enchaîné)

the rest of the press. Generally speaking, their main targets have been and continue to be established power structures and the accompanying abuses of power, «l'autorisme au sommet et un affairisme tous azimuts au-dessous» (quoted from Jamet 1983, p. 48). Since its foundation in 1915/16 by Maurice Maréchal, *Le Canard enchaîné* has been characterized by a critical, decidedly anti-military and laicist stance which has proved resistant even to strong political pressure. The language used in the weekly is marked by originality and plays on words, a factor which often makes the articles difficult for foreign readers to understand. Sometimes its inclination to ridicule and irony stimulates criticism: «La lecture du *Canard* n'est pas drôle chaque semaine, et le parti pris de dérision systématique qui est le sien reste à la fois sain et insuffisant: en cela, le *Canard* est bien le dernier surgeon de la pensée anarchiste, qui n'est ni de droite ni de gauche mais contre tous les pouvoirs.» (Stoll 1990, p. 8).

Although a variety of *scientific and scholarly periodicals* are of interest for special topics pertaining to France, it is not possible to treat them individually here; Schmidt et. al. (1983, p. 459ff.) covers the most important of them, arranged according to subject matter. Additional information on the French press can be found in the quarterly *Médiaspouvoirs* (which replaced the *Presse Actualité* at the end of 1985). Bertrand 1984 discusses French periodicals on Germany, the German language and German literature.

6.1.3 Stagnation and declining circulation in the daily press

As has already been mentioned, the growth experienced by the French magazines has had a detrimental effect on the *daily press*. During the 1950's and 1960's this sector was on the rise and a total circulation of around 13 million was reached in 1968. From then on, however, the numbers started to fall steadily. In 1984 circulation was at 9.6 million copies, and it has varied between 9 and 10 million since then (CFPJ 1988, Hirsch 1988, Albert 1991, p. 75ff.). The trend in West Germany on the other hand is going in the opposite direction, continuous increases in circulation have been registered since the beginning of the licensed press (*Fig. 69*). Only in the last few years has this curve levelled off at around 20-21 million copies. This seems to indicate that the saturation point of the newspaper market has been reached for the time being. (cf. Holtmann 1980, p. 247ff.; Schütz 1984; Schulze 1991, p. 36ff.).

The difference in the developments of the two countries is due in part to the fact that the German daily newspapers have up to now had more success in standing their ground against competition from other media, periodicals and television in particular, because of steps taken at an early date to modernize production. There is, however, another reason which is probably equally important. The absolute circulation of both newspapers and the press as a whole is much lower in France than in Germany. In other words, these printed media in general have less consumer potential in France than in West Germany. This situation is well illustrated by the fact that approximately one third of the French population between 14 and 34 years of age never purchase newspapers or magazines. (It is possible that this tendency will become much more acute with the arrival of cable television, the increased popularity of satellite television and the rise of new private television stations.) The reader density (newspaper copies per 1000 inhabitants) in France is low on the international scale as well (*Table 22*); France is ranked a mere number 27 (behind almost all the European

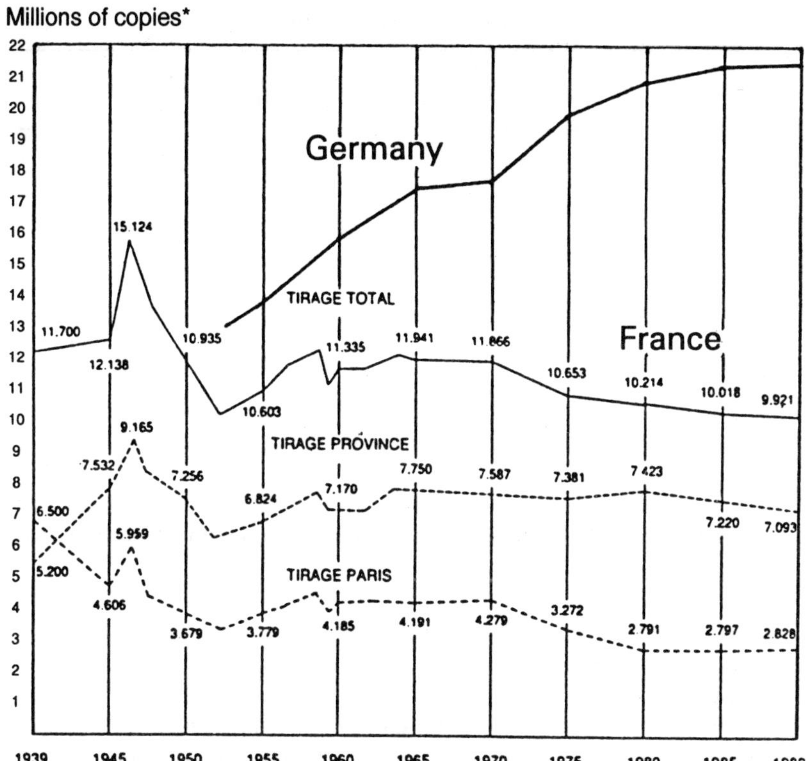

* Figures for the French press are based upon total number printed (*tirage*), for the German press, on copies sold.

Fig. 69: Circulation statistics of the daily press.
(Compiled from: Guéry 1992, p. 11; Medienbericht '85, p. 163;
Schulze 1991, p. 48)

countries and certain Asian ones as well). Furthermore, opinion polls taken in 1988 show that the low consumption of the daily press is accompanied by a degree of credibility which is substantially lower than that of television (Médiaspouvoirs 13/1989, p. 46).

A further difficulty for most daily newspapers is that they have *very few steady buyers* (Rozenblum 1980, p. 316). On the average less than 20% of the copies printed every day are sold by subscription, the majority is accounted for by *vente au numéro*, i.e. individual sales (this is the reason why so much effort is invested in designing the front pages). In West Germany subscriptions dominate the field and only

Table 22: Reader density

		Newspaper copies/ 1000 inhab.
	France	202
	West Germany	399
in comparison:	Sweden	673
	Japan	562
	East Germany	550
	Finland	535
	Great Britain	483
	Soviet Union	422
	USA	268

(Source: CFPJ 1988, p. 69; Erdmann/Fritsch 1990, p. 26)

30% of the circulation is sold at newsstands (although this form of sale is becoming increasingly common).

Circulation losses are more acute for the press in Paris than in the province. Whereas at the turn of the century the number of copies printed in Paris was considerably greater than that appearing in the rest of the country, the ratio had been evened out by the 1930's. Today the provincial press maintains a more or less constant level of circulation and accounts for more than two thirds of the total circulation of daily newspapers in France, while the share of the press in the capital continues to decline. *Table 23* is a list of the ten largest daily newspapers in France and West Germany. Only three of the French top ten are published in Paris. The main reason for this structural change is probably not so much a decrease in centralization in Paris as the fact that readers of the regional press are a relatively well-defined group. This makes it possible for the regional press to tailor the information they offer to the needs and wants of their readers: «La particularité de la presse quotidienne régionale est fondée sur le fait qu'elle s'adresse à l'individu, sujet intégré et participant à une *communauté géographique délimitée* dont il est possible de connaitre de façon plus précise que dans une mégalopole comme Paris, les caractéristiques: mentalités, habitudes, manières de vivre, niveaux de vie, préoccupations culturelles et sociales dominantes, etc.» (Mathien 1983, p. 41). This has the further effect that the readers identify themselves more with their newspapers and that the regional newspapers become more attractive for advertisers since companies prefer to promote their products in a

Table 23: Circulation of the largest daily newspapers

quotidiens	diffusion (en milliers d'exempl.)	daily newspapers	copies sold (in thousands)
1. Ouest-France	795,4	1. Bild	4745,2
2. Le Figaro	428,7	2. Westdeutsche Allgemeine	653,1
3. Le Parisien	405,3	3. Hannoversche Allgemeine	438,7
4. Le Monde	381,6	4. Express	434,5
5. Sud-Ouest	370,0	5. Südwest Presse	425,2
6. La Voix du Nord	372,2	6. Rheinische Post	395,4
7. Le Progrès	351,1	7. Frankfurter Allgemeine	391,7
8. Le Dauphiné libéré	296,4	8. Süddeutsche Zeitung	389,1
9. La Nouvelle République du Centre Ouest	267,1	9. Augsburger Allgemeine	361,1
10. Nice-Matin	253,1	10. B.Z.	343,6

(Source: Guéry 1992, p. 12f.; Erdmann/Fritsch 1990, p. 86ff.; BDZV 1991, p. 148ff.)

manner aimed at specific consumer groups. Regardless of this fact, though, the original task of the national press, i.e. dissemination of national and international news, naturally continues to be fulfilled, not only by radio and television, but also by the regional newspapers.

The Parisian press has attempted to counteract the decrease in circulation through regular *suppléments*, special editions and more appealing graphics; in addition, it has adapted to the situation inasmuch as it has turned more and more into a regional press for the area in and around Paris. There is practically no *presse nationale* left in France, the only exception being *Le Monde*.

Le Monde is a highly respected newspaper both inside and outside the borders of France. It provides its readers with comprehensive, solid coverage of a wide range of subjects. It has become an institutional forum for important national-debates. In addition, commentary by well-known writers from science and politics appears at regular intervals and ensures a broad range of opinion. *Le*

Le Monde

DERNIÈRE ÉDITION 3
BOURSE

QUARANTE-TROISIÈME ANNÉE – N° 12741 – 4,50 F   Fondateur : Hubert Beuve-Méry   Directeur : André Fontaine   MERCREDI 15 JANVIER 1986

Les chrétiens libanais déchirés

La guerre qui depuis plus de dix ans ravage le Liban a connu tous les rebondissements, les espoirs déçus, les coups de théâtre qu'aurait pu concevoir un ingénieux et diabolique metteur en scène. Du « miracle » que fut l'élection unanime de Béchir Gemayel à la tragédie de son assassinat, de la fracassante et vaine invasion israélienne à la déroute des contingents des quatre pays de l'OTAN à Beyrouth, du « triomphe » des milices musulmanes de l'Ouest à leur lutte fratricide, tous les cas de figure se sont, tôt ou tard, présentés dans ce conflit sans issue. On avait tout de même peine à croire, en dépit d'accrochages parfois très vifs, que les chrétiens régleraient leurs divergences à coups de canon dans le « réduit » où, s'estimant menacés de toutes parts, ils ont bâti la forteresse de leur survie. C'est chose faite désormais, même si le bilan – de dix à vingt morts selon les sources – paraît « modeste » aux yeux plus que blasés des Libanais recrus de comptabilité macabre.

Ce déchirement est désastreux pour des gens qui, de toute évidence, ont mieux à faire que s'entre-tuer. Il repose, pour une bonne part, sur les hargnes et rancœurs de quelques seigneurs de la guerre et sur le heurt d'ambitions rivales. Mais l'aspect clanique du conflit du Liban n'est pas une nouveauté. Il engendre parfois des épisodes que l'étranger a peine à comprendre tant est vrai le proverbe italien selon lequel « seule la cuillère connaît vraiment les malheurs de la marmite ».

En l'occurrence, l'ébauche de guerre civile dans le camp chrétien oppose trois hommes disposant de forces sensiblement égales. Le premier d'entre eux, président de la République, M. Amine Gemayel, n'a pas su ou pas pu – il y aurait fallu des dons peu communs – galvaniser ou même rassurer la communauté dont il est en principe le chef suprême.

Aujourd'hui à Damas, pour sa onzième rencontre avec le président Assad, il renâcle plutôt qu'il ne résiste à sa tutelle, trop

LA TENTATIVE DE COUP D'ÉTAT AU YÉMEN DU SUD

Violents combats à Aden entre loyalistes et rebelles

La tentative de coup d'Etat du lundi 13 janvier au Yémen du Sud n'était pas écrasée, ce mardi en début d'après-midi. Les forces hostiles au président Ali Nasser Mohamed livraient toujours, selon le Foreign Office, de violents combats dans plusieurs quartiers d'Aden. Les cent trente citoyens français de la ville ont été regroupés à la résidence de l'ambassadeur et dans un hôtel.

Des bâtiments publics et ambassades étrangères – dont celles d'Italie et d'Algérie – ont été endommagés. L'aéroport est fermé au trafic, et trois cargos, dont deux soviétiques, sont en flammes dans le port.

La capitale du Yémen du Sud est, depuis lundi, le théâtre d'une bataille entre loyalistes et rebelles. A en croire les premières indications diffusées par Radio-Aden, quatre hauts responsables du pays, dont l'ancien chef de l'Etat Abdel Fatah Ismail, ont été exécutés pour avoir organisé le coup de force.

Depuis plus d'un an, dans ce petit pays allié de l'URSS, où est installé le seul régime marxiste-léniniste dans le monde arabe, une sourde lutte pour le pouvoir opposait le président Ali Nasser Mohamed, technocrate pragmatique, partisan d'une ouverture à l'ouest, notamment vers l'Arabie saoudite, et un clan plus dogmatique, celui de l'ancien chef de l'Etat, Abdel Fatah Ismail.

Selon des sources diplomatiques et des témoignages directs cités par la BBC, l'aéroport d'Aden est sous le contrôle des forces loyalistes, tandis que des combats à l'arme lourde se déroulent dans plusieurs quartiers de la capitale. Au cours des affrontements, un important incendie a partiellement détruit l'ambassade d'Italie. Des bâtiments ancrés dans le port d'Aden auraient été aussi incendiés. Des rumeurs recueillies à Djibouti – mais qui ne sont confirmées par nulle autre source – indiquent que le président Ali Nasser Mohamed aurait été blessé et serait hospitalisé. Cela expliquerait qu'il n'ait pas encore été en mesure d'intervenir à la radio, dont la plupart des émissions régulières avaient été interrompues lundi pour faire place à de la musique folklorique.

Selon les émissions diffusées lundi par Radio-Aden, le « *complot* » est venu du cœur même du pouvoir. De fait – outre l'ancien président Ismail –, les trois autres personnalités exécutées appartenaient toutes à l'équipe dirigeante.

(Lire la suite page 3.)

LE TRIBUNAL DE COMMERCE ET « LE PROGRÈS »

Un mandataire nommé auprès de M. Hersant

Le tribunal de commerce de Paris a décidé mardi 14 janvier, après trois jours de réflexion, de désigner un mandataire, M. Paul Paclot, ancien président du tribunal de commerce de Paris, placé pour trois mois auprès de M. Robert Hersant. Ce jugement permet à celui-ci de rester à la tête du *Progrès*, qu'il avait racheté le 3 janvier à M. Jean-Charles Lignel.

En nommant M. Paul Paclot mandataire de justice au *Progrès* de Lyon, le tribunal de commerce de Paris, considérant que les faits rapportés à son audience du 11 janvier étaient « *suffisamment troublants* », n'a cependant fait que prendre au pied de la lettre la requête de M. Pierre Bezard, substitut du procureur de la République. Ce dernier demandait des mesures conservatoires : il les obtient. En revanche, le tribunal de commerce a refusé de dessaisir M. Robert Hersant de ses fonctions de président du conseil d'administration du *Progrès*, prenant acte notamment du fait que « *les salaires de décembre n'ont pu être versés que grâce à l'intervention de la nouvelle direction et qu'un administrateur provisoire pourrait se trouver finalement contraint d'effectuer, faute d'autres possibilités avérées, une déclaration de cessation de paiement* ».

Nommé pour trois mois, non renouvelables, M. Paul Paclot, ancien président du tribunal de commerce de Paris de 1969 à 1972, assistera aux réunions du conseil d'administration des sociétés Delaroche et Progrès SA. Il sera chargé d'empêcher M. Robert Hersant de prendre des « *décisions irréversibles* », qui pourraient ensuite être annulées par le jugement au fond à propos du caractère licite ou illicite de la transaction entre MM. Lignel et Hersant, sur lequel le tribunal de commerce de Paris statuera le 27 janvier.

Reste à savoir quel est le champ de ces décisions irréversibles. Selon certains avocats présents à l'audience, ce sont des décisions de M. Robert Hersant qui mettraient en cause l'autonomie du *Progrès* (comme le fait, par exemple, de confier la régie publicitaire du journal à la régie publicitaire du groupe Hersant). M. Paul Paclot est chargé de veiller au respect de l'ordonnance du tribunal et pourra rapporter à celui-ci d'éventuelles infractions. Charge alors aux magistrats de prendre les mesures *ad hoc* à l'encontre de M. Hersant.

Si M. Robert Hersant est donc « sous surveillance », il n'en continue pas moins à être à la tête du *Progrès*, bien que ses pouvoirs soient limités. L'ordonnance du tribunal de commerce constitue donc une demi-victoire pour lui, d'autant que le mandataire n'est nommé que pour trois mois, c'est-à-dire un peu au-delà des élections. Demi-victoire renforcée par le fait que le tribunal de commerce a débouté de leurs plaintes contre M. Hersant les syndicats de journalistes SNJ et CFDT.

Y.-M. L.

(Lire nos informations page 40.)

LA VISITE DE M. CHEVARDNADZE A TOKYO

Retrouvailles nippo-soviétiques

De notre correspondant

Tokyo. – Après un gel de dix ans, les relations nippo-soviétiques connaissent un « *nouveau départ* », affirme-t-on au minis-

M. Edouard Chevardnadze, ministre soviétique des affaires étrangères, est attendu le mercredi 15 janvier à Tokyo pour une visite officielle de quatre jours. Il s'agit de la première visite effectuée par un chef de la diplomatie soviétique au Japon depuis 1976. Au cours des dix dernières années, le contentieux bilatéral nippo-soviétique s'était aggravé dans la plupart des

par les Japonais, alimentaient d'autre part dans l'opinion publique l'idée d'une menace soviétique.

La relative détente Est-Ouest qui s'est dessinée à Genève n'a certes pas balayé d'un seul coup le

Prix : + 0,1 % en décembre

L'objectif de 2,5 % de hausse des prix cette année apparaît réaliste après les bons résultats de 1985.

PAGE 40

Comment calculer vos impôts en 1986

PAGE 38

Un sondage sur la flexibilité

Une majorité de Français serait favorable à l'aménagement du temps de travail.

PAGE 36

Le chômage en URSS

Contrairement au dogme, des centaines de milliers de Soviétiques sont sans emploi.

PAGE 4

Superphénix en service

Le premier surgénérateur de taille industrielle a été relié au réseau EDF. Mais on s'interroge déjà sur cette filière nucléaire.

PAGE 40

Le Monde
MÉDECINE
Péridurale :

Fig. 70

Monde is thus in the eyes of many – all over the world – one of the very best daily newspapers. The ownership and decision-making processes of *Le Monde* are exemplary as well. It is not the property of a private publisher but was instead founded as a corporation (SARL *Le Monde*) by Hubert Beuve-Méry in 1944 with its stock divided amongst its editors, founding members, publishers and other employees according to certain proportional rules. Faced with major economic difficulties, however, the newspaper was forced to found a *Société des Lecteurs* in 1985. The sale of shares resulted in a considerable capital stock, with which a series of modernizing measures could be implemented. Editorial freedom remained intact in so far as the statutes continued to prohibit any influence on the part of external interest groups, the newspaper's reading public included. The board of directors of the newspaper is elected by the staff, the editors having what amounts to the right to veto this choice. This power of veto also holds for fundamental questions having to do with organization and political orientation. At the beginning of 1991, a non-journalist was for the

Table 24: The newspaper market in the new federal states

Old Name	Circulation in 1988 (in thousands of copies)	New Name (+ new owner)	Circulation in 1988 (in thousands of copies)
former SED newspapers			
Neues Deutschland	1100	Neues Deutschland (independent, PDS)	128
Freie Presse (Chemnitz)	661	freie presse (Medien Union, Ludwigshafen)	586
Freiheit (Halle)	585	Mitteldeutsche Zeitung (DuMont Schauberg, Köln)	527
Sächsische Zeitung	566	Sächsische Zeitung (Gruner & Jahr/ Rhein. Post, WAZ)	513
Leipziger Volkszeitung	484	Leipziger Volkszeitung (Springer-Verlag/ Madsack, Hannover)	380
Volksstimme (Magdeburg)	451	Volksstimme (Bauer-Verlag)	375
Berliner Zeitung	425	Berliner Zeitung (Gruner & Jahr/Maxwell)	304
Das Volk (Erfurt)	401	Thüringer Allgemeine (WAZ 50 %)	350
Märkische Volksstimme (Potsdam)	348	Märkische Allgemeine (FAZ)	265
party newspapers			
Neue Zeit (CDU)	113	Neue Zeit (FAZ)	25
Bauern-Echo (Deutsche Bauernpartei)	94	Deutsches Landblatt (FAZ)	25
Thüringische Landeszeitung (LDPD)	68	Thüringische Landeszeitung (WAZ)	80
Sächsisches Tageblatt (LDPD)	65	Leipziger Tageblatt/ Chemnitzer Tageblatt (Springer-Verlag)	41
Die Union (CDU)	63	Die Union (Süddeutscher Verlag, München)	35
Der Morgen (LDPD)	62	Der Morgen discontinued in 1991 (Springer-Verlag)	24
Liberal-Demokratische Zeitung (LDPD)	57	Hallesches Tageblatt (Springer-Verlag)	44
National-Zeitung (NDPD)	56	in 1990, merged with: Der Morgen, discontinued in 1991 (Springer-Verlag)	–

(Compiled from: Röper 1991, p. 422f.; BDZV 1991, p. 113ff.; Medien-Jahrbuch '91, Vol. 1, p. 40) first time elected as Director. (The arrangement discussed above may pose difficulties in execution, but thus fulfils the basic demands for internal freedom of the press which journalist unions have been fighting for without avail in other French publications for many years. One can also compare this to the struggle in West Germany to repeal the so-called «*Tendenzparagraph*» in the *Betriebsverfassungsgesetz* ("Labour-Management Relations Act") of 1952, which expressly limits codetermination in institutions which influence public opinion, including the press.)

The circulation of *Le Monde* reached a peak in 1981 with 445,000 copies in distribution. This was followed by substantial losses which brought about a serious crisis – a crisis which endangered not only the financial independence of the newspaper but even its very existence. This turn of events has often been blamed on personnel costs, but this is certainly not a completely adequate explanation. A more significant factor has probably been the severe competition from other newspapers, such as *Libération* and *Le Figaro*, and also the impression on the part of many readers that *Le Monde* has not maintained the necessary amount of critical distance to the Government since 1981. The fact that *Le Monde* adopted its graphic layout from the pre-war newspaper *Le Temps* and, unlike other newspapers, makes no use of certain means such as photographs and large headlines to facilitate reader understanding, has certainly played a role. Its competitor, Libération, has been particularly successful in adapting effectively to changing reading habits – at least judging by increased circulation (cf. Liehr 1990, Freytag 1992).

There is no equivalent to *Le Monde* in the West German press; in fact West Germany, for obvious reasons, has not developed a press which can rightly be termed the press of the capital. It is hardly justified to hold up the newspaper *Die Welt*, which moved from Hamburg to Bonn several years ago, as a German counterpart. The fact that French correspondents do so in their reports in French television bears witness to the problem of *faux amis* in a cultural comparison of two countries.

The intention of the present investigation allows no more than a short overview of the changes in the German press scene since 1990. After re-unification, the trusteeship also became successor in title to the newspapers in the new federal states, and began immediately with the sale of the publishing companies. This process was, for all practical purposes, complete by the end of 1991, with almost the entire East German press market in the hands of West German (or multi-national) firms.

There was great interest in purchase of the newspapers of the SED, with their large circulation; only seven of the regional newspapers had achieved a circulation in excess of 300,000 (cf. *Table 24*). As can be seen from reader density figures (*Table 22*), newspaper sales in the GDR were considerably higher in proportion to population than they were in the old federal states. There was also significantly more variety, at least in terms of the number of publications. Once the borders were opened, interested major publishers were lured by most attractive conditions; it is scarcely surprising that there was an immediate rush to grab up the East German newspapers. In addition, efforts were made to secure a share of the potential reader and advertising market either through the sale of supra-regional West German newspapers or by founding new newspapers (e.g., the tabloid *Super!* by Burda/Murdoch). The initial results of this *«colonisation des journaux est-allemands»* (Thibaut 1992) are shown in *Table 24*. What is significant is that several periodicals publishers and international media multis have established themselves on the market in eastern Germany.

The sales policy of the trusteeship has come under repeated fire. It very quickly became clear that economic and editorial considerations were not the only criteria involved in their decisions on purchase offers. One prominent example: The *Freie Presse*, published in Chemnitz (with a circulation of 661,000 in 1988), was promised on the quiet to the *Rheinpfalz* (Medien Union) of Ludwigshafen, the local paper of Chancellor Kohl. Other instances can also be named in which individual newspaper publishing firms were "exempted" from the prescribed process of sale through invitation to tender (Die Zeit, 8 March 1991, p. 26; cf. Röper 1991, p. 426f.).

The overall tendency can be described as follows:

- Because of the loss of large state subsidies, daily newspapers in the new federal states have become significantly more expensive; this can be regarded as one of the reasons for the drop in total circulation.
- While the newly established "street sales press" has won new readers, supra-regional newspapers – *Neues Deutschland* in particular – have suffered a considerable drop in circulation.
- Even if no large scale "newspaper death" took place after 1990, further decrease in newspaper density can be expected for the coming year. Competition from other media and advertising forms (e.g., periodicals) is likely to intensify the resulting pressure still further.

6.1.4 Economic and journalistic concentration

Like other businesses, the press is subject to the general conditions of competition and to the principles of cost and benefit. The outcome of this situation is that the printed media are liable to the same concen-

Table 25: Data on concentration of the daily press

	Number of journalistic entities France	FRG
1949	155	169
1954	128	225
1958	123	201
1964	107	183
1967	98	158
1976	84	121
1981	82	124
1984	81	125
1985	82	126
1989	76	121

(Information compiled from: SJTI 1990; p. 111f.; Albert 1991, p. 81; Medienbericht '85, p. 163; Schulze 1991, p. 36ff.)

tration tendencies as other business sectors. There is but little room left for expansion in the number of buyers and subscribers; even though the prices of the newspapers do not come close to covering expenditures, price increases are held in check by strict limitations; costs for production and modernization, on the other hand, are rising. In face of all these facts, the chief way of ensuring profitability is to increase efficiency in production and distribution and to make better use of the advertisement market. The steps that must be taken in the process have induced many publishers to relinquish certain publications, to merge with other publishing companies or to seek other forms of fusion or cooperation (cf. Schütz 1974, p. 66ff.; Meyn 1974, p. 60ff.; Holtmann 1980, p. 266ff.). *This economic concentration goes hand in hand with journalistic concentration: the reduction of the number of independent publications.* For quite some time now this development has been leading to a high degree of concentration in the magazine sector in both France and West Germany – despite the fact that circulation is on the rise. Currently, about two thirds of the entire market in both countries is dominated by but a few companies (for further details cf. Guillauma 1988, p. 84; Albert 1991; Holzer 1980, p. 29ff.).

The effects of this concentration on the *daily press* are being followed with great interest. *Table 25* provides an overview of how the number of journalistic entities has developed. (By 'journalistic entities'

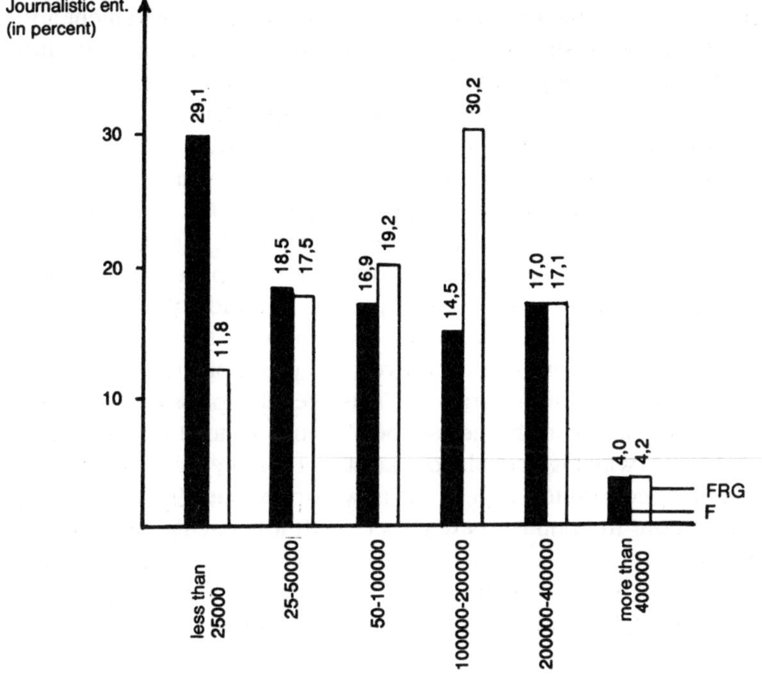

Fig. 71: Distribution of journalistic entities by circulation. (Calculated from information in: Ducarroir 1990, p. 184ff.; Guéry 1992, p. 12f.; Schulze 1991, p. 158ff.)

Schütz means full-scale editorial staffs – as opposed to local editorial staffs – which continue to bring out on their own the cover section of newspapers, i.e. the first pages containing current political news. The French statistics are based on similar criteria.)

The number of independent newspapers has decreased by half since the beginning of the 1950s, although the level in West Germany has been higher than in France except for during the period of the German licensed press. This drastic shrinkage has in both cases resulted in the formation of numerous regional monopolies, the so-called *single-newspaper regions.* Only few of these, on the other hand, were newly founded newspapers; in most cases the monopolies were brought about by smaller newspapers not being able to hold their own in the long run. Only in the last few years has this concentration process come to a temporary stop; the number of journalistic entities has even increased somewhat in certain cases. As early as 1979 Schütz thought it possible to make the following optimistic statement about the German press: "The trend towards further concentration in the sector of the daily press in West Germany seems to have come to an end for the time being; the newspaper market has achieved stability with a high degree of concentration" (1979, p. 612). Although several analogies can be found in the French press, similar conclusions on developments in that country are not warranted. On the contrary, the classification of journalistic entities by circulation (*Fig. 71*) reveals certain *structural weak points*. Nearly one newspaper out of two has a circulation of less than 50,000 copies per day and is thus on the verge of being unprofitable. Especially noteworthy is the high proportion of small newspapers below the level of 25,000 copies (nearly 30% compared to about 12% in Germany). This overall impression is confirmed when one looks at the newspapers' shares of total circulation. The daily press with high circulation statistics, i.e. more than 200,000 copies per day, constitutes 20% of all newspapers but 59.1% of the total circulation. In contrast, newspapers with low circulation (= approx. 50%) do not even account for a 10% share. This data leads one to the conclusion that the number of full-scale editorial staffs in France could quite possibly continue to decrease in the coming years.

6.1.5 Dominance of a few press conglomerates

At the business end of the matter the tendency towards concentration has resulted in the emergence of a few, influential *press conglomerates*. Their dominating presence is felt in both the magazine and newspaper sectors. The different mergers, corporate shares and interrelations (also including companies outside of the press sector), however, are so complex that it would not be possible to treat them suitably here in this overview. It is noteworthy that the involvement of foreign groups in the French press market – among them the German media companies Bertelsmann/Gruner & Jahr (Prisma Presse), Bauer – has been increasing in recent years. The growth in the size of these press groups increases not only their capacity to influence their competition at the economic level, but also their ability to exercise control and exert pressure in journalistic matters. Some of the most important corporations are Hachette, Filipacchi, Editions Mondiales, Havas, Hersant (Socpresse), Bayard Presse and Editions Aumaury. (For details on ownership see: PrAct 1985, p. 53ff.; CFPJ 1988, p. 23ff.; Albert 1991, p. 78ff.; Guéry 1992, p. 17ff.)

Fig. 72
(From: Le Canard enchaîné, 16 Jan. 1985)

The company subject to the most public criticism has been the *Hersant conglomerate.* This corporation currently controls more than fifteen periodicals (e.g. *Le Figaro Magazine, L'Auto-Journal, L'Ami de jardins et de la maison, La Revue nationale de la chasse ...*), and its share of the newspaper market was estimated at 26.4% at the beginning of 1992 (34% of the Parisian press, 23% of the regional press). Numerous take-overs and dubious dealings by Robert Hersant, the head of the corporation, have repeatedly given rise to commotions. The most spectacular change to the press world in France was without a doubt the corporation's acquisition of three Parisian newspapers: *Le Figaro* in 1975, *France-Soir* in 1976 (initially a 50% share), *L'Aurore* in 1978. In addition, the corporation owns more than 20 regional newspapers (e.g. *Le Dauphiné libéré, Paris-Normandie, Nord-Eclair ...*). Hersant's acquisition in 1986 of *L'Union* (circulation 119,000) and *Le Progrès,* a newspaper rich in tradition serving the Rhône-Alpes region (circulation 302,500 at the time), also aroused considerable attention. Trusting completely in an imminent shift in the government majority («Je suis en avance d'une loi ...»), Hersant disregarded in a provocative manner all the regulations imposed by the press legislation of 1984 (cf. 6.1.7). The most recent coup in activities of the *«papivore»* Hersant was, in 1992, the takeover of the regional newspapers *L'Ardennais* (Charleville, with a circulation of 27,000 copies going to print), *Le Courrier de l'Ouest* (Angers, with 109,000 copies) and *Le Maine libre* (Le Mans, 55,000 copies).

Many competing newspapers perceive in economic absorption by the Hersant conglomerate a threat to their own existence (cf. *Fig. 72*). The départements with established Hersant papers are indicated in *Fig. 73.* The results could give rise to speculation on whether, in the west,

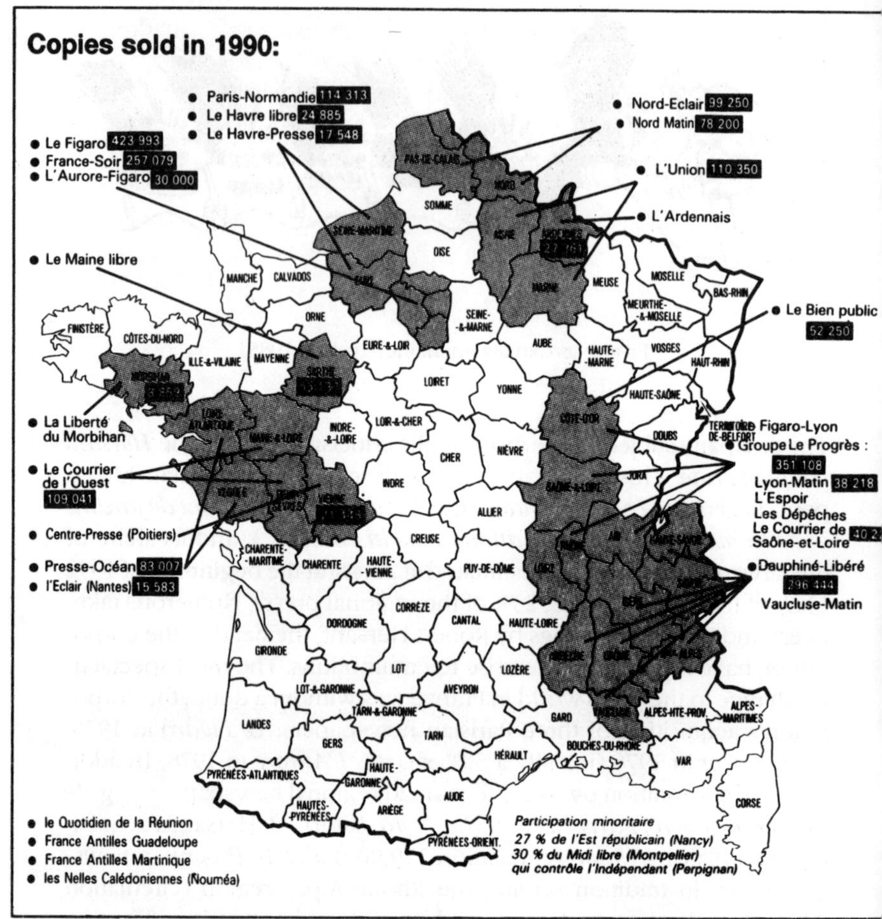

Fig. 73
(Area of circulation of Hersant's dailies)

the expansion policy might not lead to a weakening of *Ouest-France*, which is published in Rennes and until now has enjoyed the highest circulation of all French newspapers. With respect to journalistic content, the expansion of the conglomerate has contributed to increased uniformity in the press; the take-over of a publication by Hersant is usually accompanied by a shift in emphasis towards a clearly right-wing conservative stance and by an increase in sensationalism (cf. the different viewpoints offered by Brimo/Guérin 1977, Miguet 1984).

The process of economic concentration is even more marked in West Germany. Four publishing conglomerates alone (Bauer, Springer, Burda, Bertelsmann/Gruner & Jahr) account for around 65% of the magazine sector; however, there is a slight tendency in the opposite direction. The Springer corporation's dominant position in the daily press since the 1960's has been widely viewed as the symbol *par excellence* for concentration in the press and for the threat to diversity of opinion. The conglomerate owns, among others, the newspapers *Bild, Die Welt, Hamburger Abendblatt, Berliner Morgenpost and B.Z.* (Berlin) and accounts for more than 30% of the total circulation in Germany. Its share among the Sunday newspapers is even higher, namely around 90%. However, not only the degree of concentration is subject to criticism but also its journalistic practices and the way in which the competition is pushed aside (cf. e.g. Alberts 1972; Wallraff 1977, 1979; Böll 1984).

Of the publishing groups referred to here, Springer and Bertelsmann/Gruner & Jahr have meanwhile intensified efforts to penetrate into the audio-visual sector. They are thus assuming more and more the character of multi-media conglomerates (cf. 6.2.9).

6.1.6 Dependence on advertising, and news as a commodity

From an economical viewpoint, income from advertising has long since become more important than proceeds from sales. The foremost function of the press continues to be to disseminate information, for this is the only way to ensure that the buyers, subscribers and thus addressees of advertising are reached. Nevertheless, the advertising market is decisive in economic matters. This situation is strikingly reflected in Karl Bücher's well-known opinion that in the end, the editorial part of a newspaper exists only to sell advertising space.

The development towards dependence on advertising has its origins in the beginning of the 19th century. This dependency has several consequences: restrictions are placed on journalistic autonomy, the manner in which news is presented is subjected to an increasing amount of external influence, and commercial and non-commercial subject matter become more and more inseparable. The more that "paragraphs in the editorial section interact with paragraphs in the advertising section", the more the press becomes "a breach allowing privileged private interests to gain access to the public" (Habermas 1971, p. 221f.).

Table 26: Media share of advertising spending

		France	Germany
presse		56,2 %	78,9 %
dont:	quotidiens:	19,2 %	41,7 %
	périodiques:	37,0 %	37,2 %
radio		6,8 %	4,4 %
télévision		24,7 %	12,2 %
cinéma		0,8 %	1,1 %
affichage		11,5 %	3,4 %

(From: Albert 1991, p. 45)

The actual extent to which the press today depends on advertising is illustrated by the fact that advertising accounts for approx. 60-80% of the revenues of most newspapers or magazines, the variation being dependent on the size of the publication. One should keep in mind, however, that this share is subject to frequent fluctuation and that competition for advertisers is keen between the various media. When one considers the distribution of total investments by the advertising industry, one can see that the press still occupies first place in both France and West Germany, with 56.2% and 78.9% respectively (*Table 26*). In France the greater portion of this share goes to magazines, whereas in West Germany the ratio is reversed. The French daily press in particular seems to be threatened: its share of advertising is declining slightly and the dwindling number of readers might further diminish its value for advertisers. The provincial press continues to be the most well-off of all, the reason for this being its quasi monopoly in *publicité commerciale locale* and *petites annonces* (Mathien 1983, p. 114). Nevertheless, it is conceivable that the stability of this situation might be seriously upset if new competition should arise by *radios privées* becoming more common (cf. 6.2.4) and by state-run television being replaced to a great extent by *chaînes privées* with regional broadcasters. The following appeal made by a provincial newspaper reveals how threatening such a possibility is considered to be even by the regional press itself (T. 24).

T. 24:
La presse quotidienne régionale unie face au danger

La presse quotidienne régionale est en danger. Jamais depuis quarante ans, elle n'a autant qu'aujourd'hui affronté d'angoissants périls dans une période de haute turbulence. Si l'audiovisuel, symbole de modernité, doit se développer, cela ne doit pas se faire au détriment de la presse écrite, qui, depuis des décennies, a servi et la démocratie et le pluralisme, en formant la diversité de l'opinion des citoyens, en leur donnant le temps et l'occasion de la réflexion.

[...]

Aujourd'hui, la presse écrite doit affronter un double défi. D'une part, l'accès à la télévision de nouveaux secteurs d'annonceurs publicitaires qui, amenés à répartir différemment des budgets malheureusement peu extensibles, réduiront la part actuellement allouée à vos quotidiens régionaux.

D'autre part, l'éventuelle apparition de télévisions dites «privées» qui pose le problème de la redistribution des budgets de publicité dans une période de crise économique et donc, une fois encore, entraîne une ponction sur les médias existants.

[...]

Une société qui détruit sciemment un de ses moyens de communication démocratique va-t-elle dans le sens du progrès et de l'approfondissement du champ de réflexion des hommes, où qu'ils habitent, où qu'ils travaillent? Les télévisions «privées» de demain pourront-elles fournir autant de «petites» informations locales, dans le moindre village, dans le moindre canton? La civilisation de l'écrit, cette mémoire qui transcende les générations, doit-elle disparaître, faute de moyens, et laisser place nette à une civilisation orale modernisée et nivellée à travers un modèle audiovisuel? Ne doit-on pas, au contraire, rechercher une coexistence enrichissante en assurant les équilibres nécessaires?

[...] (La Montagne, 26 April 1985)

Being dependent on income from advertising not only means that the press is greatly affected by *changes in the economic situation*, it also means that the "capitalistic function" (cf. Hennig 1971) has a strong influence on the *journalistic orientation*. This is exemplified by the restrictions on journalistic autonomy as mentioned earlier. Direct coercion and boycotts are not the only measures that come to mind in this connection; there are other aspects which are of more consequence. For example, editorial sections are tacitly adapted to the expectations and needs of advertisers, and *conditions conducive to advertising* are created, e.g. in special sections not marked as advertisement (*conseils pratiques, chroniques automobiles, articles de mode* etc.) (Albert 1991, p. 49ff.; Meyn 1974, p. 56ff.). A further aspect is the verifiable tendency of a large portion of the press to exhibit conformity, to diminish the political component in reporting and to steer clear of certain opinions

Table 27: *Couplages publicitaires* in the French provincial press

Nom du couplage	Composition du couplage	Diffusion OJD 1986
Journaux de l'Ouest	*Ouest-France, Presse-Océan, L'Éclair*	837 000
Groupe Dauphiné-Le Progrès	*Le Progrès, La Tribune, L'Espoir, Les Dépêches, Le Dauphiné libéré, Lyon Matin, Vaucluse Matin, Lyon Figaro*	755 000
Quotidiens du Sud-Ouest	*Sud-Ouest, La France-La Nouvelle République, La Charente libre, La République des Pyrénées, L'Éclair des Pyrénées, La Dordogne libre*	450 000
Journaux de l'Est Associés	*Les Dernières Nouvelles d'Alsace, Le Républicain lorrain, La Liberté de l'Est*	422 000
Groupe La Dépêche du Midi	*La Dépêche du Midi, La Nouvelle République des Pyrénées, Le Petit Bleu, Le Villefranchois, Midi Olympique*	389 000
France Est	*L'Est républicain, L'Ardennais, L'Est Éclair, La Haute-Marne libérée, Libération-Champagne, L'Aisne nouvelle*	389 000
Centre France	*La Montagne, Le Populaire du Centre, Le Berry républicain, Le Journal du Centre*	388 000
Média Sud	*Le Provençal, Le Méridional, Var-Matin, Le Soir*	350 000
Les Journaux du Midi	*Midi Libre, Centre-Presse* (Aveyron), *L'Indépendant*	286 000
Groupe Normand	*Paris Normandie, Le Havre libre, Havre-Presse, Le Pays d'Auge, La Renaissance du Bessin, Les Nouvelles de Falaise, La Voix-Le Bocage, Le Courrier de l'Eure, L'Action républicaine*	230 000
Groupe Nord	*Nord-Éclair, Nord-Matin*	167 000
Inter-Ouest	*Le Courrier de l'Ouest, Le Maine libre*	163 000
Les Journaux de Bourgogne	*Le Courrier de Saône-et-Loire, Le Bien public, L'Yonne Républicaine*	140 000
Groupe Écho du Centre	*La Marseillaise du Berry, Écho-Dordogne, L'Écho du Centre*	105 000
Les Journaux du Centre	*La République du Centre, L'Écho républicain*	97 600
Quodep	*L'Eclaireur du Gâtinais, L'Éveil de la Haute-Loire, Nord Littoral, La Gazette provençale, La Presse de la Manche*	83 931
Journaux de Corse	*Le Journal de la Corse, L'Informateur corse, Le Petit Bastiais*	11 000

(Guillauma 1988, 60)

or stances which collide with advertiser interests and which deviate substantially from certain fundamental positions deemed in keeping with collective opinion (cf. Lüger 1987). Considerations on how to improve sales and secure an economic base are thus closely tied to the way in which news is selected and presented.

The advertising market is furthermore *conducive to concentration in the press.* This is due simply to the fact that newspapers with a high circulation have a great advantage over their competitors: the more people who read a newspaper, the larger the group reached by advertising. In addition, widely-read newspapers can demand a comparatively low price for advertising per 1000 readers since the price increase per ad is not directly proportional to newspaper circulation. The consequence is a negative *circulation/advertising spiral* in the course of which small press companies frequently have no alternative but to join up with advertising cooperatives (*couplages publicitaires*) or other forms of cooperation - often culminating in the merger of editorial staffs (cf. *Table 27* for details on the provincial press in France).

6.1.7 Attempts at legislative influence

In order to check the process of concentration in the press and to prevent further losses in diversity of opinion, the French Government worked out a new regulatory law for the press in 1983 (*Loi visant à limiter la concentration et à assurer la transparence financière et le pluralisme des entreprises de presse*). One of the main goals of the Government's proposal was to introduce a legal framework within which it would be possible to proceed (retroactively) against leading conglomerates. Strictly speaking, restrictions of this kind, i.e. *ordinances from 26 August 1944*, were already in effect which stipulated that no person should be allowed to control more than one journalistic entity, but they had had no practical consequences due to the lack of clear enforcement provisions; moreover, no government had been willing to introduce legal restrictions that would influence developments in the press sector, which was already threatened with economic disaster.

The law proposed in 1983 met with vehement opposition. For the Gaullist Claude Labbé it was a «projet scélérat s'attaquant aux libertés sacrées de la communication et de la presse», Alain Peyrefitte even discerned a threat to

PAS TROP DE VAGUES

– « Groupe Hersant », qui a frôlé la disqualification, arrive en tête suivi par « Loi sur la Presse », partiellement dématée...

Fig. 74
(From: Le Canard enchaîné, 17 Oct. 1984)

liberty in a free nation: «Je ne dis pas que la France est un pays totalitaire. Ce n'est pas vrai. Mais elle n'est plus tout à fait, déjà, un pays libéral.» This reaction was occasioned by, among other things, the fact that the wording of certain passages really did make it seem plausible that the measures in question might be aimed specifically at the Hersant corporation (cf. also Becker 1985, p. 159ff.).

After numerous modifications and objections (during a debate which lasted a total of 166 hours the Government had to defend its position against around 2600 petitions from the opposition calling for changes) the law was finally passed at the end of 1984 and published in the *Journal Officiel.* One significant modification made by the *Conseil constitutionnel* stipulated that conglomerates already in existence were not to be affected, i.e. there was no legal vehicle for unravelling the Hersant concern (cf. *Fig. 74*).

The most important provisions concerning the limitation of concentration were as follows (cf. T. 25):

- No more than 15% of the circulation of the national press was allowed to be concentrated in the hands of a single person (Art. 10).
- This upper limit also held for the regional press (Art. 11).
- A single person could control both national and regional newspapers as long as the national share did not exceed 10% and the regional share 20% (Art. 12 - this eventuality was not part of the first draft).

- Ownership structure had to be made public (Art. 7), and an independent commission, the *commission sur la transparence et le pluralisme de la presse*, was made responsible for seeing to it that the regulations were complied with (Art. 16).

T. 25:
Dispositions relatives au pluralisme

Article 10.

Une personne peut posséder ou contrôler plusieurs quotidiens nationaux d'information politique et générale si le total de leur diffusion n'excède pas 15 % de la diffusion de tous les quotidiens nationaux de même nature.

Est considéré comme national un quotidien, toutes éditions confondues, qui réalise 20 % au moins de sa diffusion en dehors de ses principales régions de diffusion ou qui consacre de manière régulière plus de la moitié de sa surface rédactionnelle à l'information nationale et internationale.

Article 11.

Une personne peut posséder ou contrôler plusieurs quotidiens régionaux, départementaux ou locaux d'information politique et générale, si le total de leur diffusion n'excède pas 15 % de la diffusion de tous les quotidiens régionaux, départementaux ou locaux de même nature.

Article 12.

Une personne peut posséder ou contrôler plusieurs quotidiens régionaux, départementaux ou locaux d'information politique et générale, et un ou plusieurs quotidiens nationaux de même nature, si la ou les diffusions de ces quotidiens n'excèdent pas:

1°) Pour les quotidiens nationaux: 10 % du total de la diffusion de tous les quotidiens nationaux de même nature;

2°) Pour les quotidiens régionaux, départementaux ou locaux , 20 % du total de la diffusion de tous les quotidiens régionaux, départementaux ou locaux de même nature.

(Source: Journal Officiel, 24 Oct. 1984).

Even though the mentioned regulations only affected the daily press and brought practically no direct changes to the organization of the press, it still cannot be claimed that the legislative project was a complete failure. It at least offered a starting point for inhibiting further concentration and possibly for freezing the situation at the current stage. Because of the change in Government in 1986, however, the regulations did not have time to go into full effect; *L'Union* and *Le Progrès*, as mentioned earlier, were taken over by the Hersant conglomerate with a total disregard for the press law in a sort of surprise attack, an event which pointed out the new direction which governmental policy towards the press was to take. The press law was then promptly rescinded and Hersant, who himself was a member of the right-wing majority in Parliament (as were also a number of his employees!), was granted amnesty. One particular facet of the new policy of liberalization was to forbear from laying clear boundaries for concentration. Not until the *Conseil constitutionnel* raised objections did the Government work out a revised version of the law, passed on 27 Nov. 1986, which set an upper limit of 30% of the daily press (for complete details see Blanc-Uchan 1987).

Regardless of how the situation in the press continues to develop, the emphasis of expansion for the large publishing companies in the future will probably be on the new media and on private television. In this connection, Hersant said of himself: «Homme de press écrite, je suis par la force des choses le général d'une armée en retraite, et si d'autres moyens de communication étaient libres, je dirigerais un groupe multimédia avec des chaînes de télévision et de radio» (Le Nouvel Observateur, 10 Jan. 1986, p. 24). Hersant's commitment to the television channel *La Cinq* (cf. 6.2.9), however, quickly proved to be a financial fiasco.

Practically every attempt at counteracting concentration in the press in West Germany by legislative means has met with failure. Only in a few instances has the *Kartellgesetz* (antitrust law in existence since 1957) been able to prevent mergers. Furthermore, several commissions (compare, for example, the final report of the 1968 Günther Commission and the 1978 media report of the Government) came to the conclusion that no immediate infringements on the freedom of the press can be observed as of yet, even though the current level of concentration and the large share of the market controlled by a few conglomerates do constitute a threat to diversity of opinion. One might also claim that the political situation up to now has been such that it would not have been possible to initiate drastic measures.

6.2 *Radio and television in an era of keen competition*

(Ernst Ulrich Grosse)

6.2.1 Media consumption

By now *television* has become the most widespread of the mass media in France. The French population over 15 years of age watches an average of nearly 3 hours of television per workday, most frequently between 8:00 and 8:30 p.m. during the *journal télévisé* (evening news). Radio is in second place: the French over 15 listen to the radio for an average of 3 hours per workday, usually early in the morning and at noon (statistics from 1989 taken from Mermet 1990, pp. 362f., 370). There is no recent comprehensive data on the *press*, all that is known is that the number of people who read a newspaper regularly has been declining continuously. The statistics for France show 59.7% in 1967, 55.1% in 1973, 46.1% in 1981 and 45% in 1983 (Guillauma 1988, p. 123). The curve has risen again slightly (1989: 46.7%, Mermet 1990, p. 383).

The only statistics available for West Germany are averages based on the total population, and these values reveal a somewhat different situation. The average German spends 153 minutes listening to the radio, 139 minutes watching television and 30 minutes reading the newspaper (Die Zeit, 31 Aug. 1987, p. 12).

These statistics reflect the *magnitude of media consumption* in both countries. They also provide evidence for a *"functional distribution"* in these media, i.e. a difference in the way the population uses radio and television every day. This situation has hardly been affected by the introduction of morning television (initiated in France at the end of September 1984).

6.2.2 From the O.R.T.F. monopoly to competition

In France, an increasing liberalization and privatization since the 1970s can be detected in the audio-visual sector.

Up to 1974 all government-run radio and television broadcasters in France were under the control of a single agency, the monopoly company O.R.T.F. (*Office de Radiodiffusion-Télévision Française*). Giscard d'Estaing introduced a legislative reform which resulted in the formation of seven autonomous companies. Three of these companies were responsible for planning, organization and implementation (audiovisual research, production of television movies, broadcasting technology and marketing) while four of them were radio or television broadcasting companies:

1. *Radio France* (above all *France-Inter*, *France-Culture* and *France-Musique*),
2. TF 1 (*Télévision Française 1*),
3. A 2 (*Antenne 2*),
4. FR 3 (*France Régions 3*).

In order to improve the quality of programming, the reform introduced the concept of competition into the arrangement. The effects of this step were especially significant for television programming. Conferral between the individual networks became rare – this is why evening programming overlaps in TF I and A 2, an especially obvious example being the *20-h-journaux*, i.e. the 8 o'clock news programs. The amount of finances allotted to the individual networks depended not only on viewer ratings, which determined how the mandatory television fees paid by the viewers were to be distributed, but also on a jury which passed judgment on the quality of programming.

The companies which emerged from the dissolution of the O.R.T.F. may have been quite autonomous *with respect to each other*, but this was definitely not the case *with respect to their relationship to upper levels* ,i.e. the Government and the president. Under Giscard d'Estaing, for example, the directorial positions where systematically filled with persons favourably disposed to the president. This was one of many public areas which developed into an *Empire Giscard*.

It was not until the election victory of the Left that this situation was changed – at least officially. A law passed on *29 July 1982* set up an *Haute Autorité* which was to guarantee the autonomy of the radio and television networks from the Government and, among other things, appoint the directors for the different networks. Yet doubts were voiced as to the amount of freedom this agency actually had:

"... the very make-up of this "council of wise men" and the initial steps it took raised problems. The appointment of its members, three by the head of state, three by the president of the National Assembly and three by the president of the Senate [...], has already occasioned fears with regard to the political orientation of the *Haute Autorité*. In truth, its members do not furnish in all respects the desired guarantee since the majority of them come from circles close to the Left." (Fabre-Rosane 1983, p. 45)

It was quite possible that any change in the political situation would have an effect on the *Haute Autorité*, even though a reorientation would take a while since three of the nine members were appointed for three years, three for six years and three for nine years. Cf. 6.2.9 for later developments.

At the same time, the above-mentioned law governing audio-visual communications legalized local *radios libres*, i.e. independent radio stations. *This brought about the end of the government monopoly in the audio-visual media* (the first steps in this process had been taken by the *postes périphériques* – cf. 6.2.5). The *Haute Autorité* was given the responsibility of granting licenses for the individual *radios libres*. The legalization of these independent broadcasters was part of the leftist Government's program of decentralization after 1981 (cf. 1.1.5). It is undeniable that the local and regional problems, "the life of the people in France", had been ignored by the centralized audio-visual media for a long time.

6.2.3 The German system: model for audio-visual decentralization in France

In the course of his election campaign against Giscard d'Estaing, François Mitterrand called for an end to this neglect of regional matters and proposed using the German system as a model:

He suggested, «qu'à l'exemple de l'Allemagne fédérale, les programmes nationaux ne soient plus fabriqués uniquement à Paris, mais conçus et produits par des chaînes régionales. Tel soir, Bordeaux s'adresserait à la France, tel autre soir ce serait Strasbourg ou Lyon» (Le Monde, 5 Sept. 1981, p. 8). - Jack Lang, later Minister of Education and Cultural Affairs, affirmed this plan: «Je suis pour une télévision polyphonique de toutes les Frances. Pas seulement de la petite société du spectacle parisien. Ouvrons les écrans à toutes les cultures, à toutes les formes d'expression, à toutes les régions ... Je rêve d'un système à l'allemande, où les programmes nationaux seraient constitués par les apports de chacune des régions» (Le Monde, 18 Jan. 1982, p. 19).

At the same time, the German system should not be idolized too much. To be sure: "In the Federal Republic of Germany radio and television are supervised by the *Länder*. As a result the organization of the radio and television system is decentralized and federal. There are nine broadcasting companies administered by the German *Länder* (*Landesrundfunkanstalten*). The broadcasting areas of all but a few of these companies cover the area enclosed in the political boundaries of the *Länder*. Each of these companies broadcasts programs on several radio stations and has its own television channel (regional television channels). In addition, all of the *Landesrundfunkanstalten* collaborate to produce the programming for a joint nationwide channel, the ARD. An alternative is offered by the television channel ZDF (*das Zweite Deutsche Fernsehen*), a nationwide broadcasting company set up in all of the *Länder*" (thus stated by B. Vogel in Rovan/Weidenfeld 1982, p. 123. For more details see Ménudier 1980).

Nevertheless, even though there are more channels of regional origin in Germany, the system of representation in the boards of directors, in which the chief groups and areas of society are supposed to be represented proportionally, in many cases leads in reality merely to a "balance" between the CDU/CSU and the SPD, often bringing about a "fatal symmetry". Many political and environmental movements and occurrences are presented in such a way as to ensure that nobody raises objections: "Opinions of any kind, let alone offensive or subjective ones, are so unwelcome that in the end they no longer even come up in the anxious minds of the writers and commentators." (Die Zeit, 4 July 1980, p. 1).

6.2.4 Initial steps toward decentralization since 1981

Plans for decentralization, including the audio-visual media, expressly modeled after the German system have been dealt with above. But what is the current situation really like?

1. There are more regional programs today; this is especially apparent in FR 3. However, the proportion of programs in the languages of regional ethnic minorities (e.g. Breton, Basque) continues to be low in FR 3.

2. Since Radio France initiated a pilot project with three *radios locales publiques* in December of 1980 as an attempt to "get closer to the people", the number of local radio stations has increased to 47. The long-term plan is for each *département* to receive a local public radio station of its own – in reaction to the *radios libres.* It is now possible to receive local broadcasts in half of the country.

3. The number of *radios libres* (*radios privées*) has grown to about 1800 since their legalization in 1982 (Quid 1992, p. 1166). The Government, however, has drawn up guidelines which the stations must comply with or else lose their licences: the broadcasting radius is limited to a maximum of 30 km. And licenses are granted for a period of three years, after which time a new application must be submitted to the *Haute Autorité.* For a long time it was forbidden to broadcast

Fig. 75: Radio broadcasters in France
(From: Bär/Beutter 1990, p. 155, in:
Horizons, Ernst Klett Schulbuchverlag, Stuttgart)

commercials, so that many stations were on the verge of having to shut down because of lack of funds; this ban was repealed in May of 1984. A further token of good will toward decentralized diversity of opinion is that as of 1983 every newly started local private station receives a *subvention d'installation*, an "installation subsidy". In addition, the high audio quality of music programs in FM (=VHF) stereo and frequent collaboration with regional newspapers make it easier for these stations to keep their heads above water (for further information see Bing 1984, pp. 317-320). Nine radio stations have been able to win an audience over much of the nation, with NRJ (pronounced: *énergie*) in the lead. Cf. also *Fig. 75*.

4. There were also supposed to be numerous local television stations supported solely by income from commercials. The *Haute*

Autorité (now called the CSA) is again responsible for licensing, a necessary measure especially in light of the limited number of available broadcasting frequencies (PrAct, June 1985, p. 5). To date, only two "locals" are sending terrestrially (Fr. *en hertzien*). In addition, a private nationwide television channel appeared on the scene in 1984, with two more following in 1986; these were later joined by an array of cable programs, though with little success up to now. The *concurrence des chaînes nationales* typical of the Giscard era is thus being superseded by a *new competitive structure* established in the Mitterrand era: competition between private and public radio and television.

6.2.5 The *postes périphériques*

Aside from the *radios libres*, which are being allowed to broadcast more and more commercial programming on the medium-wave (AM) band (French FM = *fréquence moyenne*) and especially on the crowded FM band (French *modulation de fréquence* = frequency modulation), there is a much older category of commercial radio broadcasters: the *postes périphériques*. These broadcasters are financed solely by commercials and transmit on the long-wave band (French GO = *grandes ondes*), as well as on the FM band. The term *périphérique* comes from the fact that their transmitters are located at the edge of the French territory, on the other side of the border to be exact: RTL broadcasts from Luxembourg, Europe I from Saarland in Germany, Radio Monte Carlo (RMC) from Monaco, Sud-Radio from Andorra (cf. *Fig*. 75). On the other hand, RTL and Europe I also have transmitters in the greater Paris area and their studios are located in Paris. During the presidencies of de Gaulle, Pompidou and Giscard d'Estaing, the *postes périphériques* were the only real competition to the government monopoly; despite being commercial they were more open-minded when it came to political information and offered extensive interviews and discussions which also included Socialist and Communist politicians. This fact, taken together with on-the-spot reporting, commentary by renowned journalists and the very latest pop music gave them their good reputation (cf. the favourable appraisal in Goguel/Grosser 1976, p. 156). The language spoken by listener ratings is very expressive indeed.

Table 27a shows how important the *postes périphériques* are (short-term fluctuations typical for listener ratings can be ignored); France-

Inter is the only real competition from state-run radio. RTL has occupied the top position for quite a while now (in the 1970s it was Europe 1). Its listener share has remained constant while competitors have lost ground under the advance of the *radios privées*.

Table 27a: Percentage of listeners (in %)

	June 1984	March 1987	Nov./Dec. 1991
RTL	23.6	21.3	21.4
Europe 1	17.6	14.7	9.0
France-Inter	13.5	15.9	8.7
RMC	7.8	7.7	4.0
others	21.8	28.5	?

(Taken from: Quid 1989, p. 1130 and Libération, 13 Jan. 1992, p. 8. The numbers indicate the percentage of the French populace that prefers the various stations.)

One can also clearly see that the *radios privées*, which in the meantime have become highly commercialized, reach a growing number of listeners: in 1987 for example, they accounted for 26.3% of the 28.5% labelled "others". The large commercial broadcasters respond to the competition by increasing listener participation in their programs and by expanding the more expensive coverage of international news. In addition, however, they are also "infiltrating" the local radios. In 1987 Europe I set up a service called Europe 2 which supplies numerous private stations, often owned by regional newspapers, with complete "music and news" programming for certain times of day. RTL has been able to sign contracts of association with many *radios libres* which then broadcast RTL programming – with a mere 20% of the airtime, called *«fenêtres locales»*, supplied by the local stations. By way of these agreements RTL and Europe I have succeeded in holding on to the lion's share of advertising revenues. In 1986, for example, RTL took in about 900 million F, Europe I took in 600 million F, and all of the *radios locales privées* put together took in only 350 million F (Le Nouvel Observateur 5 June 1987, p. 70f.).

As far as the regional distribution of popularity is concerned, RTL and Europe I clearly dominate the northern half of France, whereas the government station France-Inter has its listener strongholds in Brittany, in the south-west and on the Mediterranean coast. The first choice of listeners in the southern half of France is RMC. These results come from the first detailed research on the subject carried out by the Médiamétrie institute and based on 55,000 nationwide interviews (Libération, 7 Nov. 1988, p. 14).

The following paragraphs provide a brief description of the individual *postes périphériques.*

RTL (*Radio-Télévision Luxembourg*) broadcasts a French-speaking round-the-clock radio program deliberately tailored to popular taste. At the present, RTL television can only be viewed in Lorraine, but it will soon reach all of France via satellite and cable television. Radio programs in German also reach about 7 million listeners in West Germany every day. The French government used to own stock in the *Compagnie luxembourgeoise de télévision*, which administers RTL, and thus had some influence on programming, although this influence was not very great. The government's financial interest was based on the 15% share in RTL owned by the Agence Havas, a large publicity and travel agency in which the government had a controlling interest of 56%. When Havas was denationalized the French government lost its influence on RTL. Instead, the re-privatized Paribas Bank became the second largest shareholder in CLT (Le Monde, 22 July 1987, p. 24).

Up to now *Europe 1* has only been involved in radio, providing an attractive frame for commercials not only in the form of music, quiz and game shows but also with political talk shows. These political talk shows are especially popular during election campaigns and are of course beneficial in increasing the number of listeners and thus improving the effectiveness of commercial advertising. The French government used to be involved in the decision-making processes of this station via the government enterprise SOFIRAD (*SOciéte FInancière de RADiodiffusion*) and its 30% share in *Europe 1 – images et son.* The stock was sold on 5 March 1986 to the electronics, aviation and publishing conglomerate Matra/Hachette headed by Jean-Luc Lagardère. This corporation had grievously owned 17% of the shares in Europe 1; its current share is 51%. The increased ties between Europe I and Hachette – up to now the second largest printed media corporation in Europe after Bertelsmann – brought about the rise of a "media giant" which has already set its sights on the market in the European Community as a whole, i.e. far beyond the borders of France. Europe 1 founded Europe 2 as a reaction to the *radios privées* (cf. supra).

The French government maintained its presence in *RMC* (*Radio Monte-Carlo*); SOFIRAD even controls 83.3% of its shares. In its capacity as a *station de la Méditerranée* and *premier poste régional* RMC is trying to expand both into the Parisian area (on the long-wave band and the FM band) and far out into the Mediterranean region (with AM programs in Italian, Arabic and Corsican). Since 1984 RMC has had a television counterpart, TMC (*Télé Monte-Carlo*), in which SOFIRAD has a 35% share. To ensure that TMC did not take the necessary advertising revenue away from the regional newspapers, the French Government placed pressure on the company to work out a compromise. In this compromise local advertising spots fall under the joint supervision of the Provence daily newspapers. The newspapers thus have control over the number of commercials and are also involved in the profits. Furthermore, the non-local commercial spots are administered and distributed by *Régie n° 1*, a subsidiary of Publicis and Europe 1. Since this arrangement is to be extended in the future to TMC cable television in large cities (including Paris), it is at the same time a model for the future and a pilot experiment for compromises between regional press and regional television (PrAct, Dec. 1984, p. 58).

A new picture of the media situation in France is thus emerging, a picture in which the financially powerful *postes périphériques* take home the lion's share of the listeners and advertising income from radio, leaving behind the crumbs of the *gâteau publicitaire* ("advertising pie") for the daily press – all because of pressure from laws which are supposed to protect the weaker competitors.

Being purely commercial broadcasters, the *postes périphériques* illustrate very clearly the magnitude of the profits which can be attained by companies with a high amount of capital. RTL, for example, was able to increase its revenues by 25% from one year to the next (1983-84) without exceeding 15 minutes of commercials per hour so as not to irritate its listeners (PrAct, Jan. 1985, p. 85). This is what makes it possible for the *postes périphériques* – with RTL at the forefront - to enter the fields of satellite radio and satellite television (see 6.2.8 for more information).

At the same time these commercial broadcasters provide a clear example of a feature which is also present in the press, albeit not quite as visibly, namely that commercial advertising is not a mere tag-along in the media world but is in reality its actual *focal point*. For the reader, listener or viewer the editorial side seems to be the essence of the medium. He or she is not aware of the fact that the media producer views the portion accounting for the most space or time merely as *support publicitaire*, as advertising support. The media is aimed primarily at the potential buyer and not so much at the responsible citizen requiring information.

6.2.6 Government-run radio stations in France

France-Inter provides the general public with light programming and news. A further station specializing in information of all sorts, *Radio France Info* (RFI), has also been added.

The programming in *France-Culture* is quite different. The station offers many interviews with artists, musicians, writers and scientists (and is thus a good source of information for foreigners interested in France). A further feature is a program in which novels are presented in daily instalments, similar to serials in newspapers. In August 1981, for example, the novel *Les Chemins de la Liberté* by Jean-Paul Sartre was broadcast, naturally as a kind of radio-play.

France-Musique is dedicated chiefly to classical and contemporary "serious" music, usually in stereo. This is interspersed at intervals with lighter fare, but even this consists of "classical" jazz and occasionally an operetta or ethnic folk music – all types of music which the persons responsible deem in keeping with the level of standard of *France-Musique.*

All French radio programs, whether from government-run (with the exception of *France-Culture*) or "peripheral" stations, have one thing in common that differentiates them from German programs:

> La parole est rapide, hachée, laissant peu de place à la respiration; parfois, elle est soutenue par un support musical qui assure la continuité et remplit les silences éventuels ... Pourquoi les stations importantes n'adoptent-elles pas ... un style qui ferait place à des silences, à des pauses marquant la respiration du discours?» – The answer can be found in the competitive situation in France: «Le style est ici une *arme* dans la stratégie de la conquête des auditeurs: la permanence d'émission sonore est nécessaire pour capter l'oreille de l'auditeur passager. (Chr. Hermelin, PrAct, March 1980, p. 49f.)

The uninterrupted flow of rapid speech is supposed to prevent the listener from switching stations during a pause. *«Fidéliser leurs auditeurs»* (op. cit.) – according to this study the allegro or even presto pace of the competing radio stations is supposed to aid and abet this process.

6.2.7 The television channels TF 1, A 2 (now called FR 2) and FR 3

Despite the fact that these three channels are officially independent from the president and the Government, the political information they provide is by no means completely "unbiased". One example of this can be found in the study carried out by the *service d'observation des programmes* on the first six months of 1984:

> 39 à 49% du temps d'antenne consacré à l'information sur TF 1 et Antenne 2 vont au gouvernement, 20 à 32% à la majorité de la gauche, et 28 à 32% à l'opposition. Les régimes changent, pas les habitudes.» (F. Quenin, PrAct,

n° hors série, Jan. 1985, p. 92f.) – Schmid (1985, pp. 128-133), on the other hand, comes to a different conclusion. According to him, there may very well have been occasional cases of people in power reverting back to old habits and exerting their influence on the powerful instrument television during the Mitterrand era, and it may also be true that top positions have been filled with persons sympathizing with the Left. Following the legislation of 1982, however, there has, in Schmid's opinion, been a noticeable difference to the Giscard era: during Giscard d'Estaing's presidency one could hardly come across the explicit criticism of the Government which can currently be observed in some programs, and intervention from the Elysée Palace or the ministries has become quite infrequent. Even if this should be the case, a thorough study conducted in the period from June to August 1988 confirms that in France all of the television broadcasters give significantly more air time to the "block" comprised of president/government/majority party than to the opposition (Mauriat 1989, p. 46).

The above-mentioned cases of favouritism and accusations of "a powerful but lethargic and even rigid machine, [of] bureaucracy and corporativism" in an organization employing around 18,000 individuals (Fabre-Rosane 1984a, p. 321) were frequently cited by members of the opposition in order to lend support to their demands that the government-run television channels be denationalized. After they won the elections they were able to do so with TF 1 (previously A 2 had been under consideration) – despite resistance of various kinds.

The struggle for TF 1 was dramatic. The constitutional council invoked by the Socialists dashed Hersant's hopes in the matter on the 17th and 18th of September 1986. It proclaimed that diversity of opinion must be maintained in the French media and that one-sided concentrations of power must be avoided. This decision also put the multimedia conglomerate Hachette (cf. 6.2.5), headed by Lagardère, out of the running. A decision was finally made in April 1987 by the CNCL: the winner was a financially powerful syndicate headed by the "cement king" Francis Bouygues (25% of the stock), the world's largest construction contractor.

In the meantime, 21.9% of the shares are in the hands of four major French banks and an insurance company holds 9.5%; then follow other investors (cf. Quid 1992, p. 1167). 36.8% of the shares are listed on the stock exchange and the remaining 4.2% are in the hands of TF 1 employees. With the help of enormous investment sums, used for example to hire popular television stars for fabulous fees, TF I at times (the beginning of 1988) could claim 50% of the viewers. This brought about increased advertising revenues, which in turn enabled TF I to

Fig. 76: French television broadcaster logos (up to 1991)

spend more money on expensive programming. In order not to be left completely behind, the government-run channels A 2 (now called FR 2) and FR 3 were forced to try to make concessions to popular taste. Nonetheless, TF I has remained undisputed favourite, with more than 40% of the viewers (cf. 6.2.9 for viewer statistics). At the same time, TF 1 receives a lion's share of the "advertising pie". Almost all of the other broadcasters are faced with the problem of stretching the – insufficient – leftovers to balance their budget and meet their program schedule.

The third channel, FR 3, specializes in the regional problems of France. Since September 1983 regional programming has been expanded from 35 minutes to approx. 1½ hours and is broadcast on a number of different regional stations (Alsace, Aquitaine, Normandy etc.). The goal of decentralizing the public sector set by the left-wing Government has thus resulted in FR 3 being expanded considerably. The evening program is the same in all of the regional FR 3 stations, consisting of selected feature films, appealing documentaries and open political debates, and is thus primarily aimed at an intellectual audience.

One item that stands out in stark contrast to television in Germany is the *way in which television news is presented.* While the German news programs *Tagesschau* and *heute* "use the beginning of the show, when the viewer's concentration is at its highest, for the important political and public news items" and present the information in a "serious" tone using sophisticated language (Kübler 1979, p. 216, cf. Straßner 1982), French news is presented in an unaffected manner which sounds less serious and less official. Since the news programs are normally between 30 and 45 minutes long, they include extensive coverage of topics of general and human interest (sports, natural disasters, crimes). They strive for a personal approach in presenting information in the political portion of the show as well. It is furthermore often the case that the relatively lengthy features lack a critical approach to the subjects they deal with. The manner in which news programs are produced thus as a whole reinforces the depoliticizing trend which has already been observed in the printed media.

On the other hand, news programs take noticeable inspiration from the aesthetic values of television advertising, which is more innovative in France than in Germany (Kloepfer/Landbeck 1991). French news concentrates primarily on pictures whereas it is the words that predominate in German news shows. They also have a predilection for the subtleties of shifting camera positions, quick cuts, imaginative graphics and cross-fades (Kloepfer/Landbeck 1988, pp. 201-206; for details, cf. Landbeck 1991).

In general each channel does its best to reach the largest number of viewers it can by using methods that catch the audience's fancy - i.e. also by introducing elements of entertainment into the news.

6.2.8 The "new media"

Satellite and cable television, VCR's, *Bildschirmtext* (cf. below) and other so-called "new media" are in reality only new technologies. They are connected to the television set by way of accessory devices and open up more possibilities for television. The list can be extended to radio by including radio broadcasting via satellite (Balle/Eymery 1984).

One of the first major steps taken toward introducing these new forms of communications technology in both France and Germany was to establish pilot projects for cable television. Another way in which the two countries paved the way for the new technologies was by taking part in projects for television satellites. (On the beginnings in the 1980s, cf. Wenger 1987, Madelin 1988 and the report «Les nouveaux médias en Allemagne fédérale» in Documents, February 1985.)

Up to now, satellite television and cable have met with little success in France. The television satellites developed in co-operation with Germany (type TDF for France, type TV-Sat for Germany) have proven disappointing in terms of the economic and technological hopes placed in them (Le Monde, 7 Feb. 1991, p. 35). By the beginning of 1991, just 20,000 satellite antennas had been sold in France. In Germany too, there were takers only for approx. 20,000 TV-Sat antennas; in contrast, approx. 500,000 "dishes" had been purchased to allow reception of ASTRA satellites, which are superior both in range and program diversity (Wenger 1991, p. 31). The *plan câble* likewise turned out to be a disaster. By the end of 1990, cable had been laid for only 1.4 m. households, and a mere 16% of these connections were used (cf. Oestergaard 1992, p. 71; concerning the underlying causes: Le Monde Radio-Télévision, 18 Nov. 1991, p. 16). In Germany (only the old federal states), 16 m. households already had cable available by this time, and 53% also took advantage of the opportunity (Truffart 1990, p. 10). This is because there are many private broadcasters in Germany that can only be viewed with cable or satellite reception, while in France the largest private broadcasters (especially TF 1) can also be picked up terrestrially. Moreover, Germany has no quotas restricting the airing of American films and serials, as does France.

The era marked by governmental monopoly is without a doubt coming to an end and a new age is dawning in which the private media conglomerates with the greatest financial resources will gradually gain supremacy – as is already the case in the USA. For example, Parisian households with cable television are able to receive 17-20 channels - for the most part private and commercial. However, "uniformity in programming" still predominates (Wenger 1991, p. 147). This will only magnify the importance of the role played by serious local and government-run radio and television stations in providing alternative sources of information and in acting as a corrective factor which in the end, because of the competitive situation, has an influence back on the large private broadcasters.

This reverse tendency has already set in in the United States. By now the pendulum there has begun to swing back – to the public television stations: "While commercial television is gaining ground increasingly in Europe, the trend in the USA, the classical land of television, is moving in the opposite direction. More and more viewers are switching to public television and its informative, educational, albeit occasionally long-winded programs. According to a recently published survey, in 1977/78 only 18.6 percent of television households watched public television at least once a week during prime time; in 1984/85 the proportion was 34 percent." (Badische Zeitung, 8 Jan. 1986, p. 11).

The *Minitel* craze has rapidly become the most obvious symptom of how open the French are to "new media". A Minitel device hooked up to a telephone provides convenient access to all sorts of services: bank transactions, university registrations, purchases of merchandise, holiday and hotel reservations, etc. (and, through *Minitel rose*, even erotic contacts – this provided subject matter for popular books, such as Roger Le Taillanter's *Dans l'enfer du Minitel rose* in 1989). According to French statistics the number of installed Minitel devices increased from about 1,300,000 in 1985 and 2,237,000 in 1986 to 3,373,000 – i.e. 14% of telephone owners – in 1987 (de Montbrial 1988, p. 351), reaching approx. 5,600,000 by the end of 1990 (Quid 1992, p. 1414). West Germany is more conservative in this respect: in 1987 there were only 58,365 installed *Bildschirmtext* devices (1989: 179,831). The Postal Service, which is responsible for these devices in Germany, is attempting to attract more customers for *Btx* through improved service, easier access and lower rates.

6.2.9 New television channels in France and Germany

Since changes in the audio-visual sector come up almost every week and since the competition between multimedia conglomerates for the best starting positions for the internal European market in 1993 has long since attained European-wide dimensions, the following remarks shall be restricted to four general tendencies and phenomena.

1) When viewing the relationship between *the printed media and the audio-visual media* one can note that only the large publishers tend to become involved in nationwide private television stations. The regional newspapers are content with establishing local radio stations so as to have sufficient access to advertising revenue in the face of a partially receding readership.

2) Roughly speaking one can differentiate *four phases of development.* During the first phase (up to about 1984/85) public television, private film companies and private printed media existed side by side. In the second phase (approx. 1986/87) pressure from the "right-wing" parties finally toppled the monopoly of the public channels in France and West Germany and legalized a dualistic media situation. From then on, financially strong multimedia conglomerates began introducing new television channels financed by commercial spots. The most important ones in France were *La Cinq* from R. Hersant and the Italian television magnate S. Berlusconi, and *M 6* from the *Compagnie Luxembourgeoise de Télévision,* which already owns RTL (cf. 6.2.5), and the *Société Lyonnaise des Eaux. M 6* specializes in music programming. The channels in competition with the public ones in Germany are: *RTL plus,* which unlike CLT is controlled by a national, i.e. "German majority" (currently Bertelsmann, WAZ, Burda, FAZ) and whose corporate headquarters were thus moved from Luxembourg to Germany, *Sat 1* from the Munich film magnate Leo Kirch and the Springer publishing company, and others such as *Tele 5,* in which

S. Berlusconi has acquired a 45% interest. Further channels funded by major media conglomerates and retail chains joined the ranks between 1989 and 1992: *Pro 7*, *Premiere* and *Kabelkanal* (cf. *Table 28*); Canal Plus holds 37% of the shares in *Premiere*. The competition between movies and television has developed into a situation in which the two forms have become more and more interrelated: the financial planning of a new movie calls from the very start for it first to be shown in the theatres, then to come out on video cassettes and finally to be aired on television. The third phase of this development is already evident in both countries, although it began earlier in France (Schulz 1990): large industrialists from outside of the "cultural scene" have the necessary means for entering into the highly promising, steadily expanding media arena. (This field accounted for about 6.5% of the French job market and 6% of the French gross national product in 1987, thus reaching the level of the automobile and food industry, cf. Wenger 1987, p. 525). The clearest example of this is the takeover of TF I by a syndicate led by Bouygues (cf. 6.2.7). A fourth phase can be expected in the distant future: several giants will dominate the "media market" in the European Community through their control of satellites, extensive cable networks and a sufficient number of terrestrial frequencies, and through alliances with the large publishing and movie companies. At the moment, this tendency can be detected far more clearly in – or originating from – Germany, with the enormous economic power of its multi-media conglomerates, Bertelsmann, Kirch, Springer, etc. than in France. In any case, the EC-wide and very liberally oriented *Télévision sans frontières/Fernsehen ohne Grenzen* represents an initial step into this phase, finalized on 3 Oct. 1991 (cf. Le Monde sél.hebd., 5-11 Oct. 1989, p. 12; Das Parlament, 19 April 1991, p. 2). German federal states and broadcasters fear that this could bring on an intrusion into their cultural domain (Europäische Zeitung, March 1992, p. 17).

3) "Pay television" has a very good chance of expanding – *if* it specializes. The French fourth channel, *Canal Plus*, has been proving this since the beginning of the 1980's. 50% of its programming consists of feature films. This is supplemented by news programs and coverage of special sporting events (e.g. golf or ice hockey) which the *chaînes généralistes* have to leave out. It can be picked up on terrestrial frequencies throughout all of France with the help of a decoder. Because of the number of its subscribers (2.1 m. in 1990, for example), *Canal Plus* has become a booming business and expanded to Spain, Belgium and Germany. Although TF 1 has the largest number of viewers, it is *Canal Plus* that is making the largest profits (Schmitt 1989, p. 90).

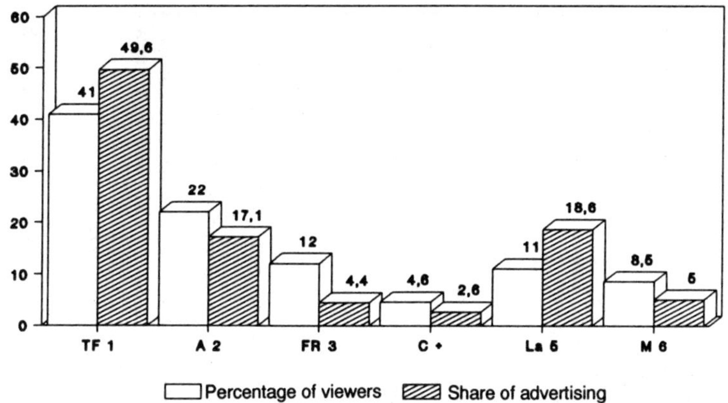

Fig. 77: Percentage of viewers and share of advertising of French television channels (1988, figures in %; from: Truffard 1990, pp. 31-34)

4) The public broadcasters have attempted to respond to pressure from their private competitors by introducing new channels. The German ARD started *Eins plus*, which shows movies and documentary films from the ARD archives, and ZDF joined forces with SRG (Switzerland) and ORF (Austria) to produce *3 SAT*; the French Government established its cultural channel, *La SEPT* (for further details, see below). The question of whether to allow commercials and whether to set a time limit on them is a matter of political contention; for the public broadcasters this question is also more urgent than the problem of new satellite or cable channels. The French government-run channels A 2 (now called FR 2) and FR 3 are struggling against insufficient financing and greater limitations on commercial time and are not able to take in advertising revenues commensurate with their share of the audience (cf. *Fig. 77*).

The question of commercial time and revenues also provided the actual impulse (or was it the required pretence?) for replacing the CNCL with an agency having more authority, the *Conseil supérieur de l'audiovisuel* (CSA) (Mauriat 1989, pp. 16-19). This was effectuated by a decree from Rocard's Government and by a law to the same effect passed in December of 1988. The CNCL had proven to be powerless against the "private channels", which regularly exceeded the time allowed for commercials (for example, six minutes per hour for TF 1) and furthermore failed to comply with the regulations governing the

Table 28: Overview of radio and television broadcasters in France and Germany (March 1993)

Radio

France	Germany
Radio France a) "centralistic" stations: France-Inter (with regional programs) France-Info France-Culture France-Musique Radio France Internationale b) decentralized stations: 47 in total, of which: - 38 local stations - 5 regional stations - 4 city stations (Lyon, Marseille, Nice and Toulouse)	*Arbeitsgemeinschaft der öffentlich-rechtlichen Rundfunkanstalten der Bundesrepublik Deutschland* (ARD): (most of the ARD broadcasters have 3-4 stations) NDR ("Norddeutscher Rundfunk", Hamb., Lower Sax., Schl.-Holst., Meckl.-Vorp., headquarters: Hamburg) RB (Radio Bremen) WDR ("Westdeutscher Rundfunk", North-Rhine-Westphalia, headquarters: Cologne) ORB (Brandenburg, headquarters: Potsdam) SFB ("Sender Freies Berlin", Berlin) HR ("Hessischer Rundfunk", Hesse, headquarters: Frankfurt/Main) MDR ("Mitteldeutscher Rundfunk, Thuringia, Saxony, Saxony-Anhalt, headquarters: Leipzig) SWF ("Südwestfunk", southern Baden, southern Württ., Rh.-Pal., headquarters: Baden-Baden)
postes périphériques (priv.): RTL (Luxembourg, studios: Paris) Europe 1 (from Saarland, headquarters: Monaco, studios: Paris) RMC (Monte Carlo) Sud-Radio (Andorra, only available in the southwest)	SDR ("Süddeutscher Rundfunk", northern Baden, northern Württ., headquarters: Stuttgart) SR ("Saarländischer Rundfunk", Saarland, headquarters: Saarbrücken) BR ("Bayerischer Rundfunk", Bavaria, headquarters: Munich) Deutschlandfunk, RIAS Berlin and DS Kultur (for Germany and Europe, headquarters: Cologne and Berlin, join radio of ARD and ZDF, new broadcaster name "Deutschlandradio") Deutsche Welle (for overseas, headquarters: Cologne)
Radios privées approx. 1800 stations in total, 9 of which broadcast nationally over radio networks (e.g. NRJ, Nostalgie, Europe 2	*Private stations:* a total of 240 (these stations, with broadcasting licences, cooperate with each other in part to funktion as one broadcaster)

Television

France	Germany
TF 1 (denationalized in 1987) *FR 2* (ex-A 2) *FR 3* (regional, national in the evening) *CANAL PLUS* (priv., estab. 1984, *télévision à péage*) [La Cinq (priv., in existence from 1986 to 1992)] *ARTE* (La SEPT, estab. 1986, available over cable or TDF since 1988, became part of ARTE in 1992) *M 6* (priv., since 1986, with thematic orientation [pop music])	*Publicly operated stations* *ARD* (first channel, jointly operated) *ZDF* (second channel, headquarters: Mainz) *Third channels* (regional channels of ARD, some joint programming with individual broadcasters, e.g. S 3 operated by SWF, SDR and SR; ORB and MDR also joined as television broadcasters in 1992) [Eins plus (cable and satellite channel of ARD, in existence from 1986 to dec. 1993)] *3 Sat* (operated by ZDF, SRG and ORF, started 1984, joined by ARD in 1993) The "Third channels" are also increasing their range through cable and satellite (eg. WDR 3, B 3, N 3) *ARTE* (on Cable after 1992, co-operation between La SEPT and ARD/ZDF; headquarters: Strasbourg)
Postes périphériques: RTL (priv., Luxembourg) TMC (priv., Monte Carlo)	
Broadcasting over cable or satellite *(currently of significance only for terrestrial reception):* *TV 5* (operated by TF 1, FR 2, FR 3, Belgian RTBF and Franco-Canadian CTQC; available throughout Europe over cable or satellite) *Canal J* (youth channel, also terrestrial in part) *MCM-Euromusique* (also terrestrial in part) *Sport 2/3* (*tv à péage*, also carried by FR 2 and FR 3, among others) *TV Sport* (Brit., only over sat., French equivalent of Germany's "Sportkanal"; Canal Plus, among others, participates) *Planète* (priv. broadcaster on cable) *Ciné Cinémas* and *Ciné Cinéfil* (priv.)	*Private television channels:* *RTL* (1984, headquarters: Cologne) and *RTL 2* (1993) *SAT 1* (1985, headquarters: Mainz) *Pro 7* (1989, headquarters: Unterföhring) *DSF* (ex-Tele 5, 1984, headquarters: Munich) *Premiere* (1991, headquarters: Hamburg, German equivalent to France's Canal Plus) *Kabelkanal* (February 1992, headquarters: Munich) *Sportkanal* (Brit. owned) *Eurosport* (Brit. owned) *n-tv* (private new channel, 1992) *vox* (1993, headquarters: Cologne)
Regional and local television channels: *Ciné Folies* (priv. broadcaster on cable insome regions) *Bravo* (priv. broadcaster on cable in 15 cities) *8 Mont Blanc* (priv., terrestrial) *TLT* (priv., Toulouse, terrestrial) *Paris Première* (priv. broadcaster on cable in the Ile-de-France region)	*In English:* Super channel, MTV Europe *In French:* TV 5 *In Turkish:* (also on cable in some areas): TRT 1 The first multilingual European news channel is called "Euronews" (1993, headquarters: Lyon)

broadcasting of feature films and Anglo-American television series. This change in the – allegedly unbiased – uppermost supervisory and decision-making agency and its personnel in accordance with the leaning of the current Government (this was the third time in only six years) is one of the symptoms of the influence which the State and the political parties continue to exercise on the audio-visual media (cf. Oestergaard 1992, p. 61f.).

This influence has also made itself felt on the commercial channel *La 5*. Shortly before going out of office in 1986, the socialists turned the station over to "well disposed" persons (incidentally, Berlusconi was among them). During the period of the *cohabitation*, the conservative government saw to it that Hersant gained influence on *La 5* as a means of combating the predominance of TF 1. In spite of this, the channel's operating deficit continued to grow; not even the Hachette takeover in 1990 did anything to improve the situation. The *Tribune de l'Expansion*, among others, passed judgement on the affair as «une chaîne généraliste de trop» (12 Oct. 1990, p. 3). The channel was forced to claim bankruptcy in December 1991; April 1992 saw, for the first time in Western Europe, the collapse of a major commercial broadcaster, an event that will weigh on the entire Matra-Hachette conglomerate for years to come. The efforts of Hachette to tread in the footprints of the multi-media conglomerate Bertelsmann have thus met with initial failure.

Jack Lang, the Minister of Culture, for whom *La 5* had long been a thorn in the side, had reason to triumph. The best airing times on the terrestrial frequencies of the liquidated broadcaster are now reserved for the German-French (and in the future, European) cultural channel, *ARTE*. This station was formed to 50% out of La SEPT, with the other half the result of a co-operative effort between ARD and ZDF (for further details, cf. Schlie 1990). At first the station encountered subdued response from the German part; as of the end of May 1992, it is offering many new productions. It could become a patron for high-quality documentaries and films as well as giving new impetus to such areas of the arts as opera, theatre and dance.

In Germany, the media "landscape" shifted dramatically as a result of the unification process. *Der Deutsche Fernsehfunk* in what was formerly the GDR was disbanded. Two new ARD broadcasters have been established: the *Mitteldeutsche Rundfunk* (MDR) and the *Ostdeutsche Rundfunk Brandenburg* (ORB); cf. *Table 28*. The former radio broadcasters *Deutschlandfunk*, RIAS and *DS-Kultur* have been merged into one station which broadcasts on two channels. This rigorous "westernization" of the entire "media scene" in the ex-GDR has prompted considerable criticism, also in France (Thibaud 1992).

Concerning future prospects for high definition television (HDTV; Gr.: *hochauflösendes Fernsehen*; Fr.: TVHD = *télévision à haute définition*) and concerning the associated conflicts of interest between Europe and Japan on the one hand, Germany and France on the other, we can here do no more than refer the reader to the appropriate sources (cf. Charon 1991, pp. 127-130; Wenger 1991, pp. 32-34; Das Parlament, 19 April 1991, p. 3).

Table 28 provides a concise overview comparing the radio and television stations of the two countries (as of March 1992). It reveals both the *differences in their radio systems* and the *partial similarities in their television systems.*

One can thus conclude that an increase in the number of channels is certainly *technicallypossible* in both France and Germany (especially if cable television is used to distribute satellite channels so that expensive satellite dishes can be dispensed with). In practice, however, this development is being held up by difficulties in *financing* it from the advertising industry and by *differences between Left and Right* in the parties of the Centre. (One should note, however, that the SPD's stance on media is quite different from that of the PS; this is a result of differences in the distribution of power and of the fact that there is a greater degree of economic concentration in the German media.) Anyone interested in new television stations must, whether he likes it or not, first deal with their *foundation*: commerce and politics. Artistic innovation, closer contact to the population, well-researched information in pictures and words – all of this does not count for much, not much at all. Most of the new television channels are in danger of deteriorating to symptoms of the degeneration of responsible political, economic and journalistic activity.

6.3 *Film and literary tradition*

(Ernst Ulrich Grosse)

In Karl Vossler's opinion, the "motion-picture novel" (*Tonfilmroman*, strictly speaking a "sound motion-picture novel") constitutes the end of a long line of development in the genre "novel" going back to the medieval romance in octosyllabic verse:

1. Verse romance.
2. Prose novel.
3. Motion-picture novel. This is up to now the form which has achieved the greatest amount of verisimilitude. [...] Today the question of whether the cinema is capable of poesy occupies the mind of every intellectual person. Adaptation to the screen at first debases the subject matter and increases the distance to the fine arts – but this ought to be no more than an initial step in preparation for the assent to yet greater heights" (1951, p. 303). Similarly Boris

Eichenbaum, one of the most important representatives of Russian formalism, expressed the opinion that now, after the eras of the theatre and the book and following the 19th century, the time has come for an era of film culture (German translation from 1965, p. 74).

Both of these attempts at setting up period classifications recognize the significance of the film. Vossler's position must, however, be corrected in two respects. Firstly, the novel continues to be the most popular written literary genre in France; consider, for example, detective novels (Simenon, Boileau-Narcejac, San-Antonio). Secondly, even though the novel of the 19th century foreshadowed certain cinematic techniques (Wagner 1972), the cinema is not descended from the *novel* alone but actually more from the *theatre*. Much of film terminology has been borrowed from the theatre, e.g. French *rôle, acteur, actrice, mise en scène*, and thus bears witness to the initial influence of the theatre on the cinema (Uren 1952).

The development of commercial movies was set off in *France* by the *cinématographe*, a device invented by the Lumière brothers and used to project moving pictures. (The French word *cinéma*, used to designate the place were movies are shown, and the corresponding English word *cinema* and German word *Kino* come from this device.) After silent pictures were developed in 1896 and "talkies" in 1929, this form of mass media had its heyday in the United States and in Europe during the 1930's. The French cinema first met with international acclaim through the work of the *Paris* avantgardists of silent movies: the Spaniard Luis Buñuel, the French poet Jean Cocteau and in particular René Clair. Surrealism and psychoanalysis – subconscious associations portrayed on film – were integral parts of their famous experiments with light and motion. Other famous directors of the time were Sacha Guitry, Julien Duvivier and Jean Renoir (known, for example, for his screen adaptation of Zola's *La bête humaine* starring Jean Gabin and Simone Simon).

Shortly after the Second World War the French cinema attained new artistic heights with Jean Cocteau's surrealistic opus *La belle et la bête* (1946) and his highly symbolic Orpheus movie (*Orphée*, 1949, both movies starring Jean Marais). These two movies exemplify one of the constant features of postwar cinema in France: the continued use of the artistically fertile technique of surrealism (the search for startling and bizarre sequences of pictures, the attempt to create a dream in film, *fantasmes, mystères*, often in flashbacks or cuts to the future which interrupt the plot). Another constant feature is the depiction of various milieus, similar to the works of Zola or to Simenon's detective novels. For example, in Jean Renoir's later movies love forms a link between two milieus: e.g. actors and the upper middle class in *Le Carrosse d'Or* (1952), intellectuals and peasants in *Le Déjeuner sur l'Herbe* (1959). This last title makes reference to the famous painting by Manet, a return to France's *own* cultural heritage – as opposed to that of the United States, to Hollywood – which is also evidenced by film adaptations of numerous novels. Two areas of this cultural heritage in particular were very common sources of inspiration:

1. "national heroes" of France: Joan of Arc, Napoleon;
2. popular novels of the 19th century, e.g. *Les Misérables* (V. Hugo), *Les Trois Mousquetaires* (A. Dumas), *Les Mystères de Paris* (E. Sue), *La Dame aux Camélias* (A. Dumas fils).

The "new wave" – *la nouvelle vague* of young film writers who were, for the most part, film critics for *Cahiers du cinéma* and who had previously only made short films – protested against the *«cinéma à papa»*. This term was coined by François Truffaut, whose article «Une certaine tendance du cinéma français» (*Cahiers du cinéma*, 1954) is considered the spark which set off this regenerative movement. Jean-Luc Godard's movie *A bout de souffle* is viewed as the "manifesto" of the *nouvelle vague* (Gerhold, in: *Film-Korrespondenz* 23/1984, p. 2). Some other adherents of this movement are Claude Chabrol and Alain Resnais. Their common resolution was as follows: similar to the way a literary author uses his *stylo*, i.e. his pen, directors should henceforth write their own scripts and then make "author movies" from these scripts using the camera and its wide variety of possibilities – the director's *caméra-stylo* (the younger generation, however, did recognize the achievements of respected masters such as Renoir and Cocteau). Thus one can again discern an influence of literature on the cinema – however merely in the *intentions* of the renewers. The execution, on the other hand, was supposed to utilize the specifically *visual* capabilities of the screen in selecting and transforming pictorial reality by camera work, lighting, editing and montage. This explains the interest in the *nouvelle vague* taken by the French semioticians (see in particular the numerous studies by Ch. Metz, cf. Prokop 1979, p. 195).

The depiction of assorted different milieus was not exactly the favourite *subject matter* of directors of the *nouvelle vague*:

"Their subjective, intimist films are often set in a quite limited milieu of artists, intellectuals, middle-class youth and idlers between Saint-Germain-des-Prés and Saint-Tropez, and in the end made 'the rebels of form' appear in the shape of 'representatives of the bourgeoisie à la mode' (L. Marcorelles). Their films concentrated more than ever on the subject of love, however their treatment of this subject was radically different from that of their French predecessors: the new-wave films reflected a new, unconventional, unbiased approach to emotionality, an attitude which – sociologically speaking – can be associated with what is refered to as the 'new middle classes' which had been on the rise since the middle of the 1950's. These films broke the taboo of sexuality and partner relationships, not so much as a result of a desire to provoke the viewers as by an unprejudiced view of reality. By dealing with this topic and by including self-confident and independent female roles as central figures in their films, these young directors not only broke with the cinematic tradition of the outgoing Fourth Republic, they also broke with the whole of its moral attitudes." (Doll, in: Schmidt et al. 1983, p. 115).

By doing this, however, the movie writers of the *nouvelle vague* boosted French cinema back to *international recognition*. This was evidenced, for example, by the worldwide reaction to François Truffaut's death in October 1984. In addition, the *nouvelle vague* remained relevant much longer than the *nouveau roman*, which went out of "fashion" at an earlier date.

The importance of France in the cinema world is furthermore manifested by: the *Césars*, awarded each year by the *Académie des Arts et Techniques du Cinéma* in Paris to the "best" French *and* foreign movies/actors; its world-renowned *festivals*, above all in Cannes and Avoriaz; and, at the commercial level, the *Gaumont corporation*, the only European movie corporation which can compete on a worldwide scale – Gaumont is currently trying to gain a foothold in the television sector as well. French movie production is still number one in Europe. In 1986, for example, 134 feature films were produced in France, a number far less than the 515 American productions but nevertheless clearly ahead of Italy (89), Spain (77), West Germany (64) and Great Britain (37) (Janin 1988, p. 123f.). The picture remained similar in 1989 (Quid 1992, p. 487).

The *nouvelle vague* also had a significant influence on the *"New German Film"*, a movement which is usually dated from the signing of the "Oberhausen Manifesto" in 1963 and which has met with continuing international success for quite some years now. The German movement has learned from and been inspired by the experiences of its French precursor and has been called the *«cinéma d'auteur par excellence»* (Sauvaget 1983, p. 206). Furthermore, "movie makers" such as Volker Schlöndorff and Peter Fleischmann learned their craft at the Parisian motion-picture academy (I.D.H.E.C.) and while assisting French directors (op. cit., p. 214). By about 1980 the New German Film was able to hold its own thanks to governmental and substantial commercial support – and also in part to simultaneous shooting of movies and television series. It became extremely popular in France:

For example, the announcements for Werner Herzog's *Fitzcarraldo* and Wim Wenders' *Hammett* appeared on the *cover* of *Une semaine de Paris - Pariscope*, one of the two leading program magazines for cultural events in Paris; Wenders' *Paris, Texas* was awarded the *Palme d'or* at the 1984 International Film Festival in Cannes.

The New German Film came on the scene during the Adenauer era to challenge the *Heimatfilme*, i.e. nostalgic depictions of "traditional" German rural life, and other cliché productions of the time. Instead of catering to desires for evasion and compensation (after the experiences of the war and in the hard day-to-day life of the "economic miracle"), the new movement wanted to present an unconventional cinematic art form, a critical and jolting picture of – primarily German – reality. However, following successes at home and after having attracted international attention many directors went *abroad* – or at least made their movies there. Volker Schlöndorff, for example made films in France and the United States after having been awarded the *Palme d'or* and an Oscar in 1979 for *Die Blechtrommel* (*The Tin Drum*). The same can be said of Wim Wenders, Werner Herzog, Peter Lilienthal, Doris Dörrie (following her movie *Männer [Men]*). Thus it seems that with the death of Rainer Werner Fassbinder in 1982 an era had drawn to a close. Worldwide recognition of the New German Film resulted in its spokesmen and their range of topics becoming "internationalized". A further aspect which might be related to this phenomenon becomes evident when one takes a look at Wolfgang Petersen's works based on best-selling books, namely *Das Boot* (based on Lothar Günther Buchheim) and later *Die unendliche Geschichte* (*The Never-Ending Story* based on Michael Ende): the directors – still? – influenced by the New German Film are becoming "Americanized". In reality, the integration of the New German Film into existing production and distribution channels started all the way back in 1966 when Schlöndorff's *Der junge Törless* (*Young Törless*) was backed by Franz Seitz. (On the other hand, the worldwide breakthrough into the movie establishment did not occur until American companies purchased several movies in 1979.) The price for this integration, however, is that the movies run less and less counter to accepted norms and that they are increasingly losing their tone of satire or critical accusation. Priority is given to movies with engaging, easy-to-understand stories, stories which may very well display a certain amount of individualism and may even contain a touch of fashionable criticism; all in all, however, they are void of any kind of objectionable ideology. In addition, special effects and other novelties à la Hollywood and scenes with "a cast of thousands" ensure box-office success at home and abroad. This explains the cutting severity in the verdict passed by one film critic on the works of Wolfgang Petersen used as examples above:

"Films like this indeed no longer have anything to do with the New German Film, whose goal has always been to maintain its unmistakable, individual "author movie" status. Films like this are producer movies in the classical style [...] Anyone who works under these conditions will sooner or later wind up in the American film business just like Petersen or Schlöndorff (even if the movies are shot in Munich to save money)" (Wetzel 1987, p. 92f.)

So much for a brief description of the cinema in recent years, a cinema more "modern" than "New German"; these developments must be considered as transitions and should not be viewed as delineating irrevocably fixed boundaries between different eras. One may join Sauvaget (1983,238) in ascribing the changes to a process by which the movie industry is bringing the *nouveau cinéma allemand* back to the fold, or one may also concur with Pflaum (in: Das Parlament, 18 April 1987, p. 3) in placing the blame on "the current political climate in West Germany" and the increased selectivity of governmental support for movie-making.

The positive response to movies by Godard and Chabrol, Wenders and Herzog raised hopes that it would be possible for artistic "author films" to hold their own, both at the national and international level – even in an age of television and American dominance on the French and German movie market.

It appears, however, that the "author films" era is gradually drawing to a close. Jean-Luc Godard's film *Nouvelle Vague* (1990; cf. Leutrat 1990) proved for most part accessible only to specialists and the initiated. His *Allemagne Neuf Zéro*, on Germany's new beginning after re-unification found no takers across the Rhine. Claude Chabrol's attempt at filming Flaubert's *Madame Bovary* received largely negative criticism. However, films from Louis Malle, Eric Rohmer and others continue to reach their audience. On current trends, cf. Mermet 1990, pp. 13 and 377.

And how is the "New German Film" faring? Co-operation between film producers and television continues to grow closer. Wim Wender, for example, has concluded a contract with Francis Bouygues' TF 1 film producing company (Libération, 15 Jan. 1992, p. 46). Alexander Kluge, formerly *the* expert on the theory of the New German Film is pursuing a career with the private television broadcasters *RTL plus* and *SAT 1*. The demand for feature films is growing along with the number of television broadcasters; the masters of cinematic art, however, seem to be fading from the screen.

The crucial question for the future will be whether artistic films require the cinematic medium (this is the opinion of most directors of consequence) or whether they are also compatible with or even profit from the television screen, either television itself or in the form of video films. In any event, movie theatre audiences began to diminish back in the 1950s, a tendency which then increased in the 1960s and '70s (e.g. France: 411 million in 1955, 170 million in 1977 – Wehrlin 1985, p. 36; 119 million in 1989, Mermet 1990, p. 374). The decline in the number of people going to the movies is continuing to this day. The growing competition from television and video films is not the only reason for this development. According to studies made by Alexander (1979) and Wehrlin (1985) it is also caused by an increase in ways in which leisure time can be spent and by the fact that a small number of large corporations have acquired a monopoly on movie production and distribution, thus making it difficult for the movie industry to take certain risks which might have been advantageous for retaliating against competition from television. This situation has led in part to artistic stagnation. Nevertheless, France in particular considers the cinema an integral part of its culture (Nowka 1983, p. 102). This is the reason for governmental support for movie-making in France, support with the goal of working out a compromise between the criteria of economic success and artistic quality. There are thus two different programs: one what is called automatic subsidies which are dependent on the commercial success of the products, and one of selective subsidies, in which movie projects are chosen according to qualitative criteria and granted *avances sur recette*, i.e. financial advances (Nowka 1983, p. 109; this book also gives a comparison to West Germany). Governmental support of the cinema is furthermore evidenced by a regulation which stipulates that 50% of the movies shown in television must be French productions – unfortunately this regulation is in part circumvented by "special provisions". In addition, both state-controlled and private television stations in France are forbidden to air movies which are less than two years old. (The rule reads: year 0 = launch in the cinema, 1/2 year = launch of the video cassette, 1 year = showing on pay-TV, 2 years = general TV broadcast. The rule also holds in Germany, but takes the form of an unwritten custom.) This is intended to ensure that the cinema remains an attractive alternative for the public. In the same way, French television stations are not permitted to show feature movies on Saturday evening, the traditional evening for going out. In this respect, France offers better film protection than Germany does. And French cinemas still show nearly 40% French films, while the showing of German films in German cinemas has dropped below 15% (Badische Zeitung, Magazin, 2 Feb. 1991, p. 4). The centrally controlled government support in France also proves more favourable overall than the situation in Germany, where the federalist structure means diverse sources of subsidies (the so-called "producers' hurdle race").

The *Cinémathèque Française* in the Palais de Chaillot in Paris provides its visitors every day with a different program of excerpts from the history of French cinema. The organization also has a branch in the Centre Pompidou. Schumacher (1986) gives information on the diversified cinema scene in Paris.

For additional information on the subject "film and literary tradition" please refer to the studies and descriptions by Idt et al. 1975, Sauvaget 1983, Michard 1983, Albersmeier 1985 and Paech 1988.

7. German-French Relations

(Ernst Ulrich Grosse)

Where does one begin an introduction to the history of French-German relations: with the Franks, the Napoleonic Wars, or possibly with the division of Germany? If one is to orient oneself according to the historical reminiscences of the countless papers and lectures which have been written on the subject, it becomes apparent that the period which may not be ignored – particularly in an introductory account – is the time between the Carolingian Empire and the Second World War. There was a distinct turning point in relations in the wake of events following this war as the growth of a partnership between France and one of the states of a divided Germany began to take the place of relations between the rivalling nation states vying for world power. With German unity in 1989/90, i.e. the end of the post-war period, this partnership took on the form of relations between two sovereign nations bound by a common interest – an interest in the stability and unification of a continent faced with a multiplicity of crises. The process of rapprochement and that of European unification, which has acted as the general framework for these relations, remain jeopardized by structural differences and nationalistic egotism – themselves "legacies" of the past. Three chronologies, one concerning the epochs prior to 1945, one on the period up until 1989 and one on subsequent developments (see sections 7.1.1, 7.2 and 7.3), will provide a general overview of the history of French-German relations. They will be consequently discussed in the text.

7.1 *Relations before 1945: antagonistic clichés or historical comprehension?*

Antagonistic clichés about their own country and people (autostereotypes), as well as about their respective neighbouring country and people (heterostereotypes), had been developing since medieval times, but solidified in the 19th century primarily due to the Franco-Prussian War in 1870/71. Among these clichés were common perceptions of the enemy as sabre-rattling Germans and peace-loving French, of "Welsch" "arch-enemies"[1], and of Germans striving to re-establish a past order. Even authors interested in reconciliation and harmony between the two nations fostered antagonistic clichés. For example, Victor Hugo wrote: «La France et l'Allemagne sont essentiellement l'Europe. L'Allemagne en est le coeur; la France en est la tête...L'Allemagne sent, la France pense» (1841, in Voss, 1961, p. 35). Henri Lichtenberger also contrasted France's *«affinement spirituel»* and *«discipline intellectuelle»* with Germany's *«énergie nouvelle»* and *«sève vitale»* and stressed the mutual inspiration between the two nations throughout the course of history (1929, in Voss, 1961, p. 7).

Research into prejudice has shown that not only the projection of common perceptions of the enemy (on "arch-enemies" [*Erbfeindschaft*] see: Pabst 1983, pp. 27, 38ff., 94f., 97; Werner 1985, p. 311) can be related back to a searching for identity (both in individuals and groups) and hence to the demarcation of oneself from other people and other groups. But this is also the case with a dichotomous, antagonistic interest in friendship and harmony. Hence, prejudice develops in response to basic human needs. It can only be displaced through more profound familiarity, careful reflection and an utmost of patience (Koch-Hillebrecht 1977, Picht 1980, see also the foreword of this book).

In any attempt to present a more prejudice-free view of French-German history before 1945, or even to a certain extent through to the present day, one must take care not to: a) generalize on the basis of individual characteristics or persons, b) assume the continuous existence through time of the essence of an identity in a nation ("the soul of a people"). Nations change historically and states vary their organization and structure. As such, relations between both nations and states are frequently subject to change. Relationships between like elements A and B in constantly varying constellations to one another do not exist. There exist, rather, relationships between changing

1 Translator's note: In German, *Welsch* first designated the Celtic neighbours (as in English where "Welsh" signifies the people of Wales up till today). After the romanization of the Celtic lands *Gallia Cisalpina* (Northern Italy) and *Gallia Transalpina* (France), *Welsch* designated the Romanic neighbours, i.e. the French and Italians (the word *walisc* in Old High German meant "Romanic"). Predominantly since the 19th century and the German-French War of 1870/71, *Welsch* has become a pejorative word for "French".

elements – so to speak A1 and B1 in feudalism, A2 and B2 in absolutism, A3 and B3 following the French Revolution, etc., whereby one must ignore the fact that in the case of Germany, a *relatively* homogeneous "element B" only came into being after 1871 with the founding of the Empire. It is therefore necessary to view relations between "France" and "Germany" in the context of their *historical development.*

A further introductory comment is necessary. When the following section 7.1.1 refers to "imperial visions" since the era of *Charlemagne*, this is a reference to such visions of great power and empires as existed in the shadow of Charles the Great and his imperium - or to those of the Western Roman Empire which served as a model for the Carolingian Empire. Also, *after* the French Revolution and *after* Napoleon, there was a manner of "imperial vision." It was more oriented toward a *world empire* with numerous *colonies* – or in Hitler's case, toward a furthered and expanded *"eastward colonization"*, i.e. the expansion of "Greater Germany" primarily to the east (and, to a lesser extent, also to the west).

There was a *change in attitude* due to industrialization (and the need for raw materials and new markets) and, consequently, due to the increasingly internationalization of trade and stock market speculation.

In the 17th and 18th centuries *French ambitions in Europe* (not to mention those of other powers) predominated. The push for colonies accelerated but was considered to be of secondary importance in comparison to the interests in Europe. By contrast, in the 19th and 20th centuries after Britain had displaced the Iberian countries from their position of dominance new ambitions arose. First in France and then later in Germany there were claims (legitimized by the appropriate ideologies) of being a "world empire" and "world people". This line of tradition leads not only from the *Second Empire* into the *III Republic*, but also the *Empire of Kaiser Wilhelm I* into the *Third Reich* – although some Germans tend to overlook this fact in a post-war attempt to forget the past. The goal of the Third Reich, with its policy of eastward expansionism, was to latch onto the tradition of the "Knights of Teutonic Order", the laying of the "foundations of the Hanseatic League" and "pre-war Prussian Germany" thereby substituting old wishes for world power with new ones. "In the East lies our future and it is to the East that the *Führer* directs our gaze... It is here that we will finally see if we have fully succeeded in educating the Germans, at nature a people of the world, to also be a people of the world in thought and deed. On behalf of the people of Germany, and hence Europe, we are once again today challenged to answer the great German calling in the East" (Löbsack 1939, p. 78).

Following Napoleon, new *imperialistic* visions (world empire, *Lebensraum* in the east, etc.) replaced the *imperial* visions descending from the idea of the *imperium Caroli Magni.* The terms "imperial" and "imperialistic" will be differentiated in this manner.

7.1.1 From Charlemagne to Napoleon: a millennium of imperial visions

Germany and France developed from the secession states of the Carolingian Empire (cf. Brühl 1990). Since the word *deutsch* (German) has only attained political and national connotations since the 11/12th centuries, one can only – hesitantly – speak of French-German relations from this time onward. A more accurate reference point, however, would be the second crusade (1147-49). It was here that French and German knights confronted each other as *milites Christi* and as rivals. It was also here that the first prejudices came into being.

Chronological Table 2: French-German Relations until 1945

800	Coronation of Carolus Magnus as emperor; Carolingian Empire
843	Partition treaty of Verdun (the West Frankish Kingdom; the "Middle Empire" Lotharingia; the East Frankish Kingdom)
962	Coronation in Rome of Otto I as emperor; Birth of the *Sacrum Imperium Romanum* (Holy Roman Empire; the addition *Nationis Germanicae*, "of the German People", is due to the late Middle Ages)
11th cent. onward	The gradual development of the linguistic concept of *deutsch* into a political concept
12/13th centuries	Spread of the Southern and Northern French culture in Europe
1477/1519	Increasing friction between Habsburg and France (1477 Burgundy to the Habsburgs; rivalry between Charles and Francis I for the Imperial Crown, 1519 Coronation of Charles V as Emperor in Aachen [Austria/Burgundy/Spain vs. France])
1517	Luther's 95 theses; the Reformation begins to spread
mid 16th century	Beginning of alliances between French kings and Protestant German rulers
1618-1648	Thirty Years' War results in the rise of France and the further fragmentation of Germany

1661-1715	Rule of Louis XIV (1670 Lorraine, 1681 Strasbourg falls under French rule)
1685	Revocation of the Edict of Nantes; Edict of Potsdam: 20,000 Huguenots taken in by Brandenburg
17/18th centuries	Second extensive phase of French cultural influence in Europe
2nd half of 18th century	*Sturm und Drang* as antithesis; development of German Neoclassicism and Neo-Hellenism in part as a reaction to the "Roman legacy of the French"
1789	French Revolution begins
1804-1814/15	Empire of Napoleon I (1804 Coronation as emperor, 1806 Foundation of the Confederation of the Rhine and end of the Holy Roman Empire, Oct.1806 military defeat of Prussia, 1813-15 Prussian revolt, so-called Wars of Liberation; France as model for Prussia and other German states)
from 1815	Conservative ordering of Europe at the Congress of Vienna
1830/48	Spread of revolutions from France to Germany (1848 Founding of German workers' organizations, Frankfurt National Assembly)
1866	Prussian victory over Austria in Sadowa (near Königgrätz)
1870/71	Franco-Prussian War, Proclamation of the German Empire in Versailles, French must cede Alsace-Lorraine and pay massive war reparations to Germany. From 1870/71 onward: proliferation of the myth of Germany and France as "arch-enemies"
since 1870-1875	Third Republic in France (proclaimed in 1875). Split into *républicains* and *cléricaux*, patriotism functions as cohesive factor
1914-1918	First World War (21 Febr.-21 July 1916 Battle of Verdun)
1919	Treaty of Versailles (9 Nov. 1918: Kaiser Wilhelm II abdicates, proclamation of the Weimar Republic)
1925	Locarno Pacts
1933	National Socialist Party (*Nazis*) seizes power in Germany; particularly after 1933 German *émigrés* in Paris
1938	Munich Pact (French-English attempt to keep peace)
1939-1945	Second World War (1940 German-French armistice; division of France, *résistance* and *collaboration*, Aug. 1944 liberation of Paris, de Gaulle forms provisional government; May 1945 capitulation of German Army)

From the 10th century Ottonians and the Old French and Middle High German "Song of Roland" on (see Köhler 1968 and Ott-Meimberg

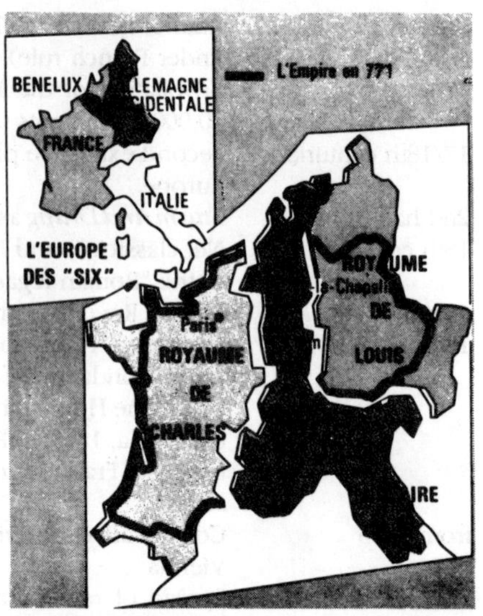

"The dream of a united Europe: THE CAROLINGIAN EMPIRE. For three quarters of a century, France, Germany and Italy find themselves reunited: a single empire, one church – a single language as well as one culture. Charlemagne dreamt of rebuilding the Roman Empire. But was not his empire rather in anticipation of the EC nucleus, the *Europe des Six*?"

Fig. 78: Partage de Verdun and *Europe de Six.* (From: Michaud/Torrès 1978, p. 95)

1980, p. 50) through Napoleon to the time of de Gaulle and Adenauer, Charlemagne's once undivided empire remained a likely point of projection for each party's individual desires, ambitions, and various attempts to legitimize them.

A particularly good example of this in the political scenario of French-German relations is the revealing actualization of the past in terms of the Carolingian era. De Gaulle and Adenauer were termed "Carolingians" by both their adherents and opponents (Herre 1983, p. 279). Similarly, the "core of Europe", i.e. the first six EEC countries (1957), were frequently likened to the Carolingian succession states of the Treaty of Verdun (843). Also, efforts at European unification were often considered to be anchored in the pattern of Charlemagne's Carolingian empire. *Fig. 78* is a good example of this. It shows the connection between an actualization of the past for educative purposes and the reverse-projection of some given present moment into the past.

Aachen (*Aix-la-Chapelle*), with its marble throne in the imperial palace chapel, the site of Charlemagne's preferred residence and court, is counted among the places possessing symbolic character in history of French-German relations. This is the background for the Charlemagne Peace Prize, founded in 1949 in Aachen, which honors personalities who have furthered Western European unification. In 1988, for example, both the French President Mitterrand and German Federal Chancellor Kohl were bestowed with this award. This was also a consideration leading to the choice of Aachen as the site of German-French state consultations on 14-15 September 1978 (see Weiss 1981. p. 47).

For contemporaries, 812 A.D. represented a symbolic event in an historic place. The more powerful and continuous East Roman Empire recognized Charlemagne as the emperor of the West Roman *imperium* in the Treaty of Aachen. In 936 in Aachen, Otto I accepted the crown as king and in 962 he was crowned emperor in Rome. This was the birth of the *Sacrum Imperium Romanum Nationis Germanicae* which – if one (incorrectly) counts back to 800 instead of 962 – lasted for one thousand years until Napoleon forced Austrian ruler Francis II to renounce the throne. It was upon this that Hitler founded his vision of the restoration of a "thousand-year Empire". But imperial visions have always been short-lived, even in the case of the Ottonians for they were constantly being challenged by rivals abroad and at home.

A rivalry between France and the Sacrum Imperium for supremacy of the West was to be counteracted by the "divine" principle of *duo regna* propagated by the Clunistic reform movement. This was a teaching which later spread through the entire church and granted the empire preeminence. Even King Phillip II (cf. 1.1.2), responsible for the development of French centralism, held this "divine right" to be self-evident (Werner 1984, p. 14). Thus, until the end of the thirteenth century, meetings of the rulers always took place on *imperial soil*, even if usually in a borderland (with the exception of Milan in 1191). "The German king and emperor never left his land for a meeting with the French king" (Voss 1987, p. 85). Furthermore, etiquette demanded that much attention be paid to demonstrations of mutual respect, both through the elaborate presentation of gifts («ietweder dem andern sant gróz und rîch prisant») and forms of address emphasizing equal rank (ibid, pp. 159, 174f., 205). Particularly in the 12th and 13th centuries the *political* primacy of the Sacrum Imperium was contrasted by French *cultural* supremacy. The Gothic movement spread from Northern France. Originating in Southern France, the courtly traditions with all of their rituals of conduct, literary materials and genre, and manners of expression were received by the rest of Europe (although Germanists in Germany tend to concentrate on the metamorphosis and development of materials of French origin). Scholastics, as well, were centred in Paris. Thus, Paris later became the model for the foundation of German universities, the first being in Prague in 1348. During the Hundred Years' War (1339-1453), French cultural prestige decreased considerably. If ever France had an arch-enemy, it was England during the Late Middle Ages in the wake of various wars, England which henceforth until the 18th and 19th centuries was labelled *«la perfide Albion»* (and not Germany). The first signs of developing French patriotism among the populace were of an anti-English and not anti-German nature. They developed before national humanism during the time of Joan d'Arc. In addition, at least until the French Revolution national rivalries were always seated among the politically and intellectually elite. The territories, the people, their land, and the fruits of their labours were the objects and means in the contention for power between states and the upper echelons of society dominating them.

The opposition between France and the Habsburgs exemplifies the development of a new phase in this rivalry. France saw itself confronted with the growing power of the House of Habsburg. This was initially so in 1477 when Burgundy partially fell into the hands of the Habsburgs. This then became even clearer after the choice of Charles V (*Charles Quint*), and not his competitor Francis I (*François Ier*), for the German emperor. Habsburg territory bounded France in the Southwest (Spain), in the North (the Netherlands) and the East (Burgundy, Northern Italy) (see *Fig. 83*). This led again and again to alliances between French kings and Protestant German rulers. It was not France and "Germany" who were fighting for the control of Europe but rather France and Habsburg. It is essential to emphasize this fact in view of the "historical" re-projection of the arch-enemy myth in the 19th and 20th centuries.

Following the abdication of Charles V (1556), his brother Ferdinand became the German emperor. (Ferdinand had already received rule of all Habsburg family lands in the Empire from his brother, a move which would later prepare the way for the Danubian Monarchy). Charles's son, Philip II, became the King of Spain. A world empire "united" under the control of the Habsburgs had ceased to exist. The potential of danger posed by a reunification of the Austrian and Spanish branches of the family remained and thus also the fears of being territorially hemmed in as during the rule of Charles V. "Thanks to Henry IV, Richelieu, Mazarin, and Louis XIV, France emerged from this conflict victorious, but even more importantly, it now possessed a 'modern' army and relatively well-developed administrative apparatus" (Werner 1984, p. 22). The Thirty Year's War had already resulted in a French rise to power. The Holy Roman Empire of German Nations was left a powerless and religiously splintered federation of states.

With France having achieved a position of predominance, the beginning of the *siècle de Louis XIV* (1661-1715) and the second great phase of French cultural influence in Europe had arrived. Numerous reproductions of Versailles and the (bourgeois) enlightenment are some of the best indications of this. Leibniz in the 17th, and Frederick II in the 18th centuries, embraced the French language. Once again there was an influx of cultural and linguistic stimuli from French into German (for examples, see Sauder/Schlobach 1986 and more specifically on the reception of Voltaire, Brockmeier/Desne/Voss 1979). Whereas an *à la mode* language and literature developed in the noble's cast, middle-class "linguistic circles" (*Sprachgesellschaften*) reacted to this movement and tried to "cleanse" the language of all gallicisms. There were, however, important mediators of French and German culture (cf. Mondot/ Valentin/ Voss 1992). Among these were French exiles, e.g. Huguenots granted asylum in Prussia (Brandenburg). (The typical Prussian characteristics and values were formed by the contact between Calvinistic Hohenzoller rulers, Calvinistic Huguenots and the Lutheran majority of the citizens. They would later shape all of Germany and are thus of historic-religious origin; cf. T. 26). – The French annexation of Lorraine, of numerous Alsatian towns and villages, and finally of Strasbourg, was a part of the *policy of réunion* carried out by French courts. This policy entailed a reassociation of territories which at some time in the past had either partially or wholly belonged to France. From this time onward, Lorraine and Alsace would be areas of dispute between France and "Germany". They would change hands time and time again, but the people themselves would never be consulted.

T. 26.
Although fleeing France was considered to be a capital crime which was punishable by death, between 1660 and 1760 about 300,000 people, or one-third of all French Protestants, fled their homeland on account of their religious beliefs. They were men and women who, having been hardened by persecution and hardship, were steadfast believers in their strictly ordered Calvinistic faith. They found sanctuary in the various non-Catholic lands of Europe. Approximately 50,000 of them fled to Germany. In Brandenburg-Prussia they were to be of historical importance for they shaped the state and helped it flourish.

On 29 October 1685, Friedrich Wilhelm von Brandenburg, Duke of Prussia, caused a sensation in Europe when he signed his famous edict in the city castle of Potsdam. In 1666, the Great Elector had dared to object to the Sun King concerning the persecution of his fellow reformers. Now he was offering the Huguenots a home in his territories. Thousands of copies of the edict were circulated in France.

The refugees were settled primarily in 47 cities. They were granted a privileged colony status which was then documented by the Great Elector and thereafter renewed by each of five Prussian kings. Not until 1809 during the Prussian Reforms were these privileges partially revoked. The status granted them autonomous control of their religion, their own language and schools, an autonomous system of administration and courts with two levels of appeal, freedom of trade, and equality with existing local guilds and associations.

As with the refugees of our times, these people had nothing outside of their creativity and a willingness to work. They were for the most part skilled tradesmen. As a "developing country" after the Thirty Year's War, famines, and depopulation caused by the bubonic plague, Prussia had the immigrants to thank for its economic upswing and increased participation in European thought and culture. Around the year 1700 every fourth resident of Berlin was of French origin.

It would most certainly be wrong to try to view the thoroughly unconventional and progressive measures of the Prussian kings as a mixture of toleration and a clever plan for the economic recovery of their country. The motivation lay deeper in the ideas and principles of their growing state. Theirs was not a nation state. States were much more the direct product of their kings' personalities. The highest goal of the growing state was law: the freedom was a living law based on the authority of the ruler. *Suum cuique* was the greatest commandment of a king and the motto of the state.

Prussian principles were founded on the inexorable and steadfast belief of the Hohenzoller rulers in the reformed church. The lords of the land shared with the Huguenots their religious faith accompanied by consequent asceticism and a strong sense of duty.

They became living spiritual role-models. The strict and rigorous Calvinistic belief in predestination might be difficult for the modern person to comprehend, but it has left its mark on the world right up to the very present, not least of all in the values underlying the American way of life.

Thus, it was the basis of faith of the French Protestants, the strictly ordered principles and values brought by French emigrants, their *esprit*, their skills and their willingness to work, couple with a German thoroughness and readiness to sacrifice, that functioned as the foundation of a positive symbiosis characterized by the unique Prussian ethics of state and culture.

This state was nearly always the most progressive and modern state in Europe. Even in the moment of its greatest misfortune, it exerted an almost magical force upon people from non-Prussian lands to declare themselves its followers.

They developed the characteristics which today are considered Prussian: sobriety, rationality, industriousness, a strong sense of duty, moderation, simplicity, charity and community, and the willingness to do something just for its own sake.

The intertwining and mutual complementarity of French-German influences are older than the rallying cries we hear today. In view of a free democratic Europe they re-present themselves all that much more compellingly. The characteristics of Prussia which formed from the life and values of the French Huguenots are in this sense indispensable.

Paul Jordan

(From: Welt-Report, newspaper supplement to the daily *Die Welt*, 26 Jan. 1985)

Feelings of German national identity were not only moulded by linguistic circles and reactions to the French policy of reunification but to a much greater degree through the process of exclusion, self-definition and self-exploration in the German literature and art movements, *Sturm und Drang* and Classicism. They embodied the clear antithesis to otherwise dominant French influences. With this in mind, one need to read no further than Goethe's essay *Von Deutscher Baukunst* ("On German Architecture") to come to this realization. The change in models from the *Originalgenie* (original genius) to the more noble classical Greek and then later to Neo-Hellenism was the result of a search for an orientation that would *diverge* from that of French culture. Since predominant French literature was rooted in ancient *Rome*, an emphasis of the spiritual relationship (both in general and of their individual) Germanness to *Hellenism* was typical of these poets who initially were held in low esteem by nobility and bourgeoisie. Classical philologist, Manfred Fuhrmann, has posed this provocative and enlightening thesis (FAZ, 27 Nov. 1982). It sheds new light on cultural history from Winkelmann's Theory of Art to W. v. Humboldt's university and Gymnasium reform.

With the French Revolution the processes of cultural *attraction and repulsion* swung into the realm of politics.

Many new studies on this topic appeared in celebration of the 200-year anniversary of the Revolution. The reader is in particular referred to the collected reviews of Erbe 1989 and the concise summary of decisive conflicts within German-French relations from 1789 until after 1945 by Bariéty 1989. A detailed account of historiographics in Germany is provided by Dippel 1989, of political implications by Thiele 1990 and of deep-rooted cultural processes by Dau 1989, Koopmann 1989, Timm 1990 and Voss 1991; on continuity and shifts in French policy towards Germany from 1789 until after 1945, cf. Hudemann 1989.

German history books tend to emphasize the *repulsion* after expressing initial sympathy, as for example with Görres and Schiller. For this reason, two aspects of *attraction* and positive reception will be emphasized here. The influence of the French revolution on Germany was immense, incalculable and nearly inestimable. It gave rise to German Jacobinism which was not intensively researched until the 1960's (for lit. see Voss 1983, XII-XIV and Kreutz 1990). The French Revolution also shaped – long distance – the concept of class struggle in Marxism and the German workers' movement (see Bouvier 1982). The proletariat can learn essential lessons from the failure of Jacobinism, the conspiracy of Babeuf, the revolution of 1848 and the commune of 1871. It now finds itself in the same relative position to the bourgeoisie (which in the meantime has become reactionary) as the bourgeoisie to the nobility in 1789. From this point of view – but not from this one alone – the French Revolution represents the final transition from feudalism to capitalism or, more generally, a change in era and state of mind. The enlightenment of the people and the class struggle must take the place of wars fought between nations. This was alluded to in verse composed by Bürger in the wake of anti-Jacobin preparations for war and its masking of "patriotic sentiments" in Germany after 1793. Illustrated is the connection between German Jacobinism and the German workers' movement.

T. 27:
For whom, you good German people,
are you so laden with weapons?
...
For princes and the noble kin
And for the vicars' vermin.

(Für wen, du gutes deutsches Volk,
Behängt man dich mit Waffen?
...
Für Fürsten- und für Adelsbrut
Und fürs Geschmeiß der Pfaffen.)

(From: Fink 1983, p. 277)

Another learning process, just as important, began later among the Prussian upper class in the wake of defeats to Napoleon's troops and the introduction of civil liberties in satellite states of the Confederation of the Rhine according to the model of the *code Napoléon.* Social change in France functioned as a model for the so-called liberation of the peasants, the abolition of the craftsmen and trade guilds, or more generally, the institution of civil rights. The conception of a conscripted army and the organization of the military were likewise shaped after the French model. Partly at Napoleon's initiative and partly following his example, ruling structures in Germany – extending far beyond Prussia – were set anew. Religiously ruled areas were secularized, most of the free cities of the Sacrum Imperium abolished. More generally: many smaller political entities were consolidated under the control of larger ones. In addition to this came changes in common civil law and the military. Only under the influence of Napoleon did Germany move on its way toward becoming a modern society and state. In as much, France awakened forces of opposition in Germany whose "inspiration" had long been silenced or avoided by German historiography.

In spite of the total change in social structures between 800 and 1800, the concept of the united empire modelled after the Carolingian and the Roman or West-Roman examples lived on. Both the need for legitimation of the French hegemony in Europe and the longevity of the Carolingian legacy are exhibited in the following quotation:

"Napoleon occasionally considered himself a Carolus Magnus of the 19th century, the emperor of an imperium which was no longer Christian but rather enlightened. Not only the French believed this, but Germans as well. Prince-bishop of Mainz and Arch-chancellor of the demised Holy Roman Empire, Karl Theodor von Dalberg, placed his hopes in the French Empereur: 'If he could only be emperor of the Occident, to resist the Russians and thereby revive the Occidental Empire, just as it was under Charlemagne, composed of Italy, France, and Germany'" (Herre 193, p. 13).

Also in terms of geography, the similarities between the Napoleonic and the Carolingian dominions are astonishing (cf. *Fig. 78* and *Fig. 84*).

Following the return of the corpse of Napoleon I from St. Helena, the hearse was driven to the sound of pealing bells (a symbol of the connection between the crown and the church) through the city of Paris to his last resting place, the Cathédrale des Invalides, bearing the imperial coat of arms and Charlemagne's (!) crown. Heinrich Heine stood by the side of the street among the French and, especially touched and caught up by the Bonapartian legend, he later wrote (T. 28):

T. 28:
The people looked so ghostly
lost in old memories –
the imperial fantasy
had been conjured up again.
I cried that day. I had
tears come to my eyes,
as I heard the long-lost cry of passion
"Long live the Emperor!"

(Die Menschen schauen so geisterhaft
in alter Erinnrung verloren –
der imperiale Märchentraum
war wieder aufbeschworen.
Ich weinte an jenem Tag. Mir sind
die Tränen ins Auge gekommen,
als ich den verschollenen Liebesruf,
das «Vive l'Empereur» vernommen.)

(quote from H. Heine: Deutschland. Ein Wintermärchen. Caput VIII)

If it were grand vassals during the middle ages (and often their brothers and sons), and later popes, and patricians and sovereign rulers who functioned as the centrifugal forces of Europe, these were, on the other hand, competing foreign powers, especially from Charles V to Napoleon. The unification of Europe through the hegemony of *one* tribe (*Franci*), of *one* dynasty (e.g. the Houses of Staufen or Habsburg), or of *one* nation (French) was never able to last indefinitely. As such, the visionary periods of imperial unity from Carolus Magnus until Napoleon were all of short duration.

7.1.2 Relations from 1815 to 1945: against the background of conscripted Armies in the nation state

The idea of conscripted armies survived the "conservative reordering" of Europe at the Congress of Vienna. With the French Revolution and the spread of a few of its basic ideas in Napoleonic times, the "civilian war" ("national war") gradually began to replace the earlier variety of war fought by professional soldiers for non-democratic absolutist governments. This new variety of war would not have been conceivable without general conscription and working requirements. This added a new dimension to French-German relations. Following the institution of general conscription and the victory in the "Wars of Liberation" (1813-1815), civilians were addressed more and more as the *active subjects* of wars. This strategy did not remain without success. A jump of one hundred years: one need only consider the conflicts of conscience experienced by *French* and *German* socialists in the year 1914. Patriotism had long become a component of socialism. And when both camps – the German socialists with a majority – finally approved the war loans, patriotic duty had won out over "international" tendencies. This example shows that the conscripted army represented but a single factor, albeit an important one, within *societies organized along lines of nation states*. Also the different development of mandatory school attendance as well as universal suffrage in the two countries converged in the same goal: having the people identify more and more with their being citizens of the state (*Staatsbürger, citoyens*) and as a rising class (*bourgeois*) with the "interests of the nation". On both sides of the Rhine, a similar development was taking place. In the case of Germany, the process of forming a nation as well as the identification process attached to it were extraordinarily tedious and filled with contradictions.

The gradual realization of the so-called *kleindeutsch* solution[2] shaped French-German relations after 1825 just as much as the "civilian army" and "civilian war" did. With Austria excluded as a part of the conservative Catholic Danubian monarchy of the House of Habsburg, Germany came into being under the leadership of Prussia. Austria's exclusion had been supported by radical-democratic tendencies before 1848, and by some currents in German Protestantism which regarded Austria as the bulwark of the Roman Catholic Church, but not by the conservatives and just as little by many socialists. Engels, Bebel, and Liebknecht, for example, envisioned the ideal as a democratic Greater Germany (Rovan 1986, p. 24f.). – May one in this context speak of a *"late nation"* and thus one which came too late for the "splitting up of the world" by the European countries? Rovan (1986, p. 24) sees in such formulas a product of the *kleindeutsch*-nationalistic view of history which has constantly denied the existence of German "polycentricism" and its "fruitful dialectics between the centre and the periphery".

The state which came into being was only a *part* of the former territories of the Holy Roman Empire. Did it not therefore have right to lay claim to territory and to enforce this by means of military might? In any case, *this* caused Germany's neighbours to view it as an unpredictable and dangerous entity and not – or at least not primarily – its desired status as a colonial power.

Until about the time of the first Austrian defeat to the Prussians in Sadowa (1866, German historiography refers to Königgrätz, a city lying a good distance from the battlefield), pro-German sentiments had outweighed others in France.

Especially the influence of the *Sturm und Drang*, German Classicism, and later German Romanticism, stimulated in France a positive atmosphere toward Germany (cf. Leiner 1989, pp. 79-85). This had been initiated – just to mention the text having the broadest effect – by *Mme de Staël*'s work *De l'Allemagne*

2 The German Empire without Austria

(1810, published in Paris 1814). Numerous French transcriptions of German works, as well as the concerts and exhibitions of German artists functioned in support of Mme de Staël's intended critique of the Napoleonic regime characterized by the conception of Germany as a «pays où règne la liberté de la pensée» and gave life to her fascinating picture of a «peuple...passionné de musique, vertueux et sincère, méditatif et cultivé» (van Tieghem 1961, p. 150). The works of such a broad spectrum of authors as Cousin, Michelet, Lamartine, Hugo, Nerval, and Renan witnessed the scope and intensity of German cultural influence in France. During this epoch, German cultural influence in France predominated over French influence in Germany. This does not contradict the fact that around 1830, during the *Vormärz* (the period before 1848) and after 1848, France itself became the model for many critical German intellectuals. Later this faded away. This is true of Heine (see Kortländer 1983, Oehler 1984) and also later of Marx, Engels, and the workers' associations which were formed beginning in 1848 (see Bouvier 1982, pp. 84-119).

Soon after Sadowa there was a rapid change of atmosphere. The French Empire under Napoleon III was no longer able to prevent further Prussian unification and even involuntarily exacerbated matters by laying claim to areas on the left bank of the Rhine (the Palatinate, Mayence). Then the candidacy of the Hohenzoller Leopold for the Spanish crown offered a pretence for war. The old French fears of a *«restitution de l'empire de Charles Quint»* reawoke (Poidevin/Bariéty 1977, p. 82). In Germany, the policy of *Blut und Eisen* (blood and iron) succeeded against France due to the tactical manoeuvring of Bismarck.

By the time of the Franco-Prussian (or Franco-German) war in 1870/71, the French conception of Germany had split in two. The earlier conception of a contemplative and peace-loving nation, of the spiritual home of Goethe and Kant, now only represented one side of the diptych. The other side showed the *patrie* of a Bismarck or Moltke, an ice-cold, sabre-rattling enemy in dazed quest of power and subjugation. The distinctions made between the two aspects, as for example in the work by the Parisian professor of philosophy, E.-M. Caro, *Les Deux Allemagnes*, would from then on become commonplace in France (Gödde-Baumanns 1981, p. 110). The German bourgeoisie continued to value Parisian fashion, painting, and literature. For decades, however, the image of France as being decadent, demographically regressive and aging predominated. Ernst Robert Curtius later so "accurately" "rectified" this conception: "not decadence, but rather calm, quiet maturity of age..." (Trouillet 1981, p. 223, see further Jehn 1977, p. 122 and Bock 1990).

How dramatically the conception of Germany changed with the war of 1870/71, and how tenacious the dark side of the *deux Allemagnes* was, have only rarely been noticed till recently. Four recent publications (Reichel 1986, esp. p. 431f.; Gödde-Baumanns 1988, esp. p. 28; Leiner 1988; Leiner 1989, pp.

140-186) have brought attention to this. Thus, popular contemporary French caricaturists tend to exploit Prussian attributes such as with the spiked helmet, the officer's monocle, the facial characteristics of Bismarck or the needle gun, whenever in a half-comic, half-serious manner they wish to warn about the potential danger of a German move toward the East or personify the supremacy of Bonn with respect to Paris (see examples in Fekl 1986).

Particularly *after 1870/71*, German nationalist circles propagated the myth of the "arch-enemy". An enemy, shared by all classes in society – only France at first, later England as well – was ideally suited to forge the new nation into one. In individual cases, the myth of the arch-enemy had already surfaced. The first attested case was in 1507 with Emperor Maximillian (Trouillet 1981, p. 39). But now the myth had really become threatening.

In France anti-German tendencies were inflamed by the temporary occupation of eastern territories until substantial war reparations had been paid, by the annexation of Alsace-Lorraine as a "former imperial territory", and, most of all, by the systematic Germanization being conducted there. «Le premier devoir de la France est de ne pas oublier l'Alsace et la Lorraine qui ne l'oublient pas», judged, for example, Lavisse in his 1884 history book *Cours d'Histoire de la France* (Poidevin/Bariéty 1977, p. 133). It is especially apparent in school history books and literature of the period that Alsace-Lorraine, patriotism and usually underlying thoughts of revenge functioned primarily as internal cohesive factors in the Third Republic, split between the *républicains* and the *cléricaux* (see Trouillet 1981, p. 139 and Christadler 1979; Christadler 1981a).

The economically powerful Empire and nation state of Wilhelm II presented the world powers, Great Britain and France, with a dynamic contender for the markets, zones of influence and colonies. In spite of repeated efforts to secure peace, by 1912 the readiness for war was growing in the nationalistic imperialist states. The media began drumming the people with ideological preparations for war and the armaments industries began supplying weapons. In the First World War, which superficially was precipitated by an Austro-Russian conflict, the two neighbours vied for control on the continent. It was, in fact, a war between the nations and it was bitterly waged. The month-long battle of Verdun alone (21 Feb. - 21 July 1916) cost the French approximately 362,000 dead and injured and the Germans 337,000. In no other conflict since the period of Napoleon had the two countries lost so many people in fighting against one another (*Fig. 79*). According to a French historian not oriented along national lines but

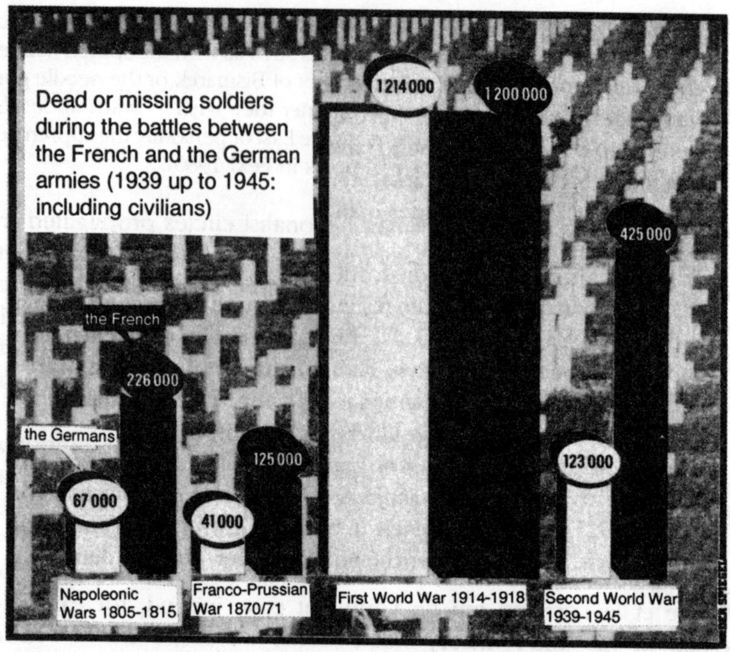

Fig. 79: The Toll of "two Arch-enemies".
(From: Der Spiegel, 21 Nov. 1977, p. 134)

rather European ones, imperialistic rivalries and a mutual fear of an existence-threatening "arch-enemy" precipitated and shaped this war. Confronted by such a perspective, the issue of guilt plays no great role any more. The final result is more important: the weakening of the European powers, the creation of the USSR and the rise of the USA to become the principle creditor for Europe and the effective victorious power (Ferro 1988).

In the same mirrored hall in *Versailles* where in 1871 the proclamation of the Empire had taken place, representatives of the Weimar Republic now had to sign the *peace treaty* following the German defeat. The choreography of Clemenceau saw to that. The treaty placed Alsace-Lorraine and the exploitation of Saar coal in the hands of the French. Germany's development was to be retarded and another rise to power prevented under the burden of decades of quasi-unfulfillable reparations. The text of the treaty shaped by the desire for vengeance and later amendments only exacerbated German-French tensions and rivalries rather than alleviating them. Today, historians in both nations generally agree upon this fact (cf. e.g. Poidevin/Bariéty 1977, p. 238).

When on the German side certain reparation demands were not met, French and Belgian troops, with the approval of England, occupied the Ruhr. German anti-Weimar, nationalist forces received their first modern martyrs. Soon, however, attempts to reach compromises were launched from various sides, including Great Britain and the USA. The era of *Briand and Stresemann* peaked in the *Locarno* Pacts (1925) negotiated between five states. Among other things, they guaranteed France Alsace-Lorraine once and for all, and Germany the left bank of the Rhine from the Palatinate downward. They also envisaged Germany's entry into the League of Nations and thereby international restoration and recognition. Also, the cultural life of the twenties and thirties was in no way dominated by the "arch-enemy" and vindictive tendencies.

Mutual cultural exchange reached a state of equilibrium, perhaps for the first time in French-German history. The active French interest in Wagner, expressionism, the *Bauhaus* movement, and in philosophers from Nietzsche to Heidegger corresponded to the fascination which French painting, sculpture, and poetry exerted on German intellectual life (see Rovan 1986, p. 73f., Harrer 1987 and Bock 1991). In this context, the following phenomena should at least receive mention:

- numerous francophile German authors (e.g. Rilke, Tucholsky, Heinrich Mann, Benn),
- the hopes of major French writers for German-French understanding (e.g. Rolland, Giono, Romains, Lichtenberger, Giraudoux, Drieu La Rochelle),
- the efforts of influential personalities from Alsace and Lorraine (e.g. Otto Flake, René Schickele, Yvan Goll) and German emigrants in Paris after 1933 (e.g. Heinrich Mann and Alfred Döblin, see Betz 1986) to build a bridge between the two cultures in spite of increasing difficulties with their own personal situations,
- the "flourishing" of cultural stereotypes not only between adversaries but even among proponents of German-French rapprochement (see Trouillet 1981, pp. 184-274, Hinrichs/Kolboom 1977b, Leiner 1989, pp. 204-235; for the function of these prejudices, see Koch-Hillebrecht 1977 and Picht 1980).

Thus even the relations between German and French youth in the period between the two world wars were "squeezed into polito-ideological corsets"; for them, "the way to normality was barred. The supposed outriders, paving the way to better relations between the two neighbouring peoples, remained in fact, and irrespective of the inertia driving them onward, prisoners of their national political cultures. All in all, they initiated no positive activity, but functioned only as a mirror of their age" (Tiemann 1989, p. 374).

On the other hand, the factors due to which nationalistic and vengeance-prone movements in Germany, from which the National Socialists emerged, were able to prevail cannot be discussed here (see Poidevin/ Bariéty 1977, pp. 273-283; Hass 1975; Deist 1979). Important in the present French-German comparison is that the "Third Reich" was based on the "irredentism" of the "Second Reich" – the Empire after 1871 – and that it redefined *biological ideas of nationality* already present in the 18th and 19th centuries into *totalitarian* ones (e.g. see Löbsack 1939, p. 76f.). All levels of society were to voluntarily subordinate themselves to the leader chosen by providence: *Ein Volk, ein Reich, ein Führer* ("One people, one empire, one leader"). The French nation state was based on the principle of the *souveraineté du peuple*, the *sovereignty of the people* which, although not founded by him, was radicalized by Rousseau. A member of the "voluntary nation" was any person who recognized its values and its culture – including Alsatians, Bretons, Basques. The struggle between "reason" and the "unrestrained power of nature", between *civilisation* and *barbarie* (see Victor Hugo 1871 and, strikingly similar, Charles de Gaulle 1934, in Pabst 1983, pp. 48 and 94f.), or from the National-socialist point of view, between an "uprooted" and purely rationalistic nation and a "native" and "organic" people (cf. Pabst 1983, pp. 63 and 97ff.) was thus incorporated into quite varied conceptions of state. It therefore comes as no surprise that mutual relations deteriorated rapidly in the wake of the very first major success of the National Socialists in the *Reichtagswahlen* (parliamentary elections) of 1930.

A last and failed attempt to secure peace was the *Munich Pact* (1938). The French and British Governments hoped this would satisfy the expansionistic desires of the National Socialists. Here the concept of Empire taken from Hitler initially went in the direction of "Bohemia", i.e. in the direction of the Habsburg/German Empire. Yet the logical continuation of this idea, a demand for "old" imperial possessions in the west, i.e. Alsace-Lorraine, was implicit. The French Government in its attempts to secure peace stood upon the ground of public disapproval of war which was expressed in the much-quoted slogan *Mourir pour Danzig?*. The areas of Sudetenland in Czechoslovakia were conceded to Germany after National-socialist foreign policy had led to the *Anschluss* of Austria. In spite of this, German troops soon marched into Czechoslovakia. The protectorate of the Reich "Bohemia and Moravia" was established. Slovakia was transformed into a satellite state. Since then, *Munich 1938* has been viewed in France as a warning (see Hörling 1985). Alfred Grosser formulated it concisely and energetically in an interview.

"In 1938 we capitulated before a dictator, we set everything on peace. We know the outcome. Like the bleating sheep in the peace movement...that can only lead to catastrophe." (Grosser 1983, p. 116)

However one may feel about this ex- or implicit comparison, it characterizes the efforts, even in a world shaped by superpowers, not to allow actions to be determined by others, but rather to decide for oneself. A strong defense is held to be imperative. This comparison, however, also characterizes the *historical consciousness* of the *grande nation* and is astonishingly wide-spread there (see Picaper 1983, Sauzay 1985).

Werner judges from the viewpoint of the historian (1985, p. 325): «Quant à la responsabilité française dans l'avènement de Hitler, elle tient au passage d'une attitude trop implacable face à une Allemagne faible à la capitulation devant une Allemagne forte.» ("In view of the French responsibility during the rise of Hitler, France held onto the change from a too inexorable attitude towards a weak Germany to a surrender unto a strong Germany.")

A final change in course with regard to the *Reich* was taken by England on 3 March and by France on 6 April 1939 with their guarantee for threatened Poland. When the German assault on Poland began on 1 September 1939, both powers declared war on Germany.

In an account of French-German relations, and according to the terminology commonly used in France, the *Second World War* can be divided into four phases.

1. *Drôle de guerre* refers to the period directly after the outbreak of the war (Sept. 1939 - May 1940). Due to a defeatist attitude in their own country and a technologically and militarily more advanced opponent, the government of France at that time did not chance opening an active front in the east. Instead, the army pulled back behind the Maginot line (for further details, cf. Heimsoeth 1990).

2. In a *guerre éclair* or *offensive éclair* – a loan-translation of the German *Blitzkrieg* – German troops thrust across Holland and Belgium, skirting the Maginot line on 10 May 1940 and taking France in six weeks. The military collapse (*la débâcle*) led to a mass exodus (*l'exode*) to the south of France.

3. The following phase is generally referred to as the *occupation* (Amouroux 1976ff.). After the cease-fire, France was essentially divided into a larger *zone occupée* and a smaller so-called *zone libre* in the southeast, separated by a nearly impassable *ligne de démarcation* (see *Fig. 85*). In the *zone libre* there soon existed an authoritarian regime

under the leadership of Pétain, with its capital, Vichy. In the beginning, this paternalistic *Etat français* was able to count on "having the approval of most of the French" (Kohut 1983, p. 111). This was due to different things which are still to be discussed. In any case, Petain's aura as a *héros de Verdun* played a considerable part.

The *résistance* began with a minority. On 18 June 1940 from London, de Gaulle incited the French to resistance at the side of the allies. In November of 1942, as American and British troops landed in the French territories of Northern Africa and introduced the counter-offensive, Hitler ordered the rest of France occupied - while officially upholding the Vichy regime. The events increased resistance noticeably and also improved coordination. Even the communists lamed by the Hitler-Stalin pact (27 Aug. 1939) until the invasion of the Soviet Union (22 June 1941) declared themselves in agreement with de Gaulle's leadership of the resistance (Jan. 1943). Excepting the resistance of a growing minority and the low-level waiting attitude of the majority – otherwise known as *attentisme* – active *collaboration* at times reached considerable proportions, a fact which for decades thereafter would be suppressed by French historical consciousness (see Ory 1977, Klarsfeld 1989). The repressive and punitive actions of the German occupation remained alive in the memories of the French: the massacre of the whole population of Oradour-sur-Glane (10 June 1944), the execution of hostages, deportations, forced labour, the persecution of the Jews. Collaboration, however, – one of the closest forms of cooperation ever between French and Germans – represented a not always unpleasant, practical life experience with the Germans for numerous Frenchmen. Primarily out of political and moral considerations were these then banned from memory. Their antipode, the *résistance*, became the shaping force after the war.

For literature about the *résistance* and *collaboration* including their after-effects see Götz 1977, Zimmermann 1982, Kohut 1982-4. A legend on the "division of labour" between Pétain and de Gaulle, which deserves closer consideration, is discussed in Rovan 1986, p. 76. De Gaulle himself has contributed to the legend. Viewed by the light of day, it represents one of the phases in a decade-long and still continuing process of memory suppression and only gradual recognition of the past in France. One French historian specialized in the field of mentality has attempted to describe and re-construe this process as the "Vichy syndrome" (Rousso 1987) through the use of films, texts and diverse opinion polls. Discussion of the literature of the *collaboration* is likewise increasing within France (Steel 1991). And the general public has become painfully aware of the extent of involvement in the *collaboration* as a result of the case of Barbie and the *affaire Touvier* (cf. Le Monde and Le Figaro, 27 Sept. 1991).

4. The *libération* began on 6 June 1944 with the landing of the allied forces in Normandy. On 8 August, their advance slowed down in the vicinity of Paris. The *résistance* had staged a revolt there the day before and encountered little resistance from the German troops: The German Commandant von Choltitz ignored Hitler's order of unconditional defense in order to protect the cultural goods of the French capital. The self-liberation of Paris was complete when a French tank division under the command of General Leclerc rolled into Paris driving out the remaining troops of occupation. De Gaulle was received with enthusiasm. On 23 October the Americans recognized the provisional government. (The liberation of Strasbourg and the part played by France in the later occupation of Germany should also be mentioned.)

By way of a partial self-liberation de Gaulle achieved a certain *weight for France* in later negotiations with the allied victors. France was not involved in the conferences of Yalta or Potsdam (for the *complexe de Yalta*, see 2.4). But it was among the permanent members of the Security Council of the United Nations (not officially founded until 26 June 1945) and was thereby granted the same recognition and veto power as were the USA, USSR, Great Britain and China. Later it was one of the four occupying powers in Germany and the four sector city, Berlin. The relationship between Germany and France had been turned on its head. In the wake of the liberation, a defeated land became a victorious power.

From the National-socialist point of view, the war was most certainly perceived and fought as a popular war, even as a "total war" - with the most bitter of consequences for Germany and Europe. France, by contrast, fought its occupation only with a part of the combined forces of its people - despite the retrospective glorification of the *résistance* and the *libération*. And for this very reason France preserved the substance of its population – an essential difference from the First World War and its consequences. That it also retained its traditionally oriented economic structure (see 3.4) and its world-wide colonial empire would later prove to be more of a burden.

7.2 *Relations after 1945: Unequal partners facing equal problems*

After the Treaty of Versailles, the Germans had been able to plunge France and Europe into misery of war for a second time in less than twenty years. This time France would have to be more permanently and effectively protected from its aggressive neighbour. Never again could a centralistic state be permitted to develop in Germany where there was a danger of its degenerating into a totalitarian, "romantic", irredentistic, aggressive state. *This is the view* that shaped French policy after 1944/45. The Anglo-Saxons and the Russians, however, (the latter after 1945) blocked plans for a lasting division of Germany and a separation of the Rhineland, the Ruhr, and the Saar analogous to the separation of areas to the east of the Oder and Neisse. France was only allowed the customs union with the Saar and the rights to Saar coal. Under the influence of the beginning "cold war" in 1946/47 and under the pressure of American economic aid to the war-torn countries of Western Europe, France reluctantly had to accept the unification of the American-British "bizone" with its own zone (Rhineland-Palatinate, South Baden, Württemberg-Hohenzollern) to form a "trizone" (cf. Hille 1983 and Scharf/ Schröder 1983). Step by step, France's foreign policy adapted to American and British foreign policies and to the "internal" German efforts which led to the creation of the Federal Republic of Germany (cf. Ziebura 1970, pp. 39-53; Weisenfeld 1986a, pp. 25-44). France never had such problems with Austria – to choose a clearly contrasting example (cf. Ravy 1977).

Viewed by the light of day, the French and the West Germans were being confronted with the same problems just a few years after the end of the war:

- the East-West conflict and the question of neutrality,
- the reconstruction and the discussion about the Western orientation which had already been effected by American economic aid.

French visions of occupying the predominant position of power in Western and Central Europe with the aid of the Soviets also failed due to the "cold war" (Weisenfeld 1986a, pp. 25-28, 33; the USA in particular thwarted these hopes: Schwartz 1991). They were not abandoned, however. They only underwent a reorientation. An alliance with the western half of Germany based on its already obvious economic power and the desired irreversibility of the division of Germany was to help France secure a predominant position of power in Europe. Other positions were also being taken in France, namely those of the socialists and the Catholic MRP (see 2.5.2). They tended to stress a "Europe of equals". They latched onto federalistic currents interested in a "European

Union" which came together after the founding of the European Council in London in 1949 but failed in face of the nationalist reservations of their members. Renewed efforts at unification, especially those of the MRP and its Foreign Minister, Robert Schuman, and the CDU under Konrad Adenauer, replaced the "European Union" with the idea of closer Western European cooperation centred around a German-French core. On 7 March 1950 Adenauer even suggested the political union of the two countries. Schumann reacted positively, and even de Gaulle as leader of the *Rassemblement du peuple français* stated on 16 March 1950 that such a union could continue the work of Charlemagne (Herre 1983, p. 269).

The following overview summarizes the political and economic relations since 1949/50. During this time economic factors have strongly influenced politics and political impulses have strongly influenced economic relations. Below, reference will be made to military and cultural relations.

Chronological Table 3: German-French Relations 1945-1988

1945	Conferences of Yalta (4-11 Feb.) and Potsdam (16 July - 2 Aug.) without the participation of France. French occupation zone, French sector in Berlin. Founding of the B.I.L.D. (see 7.2.3)
1946	French demand separation of Rhineland, the Ruhr, and Saarland
1949	Founding of the Federal Republic of Germany (23 May). Founding of the German Democratic Republic (7 Oct.). First city partnership (*jumelage*)
1950	German-French Trade agreement (30 Jan.). The "Schuman Plan" (9 May) leads to the
1951	Foundation of the European Coal and Steel Community (ECSC) (18 April)
1952	Signing of the Elysee treaty founding the European Defense Community (EDC) (27 May)
1954	French National Assembly votes down the EDC (30 Aug.). Paris Treaty concerning the future entry of the FRG to NATO; agreement on a Saarland Statute (19-23 Nov.)
1955	Foundation of the official German-French Chamber of Commerce (25 Apr.). – Referendum in Saarland: Saarland Statute voted down (23 Nov.)
1956	Luxembourg-Saarland Treaty: after 1957, Saarland belongs to FRG
1957	Founding Treaties for the EEC and EURATOM (25 March)
1958	V Republic
1963	Signing of the Treaty on German-French Cooperation (22 Jan.), Bundestag Preamble to the Treaty (16 May), Agreement on German-French Youth Association (4-5 July)
1964	Hamburg Agreement between the governments of the German Länder, making English or Latin the first foreign language
1966	France leaves NATO integrated command structure (11 March)
1969	Agreement on joint production of the Airbus (13-14 March)

1971	Agreement on expansion of the EC and the introduction of French as a possible first foreign language in FRG
1972	First German-French *Gymnasium*
1974	Economic policy agreement between new Heads of State V. Giscard d'Estaing and H. Schmidt
1977	"Anti-German" wave in France as reaction to the *Extremistenerlaß* (i.e. professional ban for members of extreme parties) and to forms of fighting terrorism in the FRG
1979	European Monetary System (EMS) created, first direct elections for the European Parliament (7-10 June)
1980	Agreement on joint venture for the development of a French and German radio and television satellite (1 Dec.)
1981-1985	French fears concerning demonstrations against the deployment of American nuclear missiles in the FRG
1985	Paris Eureka Conference (July), Eureka as Mitterrand's counter-project to the American SDI project (17 July)
1987	Joint autumn manoeuvre "Bold Sparrow" (17-24 Sept.)
1988	Formation of two bilateral councils on matters of economic and defense policies on 25th anniversary of the 1963 treaty, foundation of German-French university-level college (Jan.), official establishment of the German-French Brigade in Böblingen (21 Nov.), first meeting of the German-French High Council on Culture (20 Dec.)

7.2.1. Political and economic relations

Until now, French and West German attempts at rapprochement have always taken place in the general framework of the Western Alliance. For orientation purposes, it is helpful to divide these into two phases:

1. Until approximately the end of the fifties, the Federal Republic of Germany was concerned with overcoming opposition and resistance, particularly that of the French. German-French relations did exist in the greater European context, but their accent was clearly *bilateral.* The emphasis lay in the reconciliation between the French and the Germans.

2. Only *after* the German-French treaty in 1963 did the alliance of the two achieve a noticeably *multilateral* accent and more and more nations were drawn into the process. Nonetheless, pure harmony did not always rule – neither between the two states nor between them and their other partners. And as the number of participants in the process of European unification grew, the problems connected with it also grew.

The foundation of the European Coal and Steel Community in 1951, the establishment of the European Economic Community in 1957 and the German-French treaty of 1963 represent the three most important stations along the way to German-French and European rapprochement.

Refering first to the *European Coal and Steel Community*: Since 1949 France had been producing too much steel and receiving too little Ruhr coal. Saar coal, due to its inferior quality, represented little compensation for this. In addition, the Saar problem bogged down German-French relations. Thus, the project devised by Jean Monnet (Head of the Planning Commission) and then forwarded by Robert Schuman came into being: the foundation of a European Community for Coal and Steel. It enabled the regulation of marketing and supply problems, controlled West German production, and simplified the Saar problem. The larger market provided both countries with considerable advantages and simultaneously the problems between France and Germany were relativized and defused in the larger framework of Europe. In April 1951 France, the Federal Republic of Germany, Italy and the three Benelux countries signed the founding treaty.

In Schuman's own words, the community was to end the *«opposition séculaire de la France et de l'Allemagne»*. These words draw attention to another aspect of the treaty. In putting the entire production of coal, iron and steel, and thereby the basis of the armament industry at that time under the control of a supreme European agency, a future war between neighbours was to be precluded. At the same time, the cornerstone of an organized Europe was being laid in a limited but expandable area (cf. Poidevin/Bariéty 1977, p. 332; Herre 1983, p. 273). A number of bilateral agreements and institutions sprung up around this treaty. Among them is the German-French Trade Agreement, signed in 1950, for over more than 300 million dollars. There is also the official German-French Chamber of Commerce, founded in 1955, which since this time has sought to further economic contacts between companies and their branch offices in the respective partner countries.

However, the problem with the Saar remained unresolved. The majority of the population turned down a compromise worked out in 1954 ("Saar Statute"). This was negotiated alongside the Paris conference concerning West German entry into NATO and would have granted "European status" while upholding the customs union with France. Only following the Luxembourg Treaty on 1 Jan. 1957 did Saarland revert to German control. The loss was compensated for, however, by a few terms in the agreement which were advantageous to France (see also Weisenfeld 1986a, pp. 71-73).

The *European Economic Community* included at first the six countries belonging to the European Coal and Steel Community.

Fig. 80:
(From: Süddeutsche Zeitung, 7 Sept. 1962)

Agreed upon in 1957, it took effect in 1959. Its purpose was to scrap customs barriers between partner countries, i.e. to open up the unhindered flow of goods and, thus, create viable competition between the enterprises of the six countries. The members of the new European Economic Community also wanted to bring about the totally free movement of persons, services, and capital goods. The preparation of political union – in whatever form – was to be the result of all of these measures (see *fig. 86*).

After continual expansion of the EEC, first in 1972 with Great Britain, Ireland and Denmark, then in 1981 with Greece, and finally in 1986 with Spain and Portugal, this institution has become all that much more immobile. Despite some recent progress in this field, especially the agricultural sector has proved to be a constant source of new problems. At present, agriculture alone swallows more than two-thirds of the DM 70 billion budget of the EC at the expense of other areas.

The concept "European Communities" (EC, Germ. EG, French CE) include the European Coal and Steel Community (ECSC, Germ. EGKS, French CECA), the EEC (German EWG, French CEE), and the European Atomic Community which was founded simultaneously (EAC or Euratom, German EAG, French

CEA). The common supranational organs of the EC have been under the control of the directly elected European Parliament since 1979.

In regard to the EEC and particularly the Federal Republic of Germany, by which France measures its economic performance, de Gaulle introduced an ambitious program for the modernization of the French economy at the beginning of the V Republic in 1958 (cf. 3.5). An economically and militarily powerful France and an increasingly economically powerful Federal Republic of Germany were to form the *core for European unification.* De Gaulle and Adenauer were again in agreement over this as of 1959 (cf. Poidevin/Bariéty 1977, p. 333f.).

Figure 80 emphasizes the aspect of reconciliation. It refers to Adenauer's visit to France (2-8 July 1962), which, like de Gaulle's later visit to Germany, was to prepare the nation for the treaty between the two states.

The caricature is a reference to the last day of the state visit, or more exactly to the church service in the cathedral of Reims. The church of coronation for French kings had been hit and burned out by German grenades in the First World War. It had only been rededicated in 1938. Thus, it was a perfect symbol for the countries' common fate and their increased responsibility. Frederick the Great, Napoleon, and Bismarck gaze spellbound from the heavens upon the two statesmen who are festively celebrating the end of being "arch-enemies" in front of the cathedral.

The *German-French Treaty* of January 1963 was grounded in a common opening statement by the chiefs of state "in the knowledge that closer cooperation between the two nations represents an essential step along the path toward a united Europe, this being the goal of both nations" (Treaty 1963, p. 8). The formulation, however, disguised differing leanings. De Gaulle's foreign policy aimed at creating a Europe which emphasized its independence from the superpowers. (De Gaulle never used the expression accredited to him, *«Europe des patries».*) Since the EEC as a whole had failed this political goal, it was now to be carried out by means of close bilateral ties among nations (for further details, cf. Loth/Picht 1991; on the biographical stamp of de Gaulle's picture of Germany, cf. Maillard 1990 and Binoche 1990). Although German foreign policy of the Adenauer era was most interested in visible reconciliation and an "initial spark for the political unity of Europe" (Loch 1963, p. 36), neither of these goals was to endanger U.S. military protection against the Soviet "threat".

Essentially, the treaty established a *system of regular consultations* under which:

- the chiefs of state were to meet at least twice annually,

- the Foreign Ministers, the Ministers of Defense, the French Minister of Education and a representative of the Germans were to come together at least every three months,
- the Federal Minister for Family and Youth Issues or his representative and the French High Commissioner for Youth and Sports were to consult as often as every two months.

The treaty had the following *major goals*:

1. Foreign policy: "The two governments are to consult each other before each decision on all important questions of foreign policy, primarily in questions of mutual interest so that a similarly-directed position may be achieved." (Treaty 1963, p. 11). The strived unity and cooperation concerns, for example, the EC, East-West relations, international organizations (e.g. NATO) and development aid.

2. Defense policy: "In the area of strategy and tactics, the responsible instances in both countries are to attempt to harmonize views so as to arrive at common conceptions" (ibid, p. 12). As of yet, this clause has remained dead. There has been no standardization of military doctrines. Only two other aims of the treaty have been realized: the exchange of personnel between the armed forces and – partial – collaboration in the area of weapons (cf. 7.2.2).

3. Education and youth-related issues: the most important measures apply to language instruction and youth exchange (cf. 7.2.3).

Directly after the signing of the treaty, which still had to be ratified by the respective parliaments, heated discussion began about its foreign policy and military orientation. Before this, de Gaulle had blocked Great Britain's entry into the EEC, calling it an American "Trojan horse". Adenauer had – by chance – signalled German interest in an offer to enter into a multilateral Atlantic nuclear force (MLF) on the same day, a project which later failed. And could not such a treaty induce the Americans to pull back or even reduce their troop strength? It is not known if such a threat was ever spoken by American officials. Perhaps future historians will be able to clear up the issue following the release of archive materials. In any case, the ratification of the treaty in the Bundestag only succeeded after a preamble was added emphasizing West German membership in NATO and the partnership between "Europe" and the USA. It also demanded, among other things, an expansion of the EC through the addition of Great Britain and the removal of EEC trade barriers aimed at Great Britain and the USA (Treaty 1963, p. 4f.). In de Gaulle's eyes, this pro-American Atlantic accentuation robbed the treaty of its substance (Couve de Murville 1988).

The consequence was a long crisis in bilateral relations. There was substantial divergence on all major issues. France
- withdrew its military forces from the control of the NATO integrated command structure (1966),
- established its own *force de frappe* (General de Gaulle presented a group of high French officers with plans for this as early as 1959, cf. Weisenfeld 1986a, p. 142),
- repeatedly blocked an EC expansion which only became possible under de Gaulle's more pragmatic successor, Pompidou,
- asked the Federal Republic of Germany in vain to renounce veiled protectionism in the areas of French agricultural products such as grains, sugar, and meat, and to agree to substantially lower EEC grain prices (just to give one example). Nevertheless, France itself latched onto the tradition of Colbert in its support and marketing of modern industrial products (cf. 3.7; for examples after 1963, see Jetter 1978, pp. 86-90).

Differences in the economic structure and interests of the two countries have contributed and still contribute to this divergence. As an industrial powerful country, the Federal Republic of Germany is interested in the unhampered export of its goods. For this reason, it sought to support expansion in the EC and worked for a liberal external trade policy aimed at opening markets. France, whose industry was not thoroughly modernized until de Gaulle, had too long concentrated on traditional branches (e.g. textiles, steel) and exhibited structural weakness in capital goods (e.g. machine building industry), areas which are crucial to an industrial society and its exports (cf. 3.2). Agricultural products have represented and still represent a major part of French exports, especially to the Federal Republic of Germany and other EC member countries. Therefore, France attempted to protect its agriculture and its still developing modern industry from further EC competitors and, for the same reasons, took a more restrictive posture in EC external trade policy than the Federal Republic of Germany (cf. Menyesch/ Uterwedde 1982b, pp. 130-132). In this context it becomes clear why German agricultural export success, "also in traditionally French domains (dairy products, beef) has caused substantial excitement in its neighbouring country". They simply violated the generally accepted (although naturally unwritten) premise of the EEC: "the EEC agricultural market to the advantage of French agriculture, the Common Market for German industry" (ibid, p. 123)...

These factors and others after 1965 caused a French trade deficit with regard to the Federal Republic of Germany to gradually emerge. This deficit grew and grew. Even following the economic policy "turnabout" of the leftist government it has remained substantial (cf. *Table 29*).

Table 29: The development of the German-French trade: 1950-1990

(CAF/FOB)	1950	1955	1960	1965	1970	1975	1980	1982	1984	1987	1990
Exportations françaises vers la RFA (Mrd.F)	0,8	1,8	4,7	9,6	20,5	36,9	75,4	89,8	119,4	142,7	196,8
Importations françaises en provenance de la RFA (Mrd.F)	0,7	1,5	4,9	9,4	23,4	43,6	92,2	127,7	147,4	186,6	238,7
Solde commercial vis-à-vis de la France (Mrd.F)	−0,1	−0,2	+0,2	−0,1	+2,9	+6,6	+16,8	+38,1	+28,0	+43,9	+41,9
Part de la RFA dans les:											
– importations françaises (%)	6,5	9,2	15,8	18,5	22,1	18,8	16,1	16,5	16,3	19,8	18,8
– exportations françaises (%)	7,8	10,2	13,7	19,3	20,6	16,5	16,0	14,8	14,7	16,6	17,2
Part de la France dans les:											
– importations allemandes (%)	6,1	5,9	9,4	11,1	12,7	12,0	10,7	11,4	10,6	11,8	11,8
– exportations allemandes (%)	7,3	5,7	8,8	10,9	12,4	11,7	13,3	14,1	12,6	12,1	13,0

(From: Lasserre 1986, 243; Müller 1988, 54*; Quid 1989, 1504; Quid 1992, 1674; Fischer Weltalmanach 1992, 923)

Both states have been and remain *privileged trading partners*. For the first time in 1987, France "drove" the Netherlands – which had been a leader since 1973 due to its supplying of natural gas – to second place for German imports (cf. Müller 1988, p. 120). The illustration shows clearly, however, that the Federal Republic of Germany has played a more important role in French imports and exports than vice versa. Since 1970 the West German share of the total volume has declined slightly. However, this remains practically negligible to the German surplus and the French deficit primarily due to the high price level of German industrial goods (cf. *Table 29*, lines 4/5 and 3). Even if Jetter *exaggerates*, he does point to the deepest of the roots of the evils:

"While the Federal Republic of Germany is able to buy its food substantially cheaper from third countries, France is virtually unable to construct an efficient factory without massive supplies of German outfitting and tool machines (1979, p. 72).

In spite of significantly higher French exports to the Federal Republic of Germany in 1987, the French deficit in respect to the Federal Republic of Germany rose to a record value of nearly 44 billion French Francs (cf. *Table 29*).

To draw the quintessential out of that which has been said: France is interested in exporting agricultural products and, with the exception of a few leading industries (airplane construction, weapons), it would either like to protect or make its industry *internationally competitive.* This has been the case since de Gaulle or even more clearly since the socialist change in course in 1982/83 which does not exclude occasional fall-backs into protectionism. The Federal Republic of Germany would naturally like to sell its agricultural products. Its first priority, however, is the export of industrial products. Thus, at present there exist differences in real points of major economic emphasis. But these must be *relativized* within the larger context of world trade (cf. *Table 30*).

In terms of *exports*, the Federal Republic of Germany again moved into first place ahead of the USA and Japan in 1990, regaining the position it held from 1986 to 1988. As such, the expression familiar to French journalists and politicians since 1968, *géant economique* is fitting. However, due to its efforts since the beginning of the Fifth Republic and especially due to the course of modernization undertaken by the socialists (cf. 3.8), France has taken a remarkable fourth place even ahead of Great Britain. For this reason, France is *relatively*

Table 30: The eight leading World Trade Nations: 1989/90

1990 (1989) Imports (bill. $)	1990	(1989)	1990 (1989) Exports (bill. $)	1990	(1989)
1. USA	516,987	(493,195)	1. Germany	398,441	(342,372)
2. Germany	342,622	(269,883)	2. USA	393,592	(363,812)
3. Japan	234,800	(210,840)	3. Japan	286,949	(275,173)
4. France	233,234	(192,484)	4. France	210,168	(178,846)
5. Great Britain	224,938	(197,728)	5. Great Britain	185,976	(152,447)
6. Italy	185,505	(152,913)	6. Italy	169,265	(138,503)
7. Netherlands	126,165	(104,226)	7. Netherlands	131,839	(107,877)
8. Belgium/Lux.	120,067	(99,700)	8. Canada	127,419	(116,037)

imports cif, exports fob

interested in an open world market. For example, Giscard d'Estaing, comparatively more interested in a liberal market policy than his predecessors, brought the conferences of the seven leading world trading nations to life, and Mitterrand has characteristically pled partly for and partly – hidden – against raising national and international trade barriers. This also applies to views on the EC internal market as of 1993. Mitterrand warns of too much market penetration by *extra-Européens* (cf. 2.6), and Kohl, by contrast, warns of the development of new trade barriers:

"We do not want the European domestic market to act as a 'fortress Europe' but rather as a market which opens new development perspectives to the countries of Europe and, at the same time, offers new markets to its trading partners overseas, especially to the countries of the Third World." (Badische Zeitung, 6 March 1989, p. 9)

There have also been opportunities for cooperative efforts resulting from the close economic ties and regular consultations of the two countries since 1963. Examples of this are the bilateral, and later multi-lateral development of the Airbus since the second half of the sixties as well as the agreement signed in 1980 concerning the joint construction of two television satellites, one French and one German: TDF 1 and TV-Sat (cf. Benecke/Krafft 1986, pp. 188-191). In both cases, there have been "bitter pills" to be swallowed. The Airbus is technologically successful but faces stiff price competition from its American competitor, Boeing. The expensive TV-Sat launched into orbit in 1987 has proven to be a failure. The TDF-1 launch suffered under financing problems and competition from private satellite projects which promised greater technological advantage; the launching did take place at the end of 1988 (Madelin 1988, p. 11 and 17), but neither the TDF 1 nor subsequent German and French satellites of the same type managed more than a fraction of the performance anticipated. "Western"-oriented states of Europe can only hope to catch up with the American and Japanese lead in an area especially important in future technology, micro-electronics, by more closely coordinating their private and state enterprises. Although they have not succeeded to date, this remains a primary objective of the Eureka-Project, begun in 1985 – officially – as a civil counter-pole to the American SDI-Project for Western military research into space technology. The French desire for closer German-French cooperation on the project of a civil space shuttle (*Hermès* as a European alternative) continues to meet with deaf ears in Bonn. The Federal Republic of Germany and – after all the difficulties with *Hermès* – France agreed to participate in both projects. The accents, however, were different. French policy favoured Eureka but allowed individual companies to participate on SDI on their own. The West Germans participated in Eureka (perhaps more out of European solidarity?) but showed a greater interest in the SDI-Project. In the meantime, however, German research within the framework of the Eureka-Project has also picked up, while SDI research has been paralyzed by internal economic difficulties in America. Overall, it may be said that less bilateral and more *multilateral* "European" and "Atlantic" cooperation is taking place – admittedly with particularly close cooperation and coordination of interests between the two neighbour countries.

The problem-filled phase of the "reconciliation" appears to have been long closed. *Other problems*, which have already been referred to, have taken its place, e.g. tensions in the nuclear age, EC agricultural market, the technological lead of the USA and Japan. And there is the growth of structural unemployment, which cannot be effectively combatted by any individual state (cf. Rovan 1986, p. 187). In addition come new global problems affecting both countries: the North-South disparity, protection of the forests, soil and water – and humans... Unfortunately, there is no coordination of development and environmental policy to speak of between the two nations (despite bilateral or "European" conferences). The results which have been achieved are less than meagre. Are these *new problems* being disregarded in the national and regional decision process? Are attempts being made to cover them up or belittle them at the level of corporative management (with possible tacit toleration by state agencies who are easily intimidated by catchwords such as "job preservation" and sympathize with the demands of competition and self-aggrandizement striving for higher profit margins and dividends?) Does one – in the particularly blatant case of the environmental policy of the French Government, business associations, and trade unions – tend to ignore new problems only because the solutions to the old problems take so much energy?

Among these problems are also French fears regarding Germany fuelled on by lingering memories of *history*. A few insightful words shed light on *French historical awareness* which includes far more "scenes" from the various epochs since the *Gaulois*: «La France est sur le continent le seul pays qui ait évolué précocement et naturellement vers l'unité nationale, évolution renforcée par la Révolution française. Dans les autres pays on pourrait dire que la nation est créée par le ministère de l'éducation nationale, qui construit un passé historique et une langue nationale» (Werner 1985, p. 323; see also 1.1.2 and 1.2).

In contrast to the continuity of French historical consciousness from *Vercingétorix* to *de Gaulle* and on up to the present (cf. Kimmel/Poujol 1982, Verheyen 1992, p. 42f.), the *Federal Republic of Germany* is often said to suffer from a *"loss of history"*. Former Federal President Scheel was not off target when he warned historians, the ministries of culture, as well as all citizens and decision makers in public arena that the Germans could become a "people without a history" (FAZ, 23 Sept. 1976, p. 1).

Due to the historical awareness on the other side of the Rhine which more strongly shapes attitudes, decisions and behaviour than this is conceivable in Germany, French fears concerning the Federal Republic of Germany also have a *more significant* effect. And if one views the consequences in German-French relations, they are more significant than occasional German irritations which from time to time have been aroused by French "attempts to dictate affairs" and French "egotism." (As such, but less openly, these may also be based on a long tradition going back to reactions to the policy of *réunion* of Louis XIV and 19th century "Prussian" historiography.)

If one is to view results of public opinion polls in both countries, reconciliation has long since taken place (see, for example, Koch-Hillebrecht 1977, pp. 56-64 and 257-259; Der Spiegel, 21 Nov. 1977; Tiemann 1981, 1982; Weisenfeld 1986a, pp. 147-149). But this is on the surface. Deeper down partial and total subconscious oppositions have lived on and latent rivalry smoulders. And this appears to be far more so the case in France than in the Federal Republic of Germany. This was demonstrated by Ménudier 1981 with his discussion of the image of Germany in the French media. Four examples: in the majority French vote against the EDC in 1954, there were fears of a recurrence of German militarism (cf. Ziebura 1970, p. 74f.). Around 1973, in the country that was defeated in 1940, the *Ostpolitik* of the Brandt government aroused double fears about a – too strong – reunited Germany and about the loss of the buffer zone to the eastern block (cf. Wilkens 1990). Such "neutralism" would not only endanger the Federal Republic of Germany but also France:

> A Paris, on craint, comme l'indique Pompidou dans sa conférence de presse du 27 septembre 1973, que l'*Ostpolitik* ne détourne la République fédérale de l'Europe et ne permette une réunificaton au prix d'une neutralisation. (cf. Poidevin/Bariéty 1977, p. 338)

The situation awoke memories of the Soviet offer for reunification at the price of military neutrality (in a statement issued by Stalin on 10 March 1952) and of the German-Russian rapprochement in the Treaty of Rapallo (1922). Or possibly memories of the anti-Napoleon Prussian-Russian alliance of Taurog-gen (1812) or even the Hitler-Stalin Pact of 1939?... (cf. here Weisenfeld 1986a, pp. 56-59, 113-121) – In 1977, terrorism, and especially the West German manner of combatting it, awakened old associations of brutality, militarism, and the Prussian police state. Jean Genet's Le Monde article (2 Sept. 1977, p. 1f.) made waves, along with the French campaign against the *Berufsverbot* (a ban from state employment due to radical political views). The (former) French national institution *Le Monde* in which Genet as well as personalities such as A. Grosser and P. de Boisdeffre expressed their views, was answered by *Der Spiegel*, a German national institution, with its familiar, previously-mentioned thorough research... (A propos *Der Spiegel*, this extremely well-publicized edition represents an exception. It must be said that for years before that, the editors of *Der Spiegel* had done very little – to put it mildly – to further the state of French-German reconciliation. Can this be attributed to a Hamburg-Hanseatic point of view – or were the interests of certain advertisement sponsors of Anglo-Saxon origin or "Atlantic" orientation being taken into account?) – Between 1981 and 1985, the demonstrations of the West German peace movement against the deployment of American atomic missiles, the rise of the Greens, and the split position of the SPD all awakened French fears of their neighbouring country being neutralistic and pacifist (cf. J. Julliard: Faut-il avoir peur des Allemands?, Le Nouvel Observateur, 10 Feb. 1984, pp. 37-39, v. Uthmann 1984, Alix/Baier/Jouhy 1985, Rovan 1986, pp. 157-161 and the lit. listed in 7.1.2 under "Munich 1938").

The repeated swings back and forth between the poles of "militarism" and "neutralism" are proof of the deep-seated constancy and omnipresence of the possibility for actualization of historical experience and clichés in French public opinion. The two apparently contradictory tendencies can, in spite of all appearances, be summed up in one expression: the Federal Republic of Germany is not a dependable partner. In addition to this, but never spoken aloud, comes the gaze toward the *géant économique*. Can then this *traditional nation state* work in confidence with *such a "powerful"* but at the same time *so apparently "labile" state*, a state divided until 1990? Putting off periodically recurring French fears as "media-hype" does not help. They lie deeper – in the French history and historical awareness. History, however, is not easily erased. Only patiently worked through history and, at the same time, mutually achieved solutions to current problems can bring the partners closer. Therefore, a deeper-reaching approach to the problem must not only include "Paris" and "Bonn" (Manfrass 1984), but more than until now, regional and local levels, too.

There are already beginnings in the regions. The Rhineland-Palatinate and Burgundy, Lower Saxony and the Normandy, Schleswig-Holstein and Poitou-Charentes, North-Rhine-Westphalia and Champagne-Ardennes, Baden-Württemberg and Rhône-Alpes (expanded by Lombardy and Catalonia on 9 Sept. 1988) all collaborate in various areas as long has been the case with the economically closely knit neighbouring areas of Saarland, Lorraine, and Luxembourg (on *Saar-Lor-Lux-Raum* see Jörg 1989). With the approach of the European domestic market, the number, intensity, and the spectrum of these contacts will widen in spite of differences in governmental organization between the Federal *Länder* and French *régions* (cf. 1.2; for further indications, cf. Düwell 1991, p. 404).

German-French city partnerships (*jumelages*) have increased in number from 1000 (1981) to about 1200 (1987). Half of all city partnerships in Europe exist between the Federal Republic of Germany and France (Ménudier 1988, p. 18). That emphasizes the particularly close ties between the two countries.

There are, however, important differences. The peaceful coexistence with the eastern neighbours and the extension of relations to them is just as important to the citizens of Germany as the relations between France and Germany and the construction of Europe. Opinion polls illuminate the differences in attitude, which are dependent upon geostrategic position and the division of the Germanies (*Table 31*).

Table 31: Political Priorities

	F	GDR
La construction de l'Europe	75	43
Le rapprochement avec les pays de l'Est	11	43
Les relations avec les Etats-Unis	6	8
Sans opinion	7	6

(From: Figaro Magazine 12.11.1988, 111)

A further – and enduring – difference is to be seen in economic priorities. France is understandably interested in decreasing its trade deficit (cf. *Table 29*) by increasing the export of its goods into the FRG. In the long term, it also would like to end the dominance of the Deutschmark over the Franc simply by having the ECU (European currency unit, homonym of the French *écu* ["Thaler"/"Dollar"], the monetary exchange and planning unit of the EC) become the actual standard currency in Europe. To these ends, in January 1988 on the 25th anniversary of the Elysee Treaty, a German-French Economic and Finance Council was formed at the pressure of the French and anchored in a protocol to this treaty (for text, see Schwarz 1988, p. 42f.). Soon thereafter, however, the Deutsche Bundesbank refused to follow the "recommendations" of the Economic and Finance Council. In a verbal statement issued to the French Government on 28 Oct. 1988, the Germans stated that the Economic and Finance Council was to be viewed as a consultative and not as a legislative organ... This is reminiscent of the preamble to the Elysee Treaty, even if its effect are considerably less significant.

In spite of all the progress there still exist profound differences and divergences in interest not only of political but also of economic nature. They have been demonstrated here in two examples which speak for themselves.

Kaelble 1991, pp. 149-245, offers a detailed study of differences – and similarities – in economic and social structure.

7.2.2 Military relations

Are France and the Federal Republic of Germany also unequal partners in military matters? Are they nonetheless faced with the same problems? The first question can be relatively easily answered. The following is a quote from Helga Wex, former coordinator, now deceased, of German-French cooperation (*Text 29*).

T. 29:
Admittedly, patterns in the two states - Germany and France - are only to certain extent analogous. France is a strategic nuclear power, a founding member of the United Nations with veto power in the Security Council and one of the protecting powers in Berlin. Its military interests outside of Europe demonstrate its interest in being a world power which, however, can only to a limited extent be compared to the USA and the USSR. Germany is not a world power, does not want to and can not be one. Germany is divided and the Federal Republic of Germany is a median power in Europe, but nonetheless, due to its economic power, with world-wide interests (cf. Wex 1985, p. 6).

Further factors must be added to this. With its 1954 entry into NATO and the West European Union (WEU), the Federal Republic of Germany had to forgo atomic, biological, and chemical weapons. It agreed to the regulation of arms controls placed upon it by the WEU and to the continued deployment of troops from the USA, Great Britain, France, and Canada on German soil. Its armed forces were placed under the control of NATO's Supreme Commander. This mode of entering NATO took into account French security wishes following the failure of the EDC. France, on the other hand, withdrew from the NATO integrated command structure in 1966. It is important, however, to emphasize that it never left NATO. Its armed forces are represented at all levels of this organization and take part in all of its exercises.

Under these conditions, a harmonization of military interests as it was envisaged in the 1963 Treaty, could never succeed. Nonetheless, there has been an increase in *cooperation with respect to armaments* (see Benecke/Krafft 1986). In fact, both countries are confronted with similar problems:

- a reduction in dependency on the USA and a strengthening of their own capabilities even at the price of foregoing "cheaper" arms imports,
- full utilization of production capacity of the two countries arms industries due to increased production, but also
- problems with competition and financing of joint projects. These have already lead to the failure of diverse bi- and multilateral tank and aeronautic projects.

In contrast to the dominant conventional, only punctually limited "nuclear" doctrine of NATO, the French doctrine of deterrence is based on the two equally weighted components of its *force de frappe*: tactical atomic weapons and strategic atomic weapons, most of which are based at sea. The *force de frappe* and the tenet of *dissuasion nucléaire*, which have been elevated to symbols of patriotic consensus, pertain only to French territory. France will offer no formal guarantee for the territory of the Federal Republic of Germany, a point which was clearly stated in 1984 and reiterated in 1986. As a result, it can and will not expect German financial assistance for its costly nuclear arsenal. Private theories of French military and politicians to this effect have been consistently disclaimed. They would necessarily implicate German co-determination. Yet France has made some cautious moves toward the Federal Republic of Germany in the area of military strategy since 1984. The newly formed conventional *Force d'Action Rapide* (FAR, 47,000 troops) will not only be available in areas of the former French colonial empire or in the Middle East, but, when needed, will also thrust forward "to the Elbe" (Benecke/Krafft 1986, p. 184). The French president has declared that since 27-28 Febr. 1986, he has been prepared to briefly consult the Federal Chancellor before deploying *tactical* atomic missiles over the territory of the Federal Republic of Germany. He reserves, however, the final decision for himself alone. Comforting perspectives... Both nations have spoken out, as European cultural powers, in favour of disarmament, eg in June 1986 with the concerted protest against Reagan's attempted breach of the SALT II Treaty.

The process of disarmament that was finally initiated with the Soviet-American INF Treaty on 8 Dec. 1987 and both parties' consequent withdrawal of land-based medium-range missiles from Europe (and their world-wide elimination) provoked a certain degree of apprehension in Bonn and Paris. Was it not possible that a "vacuum" could develop in view of conventional superiority on the part of the Warsaw pact? Against this background, France has been intensifying military cooperation with the Federal Republic of

Germany in the area of conventional forces since 1987. Three spectacular events took place, partly preceding and partly subsequent to the INF Treaty:

- the military manoeuvre "Bold Sparrow" (September 1987) was the largest bilateral military exercise ever held, with approximately 20,000 French soldiers coming mainly from the new FAR and about 55,000 German soldiers (see Dokumente 44, p. 290f.),
- the foundation of a bilateral Council on Security and Defense in January 1988, along with the establishment of the Council on Economics and Finance (see 7.2.1; Text of protocol in Schwarz 1988, p. 41f.),
- the formation of a German-French Brigade, officially on 21 Nov. 1988; as of October 1990 it comprised 4200 soldiers.

This intensified military cooperation was subject to various interpretations (see, for example, Kaiser/Lellouche 1988 and Schwarz 1988, Ménudier 1988, p. 14-16, or, conversely, Baier 1988, p. 20f, and Ruf 1988). A fact often overlooked in the Federal Republic of Germany was that France had demanded a price for the extension of its military protection to the Federal Republic of Germany: the economic intercession of the Federal Republic of Germany to support the value of the Franc with the still longer-term goal of a common European currency in mind (concerning which, cf. 7.3.1).

Finally, three significant reasons can be mentioned for the phenomena surrounding dissent – from the perspective of 1988/89 - on the issue of the *Ostpolitik* (cf. also *Table 31*) and, for the French, fears of a *dérive allemande* (literally, a "German drift [to the East]" caused by tendencies toward reunification and neutrality):

1. Due to the French withdrawal from the NATO integrated command structure, France needs a partner who is solidly integrated in the NATO to act as a kind of bridge and is for this reason oversensitive to developments in *Ostpolitik* as well as anti-American demonstrations in the neighbouring country. Starting in 1966, cooperation on security policy between the two countries became "primarily a kind of bilateral crisis management to bridge the gap which had opened due to the French policy of nuclear autonomy on the one hand and the military integration in NATO on the other" (cf. Kolboom 1986, p. 22).

2. The Western bond of the Federal Republic of Germany is in accordance with French interests. It represents a buffer zone since for the first time in its history France is in the "rear", the "second link" (according to the scheme, the *one* side would defend itself, the *other* side would attack...).

3. "German-French relations since the early fifties have established an internal equilibrium dependent upon the division of Germany, Western integration of the Federal Republic of Germany, and the *préponderance légitime* of the victor and protector, France. Anything which, in the French view, could upset this balance, is a threat to the cooperation which has functioned for years, and thereby to the role of France as a European leader. For this reason, the *Ostpolitik* has always been an area of French-German relations which has required the utmost in care" (cf. Kolboom 1986a, p. 151).

The French interests in cooperation, security and power – or more precisely, the interests of the *classe politique* from the Socialists to the Neogaullists – led to a wish to preserve the status quo. A divided Germany, a Federal Republic of Germany integrated into the Western world and French military superiority: from the French point of view, these were the three essentials in relations between the two countries. However, it is not only the German *Ostpolitik* but also its *Westpolitik* and particularly the country's "too strong" a leaning toward and adaption to the United States which were – and will continue to be – followed with scrutiny. This holds especially true for the area of defense. As such, Bonn's foreign and security policy, which aims at cooperating with France and taking French interests into consideration, can truly be called a tightrope-walk.

7.2.3 Cultural relations

As an introduction, reference is made to the Journal *Dokumente* 42, Oct. 1986 and a critical dossier in the *Frankfurter Rundschau* on 28 Oct. 1986. Both highlight developments, weaknesses, and progress in cultural relations with regard to the French-German Cultural Summit on 27-28 Oct. 1986. Further orientation is offered in Ménudier 1988, p. 14-18 and 22. Menyesch/Manac'h (1984) have also prepared an extensive *bibliography*. Düwell/Pépin (1985ff.) list all important contact addresses and information and documentation concerning study abroad in France as well as German-French cultural and youth exchange programs. Two *yearly updated*, free-of-charge *information booklets* should be mentioned: *Begegnung und Austausch mit Franzosen* (Deutsch-Französisches Jugendwerk, Rhöndorfer Str. 23, D-53604 Bad Honnef) and *Studium in Frankreich* (Deutscher Akademischer Austauschdienst, Kennedyallee 50, D-53175 Bonn). *Bilateral institutions* are briefly portrayed in the brochure *Wege zur Freundschaft* put out by the Auswärtiges Amt, Public Relations Department, Bonn 1985.

Orientation on *the problems of foreign language instruction* in the two countries is given, to mention only two, in Olbert 1990 and Maillard 1986. For *images of France and Germany* (heterostereotypes) as perceived by school-age children, see Tiemann 1981 and 1982, in school books see Krauskopf 1985, in caricatures, cf. Ronge/Deligne 1987 and Dietrich/Fekl 1988. For the *translation and reception of German literature in France after 1945*, see Knoblauch-Foulquier 1981, 1983, and 1986, as well as Schonauer 1965, Hammer 1983, Morita-Clément 1985 and Neuschäfer 1990, pp. 48-52. Representative of a number of analyses on the Heidegger debate around 1987 would be Baier 1988, p. 103-124. For *translation and reception of French literature in the FRG after 1945*, see Kohut 1983, Nies 1983, Kohut 1982-84, esp. vol. 2, Kortländer/Nies 1986, Jurt/Ebel/Erzgräber 1989 and Neuschäfer 1990, pp. 52-55. *On reactions to French philosophy since 1945*, cf. Gebauer 1989 and Christadler 1990.

For reasons of space, only the culturally-related dates from *Chronological Table 3* will be handled here.

The *Bureau international de liaison et de documentation* B.I.L.D. (formed by the Jesuit father, Jean de Rivau) and the Cologne-based *Gesellschaft für Übernationale Zusammenarbeit* which soon split off of B.I.L.D. – both societies are still very active today – should be mentioned as being representative for all the groups that have created a foundation upon which reconciliation between the two nations through the self-organization of contacts, meetings, and exhibitions can be based. *German-French Societies* and city partnerships – the first in 1949 between Montbéliard and Ludwigsburg – continued the process of moving closer. The most important result and, at the same time, an indisputable success of the German-French Treaty in the area of culture was the foundation of the *Deutsch-Französisches Jugendwerk* (*Office franco-allemand pour la Jeunesse*), whose yearly budget is equally shared by the two countries. More than four million young Germans and French have taken part in 130,000 activities sponsored by the DFJW, such as group encounters, work and study stays, or seminars. Understanding among the younger generations of the two nations – not only among school and university students but more and more since the end of the sixties also among working youth – has been aided by the numerous impulses from these experiences. The results of the cultural part of the treaty with respect to *foreign language instruction in the two partner nations* has been less positive. Between 1963 and the school year of 1981/82, the absolute number of school students learning a partner language tripled in the Federal Republic of Germany. In France, with a procentually higher starting point, it doubled. This, however, correlates to the growth in school enrolment during this period. Furthermore, the *Hamburg Agreement* between the governments of the German Länder excluded French as a first foreign language in the schools. This agreement was reached at a time when bilateral relations had undergone drastic deterioration (see 7.2.1). The standardization of the educational system also played a dispositive role in this situation. The Hamburg Agreement was not *revised* until *1971*. Apparently, this was among the concessions made to the former chief of state, Pompidou. All in all, the results of this revision have to be characterized as meagre. The push for larger classes and the reduction of instruction time have hampered the F1 classes. The more favourable showing for German as a *first* foreign language in France (e.g. 13.1% of state-run and 7.3% of privately operated secondary school students as opposed to 2.5% of German students in F1 tracks [figures from 1987/88]) can be explained for the most part by the factor Alsace-Lorraine. Moreover, Spanish has long outranked German as a second and third foreign language in France. But most of all, instruction of respective partner languages in both lands is suffering due to the *overwhelming preponderance of English*. One might ask if the *French-German Gymnasiums* formed after the revision of the Hamburg Agreement (first in Saarbrücken in 1972, afterwards in Freiburg in 1975 and in Buc, near Versailles, in 1981), as well as bilingual tracks in 23 German *Gymnasiums* and 130 French *lycées* (1983) and, for example, French instruction in elementary schools near the border in Baden-Württemberg since 1984, are just token gestures, as welcome as they may be.

The Frankfurt Summit in October 1986 – also called the "Cultural Summit" – was hardly enough to inspire wide-spread interest in learning the partner languages and increasing mutual knowledge of the other country. The speakers made reference to the great importance of this. Two committees were formed to further cooperation and mutual understanding. Their status, however, was not upgraded with a protocol to the Elysee Treaty as was the case with the Economic and Defense Council. Since January 1988, a bilateral *university-level college* – centred in Mainz and Strasbourg – is supposed to be enriching the offerings of common programs of study and the "Integrated Studies" option (with consequent mutual recognition in both countries). The long-planned *German-French Cultural Council* could not be set up until two years after the "Cultural Summit". Its purpose is to support and inspire, among other things, mutual art exhibitions, the translation of selected literary works as well as co-productions in the area of film and television.

7.3 *Relations since 1989: building on a new foundation*

Chronological Table 4: German-French relations since 1989

1989	The wall comes down (9 Nov.), dissent concerning the course and the rate of German unity (beginning Dec.)
1990	Agreements on withdrawal of French troops from Germany and the German-French cultural channel (17/18 Sept.); "two-plus-four talks"; declaration of sovereignty by the 4 allied powers (1 Oct.), the new federal states join the Federal Republic of Germany/ German unity (3 Oct.)
1991	Maastricht Agreement on founding the European Union (Dec.)
1992	The German-French cultural channel, *ARTE*, begins broadcasting (30 May)

German Unity marked the beginning of a new phase in German-French relations. It not only brought about a new balance in economic and political terms, but also called into question the previous understanding: French nuclear and military might as "compensation" for German economic might.

Concerning the first set of changes, Meyer-Kalkus (1990, p. 148) speaks his mind without recourse to any of the customary diplomatic meandering: "If the economic leadership of Germany in Europe has, until now, been counterbalanced by the French role as political leaders (at least in the eyes of Paris), this is a balance that no longer exists." Unified Germany has gained noticeably in political significance. American experts are already speculating about whether Germany might not be able to relieve the USA in its cost-intensive role as maintainer of order on this side of the Atlantic. The clearest indication of the shift in balance thus far is the way Bonn took the lead in recognising Croatia and Slovenia. The remaining EC nations followed suit (some, like France, with initial reluctance). Libération (15 Jan. 1992, p. 22) did not mince words: «En reconnaissant la Croatie et la Slovénie, l'Allemagne a tourné une page de sa politique extérieure, jusque-là embryonnaire. Une attitude, très discutée, qui a ravivié des craintes.»

Dominique Moïsi, an expert from the *Institut Français des Relations Internationales*, coined a fitting slogan for another counterbalance to German economic strength, i.e. French military power: *«équilibre de la bombe et du mark»*. This issue is discussed by Kramer (1991, p. 916). Now this "balance" has also become debatable. Briefly stated, the collapse of the Eastern Block has even left many Frenchmen questioning the sense of an expensive *force de frappe*; and military expenditure has already dropped slightly. Certainly one can understand historically the deep-rootedness of the military in France's political culture, can take note of indications of continuing "incertitudes" in the aftermath of the Gulf war and pursuant to the dissolution of the Eastern Block. The manifold interconnections between military and civilian activities all the way to the DOM-TOM (cf. the discussion in Chpt. 1) should perhaps be borne in mind as well. Becker (1991) outlines all of these differences to Germany. His unequivocal conclusion is that no serious steps towards disarmament are to be expected from the French side. Nevertheless, maintaining dominance in armaments places a heavy burden on France. It tends to promote the German "economic hegemony". It further strengthens imbalance at a time when Europe has ceased to be a testing ground for two Blocks matching their

Translation: "So what's on the agenda?"
Fig. 81: Caricature on EC Summit Meeting in April 1990
(From: Plantu 1990, p. 77)

strength and talk of an ominous communist threat has ceased to be a drawing card. In this respect, it appears that Germany is "better armed for the future than her neighbour and closest ally to the west" (Becker 1991, p. 223).

There is, then, still concern about a united Germany assuming a position of supremacy. Plantu's caricature of the EC summit in Dublin (28 April 1990), with "the two Germanies" and an "allied" Gorbachov perched on the shoulders of the gigantic Chancellor (cf. *Fig. 81*), expresses the sentiment clearly. This concern may have been assuaged for the next few years in view of the difficult, expensive and arduous process of adjustment and of raising living conditions in the new federal states to "West German standards". Once the process is complete, this concern will re-emerge with all the more intensity. For the powerful centre of the continent has a dynamics of its own feared by *all* of its neighbours – and not only by France as the second strongest economic force in the EC (cf. *Fig. 82*). The veritable "run" of neutral and former "eastern" nations on the EC has to be understood in this context (cf. *Fig. 87*). It automatically puts the nation at the centre of Europe in a privileged position, as is already becoming apparent with the spread of German throughout middle and eastern Europe. This facilitates contacts and simplifies the realisation of economic and political projects. Is the much decried *hégémonie allemande* a threat after all?

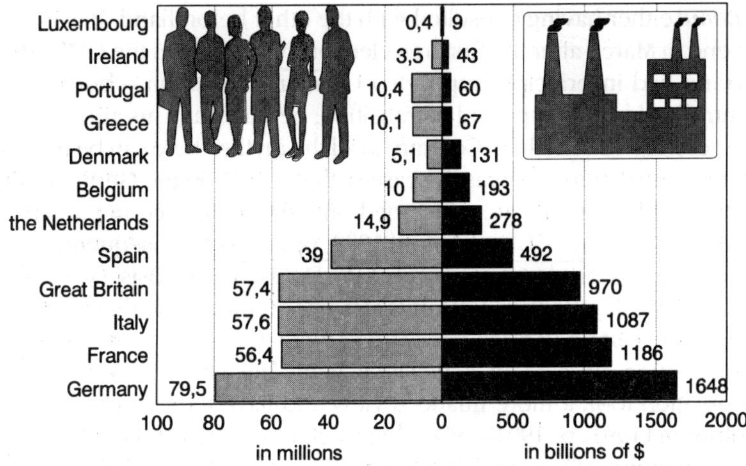

Fig. 82: Population and Economic Performance within the EC (1990)

In any case, this concern explains *the great efforts made by France* to involve *la grosse Allemagne* or *la grande Allemagne* (the phrase reminiscent of *das Großdeutsche Reich*) in EC co-operation. This course already became clear in April/May 1990, with a majority of the French population supporting it. The Kohl-Genscher "team" countered with the slogan *«wiedervereinigtes Deutschland im geeinten Europa»* ("reunited Germany in a unified Europe"). This phrase eased the minds of all the nations affected – and was necessary to achieve German unity during negotiations with the allied powers (the "two-plus-four talks") in the first place. But this slogan was not at all mere rhetoric; it reflected the conviction of those bearing responsibility. Thus, after a relatively short "ice age", French and German interests were again able to co-operate in working towards European unification.

The bilateral co-operation since 1990 – which could only be sketched in outline here due to space restrictions – must be viewed against this new background.

7.3.1 Political and economic relations

Three points must be added to what has been said above:

1. The "ice age" began when Kohl introduced his Ten Point Plan for German reunification and Mitterrand took his trip to Kiev and the GDR

without either having consulted with the other beforehand. It came to an end in March after the first free elections were held in the GDR. Mitterrand had in principle supported German unification – but with a controlled long-term period of transition; he now gave his approval to the accelerated schedule. Contrary to all the myths, there can be no talk of an "obstruction". As was the case with the SPD on the German side of the border, the debate concerned only the timing (cf. in particular Kolboom 1991, p. 45f. and Arnold 1992, pp. 29-31). Subsequently, the agreed points predominated – cf. XIV. Deutsch-Französische Konferenz, 28-30 May 1990, p. 1991. It is also important to note that the Paris media and certain Parisian intellectuals were the only ones to paint the reunification process in a negative light; the vast majority of the population took a more nuanced view and gave their assent overall. Kolboom (1991, p. 1991a) was able to demonstrate this conclusively.

2. Economically, France has been able to reap a great deal of profit from German unity. Because of increasing demand for Western goods (particularly cars, household appliances, clothing and food) in the new federal states, French exports to Germany have risen; in 1990, for example, they comprised 17.2% of overall exports (cf. *Table 29*). In 1991 there was a further increase. This has brought about a marked decrease in the French trade deficit over against Germany (cf. *Table 29* and 3.6). Of course, only the future will show whether this trend continues. Beyond this, the French economy has become the single most important foreign investor in the new federal states (for details, cf. Forster/Strauch 1991; Becker/Neise 1992).

With the single market fast approaching, handbooks "by experts for experts" providing an orientation on economic practices in the country next door are experiencing a boom. Particularly worthy of note are, on the German side, Moog 1991, and on the French side, Bommensath 1991. These two works are at the same time a real find for those with a penchant for either autostereotypes or heterostereotypes; regrettably, their effectiveness in entrepreneurial circles cannot be denied.

3. The most important event in view of the years to come – also from the perspective of German-French relations – is the *Maastricht agreement*, founding the European Union. It was signed by the heads of state and government leaders within the EC. It is above all a result of German-French co-operation (motivated by reasons outlined above). This is not widely broadcast out of deference to other EC partners, but remains a fact of which London, The Hague and Rome are all aware. And should "Maastricht" fail to be ratified by a parliament within the

EC, further negotiations will follow; the general thrust remains clear. It can be summarised as follows: 1.) Economic and Currency Union (Gr. WWU = Wirtschafts- und Währungsunion; Fr. UEM = Union économique et monétaire), with a common European currency (according to the resolution, no later than 1999) and a European central bank; 2.) on the basis of the Economic and Currency Union: a political union of confederate character with closer co-operation in foreign, legislative, internal and defense policy (for details, cf. Thiel 1992). With these measures, a lot will have been done to strengthen the EC and involve Germany in the process of European unity – even if there may be divergence of opinion regarding details of the economic and currency union on opposing sides of the Rhine (cf. the analysis of Brodersen 1991). Further German-French proposals up for debate at the Maastricht conference, specifically the plan for a European army corps as military support for the Political Union, must be regarded more as gestures of solidarity; in 1991 at least, they had scarcely a chance of being implemented (Brigouleix 1991, p. 439).

7.3.2 Military relations

The initial result of German unity was the withdrawal of French troops from south-west Germany and Berlin. With this, the post-war period also came to an end in terms of military relations. However, the German-French Brigade is now to form the core of a German-French army corps of from 20,000 to 50,000 men. This gives expression to the conviction that – despite the reserve of other EC partners – the European Union will sooner or later have to expand to include a military force. So the plans are being pursued further. The German-French co-ordination is suffering, however, as a result of old differences in defence policy: France wishes to keep the corps independent of the NATO chain of command, while Germany favours bringing it under the NATO roof, supported by both a European and a North American column. Yet France acceded so much to US policy during the Gulf War that it amounted to a break with Gaullist dogma, so there is still room for hope (Kramer 1991, p. 986f.). First of all, though, the differences in structure and mentality within the Brigade itself will have to be overcome. Several contributions in Klein (1990) offer a vivid account of these differences.

If the large army corps agreed on in October 1991 still remains "the music of tomorrow", armament co-operation suffers no less from the lack of a common concept (Carton 1991, p. 385). The only exceptions are to be found among large conglomerates. The joint founding of what has become the second largest manufacturer of military helicopters in the world is an outstanding example. The company, *Eurocopter S.A.* resulted from a co-operation between MBB (Daimler-Benz, 40%) and Aérospatiale (60%).

7.3.3 Cultural relations

Changes in this area have been less dramatic than in the political sector. Nevertheless, they have left their mark. One can speak of a *twofold movement* towards the east. French interest in Germany has grown as a result of the reunification process. Studying in the neighbouring country has become more popular. Germany exerts almost as much appeal on the younger generation as do the USA and Japan. In the ex-GDR, a number of new *Instituts français* have been established (in Leipzig, Dresden and Rostock, with Erfurt a possibility for the near future). But there is also a movement towards the east in *Germany*: due to the collapse of the communist block, "middle and eastern Europe have become a new pole of attraction, absorbing [German] energies" (Meyer-Kalkus 1990, p. 147). New Goethe Institutes, university lectureships etc. from Budapest to Moscow all cost money, and the cultural budget will, in the final analysis, be for the account of West European nations. This too nourishes old fears of German power aspirations (Meyer-Kalkus 1990, p. 148; Valance 1990, p. 199), making initiative from the German side, particularly in the cultural sector, all the more important.

Such steps should include realization of existing projects in Ludwigsburg (*Deutsche Frankreich-Bibliothek*) and in Freiburg (*Frankreichzentrum der Universität*; on these two projects, cf. Düwell 1991, p. 399f.). A new combined centre for research on France has also been established at the Mainz university library. The study of Romance languages has intensified at universities in the east of Germany – at least in terms of student numbers. Concerning the role of French in schools, however, all hopes were dashed. Only about 10% of all pupils in the old federal states learn French, while figures for the new states are currently at only 4.1% (cf. fh 23, 85; concerning the reasons, cf. Utermark 1991, Wittmann 1991, Stübs 1992).

The results have turned out better for bilateral organizations (cf. the overview in Bock 1989). The *Deutsch-Französisches Jugendwerk* has developed new programs focused on the East German states, addressed many potential intermediaries and made concerted efforts to encourage participation of the youth from the new federal states at meetings and seminars. This emphasis is also reflected in the record budget, in 1991 for example, DM 46.2 m. The *Jugendwerk* is also working out new programs with the East European countries. In view of the single market, emphasis has also been placed on multi-cultural encounter and the participation of youth from other countries such as Italy and Spain (OFAJ 1991). The *Deutsch-Französisches Hochschulkolleg* (university-level college, cf. 7.2.3) has provided considerable support for its integrated courses of study in the technical and economic sectors. The German-French Cultural Council has also intensified its activities (cf. Europäische Zeitung, Jan. 1990, p. 22), and the German-French cultural channel commences broadcasting at the end of May 1992 (cf. 6.2.9). These bilateral institutions are thus proving themselves stable coordinators and are demonstrating that a German drift towards the east, feared by the French, is only relative. The German-French-Polish initiatives already active in the political and cultural sector could also contribute in this respect. The three foreign ministers meet regularly. And the *Deutsch-Französisches Jugendwerk* has initiated a cooperation with the newly founded *Deutsch-Polnisches Jugendwerk*.

Appendix: Historical Charts

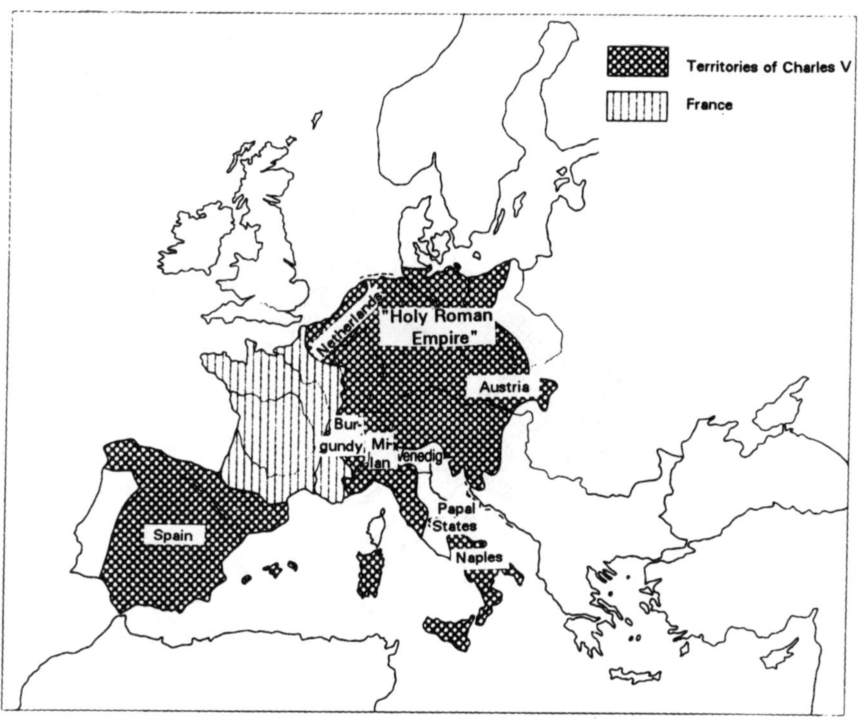

Fig. 83: The Possessions of Charles V and France

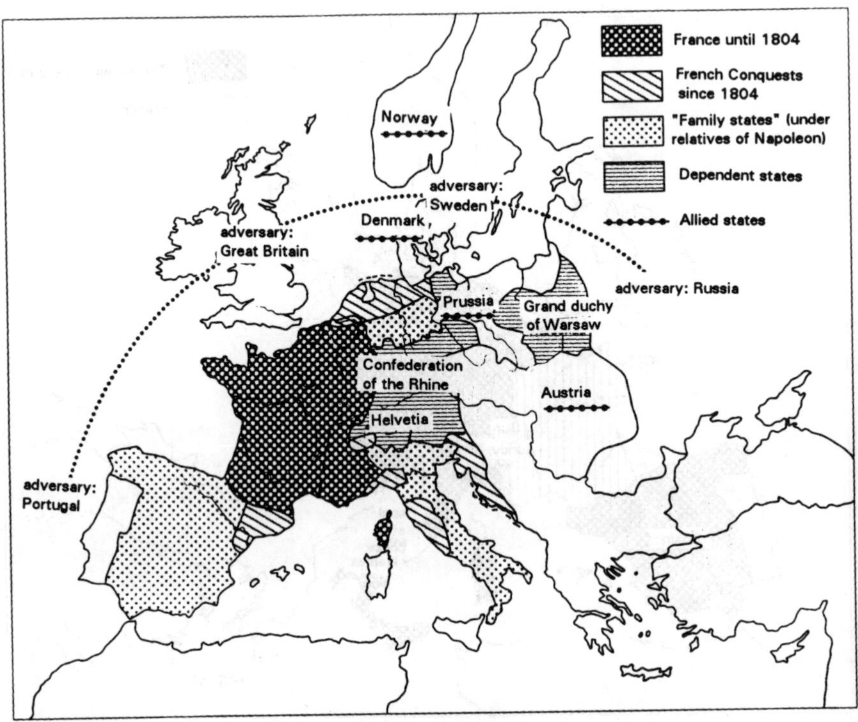

Fig. 84: Europe at the Time of the Empire of Napoleon I, 1812
(From: dtv-Atlas zur Weltgeschichte II, p. 26)

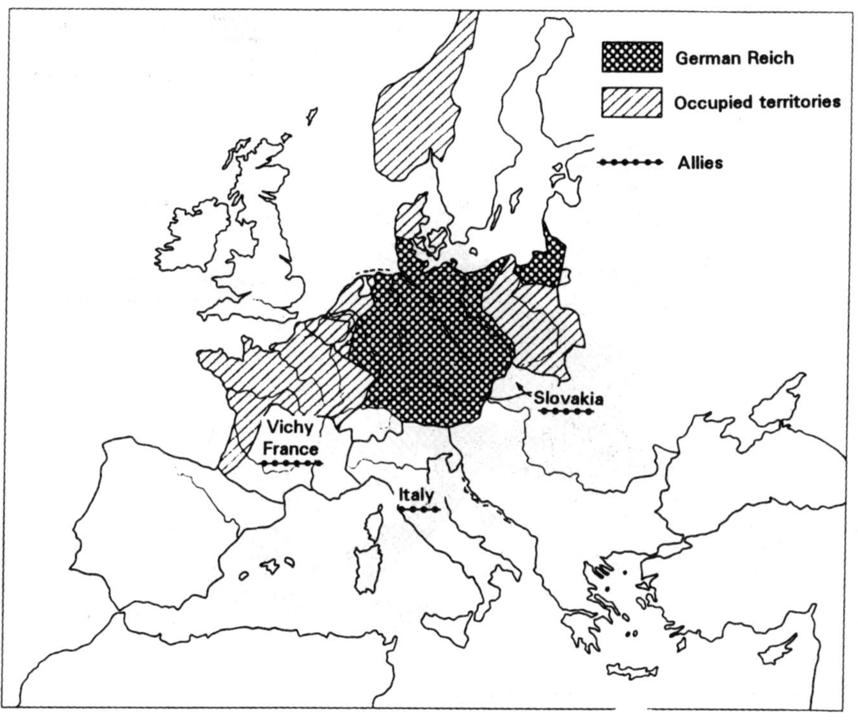

Fig. 85: The German *Reich* and the Division of France (as of 22 June 1940).

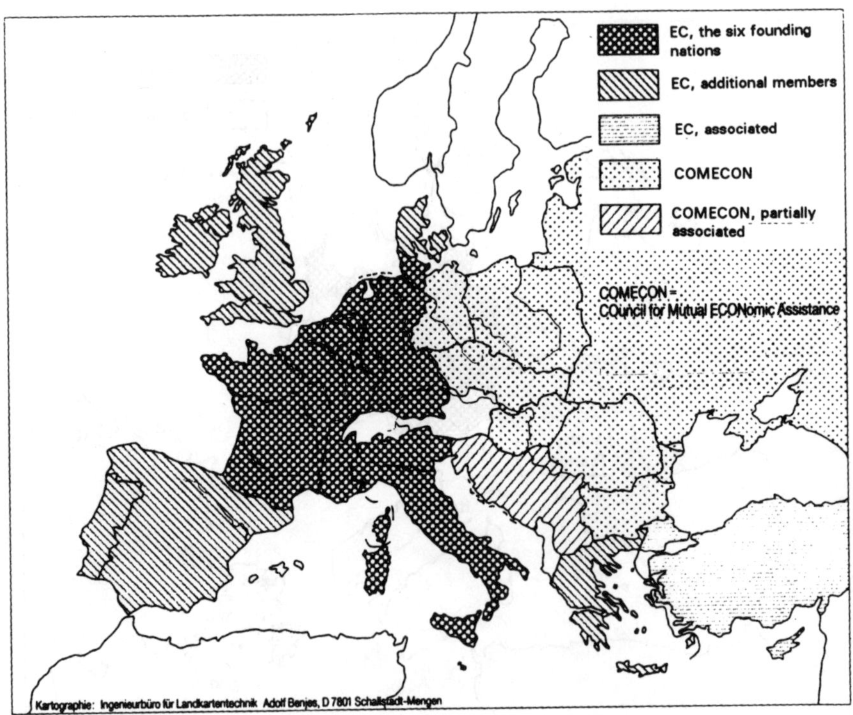

Fig. 86: European Communities in 1986.

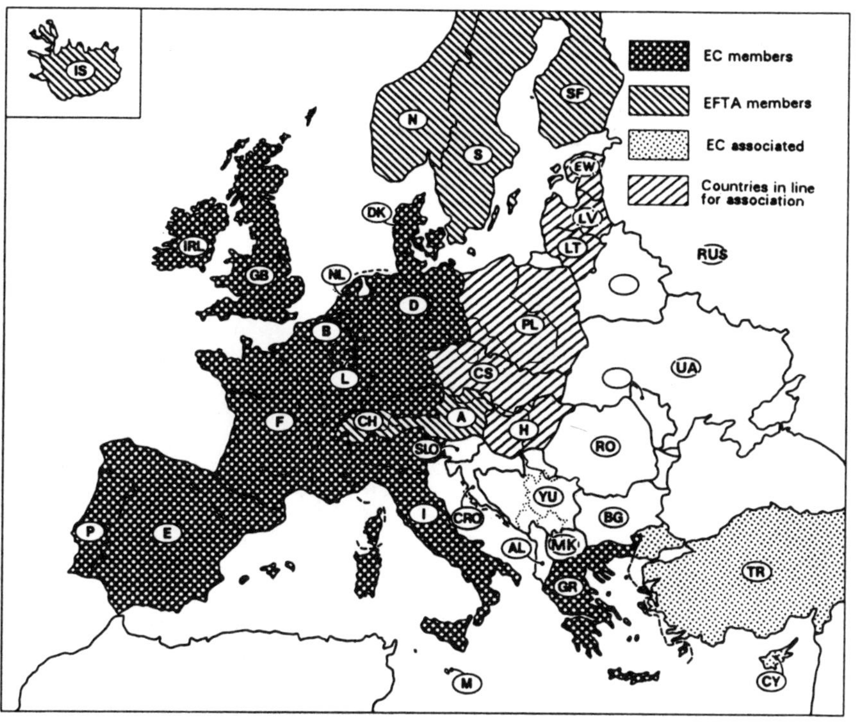

Fig. 87: European Communities in 1991

EC: now called European Union (EU),
CS: now divided into Czech Rep. (CZ) and Slov. Rep. (SK)
Byelorussia and Moldavia: still without country's identification sign

Bibliography

The index only lists the literature used in the individual chapters. *Systematically ordered bibliographies* can be found in Lasserre 1978, Christ et al. 1978, Schmidt et al. 1983, Picht/Neumann 1984, Hertel 1986; cf. also: Sozialwissenschaftliche Informationen 19/4 (1990), p. 247ff., Frankreich-Jahrbuch 1990f. Schmidt et al. 1983, p. 459ff. supplies *references* to periodicals, statistics, etc. that might serve *to update* the information provided here. Finally, Düwell/Pépin 1985ff. name useful institutions of information and contact.

Abbreviations

apuz	Aus Politik und Zeitgeschichte
BO	Bulletin Officiel du Ministère de l'Education Nationale
CEN	Cahiers de l'Education Nationale
CF	Les cahiers français
DF	La Documentation française
fh	Französisch heute
FrM	Le Français dans le Monde
ME	Le Monde de l'Education
PrAct	Presse Actualité
RegAct	Regards sur l'Actualité

Adam, G./J. D. Reynaud (1978): Conflits du travail et changement social. Paris: P.U.F.

Albersmeier, F. J. (1985): Die Herausforderung des Films an die französische Literatur, vol. 1: Die Epoche des Stummfilms (1895-1930). Heidelberg: Winter.

Albert, P. ([9]1991): La presse. Paris: P.U.F.

Albert, P./C. Leteinturier (1979): La presse française. Paris: DF.

Albertin, L. (1988): Frankreichs Regionalisierung – Abschied vom Zentralismus? in: Frankreich-Jahrbuch, 135-156.

Alberts, J. (1972): Massenpresse als Ideologiefabrik am Beispiel 'Bild'. Frankfurt a.M.: Athenäum.

Alexander, G. (1979): Das Kino im Zeitalter seiner elektronischen Reproduzierbarkeit, in: H. Kreuzer/K. Prümm, 140-154.

Alix, Ch./L. Baier/E. Jouhy (ed.) (1985): Sehfehler links? Über die deutsch-französische Mißverständigung. Gießen: Focus.

Ambrosius, G. (1983): Das Wirtschaftssystem, in: W. Benz (ed.): Die Bundesrepublik Deutschland, vol. 1. Frankfurt a. M.: Fischer, 238-297.

Ammon, G. (1989): Der französische Wirtschaftsstil. München: Eberhard.

Amouroux, H. (1976ff.): La grande histoire des Français sous l'occupation, 10 vols. Paris: Laffont.

Ardagh, J. (1968): The New French Revolution. A Social & Economic Survey of France 1945-1967. London: Secker & Warburg..

Armengaud, A. (²1976): La population française au XIXe siècle. Paris: P.U.F.

Armengaud, A./A. Fine (⁶1983): La population française au XXe siècle. Paris: P.U.F.

Arnold, H. (1992): L'amitié à l'épreuve – Das deutsch-französische Verhältnis im Jahr des osteuropäischen Umbruchs 1989/90, in: fh 23, 27-37.

Aron, R. (1959): Immuable et changeante – de la IVe à la Ve République. Paris: Calmann-Lévy.

Asholt, W./H. Thoma (ed.) (1990): Frankreich. Ein unverstandener Nachbar (1945-1990). Bonn: Romanistischer Verlag.

Aurin, K. (1978): Sekundarschulwesen: Strukturen, Entwicklungen und Probleme. Stuttgart: Kohlhammer.

Bachy, J. P. (1981): Ansätze zur Unternehmensreform, in: R. Lasserre u. a., vol. 2, 213-263.

Bade, K.J. (1983): Vom Auswanderungsland zum Einwanderungsland? Berlin: Colloquium.

Bär, H./M. Beutter u.a. (ed.) (1989): Etudes Françaises – Horizons. Stuttgart: Klett.

Baier, L. (1988): Firma Frankreich. Berlin: Wagenbach.

Balle, F./G. Eymery (1984): Les nouveaux médias. Paris: P.U.F.

Bariéty, J. (1989): Die deutsch-französische Geschichte im 19. und 20. Jahrhundert und die Französische Revolution, in: Geschichte in Wissenschaft und Unterricht 40, 385-393.

Baron, St. (1981): Nach dem Sieg Mitterrands – Parti Socialiste: Dogma oder Sozialdemokratie? in: Dokumente 37, 109-114.

Barthel, E./J. Dikau (1980): Mitbestimmung in der Wirtschaft. Berlin: Colloquium.

Bauer, I./H.Walter (n.d. [1984]): Où ça se trouve? Frankfurt a. M.: Hirschgraben.

Baumier, J. (1983): Economie: les leçons d'un 'miracle', in: G. Sandoz, 103-135.

BDZV (Bundesverband Deutscher Zeitungsverleger) (ed.) (1991): Zeitungen '91. Bonn.

Becker, J. M. (ed.) (1985): Das französische Experiment. Linksregierung in Frankreich 1981 bis 1985. Berlin/Bonn: Dietz.

Becker, J. M. (1991): Das Ende des militärischen Flirts?, in: Frankreich-Jahrbuch, 219-224.

Becker, J. M./V. Neise (1992): Frankreich bleibt an der Spitze der Auslandsinvestoren in Ostdeutschland, in: Dokumente 48, 112-120.

Beckmeier, C. (1991): Entscheidungsverflechtung an Hochschulen – Determinanten der Entscheidungsprozesse an bundesdeutschen und französischen Hochschulen am Beispiel der Studiengangsentwicklung, in: Lendemains 62, 132-146.

Becquart-Leclercq, J. (1989): Kommunalpolitik in Frankreich: Die Dezentralisation und ihre Folgen, in: Landeszentrale für politische Bildung Baden-Württemberg, 187-220.

Benchenane, M. (1984): L'émigration maghrébine, trait d'union entre l'Europe et le Monde arabe? in: fh 15, 207-218.

Benecke, L./U. Krafft (1986): Erfolge und Enttäuschungen bei der Zusammenarbeit in Rüstung und Technologie, in: E. Weisenfeld, 176-194.

Benoit, J. M./P. Benoit/J. M. Lech (1986): La politique à l'affiche. Affiches électorales et publicité politique 1965-1986. Paris: du May.

Bernard, C. (1988): Magistères: Les grandes écoles à la fac, in: Sciences et Vie Economie 41, 74-78.

Berschin, H./J. Felixberger/H. Goebl (1978): Französische Sprachgeschichte. München: Hueber.

Bertaux, P. (1973): Universités françaises et allemandes – musées ou laboratoires d'une société européenne? in: Documents 6, 51-68.

de Bertier de Sauvigny, G. (1977): Histoire de France. Paris: Flammarion.

Bertrand, Y. (1984): Germanistische Zeitschriften in Frankreich, in: Informationen Deutsch als Fremdsprache 2, 56-64.

Betz, A. (1986): Exil und Engagement. München: edition text + kritik.

von Beyme, K. ([5]1980): Interessengruppen in der Demokratie. München: Piper.

– (1991): Das politische System der Bundesrepublik Deutschland nach der Vereinigung. München: Piper.

Beywl, W./H. Brombach (1982): Kritische Anmerkungen zur Theorie der Alternativpresse, in: Publizistik 27, 551-569.

Bing, J.M. (1984): Die Schwemme der privaten Rundfunksender, in: Dokumente 40, 317-320.

Binoche, J. (1990): De Gaulle et les Allemands. Bruxelles: Editions Complexe.

Bischoff, J. (Hrsg.) (1976): Die Klassenstruktur der Bundesrepublik Deutschland. Berlin: VSA.

Blanc-Uchan, O. (1987): Le nouveau statut de la presse écrite, in: RegAct 131, 25-35.

Bluche, F./St. Rials (1983): Fausses droites, centres morts et vrais modérés dans la vie politique française contemporaine, in: Revue de recherche juridique 3, 611-626.

Bock, H.M. (1974): Zur Neudefinition landeskundlichen Erkenntnis Interesses, in: R. Picht et al. (ed.): Perspektiven der Frankreichkunde. Tübingen: Niemeyer, 13-22.

Bock, H. M. (1975): Neopoujadismus, in: Lendemains 2, 54-76.

– (1978): Gaullismus und Bonapartismus, in: Lendemains 10, 89-100.

– (1988): Die stufenweise Auflösung der Linksunion und die Perspektiven in Frankreich, in: Frankreich-Jahrbuch, 63-86.

– (1989): Deutsch-französischer Bilateralismus zwischen Begegnungsroutine und ungleicher Kooperation, in: Lendemains 54, 158-166.

– (1990): Die Politik des "Unpolitischen". Zu Ernst Robert Curtius' Ort im politisch-intellektuellen Leben der Weimarer Republik, in: Lendemains 59, 16-62.

– (1991): Deutsch-französische Kulturbeziehungen der dreißiger Jahre, in: Lendemains 62, 147-154.

Böll, H. (1984): Bild – Bonn – Boenisch. Bornheim: Lamuv.

Bommensath, M. (1991): Secrets de réussite de l'entreprise allemande. Paris: Les Éditions d'Organiation.

Borella, F. (1973, [5]1990): Les partis politiques dans la France d'aujourd'hui. Paris: Seuil

Boulnois, P. (1984): L'âge d'or de la presse magazine est il terminé? in: PrAct 186, 42-45.

Bourdieu, P. (1989): La noblesse d'Etat. Grandes écoles et esprit de corps. Paris: Minuit.

Bouvier, B. W. (1982): Französische Revolution und deutsche Arbeiterbewegung. Bonn: Neue Gesellschaft.

Braudel, F./E. Labrousse (ed.) (1982): Histoire économique et sociale de la France, vol. 4. Paris: P.U.F.

Brauner, H. (1986): Die 'stille Revolution' fand nicht statt. Die sozialistische Dezentralisierungspolitik, in: E. Weisenfeld, 86-93.

Brauns, P. (1988): Die Zeiten sind hart, aber "modern". Sprachliche Inszenierung der sozialistischen Politik in Frankreich 1983-1986. Konstanz: Hartung-Gorre.

Brigouleix, B. (1991): Mitterrand hat nicht mehr viel Zeit, in: Dokumente 47, 436-439.

Brimo, N./A. Guérin (1977): Le dossier Hersant. Paris: Maspero.

Brizay, B. (1975): Le patronat. Paris: Seuil.

Brockmeier, P./R. Desne/J. Voss (ed.) (1979): Voltaire und Deutschland. Stuttgart: Metzler.

Brodersen, H. (1991): L'Allemagne et la France face à l'Union économique et monétaire européenne, in: Allemagne d'aujourd'hui 116, 15-50.

Brühl, C. (1990): Deutschland-Frankreich. Die Geburt zweier Völker. Köln/ Wien: Böhlau.

Bruniaux, Ch./R. Tresmontant (1990): Les dispositifs de la politique de l'emploi: bilan et perspectives, in: RegAct 157, 3-19.

Bue, J./A. F. Molinie/J. L. Dayan (1987): Aménagement du temps de travail: les réalités de la flexibilité, in: RegAct 131, 3-24.

Bulka, H. D./S. Lücking (1989): Tatsachen über Deutschland. Gütersloh: Bertelsmann.

Bundesministerium für Bildung und Wissenschaft (1985): Grund- und Strukturdaten 1985/86. Bad Honnef: Bock.

Bundesministerium für Wirtschaft (BMWI) (1990): Leistung in Zahlen '89. Bonn.

Caire, G. (1971): Les syndicats ouvriers. Paris: P.U.F.

Cameron, R. E. (1971): La France et le développement économique de l'Europe. Paris: Seuil.

Canceill, G. (1984): Les revenus fiscaux des ménages en 1979, in: Economie et statistique 166, 39-53.

Capdevielle, J./E. Dupoirier/G. Grunberg/ E. Schweisguth/C. Ysmal (1981): France de gauche, vote à droite. Paris: Presses de la Fondation Nationale des Sciences Politiques.

Capdevielle, J./R. Mouriaux ([3]1976): Les syndicats ouvriers en France. Paris: Colin.

Capul, J. Y./D. Meurs (1988): Les grandes questions de l'économie française. Paris: Nathan.

Caron, F. (1981): Histoire économique de la France. Paris: Colin.

Carriere, F./P. Pinchemel (1963): Le fait urbain en France. Paris: Colin.

Carton, A. (1991): Gemeinsam rüsten? Projekte und Probleme zwischen Frankreich und Deutschland, in: Dokumente 47, 381-385.

Caute, D. (1967): Le communisme et les intellectuels français. Paris: Gallimard.

CERC (Centre d'Etudes des Revenus et des Coûts) (1987/89): Constat de l'évolution récente des revenus en France. Paris: DF.

CFPJ (Centre de Formation et de Perfectionnement des Journalistes) (1988): La presse aujourd'hui. Paris.

Chapsal, J. (1984): La vie politique sous la Ve République. Paris: P.U.F.

Christ, H. (1979): Landeskundeunterricht im Rahmen des Fremdsprachenunterrichts, in: W. Kleine (ed.): Perspektiven des Fremdsprachenunterrichts in der Bundesrepublik Deutschland. Frankfurt a.M.: Diesterweg, 74-83.

– (1985): Neuere Arbeiten zum Landeskunde-Unterricht (Sammelrezension), in: Der fremdsprachliche Unterricht 74, 153-155.

Christ, H./K.H. Engbruch/H. J. Rang (1978): Bibliographie zur Landeskunde für den Französischunterricht. Düsseldorf: Pädagog. Institut.

Christ, P./R. Neubauer (1991): Kolonie im eigenen Land. Die Treuhand, Bonn und die Wirtschaftskatastrophe der fünf neuen Länder. Berlin: Rowohlt.

Christadler, M. (1979): Kriegserziehung im Jugendbuch. Literarische Mobilmachung in Deutschland und Frankreich vor 1914. Frankfurt a.M.: Haag und Herchen.

– (ed.) (1981): Deutschland – Frankreich. Alte Klischees – Neue Bilder. Duisburg: Sozialwissenschaftl. Kooperative.

– (1981a): Politik, Mythos und Mentalität. Französische und deutsche Jugendliteratur vor dem I. Weltkrieg, in: M. Christadler, 46-85.

– (1990): Der französische Existentialismus und die deutschen Intellektuellen in der Nachkriegszeit, in: W. Asholt/H. Thoma, 224-238.

Claessens, D./A. Klönne/A. Tschoepe (1985): Sozialkunde der Bundesrepublik Deutschland. Reinbek: Rowohlt.

de Closets, F. (1982): Toujours plus! Paris: Grasset.

– (1985): Tous ensemble. Pour en finir avec la syndicratie. Paris: Seuil.

Colard, D. (1984): Frankreichs Abkehr von der 'nuklearen Maginot-Linie', in: Dokumente 40, 123-134.

– (1986): Die Wahl vom 16. März 1986, in: E. Weisenfeld, 16-23.

College de France (1985): Propositions pour l'enseignement de l'avenir. Paris: Minuit.

Commission des Communautes européennes (1990): L'emploi en Europe 1990. Luxembourg: Office des publications officielles.

Cornelius, I. (1988): Von der Pyramide zum Pilz. Die Bevölkerungsentwicklung in der Bundesrepublik Deutschland, in: H.G. Wehling (ed.): Bevölkerungsentwicklung und Bevölkerungspolitik in der Bundesrepublik. Stuttgart: Kohlhammer, 11-37.

Couve de Murville, M. (1988): Konrad Adenauer und Charles de Gaulle, in: F. Knipping/E. Weisenfeld, 168-176.

Curtius, E.R. (1931): Die französische Kultur. Stuttgart/Berlin: Deutsche Verlags-Anstalt. Neuedition: Bern/München: Francke, 1975.

Dau, R. (1989): Berührungspunkte zweier Zeitalter. Deutsche Literatur und die Französische Revolution. Berlin: Dietz.

Debré, M. (1950): La République et son pouvoir. Paris: Nagel.

Defrasne, J. ([2]1975): La gauche en France de 1789 à nos jours. Paris: P.U.F.

Deist, W., et al. (1979): Das Deutsche Reich und der Zweite Weltkrieg, vol. 1: Ursachen und Voraussetzungen der Kriegspolitik. Stuttgart/Berlin: Deutsche Verlags-Anstalt.

Delarue, J.M. (1987): Temps partiel, intérim, contrats à durée déterminée: la progression du travail atypique, in: RegAct 129, 19-33.

Delmas, C. (1962): L'aménagement du territoire. Paris: P.U.F.

Deppe, F./G. Fülberth/J. Harrer (ed.) ([3]1981): Geschichte der deutschen Gewerkschaftsbewegung. Köln: Pahl-Rugenstein.

Desrosieres, A./A. Goy/L. Thévenot (1983): L'identité sociale dans le travail statistique: la nouvelle nomenclature des professions et catégories socioprofessionnelles, in: Economie et statistique 152, 55-82.

Deubner, C./U. Rehfeldt/F. Schlupp (1978): Deutsch-französische Wirtschaftsbeziehungen im Rahmen der weltwirtschaftlichen Arbeitsteilung, in: R. Picht, 91-136.

Deutsch-Französisches Kulturzentrum Essen (ed.) (1988): Deutschland – Frankreich. Höhen und Tiefen einer Zweierbeziehung. Essen: die blaue eule.

Dietrich, R./W. Fekl (1988): Komische Nachbarn – Drôles de voisins. Deutsch-französische Beziehungen im Spiegel der Karikatur (1945-1987). Paris: Goethe-Institut.

Dippel, H. (1989): Universalismus gegen "Nationale Beschränktheit". Französische Revolution und deutsches Geschichtsverständnis im 19. und 20. Jahrhundert, in: Lendemains 55/56, 157-168.

Dloczik, M./A. Schüttler/H. Sternagel (1982): Der Fischer Informationsatlas Bundesrepublik Deutschland. Frankfurt a. M.: Fischer.

Dohse, K. (1983): Massenarbeitslosigkeit und Ausländerpolitik, in: Das Argument 138, 239-247.

Dolch, J. (1959): Lehrplan des Abendlandes. Zweieinhalb Jahrtausende seiner Geschichte. Ratingen: Henn.

Droz, J. (1977): Bemerkungen zur Spezifik des 'syndicalisme français', in: Lendemains 7-8, 31-42.

Duby, G./R. Mandrou (1968): Histoire de la civilisation française, Bd. 1. Paris: Colin.

Ducarroir, E. (1990): Evolution de la diffusion des quotidiens et principaux périodiques français de 1986 à 1989, in: Médiaspouvoirs 20, 184-196.

Düwell, H./J. L. Pépin (1985ff.): Où trouver? Kontakte zu Frankreich für Romanisten, in: fh 16 (1985), 1-97; 17 (1986), 367-372; 18 (1987), 278-283; 19 (1988), 425-434; 21 (1990), 52-57; 22 (1991), 399-405.

Dufraisse, R. (ed.) (1991): Revolution und Gegenrevolution 1789-1830. München: Oldenbourg.
Dupeux, G. ([6]1982): La société française 1789-1970. Paris: Colin.
Duroselle, J. B. (1965): L'idée d'Europe dans l'histoire. Paris: Denoël.
Duverger, M. (1974): La monarchie républicaine. Paris: Laffont.
– (1987): La cohabitation des Français. Paris: P.U.F.
– ([20]1990): Le systeme politique français. Paris: P.U.F.
Ehrmann, H. W. (1976): Das politische System Frankreichs. München: Piper.
Eichenbaum, B. (1965): Aufsätze zur Theorie und Geschichte der Literatur. Frankfurt a. M.: Suhrkamp.
Ellwein, T. ([4]1977): Das Regierungssystem der Bundesrepublik Deutschland. Opladen: Westdeutscher Verlag.
Erbe, M. (1989): "Sie und nicht Wir ..." – Zu einigen Publikationen im deutschsprachigen Raum aus Anlaß des Bicententaire, in: Lendemains 55/56, 150-156.
Erdmann, G./B. Fritsch (1990): Zeitungsvielfalt im Vergleich. Mainz: Hase u. Koehler.
EVP (1983): Politisches Programm der Europäischen Volkspartei. Bonn: CDU-Bundesgeschäftsstelle.
Fabre-Rosane, G. (1983): Eine audiovisuelle Revolution? Die weitgesteckten Ziele der französischen Rundfunkreform, in: Dokumente 39, 44-53.
– (1984): Politische Klubs sind wieder gefragt, in: Dokumente 40, 49-54.
– (1984a): Das Monopol wehrt sich. Die alten Fernsehprogramme – und ein neues – im Wettbewerb, in: Dokumente 40, 321-328.
Fauvet, J. (1959): La IVe République. Paris: Fayard.
Feist, U./H. Krieger (1987): Alte und neue Scheidelinien des politischcn Verhaltens, in: apuz 12, 33-47.
Fekl, W. (1986): Das Untergründige in den Beziehungen Bonn – Paris, in: Dokumente 42, 42-50.
Ferrandon, M.C./l. Waquet (1979): La France depuis 1945. Paris: Hatier.
Ferro, M. (1988): Der Große Krieg. 1914-1918. Frankfurt a.M.: Suhrkamp.
Fink, G.L. (1983): La littérature allemande face à la Révolution française, in: J. Voss, 249-300.
Flonneau, J.M. (1982): Une révolution nouvelle mais tranquille: la décentralisation, in: Lendemains 28, 101-111.
Forster, K./M. Strauch (1991): Wie blicken französische Firmen auf die neuen Länder?, in: Dokumente 47, 206-209.
Fossaert, R. (1980): La société, Bd. 4: Les classes. Paris: Seuil.
Frankreich-Jahrbuch (1988ff.). Opladen: Leske u. Budrich.
Freytag, J. (1992): Liberation: new journalism auf französisch, in: Beiträge zur Fremdsprachenvermittlung aus dem Konstanzer SLI 24, 82-109.
Fricke, D./F.R. Weller (1989): Frankreich – Landeskunde – Französischunterricht, in: Die Neueren Sprachen 88, 268-287, 515-543.
Frijhoff, W./D. Julia (1975): Ecole et société dans la France d'Ancien Régime. Paris: Colin.
Frisch, A. (1982): Die Verstaatlichungen – Zahl, Form, Motive, Methode, in: Dokumente 38, 6-13.

Fritz-Vannahme, J. (1984): Am Himmel überflügelt, am Boden behindert. Zur Situation der 'Neuen Medien' in Frankreich, in: Dokumente 40, 309-316.
Fürstenberg, F. ([6]1978): Die Sozialstruktur der Bundesrepublik Deutschland. Opladen: Westdeutscher Verlag.
Gallo, M. (1984): Le grand Jaures. Paris: Laffont.
Garrisson, J. (1987): Le Midi est-il français? in: L'Histoire 96, 70-75.
Gaspard, F./C. Servan-Schreiber (1984): La fin des immigrés. Paris: Seuil.
de Gaulle, Ch. (1959): Memoires de guerre, vol. 3: Le Salut. Paris: Plon.
Gautier, X. (1983): L'Allemagne fédérale et ses Turcs, in: Documents 38/3, 59-72.
Gebauer, G. (ed.) (1989): Dossier "Französische Philosophie in Deutschland heute", in: Lendemains 54, 98-139.
Gibowski, W. G./M. Kaase (1991): Auf dem Weg zum politischen Alltag. Eine Analyse der ersten gesamtdeutschen Bundestagswahl vom 2. Dezember 1990, in: apuz 11-12, 3-20.
Gilsoul-Bézier, F. (1989): Connaissance du systéme éducatif français. Paris: Casteilla.
Glass, D.V./R. König (ed.) ([3]1968): Soziale Schichtung und soziale Mobilität. Kölner Zeitschrift für Soziologie und Sozialpsychologie, Sonderheft 5.
Gödde-Baumanns, B. (1981): Grundzüge der französischen Deutschland-Historiographie 1871-1914, in: M. Christadler, 104-147.
– (1988): Unrast und Festigkeit. Beobachtung, Bild und Gegenbild im Wandel zweier Jahrhunderte, in: Deutsch-Französisches Kulturzentrum Essen, 16-39.
Götz, P. (1977): L'occupation allemande, in: J. Olbert, 255-275.
Goguel, F./A. Grosser ([5]1976): La politique en France. Paris: Colin.
Goldschmidt, W. (1974): Ökonomische und politische Aspekte des gewerkschaftlichen Kampfes in Frankreich seit dem Zweiten Weltkrieg, in: Das Argument, Sonderband 2, 1-64.
Gontcharoff, G. et al. (1983-86): La decentralisation, 7 vols. Paris: ADELS-Syros.
Gravier, J.E. (1947): Paris et le désert français. Paris: Le Portulan.
Green, A. (1990): Education and State Formation. The Rise of Education Systems in England, France and the USA. Houndmills/London: Macmillan.
Grémion, P. (1980): Ansätze politischer und administrativer Dezentralisierung in der V. Republik, in: R. Lasserre u. a., 99-157.
Große, E.U. (1978/79): La femme en France. Eine wortkundliche und frankreichkundliche Hintergrundinformation für den Lehrer, in: fh 9, 262-269 and 10, 10-19.
– (1987): Zum Vergleich zwischen französischem und bundesdeutschem Parteiensystem. Cournon d'Auvergne: Editions Orionis.
– (1992): Schritte zu einer kontrastiven Semiotik der nationalen Symbole Frankreichs und Deutschlands. 1: Die Grundlage: Greimas' Kultursemiotik,. in: Knoten 5/1, 26-34.
Große, E. U./H. Rappenecker: Perspektiven einer präventiven Umweltpolitik, in: R. Pfromm, 19-47.
Grosser, A. ([9]1981): Geschichte Deutschlands seit 1945. München: dtv.

– (1983): Das Recht auf ein offenes Wort, in: Dokumente 39, Sonderheft Jan., 107-117.

– (1986): Die 'cohabitation' – mehr als ein Modewort, in: E. Weisenfeld, 12-15.

Grossmann, B. (1983): Changement im Wahlverhalten der französischen Mittelschichten, in: Zeitschrift für Parlamentsfragen 2, 189-195.

Guédé, A./S. A. Rozenblum (1981): Les candidats aux législatives de 1978 et 1981, in: Revue Française de Science Politique 32/2, 982-998.

Guéry, L. (1992): La presse regionale et locale. Paris: CFPJ.

Guillauma, Y. (1988): La presse en France. Paris: La Découverte.

Guiol, P./E. Neveu (1984): Sociologie des adhérents gaullistes, in: Pouvoirs 28, 91-106.

Habermas, J. ([5]1971): Strukturwandel der Öffentlichkeit. Neuwied: Luchterhand.

Haby, R. (1975): Pour une modernisation du systeme éducatif. Paris: DF.

Haefs, H. (ed.) (1988): Der Fischer Weltalmanach 1989. Frankfurt a. M.: Fischer.

Haensch, G./H. Tümmers (1991): Frankreich. München: Beck.

Hänsch, K. (1973): Frankreich – Eine politische Landeskunde. Berlin: Colloquium.

– (ed.) (1978/79): Frankreich – Eine Länderkunde. Hamburg: Hoffmann und Campe.

Hammer, J.P. (1983): Von den Schwierigkeiten bei der Vermittlung deutschsprachiger Literatur nach Frankreich, in: L. Jordan et al., 153-165.

Harrer, D. (1987): Französische Literatur in der Weimarer Republik. Konstanz: Hartung-Gorre.

Hass, G. (ed.) (1975): Deutschland im Zweiten Weltkrieg, vol. 1: Vorbereitung, Entfesselung und Verlauf bis zum 22. Juni 1941. Berlin-Ost: Akademie.

Haupt, H.G. (1976): Kleinbürgertum im Frankreich der Belle Epoque, in: Lendemains 3, 64-89.

Haupt, H.G./C. Koch (1978): Schwierigkeiten mit Frankreich, in: Leviathan 6, 1-18.

Haut Comité Education – Economie (1988): Education – économie. Quel systéme éducatif pour la société de l'an 2000? Paris: DF.

Heimsoeth, H.-J. (1990): Der Zusammenbruch der Dritten Französischen Republik. Frankreich während der 'Drôle de Guerre' 1939/40. Bonn: Bouvier.

Hennig, E. (1971): Die Abhängigkeit der Massenmedien von den Werbeeinnahmen und dem Anzeigenteil, in: R. Zoll (ed.): Manipulation der Meinungsbildung. Opladen: Westdeutscher Verlag, 27-67

Henry-Gréard, D. (1982): Die Grandes Ecoles in der Zugluft der Reformen, in: Dokumente 38, 327-331.

Herre, F. (1983): Deutsche und Franzosen – Der lange Weg zur Freundschaft. Bergisch-Gladbach: Lübbe.

Hertel, W. (1986): La civilisation française. Frankfurt a.M.: Lang.

Hertzstell, I./D.R. Gross (ed.) (1980): Lehrer in Deutschland und Frankreich. Ein Vergleich ihrer Rolle und ihres Selbstverständnisses. Ludwigsburg/

Bonn: Carolus-Magnus-Kreis/Sekretariat der Ständigen Konferenz der Kultusminister der Länder.

Hillel, M. (1983): L'Occupation française en Allemagne, 1945-1949. Paris: Balland.

Hinrichs, P./I. Kolboom (1976): Kleinbürgertum oder neue Arbeiterklasse?, in: Lendemains 3, 90-114.

– (1977a): 'Ein gigantischerTrödelladen'? Zur Herausbildung der Landes- und Frankreichkunde in Deutschland vor dem Ersten Weltkrieg, in: M. Nerlich, 82-95.

– (1977b): Frankreichforschung - eine deutsche Wissenschaft. Der Weg der Landes- und Frankreichkunde in den Faschismus (1914-1945), in: M. Nerlich, 168-187.

– (1977c): Zwischen geselligem Wissen und Gesellschaftswissenschaft. Zur Entwicklung der Landes- und Frankreichkunde in der westdeutschen Neuphilologie seit 1945, in: M. Nerlich, 234-254.

Hirsch, M. (1988): Die französische Presselandschaft – Expansion trotz Krise, in: Media Perspektiven 6, 329-337.

Hirt, A. (1984): Der Erfolg linker Presse in den 80er Jahren: Libération (Typoskript).

Höhne, R. (1984): Das Dilemma der republikanischen Rechten Frankreichs seit den Europawahlen vom Juni 1984, in: Lendemains 36, 82-85

– (1985): Die innenpolitische Entwicklung in Frankreich – Die Kommunalwahlen vom März 1985, in: Lendemains 38/39, 134-147.

Hörling, H. (1985): Das Deutschlandbild in der französischen Tagespresse vom Münchner Abkommen bis zum Ausbruch des Zweiten Weltkriegs. Frankfurt a.M.: Lang.

Hofmann, A. (1991): Europäischer Kulturkanal – aufgehender Stern oder verglühender Komet?, in: Lendemains 62, 81-87.

Holtmann, E. (1980): Transformation und Krise der deutschen Presse, in: R. Lasserre et al., 235-279.

Holzer, H. (1980): Medien in der BRD. Köln: Pahl-Rugenstein.

Hudemann, R. (1989): Vom Nutzen der Revolution. 1789 und der Wandel in Frankreichs Deutschlandpolitik nach den beiden Weltkriegen, in: Frankreich-Jahrbuch, 169-181.

Hübner, E./H. H. Rohlfs (1988ff.): Jahrbuch der Bundesrepublik Deutschland. München: Beck/dtv.

Idt, G. et al. (1975): Le roman, le récit non romanesque, le cinéma. Littérature et langage, vol. 3. Paris: Nathan.

INSEE (1984a): Recensement général de la population de 1982. Principaux résultats. Paris.

– (1984ff.): Tableaux de l'économie française. Paris.

Institut der deutschen Wirtschaft (1990): Zahlen zur wirtschaftlichen Entwicklung der Bundesrepublik Deutschland. Köln.

– (1992): Internationale Wirtschaftszahlen. Köln.

Jäger, W. (1978): Die Sozialistische und die Kommunistische Partei Frankreichs, in: D. Oberndörfer, 35-132.

– (1978a): Die französische Linke, in: Der Bürger im Staat 28/1, 4-10.
– (1980): Die politischen Parteien in der Bundesrepublik Deutschland und in Frankreich, in: Der Staat 19/4, 583-602.
– (1987): Das Staatsbewußtsein der Franzosen, in: Akademie f. polit. Bildung Tutzing (ed.): Zum Staatsverständnis der Gegenwart, München: Olzog.
Jamet, M. (1983): La presse périodique en France. Paris: Colin.
Janin, N. (1988): Cinéma en France, cinéma français, in: Lendemains 50, 123-125.
Jeanneney, J. M. (ed.) (1989): L'économie française depuis 1967. Paris: Seuil.
Jehn, P. (1977): Die Ermächtigung der Gegenrevolution. Zur Entwicklung der kulturideologischen Frankreich-Konzeption bei Ernst Robert Curtius, in: M. Nerlich, 110-132.
Jetter, K. (1979): Partner und Konkurrenten, in: K. Hänsch, 64-107.
Jörg, Ch. (1989): Wie man aus drei Einbahnstraßen eine Kreuzung macht, in: Dokumente 45, 26-32.
Jordan, L./B. Kortländer/F. Nies (ed.) (1983): Interferenzen. Deutschland und Frankreich. Literatur – Wissenschaft – Sprache. Düsseldorf: Droste.
Jurt, J./M. Ebel/U. Erzgräber (1989): Französischsprachige Gegenwartsliteratur 1918-1986/87. Eine bibliographische Bestandsaufnahme der Originaltexte und der deutschen Übersetzungen, 2 vols. Tübingen: Niemeyer.
Kaelble, H. (1991): Nachbarn am Rhein. Entfremdung und Annäherung der französischen und deutschen Gesellschaft seit 1880. München: Beck.
Kaiser, K./P. Lellouche (ed.) ([2]1988): Deutsch-Französische Sicherheitspolitik. Bonn: Europa Union.
Kalmbach, G. (1990): Kulturschock Frankreich. Bielefeld: Rump.
Keller, T. (1983): Das Spiel - le match: oder Krieg der Vorurteile, in: Informationen Deutsch als Fremdsprache 1, 16-27.
– (1986): Umwelt und Krimi. Die französische Verstaatlichung der Ökologie, in: Dokumente 42, 167-170.
– (1986a): Deutsch-französische Physiognomien im Elsaß, in: G. Neuner (ed.): Kulturkontraste im DaF-Unterricht. München: ludicium, 217-240.
Kempf, U. (21980): Das politische System Frankreichs. Opladen: Westdeutscher Verlag.
– (1983): Die bürgerlichen Parteien Frankreichs: das R.P.R., die P.R. und das C.D.S., in: H. J. Veen (ed.): Christlich-demokratische Parteien in Westeuropa, vol. 2. Paderborn: Schöningh, 125-314.
– (1983a): Frankreich – Wandel bei gleichzeitiger Konstanz, in: Der Bürger im Staat 33/1, 32-37.
– (1988): Die Parteien der Rechten zwischen Einheit und Auflösung, in: Frankreich-Jahrbuch, 87-114.
– (1989): Frankreichs Regierungssystem, in: Landeszentrale für politische Bildung Baden-Württemberg, 105-139.
– (1989a): Frankreichs Parteiensystem im Wandel, in: Landeszentrale für politische Bildung Baden-Württemberg, 140-176.
Kessler, F. (1984): La durée du travail en Allemagne: 150 ans d'histoire législative et conventionnelle, in: Allemagnes d'aujourd'hui 90, 6-25.

Kimmel, A. (1990): Le phénomène Front national, in: FrM 237, 14-16.
– (1991): Innenpolitische Entwicklungen und Probleme in Frankreich, in: apuz 47-48, 3-15.
Kimmel, A./J. Poujol (1982): Certaines idees de la France. Frankfurt a.M.: Diesterweg.
Kißler, L. (1986): Vom Klassenkampf zum sozialen Dialog? in: E. Weisenfeld, 148-156.
Kißler, L./R. Lasserre (1987): Tarifpolitik. Ein deutsch-französischer Vergleich. Frankfurt a.M.: Campus.
Klarsfeld, S. (1989): Vichy-Auschwitz. Die Zusammenarbeit der deutschen und französischen Behörden bei der “Endlösung der Judenfrage” in Frankreich. Nördlingen: Delphi Politik.
Klatzmann, J. ([2]1980): L'agriculture française. Paris: Seuil.
Klein,. P (ed.) (1990): Deutsch-französische Verteidigungskooperation: Das Beispiel der Deutsch-Französischen Brigade. Baden-Baden: Nomos.
Klönne, A./H. Reese (1984): Die deutsche Gewerkschaftsbewegung. Hamburg: VSA.
Kloepfer, R./H. Landbeck (1988): Die Entwicklung von Fernsehästhetik im deutsch-französischen Vergleich, in: Frankreich-Jahrbuch, 183-209.
– (1991): Ästhetik der Werbung. Der Fernsehspot in Europa als Symptom neuer Macht. Frankfurt a. M.: Fischer.
Knight, U./W. Kowalsky (1991): Deutschland nur den Deutschen? Die Ausländerfrage in Deutschland, Frankreich und den USA. Erlangen: Straube.
Knipping, F./E. Weisenfeld (ed.) (1988): Eine ungewöhnliche Geschichte. Deutschland – Frankreich seit 1870. Bonn: Europa Union.
Knoblauch-Foulquier, Y. (1981): Französische Revuen über deutsche Prosa zwischen 1946 und 1953, in: fh 12, 19-29.
– (1983): Französische Revuen über deutsche Prosa von 1960 bis 1970, in: fh 14, 21-28.
– (1986): Französische Revuen über das deutsche Nachkriegstheater (1950-1970), in: fh 17, 469-477.
Koch-Hillebrecht, M. (1977): Das Deutschenbild. Gegenwart, Geschichte, Psychologie. München: Beck.
Kodron, Ch. (1980): Die Rolle der Lehrer in Deutschland und Frankreich im Vergleich: 5 Thesen, in: I. Hertzstell/D.R. Gross, 9-17.
Köhler, E. (1968): ‘Conseil des barons’ und ‘jugement des barons’, in: Sitzungsberichte der Heidelberger Akademie der Wissenschaften Philos.-hist. Klasse, 4. Heidelberg: Winter.
Köller, H./B. Töpfer (1978): Frankreich – Ein historischer Abriß. Köln: Pahl-Rugenstein.
Kohut, K. (1983): Literatur der Résistance und Kollaboration in Frankreich, in: L. Jordan u. a., 111-120.
– (ed.) (1982-84): Literatur der Resistance und Kollaboration in Frankreich, 3 vols. Wiesbaden/Tübingen: Athenaion/Narr.
Kolboom, I. (1975): Zum Thema Kleinbürgertum in Frankreich, in: Lendemains 2, 41-53.

– (1978): Frankreichs Unternehmer zwischen Konfrontation und 'sozialer Öffnung': Die Strategie des CNPF seit 1972, in: Lendemains 11, 125-136.
– (1984): Le Pens Nationale Front, in: Dokumente 40, 229-230.
– (1984a): Hundert Jahre 'Loi Waldeck-Rousseau', in: Dokumente 40, 274-279.
– (1986): Ein Läufer auf der Stelle? Sicherheitspolitik – komplexes Bündel von Motiven und Kräften, in: Auslandskurier 27, Sonderausgabe Okt., 22-23.
– (1986a): Unsicherheiten in der deutsch-französischen Sonderbeziehung, in: Die internationale Politik 1983-1984. München: Oldenbourg, 147-159.
– (1990): Frankreich und die staatliche Neuordnung Deutschlands 1945-1949, in: W. Asholt/H. Thoma, 51-86.
– (1991): Vom geteilten zum vereinten Deutschland. Deutschland-Bilder in Frankreich. Bonn: Europa Union.
– (1991a): Die Vertreibung der Dämonen: Frankreich und das vereinte Deutschland, in: Frankreich-Jahrbuch, 211-218.
Koopmann, H. (1989): Freiheitssonne und Revolutionsgewitter. Reflexe der Französischen Revolution im literarischen Deutschland zwischen 1789 und 1840. Tübingen: Niemeyer.
Kortländer, B. (1983): '... das Mutterland der Zivilisation und der Freiheit'. Aspekte von Heines Frankreichbild, in: L. Jordan et al., 74-79.
Kortländer, B./F. Nies (ed.) (1986): Französische Literatur in deutscher Sprache. Eine kritische Bilanz. Düsseldorf: Droste.
Kowalsky, W. (1983): 1981- Blütezeit politischer Klubs, in: Lendemains 30, 82-84.
– (1986): Die Entwicklung der französischen Gewerkschaftsbewegung, in: Lendemains 41, 104-113.
– ([2]1991): Frankreichs Unternehmer in der Wende (1965-1982). Rheinfelden: Schäuble.
Kramer, S. P. (1991): La question française, in: Politique étrangére 56, 959-974.
Krauskopf, J. (1985): Das Deutschland- und Frankreichbild in Schulbüchern. Tübingen: Narr.
Kremnitz, G. (1975): Die ethnischen Minderheiten Frankreichs. Tübingen: Narr.
Kreutz, W. (1990): Mannheim, Heidelberg und die Kurpfalz im Zeichen der Französischen Revolution, in: G. Thiele, 225-238.
Kreuzer, H./K. Prümm (ed.) (1979): Fernsehsendungen und ihre Formen. Stuttgart: Reclam.
von Krockow, Ch. (ed.) (1983): Brauchen wir ein neues Parteiensystem? Frankfurt a. M.: Fischer.
Kübler, H.D. (1979): Die Aura des Wahren oder die Wirklichkeit der Fernsehnachrichten, in: H. Kreuzer/K. Prümm, 249-289.
Kühnl, R. ([13]1979): Formen bürgerlicher Herrschaft. Reinbek: Rowohlt.
Kuntze, O.E. (1978): Wirtschaftsmacht Frankreich, in: Der Bürger im Staat 28/1, 39-45.
Kursbuch Deutschland 85/86 (1985): München: Goldmann.
Lafont, R. (1967): La révolution regionaliste. Paris: Gallimard.

Lammert, N. (1979): Das Phänomen der 'Staatsverdrossenheit' und die Strukturdefekte der Parteien, in: apuz 25, 3-14.

Lancelot, A./M. Th. Lancelot (1984): Annuaire de la France politique. Paris: Presses de la Fondation Nationale des Sciences Politiques.

Landbeck, H. (1991): Medienkultur im nationalen Vergleich. Inszenierungsstrategien von Fernsehnachrichten am Beispiel der Bundesrepublik Deutschland und Frankreichs. Tübingen: Niemeyer.

Landeszentrale für politische Bildung Baden-Württemberg (ed.) (1989): Frankreich. Stuttgart: Kohlhammer.

Lasserre, R. (1976): Sozialstruktur und politische Entwicklung, in: Menyesch, D./H. Uterwedde (ed.): Sozialstruktur und Politik in Frankreich. Ludwigsburg: Deutsch-Französisches Institut, 32-40.

– (1977): Evolution de la structure sociale française, in: J. Olbert, 243-254 (first ed. in: fh 6 [1975], 12-23).

– (ed.) (1978): La France contemporaine. Guide bibliographique et thématique. Tübingen: Niemeyer.

– (1981): Tarifpolitik zwischen sozialem Konflikt und staatlicher Intervention, in: R. Lasserre et al., 159-186.

– (1983): Concertation sociale et cogestion, in: G. Sandoz, 239-269.

– (1986): La coopération économique franco-allemande et l'Europe, in: Allemagnes d'aujourd'hui 94-95, 241-255.

Lasserre, R./W. Neumann/R. Picht (ed.) (1980/81): Deutschland-Frankreich: Bausteine zum Systemvergleich, 2 vols. Gerlingen: Bleicher.

Laurent-Atthalin, C. (ed.) (1983): Les nouveaux droits des travailleurs Paris: La Découverte-Maspero/Le Monde.

Lebas, Y. (1981): Die Internationalisierung der französischen Wirtschaft, in: R. Lasserre u. a., 81-105.

Leber, St. (ed.) ([2]1985): Die Pädagogik der Waldorfschule und ihre Grundlagen. Darmstadt: Wissenschaftl. Buchgesellschaft.

Lebon, A. (1990): Regard sur l'immigration et la présence étrangère en France. Paris: DF.

Lecher, W. (1979): Zur Lage der Gewerkschaften in Europa, in: F. Steinkühler, 171-182.

Lefranc, G. (1967/69): Le mouvement syndical, 2 vols. Paris: Payot.

– (1976): Les organisations patronales en France. Paris: Payot.

Leggewie, C. (1986): Der König ist nackt. Ein Versuch, die Ära Mitterrand zu verstehen. Hamburg: VSA.

Leiner, W. (1988): 1870/71 – Wandel des Deutschlandbilds im Spiegel der französischen Literatur, in: F. Knipping/E. Weisenfeld, 28-46.

– (1989): Das Deutschlandbild in der französischen Literatur. Darmstadt: Wissenschaftl. Buchgesellschaft.

Leisewitz, A. (1980): Die Klassen- und Sozialstruktur der Bundesrepublik, in: U. Albrecht u.a. (ed.): Beiträge zu einer Geschichte der Bundesrepublik Deutschland. Köln: Pahl-Rugenstein, 78-121.

Leithäuser, G. (1978): Nationalisierungen im Gemeinsamen Regierungsprogramm – eine linksorientierte und industriepolitische Alternative? in: Leviathan 6, 45-62.

Le Monde (1975): Dessins – Documents 74-75 (= supplém. aux Dossiers et documents du Monde). Paris.
– (1979): Vingt ans de réussite allemande. Paris: Economica.
– (1984): Les immigrés en France (= Dossiers et documents 115). Paris.
– (1986): La société française (= Dossiers et documents 130). Paris.
– (1986a): Bilan économique et social (= Dossiers et documents, n" spécial). Paris.
– (1988): Les trente ans de la Ve Republique (= Dossiers et documents 158). Paris.
Leutrat, J.-L. (1990): Nouvelle vague, in: Lendemains 60, 85-87.
Liehr, G. (1990): Die französische Presselandschaft, in: Frankreich-Jahrbuch, 173-192.
Ligou, D. (1962): Histoire du socialisme en France (1871-1961). Paris: P.U.F.
Lill, R. (1990): Konkordate, in: Theologische Realenzyklopädie, vol. 19. Berlin: de Gruyter, 462-471.
Limouzin, P. (1987): L'économie de l'Ile-de-France. Paris: Ellipses.
Loch, D. (1990, ²1991): Der schnelle Aufstieg des Front National. Rechtsextremismus im Frankreich der achtziger Jahre. München: tuduv.
Loch, Th. M. (1963): Adenauer, de Gaulle. Bilanz der Staatsbesuche. Bonn: Athenäum/Junker und Dünnhaupt.
Löbsack, W. (1939): Der Osten als Aufgabe. Ostprobleme in der nationalsozialistischen Charaktererziehung, in: Der Deutsche im Osten 2/5, 76-78.
Lojkine, J./N. Viet-Depaule (1984): Classe ouvriére, société locale et municipalités en region parisienne. Paris: Ministère de l'Urbanisme et du Logement.
Loth, W. (1992): Geschichte Frankreichs im 20. Jahrhundert. Frankfurt a.M.: Fischer.
Loth, W./R. Picht (ed.) (1991): De Gaulle, Deutschland und Europa. Opladen: Leske u. Budrich.
Lüger, H.H. (1987): Publizistische Vielfalt und Konzentrationstendenz, in: idem, Die bundesdeutsche Presse. Clermont-Ferrand: CRDP, 21-36.
– (1991): Landeskunde – Aspekte eines problematischen Begriffs, in: Beiträge zur Fremdsprachenvermittlung aus dem Konstanzer SLI 22, 4-37.
Lüsebrink, H. J./J. Riesz (ed.) (1984): Feindbild und Faszination. Frankfurt a. M.: Diesterweg.
Madaule, J. (1973): Le drame albigeois et l'unité française. Paris: Gallimard.
Madelin, P. (ed.) (1988): L'Europe des télévisions privees. Paris: DF.
Maillard, P. (1986): Retten wir unsere Sprachen! in: Dokumente 42, 399-403.
– (1990): De Gaulle et l'Allemagne. Le rêve inachevé. Paris: Plon.
Mallet, S. (⁴1969): La nouvelle classe ouvriére. Paris: Seuil.
Manfrass, K. (ed.) (1984): Paris - Bonn. Eine dauerhafte Bindung schwieriger Partner. Sigmaringen: Thorbecke.
– (1984a): Das nationale Gefüge und die Gastarbeiter, in: Dokumente 40 Sonderheft Febr., 61-68.
Marchais, G. (1985): 25e congrès PCF – Espoir et combat pour l'avenir. Rapport du comite central présenté par G.M. Paris: Comité central du PCF.

Martelli, R. (1985): Communisme français. Histoire sincère du P.C.F. 1920-1984. Paris: Messidor.
Mathien, M. (1983): La presse quotidienne régionale. Paris: P.U.F.
Mauriat, C. (1989): La presse audiovisuelle 1989/1990. Paris: Centre de formation et de perfectionnement des journalistes (CFPJ).
Maus, D. (ed..) (1981): Textes et documents relatifs à l'élection présidentielle des 26 avril et 10 mai 1981. Paris: DF.
McRae, V. (1980): Die Gastarbeiter. München: Beck.
Medienbericht '85. Bericht der Bundesregierung über die Lage der Medien in der Bundesrepublik Deutschland 1985. Drucksache 10/5663 des Deutschen Bundestages, vom 16. 6. 1986. Bonn.
Melde, W. (1980): Landeskunde und Spracherwerb. Tübingen: Niemeyer.
– (1987): Zur Integration von Landeskunde und Kommunikation im Fremdsprachenunterricht. Tübingen: Narr.
– (1989): Aprés le «Régne» du latin la «Terreur» des maths, in: fh 20, 388-398.
Mentras, H. (1970): La fin des paysans. Paris: Colin.
Menudier, H. (1980): Presse, radio et télévision en République fédérale d'Allemagne. Paris: DF.
– (1981): Das Deutschlandbild der Franzosen in den 70er Jahren. Bonn: Europa Union.
– (1988): Vingt-cinq ans de coopération franco-allemande. Paris: DF.
Menyesch, D. (1978): Das alte und das neue Frankreich, in: Der Bürger im Staat 28/1, 39-45.
Menyesch, D./B. Manac'h (1984): France – Allemagne: Relations internationales et interdépendances bilatérales. Une bibliographie 1963-1982. München: Saur.
Menyesch, D./H. Uterwedde (1978): Wirtschaftliche und soziale Strukturen in der Bundesrepublik und in Frankreich, in: R. Picht, 46-90.
– (1982): Frankreich. Opladen: Leske.
– (1982a): Wirtschaft und Gesellschaft in der Bundesrepublik Deutschland. Heidelberg: Groos.
– (1982b): Partner oder Konkurrenten? Wirtschaftsbeziehungen zwischen nationalen Strategien und internationalen Abhängigkeiten, in: R. Picht, 105-139.
Mermet, G. (1990): Francoscopie. Paris: Larousse.
Meyer-Kalkus, R. (1990): Deutsch-französische Kulturbeziehungen nach dem 9. November 1989, in: Lendemains 57, 146-148.
– (1990a): Auslandsstudium in Europa, in: Dokumente 46, 504-513.
Meyn, H. (1974): Massenmedien in der Bundesrepublik Deutschland. Berlin: Colloquium.
Michard, L. (1983): Littérature et cinéma, in: L'information littéraire 35, 37-39.
Michaud, G./G. Torres (1978): Nouveau guide France. Paris: Hachette.
Miguet, N. (1984): Hersant, un industriel pragmatique, in: PrAct 180, 34-48.
Ministére de l'Industrie (1980ff.): Les chiffres clés de l'industrie française. Paris.
Ministére de l'Industrie et de l'Aménagement du Territoire (1988ff.): Les chiffres cles de l'industrie. Paris.

Ministere de l'Industrie et du Commerce extérieur (1991): Les chiffres clés de l'industrie dans les régions. Paris.

Miquel, P. (1973): L'affaire Dreyfus. Paris: P.U.F.

Mitterrand, F. (1984): Le Coup d'Etat permanent. Paris: Julliard (first ed. 1964).

Moissonnier, M. (1977): Die Confédération Générale du Travail (1895 bis 1976), in: Lendemains 7-8, 43-79.

Mommsen, W.J. (1978): Nationalbewußtsein und Staatsverständnis der Deutschen, in: R. Picht, 30-45.

Mondot, J./J.-M. Valentin/J. Voss (ed.) (1992): Allemands en France. Français en Allemagne. 1715-1789. Sigmaringen: Thorbecke.

Monod, J./P. Castelbajac (1973): L'aménagement du territoire. Paris: P.U.F.

de Montbrial, T. (ed.) (1988): RAMSES (= Rapport Annuel Mondial sur le Systéme Economique et les Stratégies). Paris: Dunod.

Moog, A. (1991): Nachbar Frankreich. Frankfurt a.M.: FAZ.

Morawe, B. (1983): Bonapartistisches Panoptikum – Parteiensystem und Parteienkrise in Frankreich, in: Ch. von Krockow, 188-202.

– (1985): 'Ein Gespenst geht um ...' – Zur Krise der französischen Kommunisten, in: Dokumente 41, 134-142.

Morita-Clement, M. A. (1985): L'image de l'Allemagne dans le roman français de 1945 à nos jours. Nagoya: Presses Universitaires.

Morvan, Y. (1972): La concentration de l'industrie en France. Paris: Colin.

Moutoussamy, E. (1988): Les DOM-TOM – enjeu géopolitique, économique et stratégique. Paris: L'Harmattan.

Müller, B. (1975): Das Französische der Gegenwart. Heidelberg: Winter.

Müller, B.D. (1980): Zur Logik interkultureller Verstehensprobleme, in: Jahrbuch Deutsch als Fremdsprache 6, 102-119.

Müller, K. (1988): Außenhandel 1987 nach Herstellungs- und Verbrauchsländern, in: Wirtschaft und Statistik 2, 119-127; Anhang 54*-56*.

Müller-Rommel, F. (1983): Die Grünen – künftig ein fester Bestandteil unseres Parteiensystems? in: Der Bürger im Staat 33/1, 17-20.

Nerlich, M. (ed.) (1977): Kritik der Frankreichforschung. Berlin: Argument.

Das neue Europäische Parlament (1984). Bonn: Informationsbüro des Europäischen Parlaments.

Neumann, W. (1981): Tarifbeziehungen als institutionalisierte Machtverteilung, in: R. Lasserre u. a., 115-158.

– (1983): Technologiepolitik: Französische Vorstöße - Deutsche Reserven? in: Dokumente 39, 101-108.

– (1989): Technologiepolitik einer Region – Das Beispiel Rhône-Alpes, in: Frankreich-Jahrbuch, 153-168.

Neuschäfer, A. (1989): Die Bühne als Mittler. Zum deutsch-französischen Theaterdialog 1951-1989, in: Lendemains 54, 48-56.

Nicoud, G. (1972): Les derniéres libertés ... menottes aux mains. Paris: Denoël.

Nies, F. (1983): Drei Musketiere und ein kleiner Prinz? Französische Literatur in der Bundesrepublik, in: L. Jordan u.a., 138-152.

Nieser, B. (1977): Kommentierte Bildungsstatistik: Frankreich. Marburg: Forschungsstelle für vergleichende Erziehungswissenschaft.

– (1990): Bildungspolitik in Frankreich (1975-1985). Vergleichende Daten und Analysen. München: Saur.

Nivollet, A. (1987): Commerce international: la compétition France-RFA, in: RegAct 129, 3-18.

Nobécourt, J. (1977): Die Enzyklika *Mit brennender Sorge*, in: A. Grosser (ed.): Wie war es, möglich? Die Wirklichkeit des Nationalsozialismus. München: Hanser, 108-127.

Noblecourt, M. (1990): Les syndicats en question. Paris: Editions Ouvrières.

Nowka, M. (1983): Die wirtschaftliche Phänomenologie des Spielfilms als Ware. Berlin (Diss.).

Nutzinger, H. G. (1981): Betriebsverfassung und Mitbestimmung: Soziale Beziehungen im Unternehmen, in: R. Lasserre et al., 187-212.

Oberndörfer, D. (ed.) (1978): Sozialistische und kommunistische Parteien in Westeuropa, vol. 1. Opladen: Leske.

O.C.D.E. (ed.) (1974): La politique industrielle de la France. Paris.

Oehler, D. (1984): Heines Paris nach 1848, in: H.J. Lüsebrink/J. Riesz, 39-54.

Østergaard, B.S. (ed.) (1992): The Media in Western Europe. The Euromedia Handbook. London/Newbury Park/New Delhi: SAGE Publications.

OFAJ (1991): Rapport d'activité 1990, in: Allemagne d'aujourd'hui 117, 86-91.

Olbert, J. (ed.) (1977): Gesammelte Aufsätze zur Frankreichkunde. Frankfurt a.M.: Diesterweg.

– (1990): Französischunterricht und Sprachenpolitik in der Bundesrepublik Deutschland, in: fh 21, 87-105.

von Oppeln, S. (1989): Les Verts – und ihre Aussichten in Frankreich, in: Dokumente 45, 197-200.

Ory, P. (1977): Les collaborateurs 1940-1945. Paris: Seuil.

Ott-Meimberg, M. (1980): Kreuzzugsepos oder Staatsroman? Strukturen adeliger Heilsversicherung im deutschen *Rolandslied*. Zürich/München: Artemis.

Pabst, W. (ed.) (1983): Das Jahrhundert der deutsch-französischen Konfrontation. Ein Quellen- und Arbeitsbuch zur deutsch-französischen Geschichte von 1866 bis heute. Hannover: Nieders. Landeszentrale f. polit. Bildung.

Paech, J. (1988): Literatur und Film. Stuttgart: Metzler.

Parti socialiste (1972): Changer la vie. Programme de gouvernement du Parti socialiste. Paris: Flammarion.

Partikel, H. (1989): Arbeitsschutzpolitik in der Europäischen Gemeinschaft, in: F. Steinkühler, 156-168.

Passeron, A. (1984): Le parti d'un homme, in: Pouvoirs 28, 27-34.

Passet, E. (1990): Kultur-Knigge Frankreich. Köln: Hayit.

Peter, L. (1985): Zwischen Reformpolitik und Krise – Gewerkschaften in Frankreich 1980-1985. Frankfurt a. M.: IMSF.

Peyrefitte, A. (1976): Le mal français. Paris: Plon.

Pfromm, R. (ed.) (1991): Mensch – der Welt Ruin? Ökologische Perzeption und Perspektiven in Deutschland und Frankreich. Gummersbach: Theodor-Heuss-Akademie.

Picaper, H.P. (1983): Vers le IVe Reich. Ecologistes et gauchistes contre la démocratie en Allemagne fédérale. Paris: Masson.

Picht, R. (ed.) (1978): Deutschland – Frankreich – Europa. München: Piper.
– (1980): Interesse und Vergleich: zur Sozialpsychologie des Deutschlandbilds, in: Jahrbuch Deutsch als Fremdsprache 6, 120-132.
– (1981): Die Ära der Technokraten: Das Führungspersonal der V. Republik, in: R. Lasserre et al., 197-222.
– (ed.) (1982): Das Bündnis im Bündnis. Deutsch-französische Beziehungen im internationalen Spannungsfeld. Berlin: Severin und Siedler.
Picht, R./W. Neumann (1984): Basisbibliographie zur Bundesrepublik Deutschland 1983. München: Hueber.
Plantu (1990): Un vague souvenir! Paris: Le Monde.
Pletsch, A. (1991): Strukturwandel des Pariser Großraums, in: Frankreich Jahrbuch, 79-93.
Plihon, D. (1987): La balance des paiements française: un redressement précaire, in: RegAct 131, 46-57.
Poidevin, R./J. Bariety (1977): Les relations franco-allemandes 1815-1975. Paris: Colin.
Presse Actualité (1985): L'année 1984 des medias (n° hors serie). Paris: Bayard.
Priewe, J./R. Hickel (1991): Der Preis der Einheit. Bilanz und Perspektiven der deutschen Vereinigung. Frankfurt a. M.: Fischer.
Programme commun de gouvernement du parti communiste et du parti socialiste (1972). Paris: Edition sociales.
Programme commun de gouvernement. Parti socialiste, Parti communiste, Mouvement des radicaux de gauche (1973). Paris: Flammarion.
Prokop, D. (1979): Faszination und Langeweile. Die populären Medien. Stuttgart: Enke.
Prost, A. (1979): Petite histoire de la France au XXe siécle. Paris: Colin.
Quid (1984ff.), ed. D. Frémy/J. Fremy. Paris: Laffont.
Rappenecker, H. (1990): Que faire dans une classe d'allemand? Erfahrungen eines Austauschlehrers an einem lycée polyvalent, in: fh 21, 357-369.
Raschke, J. (1991): Die Krise der Grünen. Bilanz und Neubeginn. Marburg: Schüren.
Ravy, Ch./G. Ravy (1977): L'image de l'Autriche dans les manuels d'allemand en France (1950-1975). Université de Rouen: Centre d'Etudes et de Recherches Autrichiennes.
Reboul, J.-Ph./N. Tenzer (1988): Le libéralisme audiovisuel, in: Le débat 52, 98-106.
Regards sur l'Actualité 79 (1982), n° special: nationalisations. Paris: DF.
Rehfeldt, U. (1986): Die Modernisierung und die Schwerkraft der Verhältnisse, in: E. Weisenfeld, 131-139.
– (1991): Strukturkrise der Gewerkschaften, in: Frankreich-Jahrbuch, 95-111.
Reichel, E. (1984): 'Rechts' und 'links' in Frankreich – heute, in: fh 15, 393-406.
– (1986): Das Preußenbild in der französischen Literatur des 19. und 20. Jahrhunderts, in: fh 17, 419-432.
Reichel, P. (ed.) (1984): Politische Kultur in Westeuropa. Frankfurt a.M.: Campus.

Reif, K. (1981): Keine Angst, Marianne! Die französische Präsidentschaftswahl 1981, in: apuz 29-30, 34-46.
Rémond, R. (1978 a): Staat und Nation in Frankreich, in: R. Picht, 19-29.
– (1978b): Suggestions pour une explication historique de la France contemporaine, in: G. Baumgratz/R. Picht (ed.): Perspektiven der Frankreichkunde II. Tübingen: Niemeyer, 15-23.
– ([4]1982): Les droites en France. Paris: Aubier Montaigne.
Reynaud, J.D. (1975): Les syndicats en France, 2 vols. Paris: Seuil.
Rials, St. (1985): La droite ou l'horreur de la volonté, in: Le débat 33, 34-48.
Richard, G. (1979): Les institutions politiques de la France. Paris: Flammarion.
Rioux, J.P. (1983): La France de la Quatriéme République, vol. 2. Paris: Seuil.
Ripert, J. (1990): L'égalité sociale et le développement économique dans les DOM. Paris: DF.
Roche, J. (1961): Originalité de la civilisation française. in: FrM 2, 16-21.
Röper, B. ([2]1977): Wirtschaftsnachrichten in der Weltpresse. München: Francke.
Röper, H. (1991): Die Entwicklung des Tageszeitungsmarktes in Deutschland nach der Wende in der ehemahgen DDR, in: Media Perspektiven 7, 421-430.
Ronge, P./A. Deligne (ed.) (1987): Von de Gaulle bis Mitterand. Politische Karikatur in Frankreich 1958-1987. Münster: Westfäl. Landesmuseum f. Kunst u. Kulturgeschichte.
Rose, M.J. (1989): Les syndicats français, le jacobinisme économique et 1992, in: Sociologie du rravail 31, 1-28.
Rouault, R. (1990): L'enseignement privé en France. Quelle place et quel rôle dans les régions?, in: Geographie sociale 7, 117-132.
Rousso, H. (1987): Le syndrome de Vichy. Paris: Seuil.
Rovan, J. (1986): Zwei Völker – eine Zukunft. München: Piper.
Rovan, J./W. Weidenfeld (ed.) (1982): Europäische Zeitzeichen. Elemente eines deutsch-französischen Dialogs. Bonn: Europa Union.
Rozenblum, S.A. (1980): Evolution oder Mutation der französischen Presse? in: R. Lasserre u.a., 281-323.
RPR (1983): Plan de redressement économique et social. Paris: RPR.
Ruf, W. (1988): Kecker Spatz – Was nun? Perspektiven der deutsch-französischen Militärkooperation, in: Lendemains 51, 135-147.
Rupp, H. K. ([2]1982): Politische Geschichte der Bundesrepublik Deutschland. Stuttgart: Kohlhammer.
Sandoz, G. (1981): Nach dem Sieg Mitterrands – Parti socialiste: Dogma oder Sozialdemokratie? in: Dokumente 37, 109-114.
– (ed.) (1983): Les Allemands sans miracle. Paris: Colin.
– (1985): Das Dilemma der französischen Sozialisten, in: Dokumente 41, 47-53.
– (1986): Frankreich: eine andere Republik? in: Dokumente 42, 204-211.
Sauder, G./J. Schlobach (ed.) (1986): Aufklärungen. Frankreich und Deutschland im 18. Jahrhundert. Heidelberg: Winter.
Sauvaget, D. (1983): Le cinéma allemand: itinérarie d'une renaissance, in: G. Sandoz, 205-238.

Sauzay, B. (1985): Die rätselhaften Deutschen. Die Bundesrepublik, von außen gesehen. Stuttgart: Bonn aktuell.

Schäfer, W. (1989): Die französische Gewerkschaftsbewegung in der Krise. Köln: Bund.

Scharf, C./H. J. Schröder (ed.) (1983): Die Deutschlandpolitik Frankreichs und die Französische Zone 1945-1949. Wiesbaden: Steiner.

Schelsky, H. (1979): Die Bedeutung des Schichtungsbegriffes für die Analyse der gegenwärtigen deutschen Gesellschaft, in: idem, Auf der Suche nach Wirklichkeit. München: Goldmann, 326-332 (first ed. 1953).

Scherrer, V. (1987): La France paresseuse. Paris: Seuil.

Schlangen, W. (ed.) (1977): Politische Grundbegriffe. Stuttgart: Kohlhammer.

Schlie, H. W.: (1990): Die Entstehung des deutsch-französischen Kulturkanals, in: Dokumente 46, 32-36.

Schmitt, K. P. (1983): Marktwirtschaft – ein Fremdwort?, in: Dokumente 39, Sonderheft Jan., 101-105.

– (1985): Blieb alles beim alten? Regierung und elektronische Medien in Frankreich, in: Dokumente 41, 128-133.

Schmidt, B./J. Doll/W. Fekl/S. Loewe (1981/83): Frankreich-Lexikon, 2 vols. Berlin: Schmidt.

Schmitt, K. (1991): Die politischen Eliten der V. Republik: Beharrung und Wandel, in: apuz 47-48, 26-36.

Schmitt, T. (1989): Canal Plus et le paysage télévisuel français, in: Lendemains 54, 90-93.

Schnabel, F. (1980): Zwischen Dezentralisierung und Zentralisierung - zur politischen und administrativen Organisation der Bundesrepublik Deutschland, in: R. Lasserre et al., 61-97.

Schonauer, F. (1965): La littérature après 1945, in: Allemagne 1945-1965, Arts – lettres – spectacles. Paris: Documents, 48-74.

Schubert, K. (1988): "Abschied" vom Nationalstaat – "Flucht" nach Europa? Anmerkungen zum neuen französischen Europadiskurs, in: Dokumente 44, 341-350.

Schüle, K. (1983): Politische Landeskunde und kritische Fremdsprachendidaktik. Paderborn: Schöningh.

Schütz, W.J. (1974): Zwischen Kooperation und Konzentration, in: G. Mantwill (ed.) Medien und Archive. München: Pullach, 58-74.

– (1979): Kaum noch Objekte für die Pressekonzentration?, in: Media Perspektiven 9, 600-612.

– (1984): Zeitungen in der Bundesrepublik Deutschland, in: Das Parlament 15. 9.1984.

Schultze, R.O. (1983): Wählerverhalten und Parteiensystem in der Bundesrepublik Deutschland, in: Der Bürger im Staat 33/1, 6-16.

– (1987): Die Bundestagswahl 1987 – eine Bestätigung des Wandels, in: apuz 12, 3-17.

Schulz, F.F. (1990): Konzentrationstrend in Frankreichs Medienlandschaft, in: Media Perspektiven 3, 175-193.

Schulze, V. (^{2}1991): Die Zeitung. Aachen: Hahner Verlagsgesellschaft.

Schumacher, A.W. (1986) Kino in Pagoden und Palästen. Warum Filmfreunde ihr Mekka in Paris finden, in: Dokumente 42, 356-358.
Schuster, D. ([2]1974): Die deutschen Gewerkschaften seit 1945. Stuttgart: Kohlhammer.
Schwartz, Th. A. (1991): America's Germany. John Mc Cloy and the Federal Republic of Germany. Cambridge Mass./London: Harvard University Press.
Schwarz, H. P. (1988): Eine Entente élémentaire. Das deutsch-französische Verhältnis im 25. Jahr des Elysée-Vertrages. Bonn: Europa Union.
Seul, O. (1981): La presse 'alternative' en RFA, in: Allemagnes d'aujourd'hui 77, 33-44.
von Seydlitz, E. (1912): Geographie, Ausgabe B, bearb. von A. Rohrmann. Breslau: Hirt.
Sieburg, H. O. (1975): Geschichte Frankreichs. Stuttgart: Kohlhammer.
SJTI (Service Juridique et Technique de l'Information) (1990): Tableaux statistiques de la presse. Paris: DF.
Sontheimer, K. ([10]1985): Grundzüge des politischen Systems der Bundesrepublik Deutschland. München: Piper.
Spillner, B. (1978): Methoden der Kontrastiven Linguistik in der Frankreichkunde, in: H. Arndt/F. R. Weller (ed.): Landeskunde und Fremdsprachenunterricht. Frankfurt a.M.: Diesterweg, 51-178.
Statistisches Bundesamt (ed.) (1983): Datenreport. Stuttgart: Bonn aktuell.
– (1984): Wahl der Abgeordneten des Europäischen Parlaments aus der Bundesrepublik Deutschland am 17. Juni 1984, H. 5: Textliche Auswertung der Wahlergebnisse. Stuttgart: Kohlhammer.
– (1985): Entwurf zum Datenreport '84. Wiesbaden: Statist. Bundesamt.
– (1989): Länderbericht Frankreich. Stuttgart: Metzler-Poeschel.
Steel, J. (1991): Littérature de l'ombre. Paris: Presses de la Fondation nationale des sciences politiques.
Steiert, R. (1978): Die Gewerkschaften in der französischen Politik, in: Der Bürger im Staat 28/1, 57-63.
Steinkühler, F. (ed.) (1989): Europa '92. Industriestandort oder sozialer Lebensraum. Hamburg: VSA.
Stephan, R. (1978): Schule und Hochschule, in: K. Hänsch, 145-179.
Stoll, A. (ed.) (1990): Le guide de la presse. Paris: OFUP.
Stooß, F. (1981): Bildungssystem und berufliche Qualifikation, in: R. Lasserre et al., 271-323.
Straßner, E. (1982): Fernsehnachrichten, Tübingen: Niemeyer.
Stübs, H. (1992): Französisch in Sachsen, in: fh 23, 23-26.
Thibaut, P. (1992): Réunification et colonisation des médias est-allemands, in: Médiaspouvoirs 26, 156-162.
Thiel, E. (1992): Europäische Wirtschafts- und Währungsunion, in: apuz 7-8, 3-11.
Thiele, G. (ed.) (1990): Demokratisierung in der Französischen Revolution: Wirkungen auf Deutschland. Villingen-Schwenningen: Neckar.
van Tieghem, Ph. (1961): Les influences étrangères sur la littérature française (1550-1880). Paris: P.U.F.

Tiemann, D. (1981): Französische und deutsche Schüler über ihre Nachbarn am Rhein, in: M. Christadler, 170-185.
– (1982): Frankreich- und Deutschlandbilder im Widerstreit. Bonn: Europa Union.
– (1989): Deutsch-französische Jugendbeziehungen der Zwischenkriegszeit. Bonn: Bouvier.
Timm, E. (ed.) (1990): Geist und Gesellschaft. Zur deutschen Rezeption der Französischen Revolution. München: Fink.
Todt, E. (1988): La nouvelle France. Paris: Seuil.
Trotignon, Y. (1968/72): La France au XXe siécle, 2 vols. Paris: Bordas-Mouton.
Trouillet, B. (1981): Das deutsch-französische Verhältnis im Spiegel von Kultur und Sprache. Weinheim/Basel: Beltz.
Truffart, F. (1990): Le Guide des télévisions en Europe-1991. Paris: Bayard/ Médiaspouvoirs.
Tsiakalos, G. (1983): Ausländerfeindlichkeit. München: Beck.
Uhrich, R. (1987): La France inverse? Paris: Economica.
Uren, O. (1952): Le vocabulaire du cinéma, in: Le français moderne 20, 41-52 and 201-222.
Utermark, G. (1991): Der Französischunterricht in der ehemaligen DDR, in: fh 22, 1-11.
Uterwedde, H. (1979): Wirtschaft im Vergleich. Tübingen: Niemeyer.
– (1987): Die "liberale Wende" in der Wirtschaft Frankreichs, in: Dokumente 43, 253-258.
– (1988): Sozio-ökonomische Entwicklung in den 80er Jahren: Brüche und Kontinuitäten, in: Frankreich-Jahrbuch, 31-48.
– (1989): Frankreichs Wirtschaft, in: Landeszentrale für politische Bildung Baden-Württemberg, 221-239.
von Uthmann, J. (1984): Le diable est-il allemand? Paris: Denoël.
Vaillant, J. (1984): Die Linke in Frankreich nach dem Bruch der Linksunion, in: Lendemains 36, 78-81.
Valance, G. (1990): France-Allemagne. Le retour de Bismarck. Paris: Flammarion.
Verdié, M. (ed.) (1987/89): L'état de la France et de ses habitants. Paris: La Découverte.
Verheyen, G. (1992): Studium der Geschichtswissenschaften in Frankreich: Ein Leitfaden. Bonn: DAAD.
Vertrag (1963) = Gesetz zu der gemeinsamen Erklärung und zu dem Vertrag vom 22. Januar 1963 (...) Bonn: Presse- und Informationsamt der Bundesregierung.
Vincent, G. (1974): Le peuple lycéen. Enquête sur les élèves de l'enseignement secondaire. Paris: Gallimard.
Voss, G. (1984): Les industries de croissance et l'avenir économique, in: Documents 39/5, 54-64.
Voss, I. (1987): Herrschertreffen im frühen und hohen Mittelalter. Wien: Böhlau.
Voss, J. (ed.) (1983): Deutschland und die Französische Revolution. München/ Zürich: Artemis.

– (1991): Karl von Rotteck und die Französische Revolution, in: R. Dufraisse, 157-175.

– (1992): Deutsch-französische Beziehungen im Spannungsfeld von Absolutismus, Aufklärung und Revolution. Bonn: Bouvier.

Voss, K. (ed.) (1961): L'Allemagne jugée par la France. Frankfurt a.M.: Diesterweg.

Vossler, K. (1951): Die Dichtungsformen der Romanen, ed. by A. Bauer. Stuttgart: Koehler.

Wagner, B. (1972): Innenbereich und Äußerung. Flaubertsche Formen indirekter Darstellung und Grundtypen der erlebten Rede. München: Fink.

Wallraff, G. (1977): Der Aufrnacher. Köln: Kiepenheuer & Witsch.

– (1979): Zeugen der Anklage. Köln: Kiepenheuer & Witsch.

Weber, H. (1988): Cultures patronales et types d'entreprises: esquisse d'une typologie du patronat, in: Sociologie du Travail 30, 545-566.

de Weck, R. (1986): Der Störfaktor Le Pen, in: E. Weisenfeld, 46-52.

Wehler, H.U. ([4]1980): Das Deutsche Kaiserreich 1871-1918. Göttingen: Vandenhoeck & Ruprecht.

Wehrlin, M. (1985): Aspects juridiques et économiques, in: E. Segneri/M. Wehrlin: Le marché du film en Europe face aux nouvelles technologies. Strasbourg: Conseil de l'Europe, conseil de cooperation culturelle, 33-52.

Weingarten, M. (1984): Voraussetzungen des Wahlerfolgs von Le Pen, in: Lendemains 36, 86-90.

Weisenfeld, E. (21982): Frankreichs Geschichte seit dem Krieg. München: Beck.

– (ed.) (1986): Frankreich 1986 – Jahr der Wende? Bonn: Europa Union.

– (1986a): Welches Deutschland soll es sein? Frankreich und die deutsche Einheit seit 1945. München: Beck.

Weiss, G. (ed.) (1981): L'amitié franco-allemande: une réalité? Leistungskurse. Stuttgart: Klett.

Weller, F.R./K.R. Wenger (1983): Frankreich heute – ein Literaturbericht, in: Die Neueren Sprachen 82, 481-517.

Wenger, K. (1987): Medienmacht und Medienmarkt. Zur Veränderung der Medienstrukturen in Frankreich, in: Media Perspektiven 8, 517-527.

– (1989): Neue Medien – neue Programme? Eine erste Bestandsaufnahme der französischen Medienpolitik seit 1982, in: Frankreich-Jahrbuch, 133-151.

– (1991): Hochfliegend und hochauflösend: Treibt die Satellitenpolitik von Paris und Bonn in einen Engpaß?, in: Dokumente 47, 31-34.

Werner, K.F. (1984): Aktualität des Vergangenen – Geschichte der Gegenwart. 10 Jahrhunderte Deutschland und Frankreich, in: Dokumente 40, Sonderheft Febr., 11-27.

– (1985): France et Allemagne: antagonisme fatal? Une réflexion historique, in: Revue des Sciences morales et politiques 140, 309-324.

Werth, B. (1991): Alte und neue Armut in der Bundesrepublik Deutschland. Berlin: VWB.

Wetzel, K. (1987): Die Krise des Neuen deutschen Films, in: Media Perspektiven 2, 90-98.

Wex, H. (1985): Bonn – Paris: Ein Pakt für ein vereintes Europa, in: Dokumente 41, 4-8.

Wilkens, A. (1990): Der unstete Nachbar. Frankreich, die deutsche Ostpolitik und die Berliner Vier-Mächte-Verhandlungen 1969-1974. München: Oldenbourg.

Willaime, J.P. (1985): Ethos und Politik im französischen Protestantismus, in: Dokumente 41, 39-46.

Wittmann, H. (1991): Außruchstimmung. Der Französischunterricht in den neuen Bundesländern, in: Dokumente 47, 217-220.

Wurm, C.A. (1985): Die Gewerkschaften unter Mitterrand, in: Dokumente 41, 54-61.

Ysmal, C. (1989): Les partis politiques sous la Ve République. Paris: Montchrestien.

Ziebura, G. (1970): Die deutsch-französischen Beziehungen seit 1945. Pfullingen: Neske.

Zimmermann, M. (ed.) (1982): Occupation allemande et Résistance intellectuelle. Berlin: CVK.

Zürn, P. (1965): Die republikanische Monarchie. München: Beck.

20 Jahre deutsch-französische Zusammenarbeit / 20 années de coopération franco-allemande (1983). Bonn: Presse- und Informationsamt der Bundesregierung.